NEW SCHOOL

NEW SCHOOL
A History of the New School
for Social Research

Peter M. Rutkoff
William B. Scott

THE FREE PRESS
A Division of Macmillan, Inc.
NEW YORK

Collier Macmillan Publishers
LONDON

The Free Press
A Division of Macmillan, Inc.
866 Third Avenue, New York, N.Y. 10022

Collier Macmillan Canada, Inc.

Printed in the United States of America

printing number

1 2 3 4 5 6 7 8 9 10

Library of Congress Cataloging-in-Publication Data

Rutkoff, Peter M.
  New School.

  Includes index.
  1. New School for Social Research (New York, N.Y.)—
History. 2. Adult education—New York (N.Y.)—History.
3. New School for Social Research (New York, N.Y.)—
Graduate work—History. 4. Refugees, Political—
Education (Higher)—New York (N.Y.)—History.
5. Scholars—New York (N.Y.)—History. I. Scott,
William B. II. Title.
LD3837.R87 1986   374′.97471   85-20465
ISBN 0-02-927200-9

    Portions of Chapters 2 and 4 were originally
commissioned by the American Academy of Arts and
Sciences for a forthcoming publication tentatively
entitled *The Advance of Science and Scholarship in
Twentieth-Century America,* Alexandra Oleson and John
Voss, editors.
    Portions of Chapter 6 were first published as
"Social Sciences and Politics: Hans Staudinger of the
New School" in *Annals of Scholarship,* vol. I, no. 3, pp.
7-30.
    Chapter 8 originally appeared as an article entitled
"The French in New York, Resistance and Structure" in
Social Research, vol. 50, no. 1, pp. 185-214.

FOR JANE AND DONNA

CONTENTS

ACKNOWLEDGMENTS

Writing The New School's history presented a formidable responsibility and challenge. Throughout we received generous help from colleagues, participants, libraries, institutions, friends, and family. At each step of the way our work has profited from the assistance of others, many of whom we can thank only generally.

At the New School those who facilitated our research include Allen Austill, Albert Landa, Wallis Osterholz, Edith Wurtzel, Elizabeth Coleman, Sal Baldi, Jack Everett, Esther Levine, Karen Zebulon, Henry Greenberg, Jerome Kohn, Joan Grant, and Michael Lordi. At Kenyon our colleagues, Joan Cadden, Reed Browning, Roy Wortman, Martin Garhart, Jerry Irish, Philip Jordan, Jo Rice, Jami Peelle, and Howard Sacks, all encouraged and supported our work in various ways. Two of our students, Nancy Bolotin and Elizabeth Vierow, made very special contributions through their own work and research. Individuals at Kenyon and elsewhere who read parts of our work with care and (sometimes stiff) criticism include George Roeder, Dorothy Ross, Reed Browning, Robert Heilbroner, Arthur Vidich, Hans Speier, Adolph Lowe, and particularly Paul Conkin. We also wish to thank John Agresto, Ronald Overman, Robert Bremner, Stanley Kutler, David

Hollinger, Herbert Gutman, Ilja Srubar, Patrick Reagan, Dan Carter, Edward Stettner, Jergen Stein, Ludwig Stein, Magda Woss, Michael Lutzger, John Spaleck, and Jerome Bruner for their support.

The staffs and directors of the following libraries also deserve our thanks: The Kenyon Library, The Ohio State University Library, the American Jewish Archives (Cincinnati), The University of Southern Illinois–Carbondale, the Juilliard School, the New York Public Library, the Library of the Graduate Faculty of the New School, the Rockefeller Archives, the SUNY Albany Library, Sterling Library at Yale University, the Boston University Library, Harvard Law Library, the Leo Baeck Institute, the YIVO Institute, the University of Konstanz (Switzerland) Archives, the Archives de Deuxième Guerre Mondiale (Paris), the Columbia University Library, the Cornell Library, the Rutgers University Library, and the Museum of Modern Art. We received generous and timely funding from Kenyon College, the National Endowment of the Humanities, the National Science Foundation, the American Philosophical Society, the American Council of Learned Societies, the Rockefeller Archives, and the Ludwig Vogelstein Foundation. Mary Sparlin and Cathy Rennert typed and processed our manuscript again and again. We thank them both. Anne MacKinnon provided extensive stylistic help and Joyce Seltzer of The Free Press gave us the long-term support we needed, while Celia Knight and Judy Sacks aided our final preparation.

Finally, we wish to thank the many individuals who permitted us to interview them. Unfortunately, for some this represents a posthumous acknowledgment. Our thanks and gratitude to Marion Ascoli, Berenice Abbott, Etienne Bloch, Henry Bonnet, Pierre Brodin, John Cage, Rona Connable, Joseph Cropsey, Felicia Deyrup, Mrs. C. Egas, Stella Fogelman, Robert Gwathmey, Ernst Hamburger, Robert Heilbroner, Mary Henle, Sidney Hook, Erich Hula, Hans Jonas, Hanna S. Janovsky, Mme. A. Koyré, Max Lerner, Claude Lévi-Strauss, Maria Ley-Piscator, Seymour Lipton, Adolph Lowe, Thomas Luckmann, Albert Mayer, Clara Mayer, Elizabeth Minnich, Elizabeth Malaquais, Maurice Natanson, Henry Pachter, Saul Padover, Stella Saltonstall, Meyer Schapiro, Ilse Schutz, Reiner Schurmann, Hans Speier, Elizabeth Todd Staudinger, Hans Staudinger, Mrs. Leo Strauss, Genevieve Tabouis, Hannah Tillich, Meriam Beard Vagts, Michael Wertheimer, and Elizabeth Young-Bruehl. Last, our children, Joshua and Rebekah Rutkoff and Ansley and Laine Scott, who contributed in ways they do not yet understand.

INTRODUCTION

Anchoring the northern edge of Greenwich Village at 66 West Twelfth Street, the New School for Social Research has become an established feature of New York cultural life. New Yorkers from all five boroughs and the various suburbs gather here each evening to take courses on virtually every subject imaginable from Confucian philosophy to urban gardening. The adult education program has no admissions requirements and only modest course fees; its instructors are freelance intellectuals and artists. The students come to learn, drawn by what they have heard about the school: that it is a free place and an eclectic place, a place where one is bound to meet interesting people. This reputation has enabled the New School to grow and thrive.

Two blocks away, on the corner of Fifth Avenue and Fourteenth Street, the Graduate Faculty of the New School offers full-fledged doctoral programs in philosophy and the social sciences. Unlike most other American graduate schools, the Graduate Faculty combines an interdisciplinary orientation with a theoretical bent, the first a function of the influence of American philosopher John Dewey and the second a consequence of the Graduate Faculty's European roots. The Graduate Faculty has its own reputation: for scholarship of the most rigorous and serious variety. Indeed, it has been the home of several of the great thinkers of our century.

Together, these two divisions, bound by common origins and a turbulent history, make the New School for Social Research a place of unique significance to twentieth-century social thought. The eclecticism of the one and the academic rigor of the other are both integral to the place and its legend, for the story of the New School is a story of controversy, dialogue, investigation, and sometimes expediency. The New School was founded not once but twice: 1918 and 1933 are benchmarks in its history. First organized in 1918, it began as a project of a band of dissident academics associated with the *New Republic,* who chose the name "New School" to express their belief that it would provide an alternative to conventional American university education. The school, as they saw it, would be a self-governing community of scholars in which faculty and adult students would work together in a common enterprise. They expected the New School to generate a body of critical social science that would contribute to the "reconstruction" of western society along more egalitarian and scientific lines. Fifteen years later their successors created the "University in Exile," an affiliate of the New School that provided a haven for a generation of European scholars exiled by Hitler and Mussolini. No American institution of higher learning responded to the plight of these refugees, many of them Jewish or socialist, as energetically and effectively. The University in Exile was renamed the Graduate Faculty in 1935, when it was established as the permanent research division of the New School. Many of its earliest and most prestigious faculty members were European scholars who came to the New School during the bitter years of Hitler's ascendancy, and then decided to stay to continue their work.

Following World War II, the two sections came together in earnest, still devoted to the principles that had inspired their founding. The New School attracted a host of maverick artists, writers, and scholars to its faculty as its enrollments increased dramatically. Throughout the period between World War II and the 1960s, when American higher education was tending toward specialization and political quietism, the New School offered an alternative. Its steadfast "liberalism" at times resulted in a naive and overly optimistic faith in scientific rationalism and political democracy—but it also made the New School one of the few places in the country where the issues of political reform and academic freedom could be discussed with candor.

The New School we have tried to write about—the New School of legendary commitment, brilliance, and controversy—was the academic home of a precocious and diverse generation of intellectuals. As individuals, its faculty have advocated a variety of philosophies, including forms of pragmatism, philosophical rationalism, and Marxism. They have called themselves Democrats, Republicans, Progressives, Liberals, Socialists, and, in a few cases, Communists. The New School never enforced a rigid orthodoxy, but its faculty accepted as virtually indisputable the values implicit in the democratic humanism which they articulated. As philosophers, social scientists, artists, and teachers they thought of themselves as the architects and defenders of a modern, egalitarian, and cosmopolitan culture. They vociferously opposed racism, religious bigotry, national chauvinism, and nonrepublican forms of government. Their most original and important intellectual contribution was a theory of "totalitarianism" that posited basic similarities in fascism, communism, and intolerant expressions of religious belief as they contrasted these doctrines with their own model of egalitarian liberalism. Other ideas which originated with the faculty of the New School include Thorstein Veblen's "theory of conspicuous consumption," Horace Kallen's "cultural pluralism," Claude Lévi-Strauss's "structuralism," Max Wertheimer's "gestalt psychology," Leo Strauss's "neo-natural right," Wesley Mitchell's "business cycle theory," Alfred Schutz's "phenomenology," and John Cage's artistic "happenings."

We have limited our history of the New School to the fifty years following its founding, 1917 to 1967. Throughout this period, the founders and their immediate successors dominated the spirit and direction of the school. To some extent, then, the story of the New School is the story of these people who led and administered it. It is also the story of its faculty, a distinctive generation of intellectuals who emerged in western Europe and the United States prior to World War I, reached the height of their influence in New York City in the 1930s and 1940s, and then declined in impact and importance in the 1950s and 1960s. We have carried our history of the New School into the 1960s, in order to pursue to completion the trajectory of their lives and ideas.

In writing this history, we have sought to relate the formal thought of the most influential members to the institutional history of the school itself and, of course, to its larger cultural and political context, New York City. The Americans and Europeans who made the New School their home were among the most original, cosmopolitan thinkers of the twentieth century. Almost to a person, they believed in the efficacy of human reason, the necessity of popular government, the interdependency of individual freedom and social justice, and the superiority of urban life. Though some might say that, as a faith, democratic humanism has fared poorly, our culture has been profoundly influenced by the ideas it generated. Most of these extraordinary individuals tried, with unfailing commitment, to live their lives and run their school according to the ideals they held out to the world, ideals which remained remarkably fixed from the school's formulation in 1917 until the 1960s.

William B. Scott and Peter M. Rutkoff,
Gambier, Ohio, August 1984

NEW SCHOOL

1

1917: THE CONCEPTION
OF A NEW SCHOOL

THE NEW SCHOOL ORIGINATED IN controversy. On October 8, 1917, historian Charles A. Beard resigned from Columbia University to protest the firing of two Columbia faculty. Shortly after, his close colleague and friend, James Harvey Robinson, also left. Their resignations touched off one of the most publicized debates in American education over the issue of academic freedom. The discussion not only resulted in a fundamental reassessment of the principles of academic freedom in the United States, it precipitated the discussions which led to the formation of the New School for Social Research. The controversy contained all the elements of a pitched and bitter battle: a disagreement concerning American national policy, a debate over the meaning of academic freedom, and, not least, a long-standing antagonism between strong-willed and sometimes eccentric individuals and the university establishment. The argument made clear the lines that were being drawn within American universities around the country: between the interests of larger and more bureaucratized institutions and those of their increasingly politically activist faculties.[1]

Nowhere was that distinction more deeply felt than at Columbia, which had risen to new prominence under the leadership of President

Nicholas Murray Butler. Butler and his distinguished faculty had transformed the university by shifting Columbia's priorities from undergraduate teaching to research. Butler believed in academic freedom, which he defined as the freedom to engage in research of one's choice, but he did not condone dissenting political expression—whether in the classroom or in public—from within his faculty. Such a position did not go unchallenged among a faculty that included many of the leading representatives of a new generation of politically committed social scientists.

The debate at Columbia had been touched off on June 6, 1917, commencement day, when President Butler informed a Columbia alumni group that he felt the university duty-bound to support the war policies of Congress and President Wilson. Heretofore, Butler explained, Columbia faculty had been free to express themselves on the war and conscription because the government had adopted a policy of neutrality. Now, Congress had debated and settled the issue of war. What Butler had previously tolerated as wrongheadedness and folly, he now considered treasonous. There was no place at Columbia, Butler declared, "for any person who opposes or counsels opposition to the effective enforcement of the laws of the United States or who acts or speaks or writes treason." The dismissal of any such person from Columbia University, warned Butler, "will be as speedy as the discovery of his offense."[2] Four months later, Butler made good his threat, when, on his recommendation, the Columbia Board of Trustees terminated the appointments of James McKeen Cattell, professor of psychology, and Henry W. L. Dana, assistant professor of comparative literature, for having publicly opposed United States entry into World War I.

Dana and Cattell were at the center of faculty and student protests at Columbia against Congress's declaration of war. Both men advised draft-age men not to enlist and even suggested that they should refuse to register for conscription. As a socialist, Dana considered World War I antithetical to his notion of international brotherhood. Cattell was a pacifist, but not a socialist, although his protest took on heightened personal meaning when his son was arrested for refusing to register. Dana's and Cattell's actions drew strong protests from newspapers, the Columbia administration, and Columbia faculty as many called for their resignations. Charles Beard, who supported the war, defended Cattell's and Dana's right to protest publicly as well as anyone's right to be a conscientious objector.[3]

Outraged at the actions of Butler and the board, Beard resigned in protest his position on Columbia's faculty. James Robinson followed two months later. Almost immediately, the two friends set to work at establishing what they hoped would be a new kind of school. Their goal was simple but ambitious: it must be the antithesis of Nicholas Butler's Columbia. It must be committed to an expansive notion of academic freedom, and it must foster among American social scientists a desire to participate in the "democratic social reconstruction" of western society.

Of the two men whose firings had prompted the protest, only Henry Dana became involved in the New School. Dana accepted an appointment at the New School and remained until his retirement. James Cattell, ironically enough, left academic life entirely to devote himself to a series of scholarly projects, including the *Directory of American Scholars*. Yet the story of Cattell's firing illustrates vividly the conflicts that drove politically committed faculty members out of conventional universities like Columbia and shaped the objectives of the founders of the New School.

Cattell, a tenured professor at Columbia, since 1891 had organized the Columbia psychology department and built it into one of the outstanding experimental departments in the country. An innovative researcher, he had pioneered the use of the psychological laboratory in the United States. He was a member of the prestigious American Academy of Science, was a former president of the American Psychological Association, and had helped establish several scholarly journals, including the *Psychological Review,* the *Journal of Psychology, Psychological and Scientific Methods,* and *Archives of Psychology.* In addition, he edited *Society and Education, Popular Science,* and *Science.* Beyond this, Cattell had fashioned an outstanding record as a scholar and teacher. He was unquestionably one of the brightest stars of the Columbia faculty.[4]

Despite his scholarly achievements, on a personal level Cattell annoyed some of his colleagues and most of the Columbia administrators. He objected to what he considered the increasingly authoritarian character of American universities. On numerous occasions, he had criticized Butler's policies and questioned his abilities. Cattell believed that a university faculty should be completely self-governing and organized as democratically as American governments.[5] Such assertions spurred Nicholas Butler to try, with trustee encouragement, to "retire" Cattell, but faculty pressure had forced Butler to back down. In 1913, however, after Cattell published a book entitled *University Control,* which advocated full faculty control and the abolition of administrators and boards of trustees, Butler decided to renew his efforts. Once more, the faculty successfully resisted Butler's action.[6]

The antagonism between Cattell and Butler came to a head in early January 1917 when, in a letter to members of the faculty club, Cattell publicly questioned Butler's competence. When the letter appeared in several New York newspapers, a number of faculty members submitted a petition to Butler, objecting to Cattell's indiscretion. The faculty as whole, however, urged Butler not to take the letter too seriously.[7] But the university trustees and President Butler considered Cattell's letter sufficient grounds for dismissal and used the occasion to authorize Butler to monitor the behavior of the entire faculty and to fire anyone found guilty of disloyalty. To soften the blow, Butler agreed to establish a judicial body called the "Committee of Nine" to hear charges against faculty members and to make recommendations to the trustees. Philosopher John Dewey, who supported Cattell's right to free expression, was a member of the committee.[8]

Although the Committee of Nine acted as a buffer between Cattell and Butler, most of its members, Dewey excepted, clearly disapproved of Cattell's conduct as contrary to the "academic solidarity" essential to the well-being of the university. The committee censured Cattell, yet allowed him to apologize in writing to Butler. Cattell agreed.[9] However, when Edwin R. Seligman, who chaired the Committee of Nine, released the letter of apology to the press, Cattell was outraged and charged Seligman with dishonesty and breach of trust. Cattell's reaction alienated a majority of the committee, who, at Seligman's insistence, wrote the trustees: "We believe that his [Cattell's] usefulness in the University is ended." The committee declared that it was "impossible for Professor Cattell to respect the ordinary decencies of intercourse among gentlemen."[10] In his reply to Cattell, Seligman emphasized that "academic freedom has nothing to do with your case," but rather "the impossibility of any useful cooperation between you and your colleagues."[11] When the Committee of Nine reassembled in September, it formally recommended that the board retire Cattell from "active service" with pension benefits.[12]

By the time the committee had made its recommendation, Butler and the trustees had already decided to terminate Cattell's appointment: Butler went beyond the committee's recommendation, though, by also denying Cattell his pension. Butler justified his action by pointing to Cattell's antiwar activities.[13] Because Butler acted against the committee's recommendations and then defined the dismissal in terms of Cattell's disloyal activities, most press accounts described the dispute as a clear-cut battle between faculty and administration.[14] Yet many on the faculty approved Cattell's firing, although they would not have deprived him of retirement benefits. Cattell had managed to run afoul of his own colleagues as well as Butler's sense of administrative prerogative. Whatever prompted Butler to level the charge of disloyalty to the United States—his intense patriotism, impatience with the Committee of Nine, or fear that the committee would fail to recommend dismissal—it is clear that by the time he made his decision Cattell had lost the sympathy of most of his colleagues.

On October 8, 1917, a week after Cattell's firing, Charles Beard announced to his history class that this would be his last lecture at Columbia. Beard accused the university of being under the "control of a small and active group of trustees who have no standing in the world of education, who are reactionary and visionless in politics, narrow and medieval in religion."[15] Beard explained his resignation in more detail in a statement published that December in the *New Republic.* In his article he accused Butler of appointing unqualified individuals to the faculty, ignoring faculty recommendations in regard to appointments, and caving in to trustee demands to discipline "progressive" minded faculty, including himself. Beard viewed the dismissals of Cattell and Dana as only the latest and most flagrant examples of Butler's consistently reactionary policies and dictatorial behavior. He concluded that such action thwarted the prime function of a university: to advance learning.

Far from believing that the war necessitated unusual restrictions, Beard argued that it marked the beginning of a new, democratic era, and that Columbia must therefore protect academic freedom all the more scrupulously. He believed that, to enable the United States to lead the world in a postwar reconstruction that guaranteed economic justice, self-government, personal liberty, and world peace, social scientists must have the freedom to criticize all existing structures. To submit to the restraints of Butler and his own professional colleagues seemed to Beard a repudiation of his responsibilities as a social scientist. Beard's close friend and colleague, James Robinson, agreed, and in December he also resigned from Columbia.

Although the Cattell–Dana incident precipitated their action, Beard and Robinson had long been explicit about their moral commitments. Together, they had made the Columbia political science department a center of what came to be known as the "new history." In their text, *The Development of Modern Europe,* they had emphasized that westerners, consciously and systematically, had to come to grips with social and political problems.[16] After graduation from DePauw College in 1898, Beard spent a year in Chicago doing settlement work at Hull House. The following year he began work on his doctorate at Oxford, where he helped establish Ruskin Hall, a college devoted to providing educational opportunities for English factory workers.[17] On his return to the United States in 1903, he assisted in the organization of the socialist-sponsored Rand School of Social Science and participated in the work of the Bureau of Municipal Research, an early "think-tank" for urban reform.[18] He came to Columbia in 1904. At Columbia, Beard had always been something of a trouble-maker as he became the advocate for iconoclastic scholars in the political science department.

Throughout his career, Beard devoted more time to writing books directed at general audiences than to scholarly monographs. An underlying concern in Beard's numerous books was the need for his generation to free themselves from the encumbrances of the past. In his first book, *The Industrial Revolution*, published in 1901 as a textbook for English factory workers, Beard described the triumph of the human mind over "priestcraft, feudal tyrants, and warring elements." He argued that humankind had the capacity to shape its "own religion and politics, and corporately to control every form of his natural environment."[19] Yet such progress was not inevitable. Intelligent and committed individuals were necessary to bring about beneficent change, and their willingness to do so depended on education.

All education, he insisted, "must have for its object the training of the individual, so that in seeking the fullest satisfaction of his own nature he will harmoniously perform his function as a member of a corporate society.... In short, physical and social health must be made the basis of education."[20] Writing the same year in another context, Beard was even more emphatic: "Thus the work of creation is not complete—scarcely begun," he asserted. "Man, mental, moral, and social is not yet half evolved.... The work which remains seems almost infinite. But it is the grandest, noblest thing that can engage our attention and our powers."[21] Beard never deviated from this progressive faith. At Columbia, when he concluded that American entry into World War I opened the way for wholesale social reform, he found Butler's action intolerable. In Beard's mind Butler represented the forces of retrogression, the contemporary equivalent of "priestcraft, feudal tyrants, and warring elements." Far from being a force of enlightenment and human progress, Columbia had become a force of reaction.

Like Beard, James Robinson too was highly critical of the status quo and understood historical change as an overpowering "march of progress." He agreed with Beard that scholarship should serve the needs of the present. Born in 1863 in Bloomington, Illinois, Robinson had graduated from Harvard, where he also received a master's degree in biology. In 1890 he completed his doctorate in history at the University of Freiburg. He began his teaching career at the University of Pennsylvania and in 1895 accepted an appointment at Barnard and Columbia.

His two most influential books, *The New History* (1912) and *The Mind in the Making* (1921), summed up his ideas about teaching and education. Robinson's ideas on education and the social sciences, as expressed in these books, in effect, became the ideological foundation of the New School.[22]

In the *New History*, Robinson asked scholars to address their work to general audiences and history teachers to select those aspects of the past that had significance for the present.[23] By examining the attitudes and values of the past, students might begin to examine critically their own beliefs. Only then could they free themselves from outdated habits of mind and act intellectually and consistently with present needs and purposes.[24] He urged the adoption of the methods of natural scientists: a critical stance toward sources and a desire to go beyond description and seek explanations for events. A faithful application of scientific methods would heighten historians' awareness of technological changes, the growth of popularly based government, the utility of experimental science, and the evolutionary character of human society. Such a "new history," Robinson assured his readers, would create an awareness of the achievements of the past and of the possibility of progress in the future if humans so willed it.[25]

This is not to say that Robinson did not recognize the limits of this method. He stressed that, although historians and natural scientists should approach their subjects with the same critical stance, each studied quite different phenomena. Unlike the objects of natural science, humans exemplified no laws. Human deviousness, curiosity, and desire made people unlikely subjects for reliable predictions. And, unlike natural scientists, who could assume a continuity between their subject's past and present, even the most knowledgeable historians, finally, knew very little about their constantly changing subjects. Thus Robinson urged historians to remain sensitive to the many facets of human existence, to resist the temptation to specialize too much, and to draw on the work of the more narrowly focused and exact social sciences.[26]

In his *New History*, Robinson did not ask historians to rewrite history according to their own inclinations, nor did he advocate that historians become pseudoscientists in quest of mythical laws of human development. Even so, his writings reveal an unresolved tension between fact and value. In advocating the liberation of the present from the "obsolete values" of the past, Robinson avoided the question of what criteria historians might use to determine the obsolescence of the past. He, like Beard, used uncritically such loaded words as "progress" and "freedom." Both assumed that democracy, individual liberty, experimental science, collective action, and material prosperity were much more than the values of particular societies at particular times. For them such values were practically universal, beyond dispute, and anyone who rejected them was, like President Butler, "reactionary and visionless in politics, narrow and medieval in religion."

These assumptions point to a logical problem, perhaps a contradiction, in the thinking of Robinson and some of his colleagues. Already evident in his *New History,* the problem became explicit in *The Mind in the Making* (1921), where he traced the evolution of what he called the "critical mind" from humanity's animal origins to the modern, scientific mode. Drawing on the work of Dewey, Veblen, and anthropologists Franz Boas and Alexander Goldenweiser, Robinson argued that there was no such thing as "human nature" and that all human thought was culturally specific. Critical thought first emerged in classical Greece but was supplanted for nearly 1,500 years by the prescriptions of Christianity. With Galileo and others, however, European thinkers recovered their critical consciousness. Thus Robinson rather oddly established his "critical mind," to him a universal human ideal, as the cultural product of a particular historical setting.[27]

Robinson then proceeded to justify his history of thought with an almost rationalist description of the human mind. He declared that the purpose of the "new history," and critical thought in general, was to create a critical, open-minded attitude.[28] "Instead of permitting our observations to be distorted by archaic philosophy, political economy, and ethics," we should "free our minds so as to permit honest thinking."[29] "I have no reforms to recommend," insisted Robinson, "except the liberation of intelligence."[30] He then described the mind as both "conscious knowledge and intelligence, as what we know and our attitude towards it—our disposition to increase our information, classify it, criticize it, and apply it."[31] All humans, he tells us, have the capacity for critical analysis, a cleansing and liberating process without which thought becomes merely "rationalizations" of what we already believe rather than knowledge of ourselves and nature. Thus the human mind itself, when free from atavistic distortions, possesses an inherent capacity to distinguish true from false.[32] Robinson believed that this universal rationality made democracy both a moral and a scientific imperative. He wrote: "But there is still a more fundamental discovery underlying our democratic tendencies. This is the easily demonstrated scientific truth that nearly all men and women, whatever their social and economic status, may have much greater possibilities of activity and thought and emotion than they exhibit in the particular conditions in which they happen to be placed; that in all ranks may be found evidence of unrealized capacity; that we are living on a lower scale of intelligent conduct and rational enjoyment than is necessary."[33]

Robinson and Beard understood themselves to be the advocates of an objective and scientific mode of analysis. They described their disagreement with Butler and Columbia as not simply a matter of conflicting values, but a dispute between "rationalization" and "rationality" or, in Kantian terms, between the "naive" and the "critical." Nonetheless, despite Robinson's and Beard's assertion that their "new history" represented an affirmation of a scientific mode and eschewed all *a priori* values, in truth they judged the past according to their own preferences. They rejected sexual and racial prejudice, expressed a distaste for nationalism and religious belief, and endorsed governmental intervention in areas of economic and social behavior. For them, the purpose of the "new history," and the New School as well, was to bring minds into agreement with these values.

Robinson's ideas on history, and on education generally, were neither original nor indeed especially controversial. Some may have taken exception to certain comments, and many no doubt would have felt uncomfortable with his thinly veiled agnosticism. Few American educators, though, including Nicholas Murray Butler, would have denied the dynamic character of knowledge and education or their utilitarian and moral effect. Robinson's genius lay not in penetrating, original analysis, but in his ability to synthesize, popularize, and inspire. Like Beard, Robinson directed his writings as much to a general, educated audience as to his professional peers. He was willing to simplify complex intellectual issues and espouse high-sounding, but often analytically shallow, platitudes, especially where they advanced his pedagogical purpose: to mobilize his readers and students to action. Robinson and Beard, impatient with the painstaking scholarly procedures of their colleagues, pictured their critics as morally insensitive obscurantists. There was much about Columbia and other American universities to justify their indictment. Still, their characterization was on the whole unfair.

Although their resignations deprived them of the institutional framework that had provided congenial companionship and intellectual stimulation, Beard and Robinson found a substitute for Columbia in the intellectual circle associated with the *New Republic,* a "journal of opinion" founded in 1915 by Herbert Croly, with the financial backing of philanthropists Dorothy and Willard Straight. Croly's opinions turned out to parallel those of Beard and Robinson. All three supported President Wilson's decision to intervene in World War I; they believed that the war marked the opening of a new, democratic, and peaceful era. They agreed that "rational" and "informed" leadership could bring progress and that, because the United States would be the key to postwar reconstruction, American opinion-makers and educators bore a particularly heavy responsibility. This was to be the American era, and they wanted to be certain that the United States lived up to its responsibilities.[34]

Robinson and Beard found at the *New Republic* the kind of intellectual discourse that they believed Columbia had sought to suppress. Here they could publicly advocate specific reforms without fear of jeopardizing their professional standing. At Columbia they had felt stigmatized as political agitators; at the *New Republic* they could be moral philosophers. Nonetheless, their status at the magazine had its drawbacks. Even though they both came from reasonably well-to-do families and had authored successful textbooks, they could not work indefinitely without pay: neither were they offered positions as coeditors. Equally important, although the *New Republic* could guarantee them readers, it could not provide the direct stimulation of students. Beard and Robinson found the lure of the classroom irresistible. They wanted an environment that combined the teaching and professional rewards of Columbia with the freedom and moral commitment of the *New Republic*. They needed a "new school."

Had Robinson and Beard blamed their resignations solely on Butler and Columbia they might have simply sought university positions elsewhere. They believed, however, that Butler and Columbia were symptomatic of a much larger problem that encompassed all higher education in America and which could only be resolved by creating something entirely new. For some time before October 1917, Beard and Robinson had been unhappy at Columbia. As early as 1916, they had discussed with Herbert Croly the possibility of establishing an independent social science institute to offer lecture courses and research opportunities for adult students. Long a pet project of Croly's, such an institute would constitute a cooperative community of scholars drawn from various social science disciplines. Adult students, motivated by curiosity, not coercion, would enroll for "no other purpose than to learn." The faculty would control all institutional policy, including finance, curriculum, and faculty appointments, and would be freed from the tedium of undergraduate instruction. Beard and Croly also hoped for a place that would encourage free inquiry and a loose interpretation of the bounds of the traditional academic disciplines. When Beard and Robinson resigned from Columbia in 1917, their earlier discussions took on new meaning. One of their first steps was to adopt the idea of adult education, recognizing as they did that American universities had sorely neglected this important area. It was a genuine cause, and one appropriate to their rhetoric. Thus endowed with a mission, they began to plan in earnest.[35]

In Herbert Croly and Dorothy Straight, Robinson and Beard found sympathetic and resourceful patrons. Croly used his position at the

New Republic to assemble other like-minded and interested intellectuals and civic leaders. Heir to the Whitney fortune, Dorothy Straight saw in Beard's and Robinson's new school the means to train future "progressive" leaders who would participate in the reordering of American society along lines projected by the *New Republic*. Her husband Willard, then serving in Europe, warned her away from Beard and Robinson: "I'm getting a little restive and uncertain about some of these forward looking people. Robinson and Beard wouldn't get you—I mean anyone—anywhere except in trouble—if you followed them too far." Straight ignored her husband's advice. In February 1918 she transformed the New School from a provocative subject of discussion into a realizable dream by pledging $10,000 a year to the project for ten years.[36]

At Beard's and Robinson's urging, Croly organized weekly planning sessions for the school at the four-story brick New Republic offices at West Twenty-first Street. These meetings were but an expansion of discussions which Croly frequently organized at the New Republic building on behalf of various projects which interested him. The regulars included jurists Learned Hand and Felix Frankfurter, John Dewey, novelist Winston Churchill, economists Wesley Mitchell and Thorstein Veblen, former dean of Barnard College Emily Smith Putnam and her husband, publisher George Putnam, associate editors of the *New Republic* Walter Lippmann and Alvin Johnson, philosopher Horace Kallen as well as several New York civic leaders and philanthropists. These included Mary Harriman Rumsey, a close personal friend of Dorothy Straight's and daughter of financier E. H. Harriman. Rumsey at the time was serving on the federal Food Price Board and the Community Industrial Relations Committee. Others were Caroline Bacon, who taught history at Smith College and worked with the League of Women Voters; Thomas Chadbourne, a corporate lawyer, who directed several New York transit companies and was vice chairman of the War Trade Board; Charles Burlington, an attorney, who had helped direct the successful New York City mayoral campaign of reform candidate John Purnoy Mitchel of 1913, served as head of the Civil Service Reform Association, and had been president of the New York City Board of Education.[37]

The founders of the New School had been brought together by their participation in various activities associated with Columbia University, the Bureau of Municipal Research, the *New Republic*, and the Women's Suffrage Party. These influences made themselves felt in the first piece of literature produced for distribution to the public, "A Proposal for an Independent School of Social Science," in which the organizational committee announced the formation of the school and outlined their ideas. "The economic development of the past twenty-five years," they declared, "called for a new type of leadership in every field of American life." In business, government, labor, and education, "scientific methods and independent research must be applied to the changing social order." A "New School" was called for, where "well qualified investigators and thinkers can enjoy the advantage of one another's thought and discoveries, and where they can talk freely upon any theme they judge fit to such grown up and responsible men and women as may wish to seek their instruction." Such a school could become "as powerful in modern life as some of the great universities were in the Middle Ages." It could dominate the "fields of higher education in political and social sciences, much as Johns Hopkins University dominated the American university world for twenty-five years. Such a school," they declared, "would become the center of the best thought in America, would lead in emancipating learning from the narrow trammels of lay boards of trustees, and would be a spiritual adventure of the utmost significance. Nothing like it has ever been attempted." They asserted, "This is the hour for the experiment; and New York is the place, because it is the greatest social science laboratory in the world and of its own force attracts scholars and leaders in educational work."[38]

An infatuation with the "scientific" mode characterized the discussions and publicity surrounding the formation of the New School. In a few cases, the founders of the New School expressed confidence in the inherently progressive character of scientific knowledge and its application, and on the accomplishments of scientists, who since the seventeenth century had revolutionized western notions of the physical world and enabled humanity to harness and exploit that world in a manner previously unimaginable. Now, they believed, social scientists, liberated from tradition, religion, and special interests, could use the methods of natural science to create a new world free from war, famine, injustice, and ignorance. But to meet these social and moral responsibilities, they would have to free themselves from the constraints of the institutions where they had been trained and where they taught. The normative influences of American universities produced social scientists too specialized and politically conservative to look at society as an integrated whole. Most social scientists pursued narrowly focused research, which resulted in reliable but almost useless scholarship. Furthermore, social scientists, at least in the United States, worked almost exclusively within universities controlled by business-oriented boards, which penalized scholars who criticized existing social arrangements, and which fostered conformity, mediocrity, and political quietism. Only when educators freed social scientists from such universities and organized research around social problems would they be able to provide the necessary leadership for social reconstruction. This was the political challenge that the New School hoped to meet.[39]

The educational philosophy of the New School was influenced, substantially and explicitly, by the ideas of John Dewey and Thorstein Veblen. The preeminent educational philosophers of their time, both men were intimately involved with the school from the outset and were personal friends of Beard and Robinson. Dewey at first intended to join the New School faculty, taking a leave from Columbia in 1918 to consider the decision. Although he returned to Columbia in 1921, he maintained his ties to the New School by periodically lecturing, serving on various of the school's advisory boards through the 1940s, and celebrating his seventieth, eightieth, and ninetieth birthdays at the New School. Thorstein Veblen was a member of the original New School faculty, joining in the same year he published his influential work *The Higher Learning in America.*[40]

In 1917 John Dewey stood alone as the foremost American philosopher of education. His laboratory schools at Chicago and Columbia and his classic statements on education, *School and Society* (1899) and *Democracy and Education* (1916), placed his ideas at the center of discussion of American educational reform.

Dewey's attempt to relate political democracy, the experimental method, and industrial reorganization meshed closely with Beard's and Robinson's notion of a "new history." Instead of viewing knowledge as a transcript of some reality, Dewey described it as an "instrument" that enabled humans to understand and in some cases manipulate their environment. It served human ends. As a resource, like any other tool, it was always subject to further refinement. "The funded capital of civilization," knowledge, was made up of propositions that worked in a given circumstance.[41]

Applying this theory of knowledge, Dewey defined education largely as a process of creating in students critical and inquisitive minds. Experimental methods taught students to test their preconceptions and to explore new possibilities. Dewey refused to believe that education was the province of a particular phase of life, or that it should be merely a means to achieve material security. A proper educational system integrated study and exploration into all aspects of a student's life and created individuals who would continue to learn and grow throughout their lives. Dewey so valued continuing personal growth that he elevated education from a utilitarian to a moral necessity. "To maintain such an education," he wrote, "is the essence of morals. For conscious life is a continual beginning afresh."[42] The logic of Dewey's "progressive education" went well beyond the scope of the existing organization of American education. It was a manifesto for adult education that stressed intellectual growth more than vocational training.[43]

Thorstein Veblen concurred with Dewey on the importance of critical thought and the need for adult education. But Veblen focused his attention on the structural flaws within the university itself.

Veblen's *The Higher Learning in America*, which expanded Cattell's critique of the American university system, provided a virtual blueprint for the New School. In it Veblen argued that contemporary civilization valued knowledge and research above all else, the prevailing emphasis on profit-making and consumption notwithstanding. In spite of this, however, society had placed the entire task of developing new knowledge on its universities, to which it had perversely added the job of teaching undergraduates. Although both were crucially important functions, according to Veblen, the coexistence of the two—research and undergraduate instruction—worked to the detriment of both. The enormous size of universities and the faculties' quite proper preoccupation with research allowed no more than the most impersonal relations between students and teachers. To cope with the burden of teaching such large numbers of students, universities resorted to bureaucratic organizations that placed graduation and good behavior above the desire to learn. Students were treated like inmates, not scholars, and lived under a system that emphasized grading, supervision, and punishment.[44]

The mixing of teaching with research had equally pernicious effects on scholarship. Faculty members were forced to devote most of their time preparing students for life and citizenship, functions more suited for schoolmasters than scholars. Courses reflected the needs and abilities of young adults, not the research interests of the faculty. Furthermore, because most college students were young and inexperienced, faculty members had to act as guardians of student morals and supervisors of conduct. All these responsibilities diverted scholars from their true purpose—the pursuit of knowledge.[45]

Veblen also found disturbing the structural similarity of American universities and business enterprises. Businessmen sat on the boards that chose presidents and set policy for the institutions. These business-oriented trustees conceived of the university as a factory charged with the production of graduates and publications, not as a community of scholars engaged in free inquiry. Administrators used salaries and promotions to foster competition between faculty members and loyalty to the institution. Instead of allowing scholars the freedom to pursue their curiosity, administrators admonished them to produce practical, usable scholarship. This, according to Veblen, resulted in faculty intimidation as well as rewards for the mediocre. Most trustees considered exceptional, iconoclastic minds among the faculty to be distinct liabilities.[46]

Veblen advocated the separation of research and scholarship from undergraduate education. Undergraduates would be better served in small colleges staffed with people dedicated to the teaching and supervision of the young. The goal of these colleges would be to inculcate civilized values. University faculty would then be free to concern themselves solely with research and the training of graduate students. Veblen believed that, since scholars alone could appreciate and evaluate the work of other scholars, research universities should be self-governing and free from the meddling interference of trustees and presidents. In such an environment scholars could pursue their true vocation, the quest for new knowledge. Moreover, by separating "critical" scholarship from undergraduate education, boards of trustees need no longer fear the disquieting impact of faculty research on the minds and morals of young students. Such a reorganization would allow the university to fulfill the highest and most noble ends of modern civilization. Anything less, insisted Veblen, and the United States would soon become a civilization of profit-seekers and consumers of meaningless goods.[47]

Like Beard and Robinson, Veblen had developed his ideas about educational reform over many years; indeed, most of *Higher Learning in America* was completed before 1910. The war, however, brought an urgency to his work and inspired him to draw explicit connections between the needs of society and the responsibilities of scholarship. This was the theme of the four-page article, "War and Higher Learning," that he added to the introduction of his book when he published it in 1918. Veblen argued that, with the outbreak of war in Europe, the United States now bore the awesome responsibility of preserving higher learning in the West. The war, he concluded, had all but destroyed the integrity of European universities. They had been depleted by conscription of their faculty, students, and resources but, worse, they had suffered the more serious damage of transformation from institutions of higher learning to instruments of patriotism. By its very nature, asserted Veblen, scholarship is "international in character and cannot be taken care of except by unrestricted collusion and collaboration among men of all those people whom it may concern."[48] That European faculties had consented to the politicalization of their own universities indicated to Veblen the seriousness of the corruption.

Only in America, according to Veblen, did the ideal of the university as a community of scholars survive. In the future, Europe would look to the United States for intellectual leadership. American intellectuals, during the coming darkness in Europe, should be responsible for preserving the ideals of learning and free inquiry against the invidious intrusions of national chauvinism. In addition, as part of this work, they should create within the United States a refuge for European intellectuals who could no longer continue their work at home. "A beginning may well be made by a joint enterprise," he suggested, "among American scholars and universities for the installation of a freely endowed central establishment where teachers and students of all nationalities . . . may pursue their chosen work as guests of the American academic community at large, or as guests of the American people in the character of a democracy of culture."[49] Thus Veblen articulated intellectual and moral commitments that, although unrecognized for more than a decade, were implicit from the start and ready to be acted upon when the need arose.

In retrospect, the founders of the New School may appear somewhat quixotic and self-righteous. They accused university administrators of moral indifference and their colleagues of careerism, meanwhile describing their own ideas as both "scientific" and "progressive." In fact, neither Columbia University nor their faculty colleagues were as self-serving or morally indifferent as they pictured them. In 1917, during Butler's presidency, Columbia was regarded as one of the foremost research universities in the world, and in the United States its faculty was unexcelled in its scholarly accomplishments. Furthermore, the Columbia faculty included a remarkable number of individuals whose work rested on strong moral presumptions. Indeed, the New School borrowed much of its "socially committed" curriculum from Columbia.[50] Even so, it would be a mistake to dismiss the criticisms that were leveled against Columbia and American higher education in general. Despite the self-righteous tone of their criticism, the founders of the New School raised disturbing and still unresolved questions about the university and the role of the social sciences. The growth of faculty participation and research opportunities after World War I did not blunt Veblen's barbs: in general, American universities continued to encourage publication largely for the sake of institutional prestige, reward mediocrity as often as merit, and exert enormous pressure on dissident faculty to conform to university as well as social conventions. That the faults were the result of human, as much as institutional, frailty did not make them less true.

More significant, Beard, Robinson, and the other organizers of the New School sensed that the various social science disciplines were undergoing important changes. Even as social scientists became more specialized and more scientific in methodology, they seemed to be shifting their attention away from social problems toward purely technical concerns, becoming more and more embarrassed by explicit political commitments. Moral fervor and professionalism had come to seem incompatible. One result of this transformation from advocacy to objectivity was greater methodological rigor and more reliable scholarship.[51] On the other hand, the demeanor of "scientific objectivity" with its arcane technical language and elaborate scientific procedures tended to obscure the unstated moral and political commitments of social scientists.[52] Experts could represent themselves as "value-neutral" technicians, even when their advice was the product of partisan assumptions, conscious and unconscious. Moreover, unexamined professionalism encouraged social scientists to avoid confronting the moral implications of their work. If to be professional meant to be value-free, then a social scientist must at all costs avoid questions of moral purpose and responsibility.

The founders of the New School had entered graduate school at a time when in the United States social science and social reform were still considered compatible. In the two decades before World War I, however, they found themselves under greater pressure to conform to professional values that they did not accept. The moral fervor of the war had intensified their feelings of alienation from the professional and institutional establishment and finally drove them into open revolt. Rather than adapt, they challenged the assumptions of the new professionalism and insisted that advocacy and objectivity were not only compatible, but were of small value when separated. Without moral concern and commitment, social science had no reason to exist. Whatever incidental contributions so-called value-neutral social scientists might make to human well-being, when push came to shove such persons invariably defended the status quo. The Columbia faculty's concurrence with President Butler over Cattell's dismissal lent weight to Beard's and Robinson's charges.

Beyond these professional disagreements, Beard, Robinson, and the other supporters of the New School protested the cultural values that, in their estimation, Butler and other American university presidents affirmed. In 1920, in the wake of the founding of the New School and during the height of the Red Scare, Butler described Columbia as a bastion of traditional American culture as well as an institution of higher learning and research. "Columbia," he declared, "is both American and Christian and it cannot in its institutional capacity properly go beyond this and be drawn into either political or religious controversy."[53]

Narrowly defining traditional American values, Butler believed that Columbia must pursue the "truth" within the context of those values. The New School professors, however, found these values parochial and inadequate for their own vision of the future. For them, academic freedom included the right and even the obligation to subject every preference, institution, and presumption of knowledge to critical inquiry, unhampered by political, religious, or philosophical conventions. They saw themselves as advocates of a cosmopolitan and progressive humanism that contrasted profoundly with Butler's defense of the American status quo.[54] The enthusiasm of the founders of the New School enabled them to attract donors, faculty, and students, even as their sometimes vague rhetoric helped gloss over the differences that existed between them. The founders fervently believed that the New School would make a difference; it was not, in their minds, just another experimental school.

Although their utopian enthusiasm lasted but a short time—by 1923 few of the founders remained at the New School, and those who did no longer hoped for a fundamental social reconstruction—the New School never repudiated their democratic cosmopolitanism or their expansive notion of academic freedom. The convictions of the founders endowed the New School with a flexible attitude toward education and research and, as well, a strong sense of the limits of its own toleration: theistic philosophy, racist social theory, and antidemocratic political thought were strictly excluded. With room for virtually everyone, except the advocates of what they considered regression, the founders of the New School were above all committed to human progress as they understood it.

2

THE DOORS OPEN IN CHELSEA

ON DECEMBER 28, 1918, the *New Republic* carried an advertisement for the New School for Social Research. It announced a preliminary set of course offerings for the following February, a full slate for the next October. The New School invited "intelligent men and women" to study the "grave social, political, economic, and educational problems of the day" as well as to prepare themselves for careers in journalism, municipal administration, labor organization, and social science teaching.[1] When the New School opened its doors to students in February 1919, it had just moved into its first home on West Twenty-third Street in the Chelsea neighborhood of Manhattan. The campus consisted of six brownstone mansions, newly renovated to provide comfortable quarters for the faculty and students, paid for largely by Dorothy Straight. The offices of the *New Republic* were practically around the corner, on Twenty-first Street, and Greenwich Village—already a center for New York's avant-garde community—stretched directly to the south. The setting could hardly have been better for the experiment in education that the New School represented.

The founders of the New School—with the exception of James Robinson—had accepted without qualification Veblen's assertion that scholarly research and conventional teaching were incompatible. And although they had always conceived of themselves as founding a "school," complete with students, they all agreed that teaching should remain ancillary to research. The New School staff understood adult education to be comparable to an apprenticeship, in which the student would learn from a senior scholar much as a young person might learn from a master artisan. Such a relationship, while preserving the primacy of research, allowed friendship and cooperation between faculty and students that was rare—or even nonexistent—in more traditional institutions. Likewise, the staff embraced Veblen's ideas about faculty control of institutional policy and tried to put them into action. Whatever else they may have accomplished, these experiments helped the New School to firmly establish the informal style that became its trademark. Because its students were adults and its faculty resented institutionalized formality, no serious gulf developed between students and faculty. Even after full-time administrators were appointed to run the school in 1922, they managed to preserve an almost family-like ambience.[2]

Such an environment—informal and egalitarian, a marked departure from the hierarchical organization of most American universities—was a goal from the first. In the earliest surviving document relating directly to the New School (dated January 16, 1916), Emily Putnam chided James Robinson for failing to be "revolutionary" enough. Putnam insisted that faculty control be the guiding principle of the school. The faculty should make appointments, determine the curriculum, and approve all financial decisions. To guarantee "fluidity" as well as encourage intellectual independence she even suggested that faculty appointments be limited to five-year, nonrenewable contracts. She signed her letter "Yours for Anarchy."[3] When Putnam drafted the letter in 1916, she wrote as a minority voice, although she claimed to have the sympathy of Beard. By 1918, however, the New School group as a whole had come to accept her radical proposals, including banning tenured appointments. During its first four years the New School sought to implement faculty control, academic freedom, and equality among faculty. Under the leadership of Putnam, Robinson, and Beard the New School consciously organized itself as a community of scholars consistent with Veblen's guild notion of scholarship.[4]

The anarchist sentiments that Putnam had expressed were not written merely for rhetorical effect. For most of the organizers, the New School was to be the antithesis of Columbia and other American universities. Robinson opposed even the idea of a governing board, but was overruled when others pointed out that the school would not be able to secure a charter without a board of trustees. Even so, the board was to restrict itself to issues that affected finances and the physical plant. The faculty retained control over appointments, research, and curriculum. Beard went so far as to argue against the acquisition of any kind of permanent building. He preferred renting loft space so that at any moment the faculty would feel free to "cancel our lease, pack our papers into handbags, and go our way in peace. To own a building was to chain yourself down and force all sorts of compromises upon your free spirit."[5] Again, prudence prevailed. None of the major donors would have anything to do with Beard's storefront college. Beard also feared that a comfortable endowment would make the school complacent and conservative. As a result, although the school secured ten-year pledges of support amounting to nearly $300,000, much of it from Dorothy Straight, it did not establish an endowment.[6] When the New School failed to fulfill the expectations of its donors, many withdrew their pledges, leaving the school in a precarious situation.[7] Ironically, this temporary crisis contributed to the decision to cut back on research at the New School after 1922, a development that Beard found most distressing. All in all, despite the failure of the most radical proposals, the New School emerged comparatively free of the usual academic structures.[8]

The decision of the organizers of the New School to dispense with most "academic encumbrances" was a sound strategy, born of necessity as much as idealism. The New York Board of Regents required a $500,000 endowment before it would accredit any private institution of higher learning. Lacking such an endowment, the founders secured a charter from the District of Columbia, which at the time granted educational charters almost on request. Similarly, by dispensing with dormitories, eliminating undergraduate responsibilities, and offering night courses, the New School both reduced its startup costs and increased its attractiveness to potential faculty. Teaching was restricted to between three and five hours of in-class instruction per week, freeing faculty to devote most of their time to research and writing.[9]

At the same time, the scheduling of classes in the late afternoon and evening enabled the school to hire instructors on a fee basis from other schools. New York City academics found the New School an attractive means to augment their incomes. This reduced even further the New School's overhead expenses and eliminated faculty fringe benefits, allowing it to offer quite generous salaries. The combination of light workloads and high salaries made it possible for the school to recruit distinguished lecturers from Harvard, Cornell, Princeton, Yale, City College, New York University, and Columbia. In this regard, the New School was ingenious if not revolutionary. By directing its program to adults the New School tapped a previously unexploited educational market and, at only minimal expense, drew on the faculty of other academic institutions as well as the educational resources of the city at large.[10]

As announced in the *New Republic*, the New School opened for classes in February 1919. In October it established a three-term academic year: October 1–December 22; January 2–March 25; and April 1–June 23. The school operated on this schedule until 1923, when it shifted to a fall, winter, and summer format. Through 1923 most courses were offered in three sequential parts, one each session. The catalog recommended that students enroll in the fall for all three, but the school allowed students to register for any one of the parts in any of the three sessions. Each course met once a week for an hour-and-a-half lecture, either in the late afternoon (5:30) or early evening (8:30). In addition, students were encouraged to organize their own discussion groups. The New School offered to provide classroom space for these discussions, but not instructors. After 1923, when the board reorganized the school, it dropped the spring session, converted the three-part courses to two parts, and offered only miscellaneous courses during the summer session. Otherwise, the pattern of evening and late-afternoon courses, meeting once a week for lectures, has persisted to the present.[11]

In its first four years the New School maintained a core faculty of its own. Most of this "permanent" faculty taught courses in all three sessions, year after year, and only at the New School. The stalwarts included economists Thorstein Veblen, Wesley Mitchell, and Leo Wolman, classicist Emily Putnam, historians Charles Beard and James Robinson, anthropologist Alexander Goldenweiser, philosopher Horace Kallen, and literary critic Henry Dana. In addition visiting lecturers, such as Harvard law professor Roscoe Pound, freelance journalist Lewis Mumford, British political scientist Harold Laski, *New Republic* drama critic Stark Young, sociologist Harry Elmer Barnes, anthropologist Franz Boas, and City College philosopher Morris Cohen, occasionally offered courses. John Dewey, who had left Columbia to join the New School, returned to Columbia after a two-year leave of absence, teaching at the New School only as a visiting lecturer.

Unfortunately, the loose structure of the early years resulted in few written records of the school's activities. The board of directors appointed James Robinson as "director." He coordinated faculty and board meetings and, with the school's executive secretary, drew up the catalogs, arranged course schedules, made classroom assignments, billed students, and paid the debts. The small faculty met regularly and approved all teaching appointments.[12] Relaxed and informal in administration, the New School relied largely on the professional standards of the faculty to ensure proper conduct. Only once did the actions of a faculty member appear to have been at issue. In 1926 the school terminated the appointment of psychologist John Watson for what Beard's daughter later described as "sexual misconduct."[13] Watson seems to have left with few regrets, and the charge of misconduct was never specified or made public. Whatever the difficulty, the incident suggests that the New School was willing to enforce certain standards of professional conduct, but apparently had little need to do so.

In these early years, relations between the faculty and board seem to have been amiable. Four of the eleven board members served on the faculty—Mitchell, Putnam, Beard, and Robinson—and so there was little potential for tension. Within the board itself, however, there was disagreement as to the primary mission of the New School. Two positions evolved, one advocated by Herbert Croly and the other by James Robinson. Croly conceived of the New School as an American equivalent to the French *Ecole des Sciences Politiques.* As such it would sponsor scholarly research as well as train business, governmental, labor, and educational leaders. In Croly's words, the New School should be "an instrument of both social purpose and social research." Robinson, on the other hand, was less interested in vocationally related instruction as he considered adult education an end in itself. Most of the board believed that the New School should do both. Not until 1922, when the school ran into financial difficulties, did this fundamental disagreement manifest itself as a policy dispute.[14]

In its first four years, the faculty worked as a tightly knit group of like-minded, if independent, scholars who were members of a very unique club. After 1923, except for Kallen, Veblen, Wolman, Dana, and Goldenweiser, the remainder of the regular faculty left the New School. From 1923 until 1933, the school depended almost exclusively on nonfaculty lecturers for instruction.[15]

The clubiness of the early New School was reinforced by the campus itself. Its six Victorian mansions were set three in a row, back to back, in the formerly fashionable Chelsea neighborhood of London Terrace. At the time it was accessible only by the Ninth Avenue Elevated or by automobile. It was in rundown condition when purchased, but Dorothy Straight underwrote the renovation while Charlotte Hunnewell Sorchan, an interior decorator, and Herbert Croly, who had earlier edited the *Architectural Review,* agreed to direct the remodeling. The houses, once renovated, included a lounge, an assembly hall that seated 250 people, several classrooms, seminar rooms, studies, a library, a bookshop, and offices. The upper floors were converted into faculty apartments. Virtually all the rooms had working fireplaces, which provided both heat and an atmosphere conducive to informal faculty–student relations. The backyards of the houses were joined to create a small courtyard which contained a pool, benches, sculpture, and shade trees. After lectures and concerts—some by such notables as economist John Maynard Keynes, philosopher Bertrand Russell, dancer Doris Humphrey, and composers Aaron Copland and Henry Cowell—students, faculty, and guests mingled over coffee and cookies or broke up into groups and wandered over to neighborhood coffeehouses for prolonged discussions.[16] One former student remembers trooping out after a lecture with six or eight other students from Barnard, Columbia, City College, and NYU to hear Margaret Sanger lecture at Cooper Union on birth control, in the process nearly getting arrested.[17] The 1919–1920 Red Scare made the New School's first years seem all the more exciting. Horace Kallen recalled with great delight discovering what he took to be two undercover agents attending his lectures on the "Evolution of the International Mind" and the subsequent writeup of the New School by the antiradical Lusk Committee of the New York State legislature.[18]

By far the most gratifying element of the school's first years was the camaraderie among its faculty. Leo Wolman, a labor statistician, whom Wesley Mitchell had recruited from Johns Hopkins, recollected the constant coming and going of distinguished lecturers as well as the close relations that he developed with the other regular faculty. Wolman described his experience at length: "They all came, and we had a hell of a good time together. . . . I knew Robinson well. Robinson was around you see. I lived on the top floor at 427 West Twenty-fourth Street, where there were two apartments. Kallen lived in the back one, and I lived in the front one. Harry Elmer Barnes was below us, and Veblen was next door, and Henry Wadsworth Longfellow Dana was around a lot. He lived next door. People would turn up, like Patrick Geddes, the city planner, a friend of Lewis Mumford and [W. H. R.] Rivers, the anthropologist, and as I said before, the fellow from the London School [Graham Wallas], a big, very able fellow, all kinds of people."[19]

One of the more distracting events of this period, though, proved to be neither intellectual nor even social. Early one July morning in 1922, Horace Kallen awoke to find a hand on his foot. Fearing the intruder would enter his sister's adjoining room, Kallen jumped up in the dark and grabbed at the person, only to be hit in the nose. "I started bleeding like a stabbed pig," related Kallen a few days afterward. The burglar broke free and ran away but left a cap behind with a chaffeur's badge attached. With the badge and Kallen's identification, the police apprehended the intruder. He turned out to be only twenty-two years old.

Kallen immediately felt sorry for the man and tried to have his charge dropped. Even so, Kallen failed to see any humor in the incident as it had upset his already ill sister and left him "in a decidedly nervous state," so much so that he soon left his school apartment.[20]

Nonetheless, for everyone else Kallen's ordeal made for a great story as they pictured the very serious Kallen wrestling a burglar, bleeding like a "stabbed pig," his sister all the while screaming for the police, and then, with justice about to be rendered, Kallen pleading for clemency on behalf of the culprit. After forty years, even Kallen came to appreciate the fun and, in retrospect, seemed to have enjoyed the fellowship of the early years in Chelsea fully. Nearly all the early participants looked back on the New School's first four years as something special, a time when the school seemed to live up to the utopian vision of its founders. In their eyes it was, or was trying to be, a democratic community of independent scholars, engaged in an exciting and serious enterprise, immune to the constraints of the outside world.[21]

With all the camaraderie, there was never any question of the serious purpose of the school. The New School had been founded to help reconstruct society, not indulge individual whim or foster scholarly prima donnas. No one rested on his or her past accomplishments as the board asked for an annual accounting of faculty work.[22] The proposed ten-year budget that was drawn up in 1918 allocated $99,000 for each of the following years, $58,000 of it for salaries. This included $8,000 for one senior instructor, $6,000 each for four other senior instructors, $4,000 for a part-time senior instructor, another $2,000 for a second part-time senior instructor, $15,000 for six teaching instructors paid $2,500 each, and another $5,000 for guest lecturers. By the standards of the time these salaries were competitive with any academic institution in the country. The board planned to raise almost all the money from private donations. Tuition, during the first four years, provided on the average only about 28 percent of the annual budget.[23] Since the school allowed faculty members to spend only a small portion of their time teaching, these salaries were virtually research stipends. The first annual report stated this clearly: "The object of the school will be to give properly qualified and earnest men and women, whether they have an academic education or not, an opportunity to carry on serious research in the fields of government and social organization."[24]

Despite the faculty's commitment to research, enrollment statistics and course offerings indicate that teaching at the New School was good enough to draw students. In fact, the adult education courses drew far more students than anyone had anticipated. In its first full academic year (1919–1920) the New School enrolled 348 students. In the academic year 1923–1924 registrations increased to nearly 800 students.[25] Nearly half of the 127 courses taught from 1919 to 1923 were in economics and political science; another third were in history, philosophy, and anthropology; and 15 percent were in psychology, social work, and education. In the first five years the New School offered only six courses in art, literature, drama, dance, music, or physical science. In both teaching and research, the New School devoted almost all its energies and resources to subjects related directly to public affairs, social work, and social science.[26]

The heavy emphasis on public affairs and social science affected the character of the student body. Of the 3,435 students who registered for courses from 1919 to 1923, about 16 percent were educators, 10 percent social workers, 15 percent professionals or business executives, 10 percent students from other institutions, 5 percent laborers, and 11 percent "housewives." Not surprisingly, almost everyone had attended college (80 percent) and most had graduated (60 percent).[27] The most striking feature, though, was the relatively large number of women. During a time when women made up only about 40 percent of American college students and 35 percent of college students in New York State, at the New School two-thirds of the students were women, even though the afternoon and evening classes had been established specifically to attract working people, whom it was assumed would be largely men.[28] The other noteworthy feature is the relatively large number of persons who had what appear to be Jewish surnames, from 25 to 30 percent of the students.[29]

The proportionately high representation of women and Jews can be explained by several factors. At a time when other educational institutions openly discriminated against women and Jews, the New School solicited both. The New School faculty contained prominent women and Jews, as did its board of directors.[30] During the first four years, the New School particularly sought the support of labor unions, charitable groups, and secondary school teachers—groups with high female and Jewish representation. And, among labor unions, the school received its strongest support from the International Ladies Garment Workers Union, a largely Jewish union.[31] The New School, which gained an early reputation for "respectable radicalism," seems to have appealed to intellectually minded women pursuing careers, and women involved in reform movements, many of whom happened to be Jewish. Moreover, at Columbia as head of the political science department, Edwin Seligman, a member of a prominent New York Jewish family, acted as a kind of father/mentor to both Robinson and Beard as he had protected them and the other political science "radicals" from harassment by the Butler administration. At various times in the New School's early years Seligman aided the school, and with Horace Kallen and Felix

Frankfurter, provided the school with an entrée to Jewish organizations and foundations.[32]

The first four years were an intoxicating time for the New School. It had attracted a faculty of luminaries, raised nearly $300,000 in contributions, sponsored numerous publications, drawn a diverse student body, and established itself as an important school for adult education.[33] By 1922, however, when the people involved with the New School looked back and assessed the progress of the school, these accomplishments seemed of small moment when compared with the expectations of 1917. There had been no radical social reconstruction of western society following World War I, the New School had made only a marginal impact on social science and higher education, and the students, without the incentive of grades and degrees, had failed to throw themselves into research. The original excitement had begun to dissipate. The school's chronic indebtedness, the difficulty of operating an egalitarian educational institution, and the growing recognition that teaching the popular lecture courses must be given higher priority all contributed to growing dissatisfaction. In early 1922 the New School had reached a major crossroads.[34]

By April the demoralization of the faculty reached crisis proportions. Although personal animosities, chronic financial problems, and the waning novelty of their endeavor no doubt contributed to the mood, faculty members expressed their disillusionment in terms of institutional policy. Should the New School divest itself of its profitable adult lecture program? Should it shelve the expensive but valuable research program? Or should it try to continue to offer both? Virtually everyone seemed to agree that, to survive, the New School had to be reconstituted. Herbert Croly insisted that, although donors might support a prestigious research institute, they would be reluctant to contribute to the New School as long as it operated as a lecture bureau. James Robinson, on the other hand, felt that adult education had been the New School's most successful enterprise, and one that had largely paid its own way.[35] Board member Caroline Bacon, undaunted by the cries of despair, denied that the situation was desperate. True, there existed a probable deficit for 1922 of $6,213, but that was a relatively small sum considering that the fiscal year would not end for another two months. Bacon assured the board that the deficit could be made up if only the school's future could be clarified.[36] Such a clarification, however, seems to have been virtually impossible under the circumstances. Robinson and Croly, the acknowledged leaders of the school, seem to have been eager only to be done with the whole thing, and Beard and Mitchell were either unwilling or unable to guide the school through its crisis. Faced with a virtual default in leadership, Caroline Bacon realized that it would be necessary to go outside the faculty to find a solution. At Herbert Croly's recommendation she invited Alvin Johnson, then associate editor of the *New Republic,* to step in to mediate the board's differences and to present a plan to reorganize the New School.[37]

Alvin Johnson had been a member of the board of directors of the New School from the school's inception, but until Bacon's request he had taken only a casual interest in its affairs. Consequently, Johnson was able to present himself as an impartial mediator, free from the accumulated personal antagonisms of the previous four years. Speaking at a board meeting on April 26, Johnson made a sweeping proposal for reforms, complete in all but the smallest details. His suggestion, in essence, was that the New School extricate itself entirely from adult education and reestablish itself as a research institute.[38]

As an institute of social research the New School would, according to Johnson's plan, invite scholars to carry on specific research projects on such subjects as international relations, banking and finance, agricultural problems, and urban housing. The institute would provide each scholar with facilities, research assistants, and a research budget. On completion of each project, the institute would publish the results in a monograph series. Depending on the scope of the undertaking, institute sponsorship would vary from one to five years. At the end of the fellowship period, scholars would leave the institute and new fellows would replace them. Johnson proposed that positions be created for three senior research fellows, two junior fellows, and ten assistant fellows, at a total salary of $32,000. He also included funding for research expenses, overhead, and a salary for a secretary-manager, bringing the annual budget to $57,000, or almost exactly the current budget.

Very quickly, Johnson predicted, such an institute would attract the best social scientists in the country, and most universities would encourage their faculty to participate. His plan allowed for lectures by distinguished scholars, but he insisted that "such lecture courses ought not to be permitted to embarrass the finances or confuse the government of the research institute."[39] Whatever Johnson's purpose, his proposal for a research institute put Herbert Croly on the spot. Johnson had presented a plan—a practical plan—that met each of Croly's demands. All that remained was for Croly to embrace the plan and pledge to raise the necessary funds. Instead, the ordinarily opinionated Croly chose to withdraw from the debate and leave the governance of the New School to others. Johnson himself always believed that Croly, facing financial problems at the *New Republic,* wanted to terminate the New School so that Straight would provide his magazine with more support.[40]

James Robinson, the school's strongest advocate of adult education, had come to the meeting with a plan of his own. His position
throughout the debate had been that social research and adult education were reconcilable goals, but he conceded that it was not feasible to
fund both. At the meeting on April 26, he argued that, since the lecture
program was in part self-supporting, the New School should reorganize
itself as a school for nonvocational adult education and drop the
research program altogether. Always the teacher, Robinson detailed
the unprecedented need for adult education. Breakthroughs in technology, physics, chemistry, biology, and psychology made popular
literacy in the sciences and social sciences imperative. With an expanded lecture program, the New School could mediate between
research scientists and the educated public. Furthermore, he proposed
organizing "New School Clubs," or study groups, throughout the country which would use New School textbooks and a quarterly bulletin as
study material. Like Johnson, he also recommended abolishing the
faculty as such and hiring lecturers on a per-course basis. All told,
Robinson anticipated annual expenses of $69,000 with an income of
$16,000 from tuitions. That is, whether a research institute or a lecture
program, the New School seemed to require an annual subsidy in excess
of $50,000.[41]

Johnson had come well prepared. Just as the board appeared to be
at an impasse between an expensive research institute and an equally
expensive adult education program, Johnson brought forward a second
plan. In support of Robinson's position, Johnson agreed that research
and adult education were indeed compatible, but that at the moment
the New School simply could not afford both. Johnson estimated that a
well-conceived lecture program could bring in as much as $20,000 each
year, leaving a deficit of only $5,000 for the adult education program.
For another $38,000, the New School could sponsor a scaled-down re-
search institute, with positions for two senior researchers, two junior
researchers, and eight assistants. A full research institute, like that
described in his first plan, would have to await additional funding.
Finally, Johnson insisted that the New School be reorganized along less
egalitarian lines. He recommended the appointment of a director for the
adult education program, who would determine course offerings and
hire lecturers. In deference to the faculty, Johnson proposed a separate
governing board for the research division, which would assure scholarly integrity and academic freedom. He suggested that this advisory
board consist of distinguished scholars such as John Dewey, Felix
Frankfurter, Wesley Mitchell, and Louis Brandeis.[42]

In effect, Johnson refused to give up anything. He wanted the New
School to continue its social research and at the same time take full ad-

vantage of its popular lecture program. To the extent that it could be afforded, research would continue in the form of faculty work and an occasional postdoctoral fellowship. As endowment became available, research would be expanded. But for the immediate future, Johnson argued that the school should place its emphasis on the self-sustaining adult lecture program.

Johnson's compromise proposal carried the board as it asked him to assume administrative control of the New School. Johnson had made the New School's cause his own; as director he would give the school its first effective leadership. Johnson wrote Dorothy Straight the next day, "To put it baldly, I have usurped the administrative powers of the school, and mean to hang on to them until they can be turned over to someone who shows promise of doing a real job. I don't like either usurpation or administration, but I am personally convinced that a big job can be done by the school, and I don't see how I can keep out of it so long as that is my conviction."[43]

Alvin Johnson's handling of the 1922 crisis and his explanation to Straight typified his leadership at the New School. Whatever the situation Johnson invariably managed to cut through confusions and personal animosities, showing little patience for obstructionists. He preferred to settle differences through personal diplomacy but, that failing, he did not hesitate to confront individuals whom he believed foolishly endangered the New School. If that meant alienating the school's founders—Beard, Robinson, and Croly—so be it. If it meant sidestepping the board, Johnson did so. If it meant firing star faculty such as Veblen, then Johnson acted. Still, he much preferred to work through groups and especially his boards of trustees. Johnson always carefully cultivated board members, chose persons who would either support his decisions or defer to his judgments, and always took the precaution of sounding out individual board members when important votes were pending. Much as the school in time became a creature of Alvin Johnson, so did the members of the board. At those rare times when all Johnson's efforts failed and the board balked at one of his schemes, he simply constituted a new, autonomous board to oversee the controversial project. Then, after the controversy subsided or dissident board members retired, Johnson would combine his trustees into a single board and make the new activity an official part of the New School.

Johnson ran the day-to-day activities of the New School in a similar manner, firm, but personal, and always on the lookout for something new. As president of the New School, Johnson exhibited three invaluable traits—a remarkable capacity to attract creative individuals, a profound respect for talent, and an uncanny ability to accomplish ambitious projects with little or no money. He not only identified enthusiastically with other people's ambitions, but could communicate their ambitions to wealthy benefactors and board members. At first glance, few would have guessed that this tall, scholarly man with a full head of white hair was other than a capable but staid academic. Johnson, though, was not staid. He enjoyed his whiskey, delighted in telling ribald stories, and took on projects and individuals no other institution would touch. Moreover, Johnson had a common, if calculated, touch which put people at ease as he represented himself as a child of the toiling classes. Whether acting as an economist, editor, or administrator, he always took the side of laborers, farmers, and minorities in general. He was an early and articulate spokesman for Negro civil rights, opposed all manifestations of anti-Semitism, and supported women's rights. When he formally retired in 1945, Johnson took over as editor of the *Yale Review,* even as he tried to set up a rural resettlement community for landless farmers in North Carolina. These were the polarities of his life, an equalitarian commitment toward the disadvantaged and an unequivocal affirmation of the value of refined culture—democracy and learning. Under Johnson these were also the polarities of the New School, an institution as idiosyncratic as Johnson himself.

In retrospect, it is difficult to imagine that until April 1922 Alvin Johnson had been largely indifferent to the fortunes of the New School. The school's disavowal of dogmatism, its commitment to social reform through research and publication, its informal and unpretentious manner as well as its naive enthusiasm characterized Johnson as much as the New School. When he accepted the directorship of the New School, he immersed himself in its spirit and activities. Johnson expanded adult education, worked to reestablish the research division, and organized numerous programs to train business executives, labor leaders, educators, and civic leaders. Similarly, he reaffirmed the New School's policy to act as a forum to address contemporary issues and propose solutions for social problems. And like the earlier founders, Johnson fervently believed in the possibility of human progress.[44] Thus, even though he drastically reorganized the school's administrative structure and momentarily shifted the school's emphasis from social research to adult education, he did so to save the New School from itself, not to transform it. In later years, Johnson often poked fun at the administrative naiveté of Robinson and Beard but he never ridiculed their vision. When all was said and done, their vision prevailed. Croly left in anger, Robinson and Beard in disillusionment, and Wesley Mitchell in search of new challenges. After 1922, the personnel was different, the emphasis had shifted, and the administration had been reformed, but the ideals remained unchanged.

No one could have been better suited to head the New School than Alvin Johnson. The child of Danish immigrants, Johnson considered himself a bona fide pioneer and a midwesterner to the core. Characteristically, he described his birth on December 10, 1874, as "the day I chose to be born." He was educated in Nebraska public schools and studied classical and German literature at the University of Nebraska. Throughout his life Johnson delighted in the contrast between his humble rural background and his urbane learning, playing the part of the country-bred scholar who with equal ease could quote Ovid and Schiller in their original languages. Johnson enlisted in the army during the Spanish–American War, but was never assigned to combat. After his discharge, he proceeded to Columbia University to enroll in its prestigious Graduate School of Political Science. Columbia accepted Johnson into its program in economics.[45]

Johnson found both Columbia and New York grand beyond his wildest hopes. Intimidated neither by the city nor the university he adjusted quickly. By his own account he had a wonderful time in class and out. He excelled at Columbia as he had at Nebraska. In 1910 at the request of Professor Edwin Seligman, Johnson prepared a research paper for the Committee of Fifteen, the precursor of the Bureau of Municipal Research, on the responses of European governments to prostitution. The subject was right up Johnson's alley as he delighted as much in the subject as in the scholarly opportunity. After extensive research, he concluded that European efforts to regulate prostitution through licensing and medical examinations had largely failed as both supply and demand outstripped the government's most strenuous efforts at regulation. To Johnson the best policy seemed for the government to take a hands-off attitude and instead concentrate its efforts on improving the social and economic environment in which young women from destitute families found themselves. His report concluded that all efforts at reform and regulation were doomed to failure until the poor were offered both education and decent employment. The committee found Johnson's proposals sound and with his permission published the report under its own name as it became a standard work on the subject. Johnson's willingness to tackle a subject encrusted with social taboo; his commonsensical, if undramatic, solution; and his willingness to remain anonymous, all exemplified his leadership at the New School.[46]

From 1900 to 1914 Johnson taught successively at Bryn Mawr, Columbia, Nebraska, Texas, Chicago, Stanford, and Cornell. Although respected as a teacher and economist, Johnson found academic life unrewarding. In 1914 he accepted a temporary job with the Carnegie Corporation, and then in 1916 he took a year's leave of absence from Cornell to work for the *New Republic*. Johnson returned to Cornell, but in 1917, when the United States entered World War I, he resigned to become assistant editor of the *New Republic*. Soon after, however, Wesley Mitchell succeeded in luring him to Washington to work for the Council of National Defense under Bernard Baruch and later the War Industries Board. Like so many others at the New School, Johnson was convinced by his wartime experience of the validity of governmental planning and economic intervention. After about a year in Washington, Johnson returned to the *New Republic,* hoping to help swing public opinion toward a nonvindictive peace settlement. He stayed on even after President Wilson caved in to Allied demands at Versailles for enormous reparation payments from Germany. Together with Herbert Croly, he edited the magazine until 1922.[47]

Although Johnson was not a member of the faculty, he had participated in the organization of the school in 1917 and had served on the board since then. He was no stranger to the New School or to its guiding principles. His ideas on education and politics had been shaped by the same factors that had led to the formation of the New School. His background was remarkably similar to that of Beard, Robinson, Veblen, and Mitchell, midwesterners who had chosen New York as their home and who had gravitated toward the faculty at Columbia, the Bureau of Municipal Research, and the politically activist staffs of the *New Republic, Seven Arts,* the *Dial,* and the *Nation.* A social scientist with political commitments, Johnson was unsuited for the routine of academic life and its narrow professionalism. He had been profoundly affected by the experience of World War I, which he too saw as the watershed between the nineteenth and twentieth centuries. When he took over the New School in April 1922, he did so as an insider. Johnson, finally, at age forty-eight, had found at the New School his professional niche.

Johnson's determination to make the New School work received unexpected support from a delegation of students headed by Clara Mayer, publisher W. W. Norton, and Mary Ely, head of the American Association of Adult Education. Together, they promised to raise the funds necessary for the school's survival along the lines Johnson had proposed. With this backing, together with the support of board members Caroline Bacon, Florence Corliss Lamont, Daniel Cranford Smith, Wesley Mitchell, and Emily Putnam, Johnson assembled a faithful circle of patrons.[48] One of the most significant results of the crisis was Johnson's recognition of the largely untapped potential of

New School students. It became clear that the New School, if it paid serious attention to student suggestions, not only could count on them as generous donors, but could also attract more tuition-paying auditors to its courses. Johnson immediately recognized something that Robinson had glimpsed, but that Beard, Croly, Mitchell, and Veblen had missed entirely: students were crucial to the New School's well-being. In his 1925 Annual Report, Johnson expressed his position clearly: "The educational policy and program are determined by the faculty and students and not by any other administrative body. The students have the privilege of organizing courses on their own initiative and responsibility." Through informal consultation and student representation on the board, Johnson developed the curriculum "according to the expressed needs of its students."[49]

As the school year ended, Johnson set to work to put his program into effect. Before the fall, he had to reorganize the faculty, set up a lecture program, and put the school's finances into order. To his great fortune, Clara Mayer, who had come forward with an offer of help during the fiscal crisis, soon stepped in to assist with the other facets of his enormous task. The daughter of a wealthy New York realtor, Mayer had attended Barnard and found Robinson's lectures in intellectual history her most provocative college course. When Robinson resigned to organize the New School, Mayer enrolled in several evening classes. She became active in the New School Associates, a student organization, and contributed to various of the school's programs. In 1922, when the New School appeared on the verge of closing down, Mayer helped organize a committee of students to raise the funds necessary to weather the crisis. For her help, Johnson appointed Mayer to the board and hired her as secretary of the New School, later assistant director, and finally dean of adult education. Mayer recruited her mother and several brothers and sisters to the school's cause.[50] Over the next fifty years only Alvin Johnson played a more important part in the life of the New School.

The reorganization left the New School without its academic stars. Beard, Robinson, and Croly left immediately, Mitchell left in 1924 to return to Columbia, followed by Leo Wolman in 1931. Henry Dana remained as instructor of comparative literature, Horace Kallen continued to offer courses in philosophy and psychology, Alexander Goldenweiser in anthropology, and Veblen in economics. The remainder of the lecturers only taught irregularly, either one course per term or full time periodically. Such part-timers included sociologist Harry Elmer Barnes of Smith College, *New Republic* drama critic Stark Young, and philosopher Harry Overstreet from City College. The lecture offerings of social science, philosophy, psychology, and social work resembled the pre-reorganization fare. Similarly, a number of board members stayed on, such as Herbert Croly, Wesley Mitchell, Caroline Bacon, Dorothy Straight, and Emily Putnam, even as the New School publicly affirmed its commitment to research to the point of Johnson setting up an advisory board. The advisory board included Nebraska-born novelist Willa Cather, jurists Roscoe Pound, Felix Frankfurter, and Learned Hand, journalist Walter Lippmann, editor of the *New Republic* Bruce Bliven, Sidney Hillman of the Amalgamated Clothing Workers, Eleanor Roosevelt, and the one-time president of the United States Chamber of Commerce, Julius Barnes. Like the New School's research program, the advisory board was little more than window dressing intended to project an image of respectability and permanence despite the loss of key faculty. The continuities were significant, but so were the changes.[51]

The reorientation of the New School under Johnson manifested itself in the school's curriculum and in its public statements. The 1923–24 *Announcement,* the first issued after Johnson's reorganization, described the school's present purpose as consistent with its founding goals: "to seek an unbiased understanding of the existing order, its genesis, growth, and present working as well as . . . it's revision." The catalog reassured its readers that the New School would remain committed to "intellectual liberalism," which it claimed was possible only in an institution that catered to adults rather than to immature and impressionable college-aged youth. Apart from a passing reference to the need for an endowment to fund research, the school's revised *Announcement,* cowritten by Johnson and Mayer, emphasized a program of lecture courses which were financially dependent on tuition alone. It predicted that tuition from lectures would soon make the entire New School self-supporting. Finally, the *Announcement* emphasized the important constraints that delivering public lectures imposed on scholars. By being held accountable to tuition-paying auditors, scholars could not afford to dwell on the arcane and technical. Rather, they had to present their material in an understandable format. In short, even without a research faculty, the New School represented itself as performing several important educational functions. It offered a forum for diverse views on public and intellectual topics; it considered itself a bastion of academic freedom; and it acted as a vehicle to bring to the public in comprehensible form the latest discoveries in the social sciences. The research division remained "on the books," ready to be resuscitated as funding became available.[52]

More revealing than these general claims were the changes in course offerings. The 1923 catalog shows that, to the standard offerings in social science, public policy, and vocational courses, the New

School added several new lecturers. These included: John Watson on behavioral psychology; Morris Cohen on the thought of the nineteenth century; Stark Young on the art of the theatre; Henry W. L. Dana on social currents in modern literature; and Lewis Mumford on architecture in American civilization. Johnson, at the urging of Mayer, had committed the New School to several new subjects: psychology, philosophy, intellectual history, literature, and art. With Harry Elmer Barnes picking up Robinson's course on the human mind, more offerings in philosophy and psychology, and the new cultural orientation of the courses in art and literature, the New School seemed to have adopted the human mind broadly defined, rather than social science and social work, as its dominant interest.

Johnson skillfully played down the magnitude of the change these courses represented, and implied that student participation in policy-making had been the New School's practice from the start.[53] Nonetheless, it represented a significant departure. Influenced by Veblen, the New School had previously accepted the notion that the faculty, as scholarly artisans and producers, should control school policy, including faculty appointments and curriculum decisions.[54] Johnson shifted authority away from the faculty/producers to the student/consumers. As director, he believed that it was his responsibility to meet the market demands of students. Johnson hired faculty, terminated appointments, and organized student initiative for the two most important curriculum changes of the 1920s, the expansion of the psychology offerings and the introduction of lectures in literature, music, and art.[55] Nowhere was the change from Veblen's guild ethic to Johnson's consumerism more evident than in Johnson's firing of Veblen himself.

Veblen had always been contemptuous of students, believing that most sought entertainment, not learning. His *Higher Learning in America* was a peroration against undergraduate teaching in favor of scholarly autonomy. When he had joined the New School, Veblen understood that the institution's primary purpose was to provide scholars a convivial, free, and secure environment in which to research and write. Faculty members were to work with select students as well as on their own research projects, with lecturing only a secondary concern. Ironically, Veblen's fame as a writer and social critic proved to be one of the New School's most important drawing cards. Students flocked to his courses only to find Veblen determined to drive them away. He mumbled, rambled, and answered questions with sarcastic impatience. In desperation, Johnson surreptitiously placed a microphone on Veblen's lectern so that students could at least hear him. When Veblen realized what Johnson had done, he grabbed the microphone and threw it into the trash can. Once again, no one could hear him and in a couple of weeks his class dwindled from nearly a hundred students to half a dozen. After class Veblen implishly related to Wolman, "Johnson thought he would make me popular. But I fooled him."[56]

In 1925, faced with Veblen's refusal to teach the students who indirectly paid his salary, Johnson reluctantly fired the person most responsible for the idea of a new school. In 1918, when Veblen had first come from the University of Missouri to join the New School, he had confided to Wolman, "Well the London School of Economics has been a rebellion against older schools and it failed. I hope and pray that the New School will not be a similar failure, but I pray more than I hope."[57] Firing Veblen was probably the most difficult decision that Johnson ever made regarding the New School. He must have understood it as virtually an act of patricide. He felt deeply torn, and on numerous occasions he jokingly, but defensively, justified his action. Johnson's determination to reestablish a research division at the New School, his insistence that the research division remain autonomous and separate from adult education, and his subsequent organization of the University in Exile in 1933 all suggest that he valued the artisan/scholar more highly than the consumer/student, even in the face of what he considered financial necessity.[58] That he chose as he did in Veblen's case only demonstrates his determination to act in the best interests of the school.

In the years that followed the trends away from social science and toward cultural subjects, from research to adult education, accelerated. In the 1926 course catalog only nine of the twenty-seven courses fell into the categories of public policy, social science, or vocational training; from 1919 to 1922, nearly 75 percent of the courses at the New School had been in these three areas. Moreover, psychology courses had increased to five and cultural offerings had been expanded to include modern art and the motion picture. The most dramatic addition of all, though, was a course in psychoanalysis taught by Sandor Ferenczi, a distinguished Viennese psychiatrist who had worked with Freud.[59] The 1927–28 catalog explained such shifts as consistent with the New School's policy to offer "whatever seriously interests persons of mature intelligence." The New School no longer described itself as an instrument of social reform. Rather, it asserted, "Most of the work of the New School is cultural rather than vocational. . . . The students of the New School are in a great majority persons who have found their economic adjustment to life or are in the way of finding it. They come to the New School primarily to satisfy purely intellectual needs."[60] Consistent with that commitment, the catalog contained a preponderance of courses in philosophy, intellectual history, psychology, art, and literature. It also announced the New School's sponsorship of a new magazine, tentatively entitled *American Prose,* to be edited by writer and publisher Gorham Munson, as well as a series of lecture-recitals by composer Aaron Copland.

A comparison of the curriculum from the 1919–1924 period with that of the period from 1925 to 1930 makes the character of these changes quite clear. The staple social science courses, 60 percent of the New School's offerings in the 1919–1924 period, had dropped to barely 25 percent. Psychology, art, and literature, barely represented in the first period, had become important fields of study. And, despite the catalog's claim to the contrary, the percentage of vocationally oriented courses in social work and education had more than doubled, from less than 9 percent to nearly 20 percent.[61] These figures reveal a set of basic insights about the school and its students, insights that certainly informed the efforts of Johnson and Mayer during these years: first, that the "serious" courses which the founders had favored were no longer sufficient to support the school; second, that courses in psychology, the arts, and literature were popular; and finally, that the demand for vocational courses was greater than they had at first expected.

The changes that occurred under Johnson and Mayer were more an enlargement of perspective than a change in priorities. By expanding the New School to include cultural and artistic courses, Johnson and Mayer carried through on Robinson's idea of intellectual transformation. In his intellectual history course at Barnard, Robinson had lectured Mayer on the interrelationship of political, technological, and cultural change. He insisted that modern science and urbanization manifested themselves in art, literature, and architecture. Broadly understood, social research should include both music composition and wage and price studies. Johnson's and Mayer's decisions following the reorganization reflected this understanding. Moreover, rather than simply adding courses in psychology, literature, and the arts, they chose what they considered "modern" expressions of these forms. Art critic Leo Stein lectured on modern art, dancer Doris Humphrey on modern dance, composer Aaron Copland and music critic Paul Rosenfeld on modern music, writer Waldo Frank and literary critic Henry Dana on modern literature, publisher and writer Gorham Munson on modern writing, drama critics Anita Block and Stark Young on modern drama, Sandor Ferenczi on Freudian psychology, and freelance writer Lewis Mumford and urban planner Patrick Geddes on modern architecture and urban planning. Each of these individuals introduced their students to "modern" cultural developments even as the New School acted as a patron and forum for their work. In this manner the New School came to represent "modernism," broadly defined as artistic creativity, social research, and democratic reform.[62]

The differences between the student body of the 1919-1924 period and that of the 1925-1930 period paralleled the changes in curriculum. From 1919 to 1924 three groups—educators, social workers, and office workers—made up one-third of the New School's course registrations. From 1925 to 1930 these three groups accounted for 40 percent of registrations. In the 1919-1924 period college students represented 10 percent of the registrations, wage earners about 5 percent, and "housewives" more than 11 percent. In the 1925-1930 period registrations of college students dropped to less than 5 percent, wage earners to 2.7 percent, and housewives to 6.5 percent.[63] The educational profile changed as well. In the 1919-1924 period 80 percent of the students had attended college, 60 percent held college degrees, and about 7 percent held professional certificates but had not attended college. From 1925 to 1930, 52 percent had earned a college degree, another 20 percent had attended college but had not received a degree, and 17 percent held professional certificates. Some things, however, had not changed. Business executives and professionals were represented in the student body in about the same percentages, about 16 percent in the first period and 15 percent in the second.[64] People who had attended college but had not graduated stood at about 20 percent in both periods. The percentage of women and of individuals with Jewish surnames remained about the same: 65 percent of the students were women in both periods, and about 30 percent of the students in both periods appear to have been of Jewish descent.[65]

The shift from social science offerings to cultural courses had only a marginal effect on these last four categories of students. Under the leadership of Johnson and Mayer, the New School became significantly more attractive, however, to educators, social workers, and office workers, persons apparently more interested in recent cultural developments than in the social sciences. At the same time three other groups found the New School's cultural emphasis less attractive: students, laborers, and housewives. In the 1919-1924 period these three groups together comprised 26 percent of the school's enrollment. In the 1925-1930 period they accounted for only 14 percent and their percentage declined steadily during the next five years as well. They made up only 11 percent of New School registrants in the period from 1931 to 1936. College students, no doubt, found the research orientation and the more specialized courses of the earlier period more interesting, and laborers probably responded to the greater number of labor-oriented courses. It is not as clear why housewives found the new cultural emphasis less attractive. Perhaps, like the students, housewives wanted challenging research projects and advanced courses, or maybe they found the somewhat more radical tone of the early years more appeal-

ing. One thing seems certain: in the 1920s, contrary to many stereo-
types, New York housewives showed little interest in lectures in
psychology, psychoanalysis, recent fiction, music, the theatre, or art.
Of all the occupational categories, students and housewives seemed
most attracted to the research orientation that had characterized the
early era of the New School.

The changes at the New School had produced disillusionment
among the faculty. Many, like Beard, Croly, Robinson, and Mitchell,
left in 1922 when the research division was dismantled. Others stayed
on as lecturers, but came to feel that the changes of the twenties had
undercut the school's original purpose as a research institute and
school for the social sciences. Even Leo Wolman, who cared about the
school and served on its board for many years after his departure, left in
1931 to accept an offer from Columbia. In 1961 Wolman reflected on
why he had left the New School. "The New School was a kind of lecture
bureau," he suggested. "It wasn't really a school. Many men on the
faculty came to think that, you see. Mitchell finally went back to Columbia. Beard got out. Then Alvin Johnson came in and took it over and
tried to rebuild it in a way." But for Wolman the results were disappointing, particularly in regard to the students who attended the lectures. "Well, they weren't really students. They were people who came
in to listen to lectures, that's all. Not students in the sense in which you
use it here [Columbia], as you get it in school. That's why I said that it
became a school only later. . . . Johnson during the war, created the
'University in Exile' for those foreign, dispossessed scholars, from Germany mainly, Austria and Italy. That enabled him to create a graduate
school and have the right under state laws to give diplomas and that
sort of thing. They put it on its feet."[66]

Coming from a friend, Wolman's observations were telling. Johnson and Mayer might have resented the remark and no doubt would
have considered it an unfair caricature of the New School's adult education program. But both would have agreed that without a research
faculty the New School could not achieve its most important objective.
In the 1950s Mayer wrote, "One of the principal reasons for the existence of the New School consists in passing on the new knowledge
with a minimum of delay. And the corollary is that those who teach are
for the most part one and the same with those responsible for the
original exploration and discovery—we don't wait for textbooks, not
only because it takes too long but because too much of the thrill of
knowledge is lost in them."[67] Throughout the 1920s in their annual
reports, even as Johnson and Mayer energetically expanded the New
School's lecture program, they repeatedly argued for the need to
reestablish a research faculty. They pointed out that a research faculty

would strengthen student loyalty to the school, increase the number of students who returned for additional courses, and allow the New School to secure the right to grant degrees.

Without an endowment, however, such a program was out of the question and, indeed, would not have been approved by the state regents. "It had not been possible," wrote Johnson and Mayer in the 1925 catalog, "to make adequate provision either for the systematic grouping of courses, general or special . . . or for the projects of research that naturally arise out of the courses of instruction. For such work, obviously essential to the vitality of the institution, a higher degree of permanence is requisite. . . . If the New School were financially in a position to encourage this type of work," they continued, "it could make contributions of immediate practical importance to the literature on labor, agriculture, banking, applied psychology, education, religion." Furthermore, "in the field of social research there is a need for an institution free from the conventions and restrictions of existing bodies."[68]

Even with financial limitations, under Johnson the New School continued to conduct limited research. Not a person to give in to adversity, he believed that with as little as $25,000 in endowment the New School could accomplish important work. And although it was barred from granting degrees, the New School in the meantime could issue "certificates" for successful completion of courses which other schools might honor. Such a program would require instructors to keep track of attendance, give examinations, and assign grades. While this might compromise the informal character of the New School, it would establish its serious academic credentials.[69]

In sum, Johnson had always been of one mind with the other organizers of the New School in his desire to foster socially relevant research. He and Mayer had expanded adult education because the New School had to generate its own income, and in fact their plan had been successful: although student fees had comprised only 22 percent of the school's income in 1919, by 1929 they accounted for 49 percent.[70] In the process, they had come to appreciate adult education as an important enterprise in its own right. Nonetheless, Johnson and Mayer continued to work toward the revitalization of research at the New School.

Unlike Charles Beard, Emily Putnam, and James Robinson, neither Johnson nor Mayer was hostile to the formality of institutions. Their fondest dream was to build the New School into a distinguished center for social research, adult education, and modern art. To achieve this the New School had to secure an endowment. In addition, they forged another goal for the school, a goal that would prove as significant as anything else they accomplished. During these years, they came to believe that a functional and visually impressive building—a new building—was necessary to attract students and endowments to the New School.[71] In 1928, faced with the termination of the school's ten-year leases on its Chelsea quarters, Johnson, with Mayer's help, undertook a fund-raising campaign to finance the construction of a building that would express the needs and spirit of a new time, the architectural equivalent of Johnson's vision of the New School. Central to his vision was the informality that the New School adopted in its first ten years in Chelsea, an informality that contrasted sharply with the growing bureaucratization of American education in general. It also included a growing appreciation of the significance of modern artistic expression and the critical role of the arts in defining a modern society.[72]

3

GROWING UP ON
WEST TWELFTH STREET

FOLLOWING ITS REORGANIZATION IN 1922, the New School thrived as
never before. Not only were lectures crowded and additional courses offered each year, but the school's ongoing expenses were covered by lecture fees. The New School successfully made the transition from an experiment to an established institution. By 1927 Johnson had concluded
that the cozy quarters in Chelsea would no longer do. The ten-year
leases negotiated in 1919 were due to expire in two years, the school
was inconvenient to the main lines of transportation, and the buildings
themselves placed severe limits on future growth. The Chelsea location
had been appropriate for a small, well-funded research group of like-
minded scholars. It was poorly situated for an expansive institution of
adult education whose financial life depended on its ability to attract a
large number of fee-paying students. Moreover, both Johnson and
Clara Mayer were eager to expand the school's offerings in the fine arts,
a venture that would require considerably more space. Finally, Johnson
believed that the informal, almost ad hoc character of the Chelsea campus discouraged prospective donors. Wealthy patrons hesitated to in-
vest in such a temporary and visually unimpressive enterprise. If the
New School were to survive, Johnson realized that it would have to

dream grandly and act boldly. Otherwise, the New School would go the way of so many other interesting but underfinanced educational experiments.

An entrepreneur, a builder, and above all a visionary, Alvin Johnson was not by nature a caretaker.[1] The child of rural parents, educated in public schools and at the University of Nebraska, he could make no claims on the socially prominent of New York. Before coming to the New School his success had rested on his considerable abilities to get jobs done, whether for Edwin Seligman at Columbia, the Carnegie Foundation, Bernard Baruch at the War Industries Board, or Herbert Croly at the *New Republic*. In each case Johnson had been the hired man. His employers valued him for what he could do, not for what he represented. Now, however, as director of the New School, he had become his own man, although a man with no ready access to wealthy donors or foundations.

Johnson's lack of social connections and his relatively modest financial condition left its mark on the New School. Unlike other cultural institutions founded in New York in the 1920s, such as the Museum of Modern Art and the Whitney Museum, the New School could not count on the Rockefellers, the Whitneys, the Goodyears, or the Guggenheims to pull it through. And because the New School eschewed all forms of sectarian doctrine, whether religious or political, it could not draw on true believers, as could the socialist Rand School or the anarchist Ferrer School. Adult education and social research lacked the social prestige or doctrinal purity normally needed to attract patronage. As a private, nonsectarian, but egalitarian institution the New School enjoyed no natural patrons. Faced with such a discouraging prospect, Johnson had no choice but to beg, borrow, and market the New School into prominence.

New York in the 1920s teemed with poorly educated but prospering young people, many of whom were from lower-middle-class families, either the children of immigrants or new arrivals from small-town America. Johnson's training as an economist perhaps quickened his appreciation of this vast and largely unexploited market. He sensed that many New Yorkers with backgrounds similar to his own were starving for cultural edification but found themselves either intimidated by or excluded from the city's prestigious art museums and more formal academic institutions.[2] Continuing James Robinson's interest in cultural education Johnson, as early as 1925, added courses in literature, art, theatre, and music. Through newspaper advertising campaigns, he made it clear that all were welcome at the New School.[3]

The means to exploit this market were at hand. In the 1920s music, painting, dance, drama, and literature were all undergoing radical change. As the nation's cultural mecca, New York contained thousands of bright, young, and able artists, determined to find their livelihoods without compromising their esthetic goals. Johnson envisioned the New School as an intermediary between culturally deprived but economically secure adults and artistically innovative but financially insecure artists. By making the New School a center for "new" art forms, Johnson could at one time attract fee-paying students, wealthy patrons, and talented faculty. The school would offer the new class of economically secure workers and professionals a means to cultivate their knowledge of modern art and at the same time patronize young artists.[4]

Johnson set his grand scheme in motion with an "endowment" campaign. At first he tried the conventional route of appealing to established foundations, such as the Rockefeller, Carnegie, and Rosenwald foundations. They turned down his request for funds.[5] Undaunted, Johnson asked his board of trustees collectively to pledge $50,000 a year for five years. To his surprise the board agreed, on the condition that he raise another $25,000 a year for five years from the New School students themselves.[6] By late 1929 Johnson had secured pledges for the full $75,000 a year for five years, which gave him a cushion to complete a building campaign, move into the new building, and expand enrollment before he had to worry about the increased costs of an enlarged curriculum and physical plant.[7] As it turned out, the success of the endowment campaign insured the success of the building fund drive. With the five-year pledges secured, Johnson managed to manipulate the New School's existing resources in a manner that allowed him to construct his new building with little additional funding. Almost all the remaining funds, in strictly monetary terms, were as much fiction as fact.

Johnson launched his building fund campaign with the $23,000 that the school had received from its leaseholders for improvements the school had made on the London Terrace property in Chelsea. With this in hand Johnson formed an executive committee, consisting of himself and businessmen-trustees George Bacon, George H. Davis, and Joseph Milner. After a study of New York's transportation patterns was conducted by Davis's firm, the committee concluded that the New School should be situated near one of two transportation junction along Fifth Avenue, at Forty-second Street or on Fourteenth Street. The committee quickly decided that real estate prices near Forty-second Street were out of reach and narrowed its search to the Fourteenth Street area. As usual, luck was with Johnson. Daniel Cranford Smith, a retired businessman and friend of the school, happened to own three adjoining houses on Twelfth Street between Fifth and Sixth avenues. In a legendary feat of salesmanship, Johnson talked "Uncle Dan" into selling his property for $155,000, the only condition being that the school take over the existing $65,000 mortgage. Rather than take cash, Smith agreed to accept a second mortgage on the property in return for $155,000 in 6 percent bonds issued by the New School. By taking a second mortgage, Smith enabled Johnson to borrow another $200,000 on the first mortgage. Johnson paid off Smith's original $65,000 mortgage, held title to the property, and still had $135,000 toward the building fund. Smith's generosity made it possible for Johnson in effect to borrow $355,000 ($155,000 from Smith himself and $200,000 from a bank). In return, Johnson offered Smith a penthouse apartment in the new building at a nominal rent, a lifetime of free courses at the New School, and his eternal gratitude.[8]

With such an auspicious start, Johnson proceeded immediately to construction details. For this he turned to the Taylor Construction Company, whose principal partners were Charles and Albert Mayer, Clara Mayer's brothers. The Mayers agreed to construct the building for a very low cost of $.67 a cubic foot and personally recommended an architect, Joseph Urban. In addition, the Mayer family contributed $100,000 to the building fund. When Urban's design called for more street frontage than the original three lots provided, Johnson bought an adjoining lot on Twelfth Street for $20,000. Joseph Milner then applied his real estate expertise to the task of combining the four lots into a single title, complete with first and second mortgages. With a cash expenditure of only $20,000, Johnson had purchased the property for his building, raised $235,000 toward a construction loan, and secured a friendly builder and architect, neither of whom asked for advance payment. And he still had $3,000 left in cash![9]

As projected by Urban, the building costs would total $500,000, of which Johnson still needed another $265,000. Over the course of the next year he raised all but $50,000 of the balance by selling 6 percent second mortgage bonds to board members and other friends of the school. Later, in the midst of the Depression, the New School defaulted on most of this debt: fortunately, the bonds were held by friends, who wrote them off as outright if somewhat involuntary donations.[10] By then, though, Johnson had his new building, and fees from the expanded curriculum had made the school self-supporting when the five-year pledges ended in 1933. Forced by the major foundations to turn elsewhere for funds, Johnson—with the help of his business friends Daniel Smith, Caroline Bacon's husband George, Bacon's law partner George Davis, realtor Joseph Milner, and Charles and Albert Mayer— had performed a daring act of financial wizardry, a feat that transformed the New School from a promising experiment into a permanent institution. Johnson's entrepreneurial daring, combined with his capacity to appeal to sympathetic business entrepreneurs, would provide the financial resources for later and equally adventurous undertakings.

The Twelfth Street site had been chosen for its accessibility, experience having shown that students would attend night classes only if they found it easy and safe to come and go. Express stations on the IRT and the BMT subway lines were within short walking distance, as was the Sixth Avenue Elevated, the Hudson Tunnels, the Fifth Avenue bus lines, the Fourteenth Street subway, and the soon-to-be-completed Eighth Avenue subway.[11] As a result the New School stood within easy reach of every resident in the New York metropolitan area, even those without automobiles. For a market-oriented institution like the New School nothing could have been more important. Still, the Twelfth Street site proved more than simply convenient. In moving out of Chelsea, the New School had moved into Greenwich Village.

More than its academic neighbor New York University, or even Cooper Union, the New School embodied the informal, rebellious, and irreverent ethos of Greenwich Village. The New School fit in well with the bohemian population that lived in the Village prior to World War II.[12] Its new emphasis on art, its broad commitment to social reform, its political radicalism, its naive enthusiasm, and its flagrant disregard for conventions, academic and otherwise, made the New School seem a natural outgrowth of the Village rather than a recent transplant. In the Village, its lack of conventional status, its hand-to-mouth existence, and its experimental character became distinct virtues. The presence in the neighborhood of numerous new and used bookstores, artists' lofts and studios, and small, inexpensive restaurants, cafés, and bars provided a perfect ambience for the New School's low-key academic innovation. Assuming some of the "arty" and exotic quality of its surroundings, the New School for thousands of New Yorkers became the academic heart of the Village.[13]

By 1920 New York, like other major cultural centers in the twentieth century, had lost much of its personal character. Intellectual and artistic life had become increasingly institutionalized so that few places existed where less conventional avant-garde artists, writers, scholars, and other intellectuals could establish themselves. Although there were select circles of intellectuals at the *New Republic,* various "little magazines," the newly organized Museum of Modern Art, New York University, City College, and Columbia, such groups were often self-contained, and entry to one did not assure entry to another. Equally important, moments of confrontation and dialogue between intellectuals and the general public had become rare, even noteworthy, events.[14]

The New School, under Johnson's leadership, tried to fill this void, just as the artists and intellectuals of Greenwich Village had developed their own informal circles as a self-conscious alternative to the more established and elitist cultural life of New York. At the New School anyone in New York, by paying a modest fee, could attend lectures by such distinguished speakers as jurists Roscoe Pound and Felix Frankfurter, poet Robert Frost, art patron Leo Stein, art historian Meyer Schapiro, painter Thomas Hart Benton, writer Thomas Mann, essayist Lewis Mumford, composers Aaron Copland and Henry Cowell, dancer Doris Humphrey, political commentator Max Lerner, philosophers Bertrand Russell, Morris Cohen, Sidney Hook, and John Dewey, anthropologists Franz Boas and Margaret Mead, psychiatrist Erich Fromm, and dozens of other eminent thinkers and doers.[15] The New School not only gathered together New York intellectuals, it brought them in contact with broad popular audiences. For those who lacked access to the city's more expensive and exclusive institutions, the New School in Greenwich Village offered extraordinary opportunities.

Yet Johnson envisioned the New School as much more than a cultural clearinghouse. He imagined it as a dynamic center of modern culture in which adults could learn to appreciate new art forms, or even become artists themselves. Like the other founders of the New School, he viewed social science as a transformative agent; properly executed, it could liberate humanity from antiquated beliefs and habits and provide the means to reform society along more democratic and cosmopolitan lines. To these ends, the arts were as instrumental as the social sciences. A reconstructed society would need a reconstructed, "modernist" esthetic for the performing and plastic arts as well as for design and architecture. Johnson's choice of an architect exemplified his commitment to "modernist" culture; he insisted that the New School's building be "ultra-modern."[16] In 1929 New York architects were just becoming familiar with the work of Le Corbusier, Gropius, and Mies van der Rohe. The architectural exhibit at the Museum of Modern Art that popularized their work did not take place until 1932. But Johnson, through his friendships with Lewis Mumford and Albert Mayer and as a consequence of his trips to Europe in the early twenties for the *New Republic,* had become infatuated with what was known after 1932 as the "International-Style." For this reason, he was delighted by Joseph Urban's interest in the New School project.[17]

As a young architect in Vienna, Urban had enjoyed a distinguished career. His works included the Ratshaus in Vienna and the Czar Bridge in Leningrad. For these and other projects he attracted international acclaim and numerous prize medals. As a member of the Viennese Secession movement, Urban had participated in one of Europe's most avant-garde circles. Led by Adolph Loos, the Viennese Secessionists anticipated many of the architectural departures which after World War I came to be known as "modernist." In 1911 Urban came to the United States to design sets for the Boston Opera and then moved to New York to become the set designer for the Metropolitan Opera.[18] In 1929 Johnson caught Urban at an opportune moment. For several years Urban had been wanting to design a building in the "modern" style. An adult education building devoted to social science and modern art seemed an ideal project in which to combine his ideas as a theatre designer with the new architectural styles. Urban eagerly accepted Johnson's offer. Johnson outlined the school's functions, the cost limitations, and the specific needs the building would have to meet. Otherwise, he allowed Urban to design his own building. Johnson and Urban agreed that it should serve as an example of "functional" sculpture on an architectural scale.[19]

Except for two murals, Urban designed the Twelfth Street building from top to bottom, down to the last detail, including light fixtures, furnishings, and ashtrays. The result was a remarkably unified structure of uncompromisingly contemporary design. Although Urban considered "functionalism" his point of departure, he defined "functional" to include esthetic effect, the psychological needs of the building's users, and the values that the New School represented. Urban saw the building as an architectural affirmation of the New School's dedication to what Johnson called "democratic liberalism," which sought "to meet realistically and with understanding the challenge and the thrust of vital contemporary issues." The building contained several features that demonstrated Urban's effort to "house an idea."[20] The most dramatic was the oval auditorium in which Urban recaptured the intimacy between speaker and audience characteristic of classical Greek theatre. He placed the stage so that it projected itself visually into the audience, making on-stage lecturers feel themselves enclosed by their public. Beneath the auditorium Urban carried this notion even further with a sunken, circular dance floor. Here dancers had to come and go through their audience. The audience, meanwhile, watched the dancers at eye level rather than looking up at their legs from below. In addition, Urban chose not to install fixed seating, leaving the audience free to move around as it chose even as it allowed directors to arrange seating appropriate for each occasion. He hoped to dissolve the artificial dichotomy between life and art by bringing performers and viewers into a natural, and literal, face-to-face relationship.[21]

Urban's effort to bring art to life and life to art characterized the entire building. In the structure itself he incorporated what was for the time an unusual quantity of windows. He glassed in almost one-third of the facade of the building in four-foot, horizontal bands of windows that ran across the entire front of the building marking off each story. This opened up the building to the outside and reduced the need for artificial lighting during the daytime. The upper floor contained a penthouse-art studio, which looked out on a large, street-side terrace and afforded access to two other small terraces. Inside, the building included a library, seminar rooms, several additional studios, a large dining room, a lounge, and an exhibition gallery. The two "noncreative" spaces, the lounge and the dining room, were arranged to promote discussion and social intercourse. Throughout the rest of the building, a surprising emphasis was placed on the arts and artistic activities. Urban provided for a 600-seat auditorium, a dance studio, three art studios, and an exhibition gallery. Even in the seminar and dining rooms he set aside wall space for full, ceiling-to-floor murals. It became nearly impossible to come into the building without confronting some form of art and, more important, without being drawn to participate at some level.[22] All in all, Johnson could not have been more pleased.[23]

Aside from the structure itself, the most spectacular features of the new building were its murals, which came to the New School through a characteristic blend of luck and self-promotion. Urban had envisioned murals in the dining room and seminar rooms, but the New School lacked funds for their execution. By chance, however, Alma Reed, owner of the Delphic Studios, an avant-garde gallery, happened to read an article in which Urban described the proposed structure. For some time Reed had been seeking a building suitable for a mural by her client, Mexican muralist José Clemente Orozco. Urban's description of his design for the "progressive" educational activities of the New School seemed perfect for Orozco's social-realist style. Reed believed that Orozco's success in the United States depended on his capturing the attention of New York critics. She contacted Lewis Mumford, who shared her enthusiasm for Orozco's work, and Mumford introduced her to Johnson. Reed suggested that Orozco execute the mural for the cost of materials. If on completion a friend of the school became taken with the work and wished to pay Orozco a commission, so much the better. Johnson could hardly believe her offer and cautioned that Orozco should not expect payment. Reed agreed, and Orozco insisted only that he have complete freedom to choose and develop his own theme.[24] With his characteristic grandiloquence Johnson concurred: "Paint me a picture. Paint as you must. I assure you freedom."[25] Although critics—including a trustee—later objected to Orozco's inclusion of Lenin and Stalin, Johnson stood by his promise.[26]

Thomas Hart Benton found himself in a position similar to Orozco's. Also a client of Reed's, Benton had acquired a limited reputation in New York but had failed to command a serious audience. He too believed that a large mural in a major building in New York was just the boost his career needed. Annoyed that Reed had not included him in the New School deal, Benton contacted a friend, Ralph Pearson, who taught art at the New School. Pearson stormed into Johnson's office, demanding to know why Johnson had commissioned a "foreign" artist and ignored such an able American as Thomas Hart Benton. Quick to see an opportunity, Johnson responded by also inviting Benton to paint a mural on the same terms as Orozco. Benton agreed.[27]

Benton and Orozco, like the other artists Johnson recruited to teach at the New School, called themselves "modernists," but their use of the label "modern" should not imply a common style or set of ideas. Rather, as a group they acknowledged that creative artists invariably responded to the stimuli of their own times and cultures. They could not be bound by *a priori* principles handed down from the past. The canons of nineteenth-century art seemed to them esthetically irrelevant for the twentieth century. They believed that creativity and destruction were inseparably linked and that creativity required the replacement of old ideas and conventions with new, and often better, ones. As young artists, they used this notion as a psychological lever against established artists and conventional forms. "Modernism" became a battle cry of the young against the old.[28]

Time and again, the artists associated with the New School asserted that they were not in "revolt against formalism," but against particular forms. In their discussions, whether about painting, dance, or music, they agreed that nineteenth-century art reflected the social, national, and racial bias of nineteenth-century Europe. Far from rejecting formal considerations, they argued that they were creating new art forms appropriate for their own time. Like Beard, Robinson, and the other founders of the New School, the New School artists considered themselves the cultural vanguard of a new, more rational, and egalitarian society. They were committed to a universal, or cosmopolitan, art which transcended particular cultures and classes. Moreover, they presumed that anyone could be creative and that modern art served the public function of interpreting and articulating the complexities of contemporary reality. They understood themselves as egalitarians and humanists as well as modernists.

It is a tribute to Johnson that he recognized both Benton's and Orozco's extraordinary talents, even before they were recognized generally by American art audiences. Reed at first found Benton's action underhanded and feared that his work might upstage Orozco's in the eyes of American critics. Nonetheless, she eventually came to take great pride in the role Delphic Studio had played in introducing to New

York art circles the murals of Orozco and Benton.[29] Johnson could hardly contain himself. Not only had he managed to construct one of New York's first modernist buildings, he had also secured murals by two of the twentieth century's most important muralists. More impressively, he had accomplished it all in the teeth of the Depression with little or no money.[30]

Orozco's murals consisted of five frescoes, each about six feet by forty feet, one on each wall inside the dining room and one on the wall outside the entrance to the dining room. Every morning for nearly forty days a plasterer prepared a fresh section, on which Orozco painted before the plaster set. Orozco chose red as his primary color, which he highlighted with shades of gray, black, and brown. In the New School murals, he experimented with "dynamic symmetry," a technique in which shapes were created through combinations of squares and isosceles triangles.[31] Dynamic symmetry, with Orozco's harsh earth tones, gave the frescoes an abstract, even mechanical, appearance. Devoid of curves or fluid movement, the various frescoes jarred against one another, resulting in an even greater sense of harshness. The overall effect was one of somber, if irresistible, human determination.[32]

Orozco had begun his artistic career during the Mexican Revolution as a political cartoonist. After the revolution the new republican government commissioned him to execute several "revolutionary" murals on public buildings. In these Orozco sympathetically pictured the plight of the Mexican peasant and with extraordinary power portrayed the vicious class system that exploited them. In the political merry-go-round of postrevolutionary Mexico, there was no place for an artist of Orozco's uncompromising vision. In 1928 he came to the United States, hoping to establish an international reputation as a muralist. Altogether, he completed three sets of murals in the United States, all at educational institutions: Pomona College in California, Dartmouth College in New Hampshire, and the New School in New York. Because of its location, Orozco cared most about his New School mural.[33]

The five New School frescoes were entitled *The Table of Brotherhood, Homecoming of the Worker of the New Day, The Struggle in the Orient, The Struggle in the Occident,* and *Creative Man.* In *The Table of Brotherhood,* Orozco pictured eleven men seated around a table as equals. They included two Asians, an African, a Sikh, a Tartar, a Mexican-Indian, an American black, an American art critic, a French philosopher, a Zionist, and a Dutch poet. On the opposite wall, in *Homecoming of the Worker,* he depicted a male worker returning home to his wife, children, food, and books—the good things of life. On the east wall, *The Struggle in the Orient,* Orozco outlined a grim picture of enslaved masses relieved only by the leadership of Gandhi confronting the brutality of British imperialism. In contrast, on the west wall, in *The Struggle in the Occident*, Orozco juxtaposed the peasant revolution in Mexico with the Marxist revolution in Russia led by Lenin and Stalin. In the final fresco, outside the dining room, Orozco offered the heartening prospect of *Creative Man*, in science, art, and labor.[34] Orozco's sympathies stood clearly on the side of the oppressed of the world, their revolutionary leaders, social idealists, and productive laborers, artists, and intellectuals celebrating them.[35]

Although Orozco's New School murals were powerful and moving, New York art critics damned them with faint praise.[36] In retrospect, they have come to be seen as the weakest of the three sets of murals he executed in the United States.[37] It is thought that, despite Johnson's assurance of complete freedom, Orozco consciously sought to create a series of frescoes that embodied the values, as he understood them, of Alvin Johnson and the New School. This self-consciousness, combined with the artificiality of his use of "dynamic symmetry," perhaps drained the frescoes of much of their vitality. It was almost as if Orozco had tried too hard to please Alma Reed, Alvin Johnson, and the New York art world at the sacrifice of his own artistic impulses.[38]

This was not the case with Thomas Hart Benton. Benton was born in Missouri, had studied in Paris, had spent the previous twenty years developing his unique style. After returning to the United States in the 1920s, he settled in New York, married a daughter of Italian immigrants, and worked furiously to gain the attention of the New York art community. Benton achieved some success, but until he painted the New School murals he had failed to gain widespread recognition.[39] Like Orozco, Benton was known to be a committed modernist, but his murals could not have been more different than Orozco's. Benton painted his murals on moveable linen panels, which he completed in his own studio, using egg tempera in bright, vibrant hues. Rather than portraying symbolic male figures in somber abstraction, Benton filled his canvases to overflowing with dozens of cartoon-like individuals, male and female, working and playing in numerous aspects of life. He documented America of the 1920s, not "emerging mankind." So full and chaotic were Benton's murals that he had to place one scene on top of another, separated by architectural moldings in the style of the rotogravure section of contemporary Sunday newspaper supplements. Unlike Orozco, who had consciously imposed on his murals technical and ideological restraints, Benton let himself go. In the process he found himself as an artist. The New School murals represent his very best work and proved an instant success. As he had hoped, they established his reputation as a major artist.[40]

Despite their explicitly American character, Benton's murals shunned nativist or chauvinistic imagery. He did not present America the powerful or America the bountiful. Instead, he offered a panorama of America the diverse, the energetic, and the playful. His murals pictured the basic industries of the United States: agriculture, mining, steel, lumbering, and transportation; its sources of power: electricity, steam, internal combustion, and coal; and its regional diversity: South and West as well as the teeming and tawdry city. In his nine panels he managed to capture an amazing range of activities, including a jazz band, a baseball game, a Salvation Army band, a subway, a religious revival, a stock exchange, lovers embracing on a park bench, prostitutes soliciting customers, herders, an Indian, a sharecropper, and—in a corner at the bottom of the City Activities section—Alvin Johnson and Thomas Hart Benton, two midwesterners savoring a drink of whiskey while looking over the American panorama.

Because Benton's New School murals betrayed no ethnic, religious, class, regional, or national prejudice his affirmation of America encompassed almost as wide a range of humanity as Orozco's had. Like Orozco's, Benton's heart was clearly with the industrious masses who had come from all over the world to make up the United States. Benton reserved his rare negative images for stock brokers, revivalist preachers, and social snobs.[41] The most important difference between the Benton and Orozco murals was Benton's refusal to articulate an ideal beyond the diversity, freedom, energy, and human dignity that he found in such abundance. He did not preach, he foresaw no revolution, and he offered no prospect of a better world. He presented American life as he understood it, and he obviously reveled in it. He did not draw back from it vulgarity, its escapism, its eroticism, its boredom, or its brutality. While Orozco's political vision provoked viewers' consciences and attacked their complacency, Benton's national portrait endlessly fascinated its audiences. The two sets of murals complemented one another: Orozco delineated the plight and dreams of the world's poor and enslaved; Benton sympathetically presented the common people of the world's richest, freest, and most industrious society.[42]

On January 2, 1931, the New School officially opened its doors at 66 West Twelfth Street. For those who attended the opening the shift from social science to art was everywhere evident: in the building itself, the Orozco and Benton murals, and the fixtures and furnishings that Urban had especially designed. Johnson proudly showed off his brightly lit and colored facilities for dance, theatre, painting, sculpture, and music. To top off the celebration the New School sponsored two exhibits, one of contemporary domestic furnishings and the other an international show of modern painting. Edwin Park organized the first exhibition, which included rugs, furniture, textiles, ceramics, lighting fixtures, and linoleum. All of the articles shown were contemporary in style, American designed, and machine manufactured. The *Societé Anonyme,* under the direction of Katherine Dreier, arranged the painting exhibit, which included works by such European and American modernists as Léger, Kandinsky, Klee, Kuniyoshi, Man Ray, Mondrian, Zorach, Weber, and Ernst. These two exhibits anticipated the thrust of the New School's art programs: modernism and functionalism, innovation and use.[43]

Johnson's decision to emphasize the arts came at a particularly fortunate moment. American artists, particularly those influenced by European modernism, had not yet established their reputations. Further, in the twenties and thirties, American artists, whether dancers, composers, or painters, had so far not created infrastructures comparable to those of other professions. They enjoyed little institutional support, had no organizational cohesion, and could claim few patrons.[44] The New School's success in enticing individuals such as Orozco, Benton, and Urban as well as two major art exhibitions with little or no money attested to the dire straits in which contemporary American artists found themselves. The Depression of the 1930s severely aggravated an already dismal situation.[45]

Johnson understood the opportunity it presented to him. The Depression created a reservoir of talented but economically pressed artists eager to teach at the New School. Moreover, he realized the affinity that existed between the New School's scholarly and academic concerns and modern artists. He saw parallels between academic freedom and artistic freedom, between social research and artistic creativity, and between the ideas of social progress and the role of the avant-garde.[46] The New School's flexible interdisciplinary approach and its receptivity to everything new and contemporary made it an especially attractive institution for young artists. Here artists could secure part-time employment, discuss their work with other artists inside and outside their own fields, have access to first-rate facilities, meet potential patrons, and try out their ideas on eager and attentive adult students. With no established art department to contend with, artists were free to create their own definitions and procedures. Consequently, beginning in the late 1920s, the New School attracted an extraordinary number of remarkable young artists, particularly in music, dance, and the visual arts. As a group, they made the New School during the 1930s one of the most exciting centers of modernist expression in the United States.

The transition from a predominantly social science curriculum to broadly defined cultural courses had begun in the first year of

Johnson's directorship. In 1923-24 Henry Dana, who had been fired from Columbia in 1917, taught the first course at the New School on modern literature, drama critic Stark Young gave a course on modern drama, and Lewis Mumford taught a course on architecture.[47] Two years later, writer and critic Waldo Frank gave what was probably the first course on modern art taught at an American academic institution, while music critic Paul Rosenfeld offered what was likely the first course on modern composers.[48] Rosenfeld was a crucial figure in recruiting young artists for the New School, especially composers. A member of Alfred Stieglitz's circle, Rosenfeld regularly contributed articles on modern art and music to such little magazines as the *Seven Arts, Vanity Fair,* the *Dial,* the *Bookman,* and the *New Republic.*[49] He established a reputation as an able critic and an enthusiastic advocate of the "new" arts. His books *Port of New York* (1924) and *An Hour with American Music* (1929) brought to the attention of the public painter Georgia O'Keeffe and poet Carl Sandburg, writer Waldo Frank, and composers Aaron Copland, Roy Harris, Roger Sessions, Walter Piston, and Virgil Thomson. At his death in 1946, Rosenfeld was generally considered the pioneering dean of American music criticism.[50] It was Rosenfeld who recruited composer Aaron Copland to take over his lectures in modern music at the New School in 1927.[51] Copland's appointment marked the emergence of the New School as an important center for modern music in New York City.

By 1927 Copland had gained recognition as an important young modernist, but he lacked a solid base of support. The New School position not only provided him with an opportunity to articulate his ideas publicly, it also gave him the time to work on his compositions. Otherwise, he would have had to become a music teacher. In 1927, with Roger Sessions, Copland organized the famous Copland-Sessions concert series at the New School. This series included the first recitals for Copland and Sessions, as well as for Virgil Thomson, Roy Harris, and Walter Piston. The Copland-Sessions concerts, which in effect brought American composers their first recognition in the world of serious music, were as important for this group of young American composers as Benton's mural was for him. In 1932 Copland helped found the Yaddo Music Festival at Saratoga, New York, and in 1939 he published his New School lectures, *What to Listen for in Music,* which he followed in 1941 with his classic defense of modern composition, *Our New Music.*[52] Copland's determination to popularize modern composition through the promotion of young American composers fit in well at the New School. Johnson considered this adult education at its best. Not only was the New School contributing to the transformation of

American musical tastes, it was also providing necessary support to a gifted young composer.

In 1930 Henry Cowell joined Copland at the New School. A born promoter, Cowell set about organizing the New School's division of music and dance. A Californian by birth, Cowell had, of economic necessity, taught himself music and composition. Without the influence of tradition-bound teachers, he moved easily into modern atonal music and excelled in technical innovations. His contributions include what he called "tone clusters," which amounted to hitting several piano keys simultaneously with his fist, and his famous piano "plucking," a technique by which Cowell plucked the strings themselves with a fork.[53] Such activities gave him a well-earned reputation as a musical maverick. Like Copland, he was also one of the most important early boosters of dissonant and atonal music in the United States. Almost singlehandedly, he resurrected Charles Ives's reputation as an important American composer through his biographical study of Ives's work. In 1933 he organized a symposium at the New School of the best contemporary American composers and edited their reflections on one another's work in a landmark book, *American Composers on American Music.*[54]

In 1931 Cowell brought to the New School his close friend, musicologist Charles Seeger.[55] At the same time the school hired Russian composer Joseph Schillinger and Swiss pianist Paul Boepple, a proponent of Dalcroze Eurythmics.[56] In 1935 two distinguished European modernist composers joined the faculty, Ernst Toch, who taught until 1937, and Hans Eisler, who remained until 1942.[57] Under Cowell's leadership the New School supported an extensive program of concerts and festivals, including an annual folk festival entitled "Dances of Many People." Together with Seeger, Cowell made the New School a rallying point both for technical innovation and nonwestern music.[58]

From one perspective the new music at the New School was quite diverse. It included Copland's jazz-inspired modernism, Cowell's curious technical innovations, Toch's neoclassicism, Seeger's international music, and Eisler's "proletarian" compositions. Still, they were as one in their commitment to new musical forms and their belief that these new forms were implicitly "democratic." As a group, they bristled at the charge that modern music was no more than a subjective rejection of form and structure. Modern composers, they argued, rejected only the antiquated, obsolete forms of nineteenth-century romanticism. In adopting new tonal structures and rhythms, modern composers were actually creating new, more complex, and subtle forms. "Modern music," wrote Copland, "is principally the expression in terms of enriched musical language of a new spirit of objectivity, attuned to our own times."[59] In a similar vein, Toch insisted, "Form is to forms as the Universe is to a mountain or a tree .... In the highest art content and form coincide. How, then, could Form be reduced to a few forms when content is limited only by the Universe?"[60]

Copland, Eisler, Toch, and Seeger each denied that modern music had become subjective and irrationally self-indulgent without regard for its audience. Copland argued that music acquired meaning only when it reached a comprehending audience. "Art and the life of art must mean something, in the deepest sense, to the everyday citizen. When that happens," lectured Copland, "America will have achieved a maturity to which every sincere artist will have contributed."[61] They recognized that the "new facts" of modern music might at first sound dissonant to Americans; but they believed that in time the form, melody, and beauty of modern compositions would become clear and understandable to listeners as Beethoven and Brahms had been to their audiences. Beyond the issue of comprehension, music contributed to the fullness of life and should be made accessible to the general public. They claimed that modern music was fundamentally egalitarian. It broke with the aristocratic forms of the nineteenth century and brought music out of the concert house and into public spaces.[62] Moreover, nineteenth-century music suffered from acute cultural particularism. They wanted their music to be international, not European, comprehensible to all people, not simply the genteel classes of Europe and the United States.[63]

This desire to expand the audience for serious music, both among nations and within society, lay at the heart of Copland's simplified and popular compositions written later, such as "Appalachian Spring," "Billy the Kid," "The Tender Land," and his numerous movie scores.[64] Likewise, Seeger intended his musicological studies of nonwestern music to help universalize musical forms. He sought out the commonality within the great variety of human music. Seeger wanted a new music that not only drew on all musical traditions but could also be comprehended by all people.[65] Similarly, Hans Eisler, a Marxist, wanted his "proletarian music" to reach the masses, where it might help transform society by mobilizing workers into political action.[66] Rosenfeld, Copland, Cowell, Seeger, Toch, and Eisler all hoped to accomplish through music the same end that James Harvey Robinson had hoped to accomplish through his *New History.*

In the 1930s, while modern music flourished under the aegis of the New School, modern dance made its way to West Twelfth Street. Pioneered before World War I by Americans Isadora Duncan and Ruth St. Denis, modern dance in the United States remained a largely unacknowledged art form.[67] However, its emergence paralleled the course of dissonant and atonal music, and modern dancers and composers frequently collaborated to synthesize the new music with new dance. It became almost a truism that where one went the other followed. This mutual affinity resulted in their close association at the New School and later at Bennington College and the Juilliard School.[68] It is not surprising, then, that it was a composer, Henry Cowell, who recruited Doris Humphrey to the New School faculty. At the New School, Humphrey worked with Aaron Copland, producing numerous subsequent collaborations. In 1933, with Martha Graham and Charles Weidman, Humphrey organized an important modern dance series at the New School which anticipated their famous dance workshops at Bennington College.[69] Also at the New School, under the guidance of Paul Boepple, Humphrey renewed her work with Dalcroze Eurythmics, a theory that combined a systematic study of muscular movement with music.[70]

Beginning in 1931 and lasting until 1940, Humphrey offered a workshop in modern dance at the New School as well as a regular lecture series. She found teaching at the New School particularly convenient, as her own dance studio was only a few blocks away on Eighteenth Street. Humphrey, like Copland, used her lectures to work out her ideas in detail and to popularize them beyond her own students.[71] Here she articulated her principle that dance movement existed in the arc between balance and unbalance, between motionlessness and uncontrolled falling, between order and chaos. Dancers created their art, declared Humphrey, by transforming this arc through controlled, rhythmic motion. Humphrey believed that her insight had freed dance from traditional formulas which restricted dancers to a set number of movements and made their work appealing only to western audiences. Modern dance, she asserted, rested on universal physical laws, not culturally or historically determined values. Dancers were now free to create an infinite number of new forms, which could be communicated to all people regardless of their cultural background.[72]

When Humphrey came to the New School, John Martin, the *New York Times* dance critic, joined her. Martin, who had begun to write his column in 1927, lectured at the New School from 1930 to 1945. In 1934 with Doris Humphrey, Martha Graham, and Charles Weidman, he organized the Bennington College modern dance program. Through this work and his statements on modern dance, *The Modern Dance* (1933), *Introduction to the Dance* (1939), and *The Dance* (1947), Martin decisively influenced the development of dance in the United States. His lectures and articles created an informed constituency for modern dance, even as his ideas affected the thought of American dancers themselves.[73] As it had for Copland, the New School provided Martin both a forum for his ideas and a convenient means to work closely with such dancers as Humphrey, Graham, Weidman, and Hanya Holm. Unlike his *New York Times* readers, Martin's New School students could answer back and, more important, they could test his ideas by talking to and observing Humphrey and other dancers.

Artists, Martin claimed, have the task of reconciling the function of their art with their chosen materials and with the capacity of their audiences to understand. These three factors, Martin asserted, determine form. But form, he cautioned, should not be confused with pattern. To reject a stylish pattern of the past was not to reject form. "The impulses of art, its motivations and its necessities are universal," he affirmed, "but the forms in which it is materialized are inevitably localized."[74] Martin felt that the slavish following of conventional forms invariably led to mechanical, uninspired, and predictable results. An audience, in such cases, learned little and gained little. Good art, he insisted, forced its audience to grow: it transformed them.

According to Martin, modern dance was neither arbitrary nor formless. Instead, it was a functional outgrowth of its environment. "Indeed," he wrote, "modernism in the large sense is that tendency in any period which first senses and makes tangible the new directions of its time before they become an accepted part of daily life. . . . Obviously, no matter what form it takes, it is inevitably strange and unpopular in the days of its ascent."[75] Even so, Martin did not consider modern dance in any way alien to American culture. He argued that the "shaping force behind American dance, the thing that makes it dynamic, the thing that makes it a dynamic art instead of pictorial or meditative one—is the traditional American approach to living. In this scheme of things man himself is the center of the universe, the master of the environment, conscious of his power and its basis in the law of his being."[76]

Martin supported the expansion of artistic opportunity in the United States. He proposed political action by the federal government to address issues of cultural as well as economic inequity. "That paradox," he declared, "which allows great sections of the population to starve in the midst of material resources is exactly reflected in the realms of the mind and imagining where there is a wealth of cultural resources available only to the few." "Surely," he continued, "in a period like the present, with its arguments of escape from difficulties of individual conviction into comfortable authoritarianisms, no agency can be overvalued which relates man consciously and actively to his environment."[77]

Like those in music and dance, the New School's program in the visual arts burgeoned in the thirties. Since 1925 the New School had in a piecemeal fashion added courses in art appreciation and esthetic theory, but the art program was not established on a firm basis until 1930, when Ralph Pearson introduced his "Design Workshop." This course provided the framework for the New School's rapidly expanding offerings in the studio arts. In 1931 the New School added lectures on the moving picture, modern architecture, international architecture, and Thomas Hart Benton's course, entitled "Craftsman and Art." At the same time the New School also started a regular exhibition program, beginning with its European and American modern show. Other shows included a modern house exhibit in 1933; the first all-union art show, "United American Artists, CIO" in 1939; and the politically significant photography shows "Manhattan Playgrounds" and "Toward a Harlem Document," also in 1939. On a more informal basis, the New School frequently showed the work of local Village artists.[78]

In the visual arts, as in other areas, the New School's political predilections showed through.[79] Several New School painters exhibited at the radical John Reed Club. In 1936, at Pearson's instigation, the school cosponsored the first American Artists' Congress, a united front organization of over 400 artists who opposed "War, Fascism, and Reaction." Beyond its radical political affiliation, the 1936 congress represented one of the first efforts by American artists collectively to address professional and economic issues. Among the speakers were New School instructors Stuart Davis, Lewis Mumford, José Clemente Orozco, Meyer Schapiro, and Ralph Pearson, and virtually everyone else who taught art at the New School in the thirties signed the "call to organize."[80] The previous year the New School had sponsored the organizational meetings of the American Writers' Congress, the writers' equivalent of the artists' congress as the school, throughout the thirties, served as a center for political activities in the arts.

More important than these various activities were the artists themselves who taught at the New School. Besides Pearson and Benton, the list included Nicaraguan painter and muralist Camilo Egas (1932–1962); Berenice Abbott (1935–1965), a preeminent photographer of New York City; painter Stuart Davis (1934–1950); Spanish sculptor José de Creeft (1933–1939, 1944–1970); Lithuanian-born sculptor William Zorach (1936–1940); art critic and historian Meyer Schapiro (1935–1954); German painter Kurt Roesch (1933–1936); Japanese-born painter Yasuo Kuniyoshi (1934–1950); and American sculptor Seymour Lipton (1939–1965). Together, they represented much of the very best in American painting, sculpture, and photography in the 1930s.[81]

Still, the central personality and guiding spirit of the New School art curriculum in the thirties was Ralph Pearson. In 1930 Johnson appointed Pearson to supervise the New School's art division. Pearson continued to teach the lecture courses in architecture that Mumford had originally taught and an art history course that he had inherited from Leo Stein and Meyer Schapiro. It was Pearson's introduction of the "Design Workshop," however, that transformed the New School art division from a miscellany of art courses into a genuine art school. Pearson called his workshop method the "new art education."[82]

Pearson's ideas were published in a book entitled *The New Art Education* in 1941. Like John Martin, Pearson was influenced by Dewey's *Art and Experience.* Pearson believed that a teacher's primary responsibility was to bring students to realize that as artists they must infuse their artifacts with an "artistic vision." Such visions were not restricted to an artistic elect. All persons were capable of artistic expression. "Sufficient for the moment to say," he wrote, "these activities of spirit, mind, and heart tap the deepest and richest veins of human experience. They are the kind of activities which are furthest removed from the animal, most characteristic of man as man. They allow men to achieve the civilized life."[83] Through education, he argued, art and creativity could become the cornerstones of modern society. "Education effectuates creative living. Education which liberates the human mind from blind faiths, the bigotries, the taboos of the ages, which teaches it to combine feeling and thinking, to control emotions with reason, to deal creatively with all the materials of the environment—this is the kind of education that is a force in man—a powerful constructive force."[84]

While no single label does justice to the range of artistic expression represented at the New School in the 1930s, all the artists who taught at the New School had much in common with the school itself. They were young, considered themselves "modernists," had not yet received significant public recognition, and all needed their salaries. They also, in one way or another, saw themselves as outsiders. To a person, those who were not Jews were either immigrants, refugees, or American provincials. Almost invariably, they came from families of modest means, and all had come to New York to make a name for themselves.[85] In fact, these similarities in background say almost as much about American artists in general during this period as about New School artists in particular. Most American artists came from modest backgrounds and grew up outside the major American cultural centers of New York, Boston, and Philadelphia. Many of those who did come from metropolitan areas were children of Jewish immigrants.[86]

It seems more than coincidental that the artists who taught at the New School resembled in their backgrounds and professional ambitions nearly everyone else who became associated with the New School under

Alvin Johnson's directorship. During the Depression, the New School served a function similar to that of the federally financed WPA program for artists. On a small scale, it offered unestablished artists an opportunity to continue their work at a time when only a handful of American artists could make a living at their art. For Aaron Copland, as for others, his New School appointment came as a godsend, sparing him the grueling and artistically deadening experience of earning a living on the Adirondack and Pocono resort circuits.[87] The New School nurtured these individuals through the Depression with their artistic skills intact. Through its expanded adult education program, it offered them a convenient, if spartan, refuge.

In looking back at the work and public statements of these artists, it is clear that as a group they were extraordinarily aware of developments in all artistic fields as well as of the international nature of contemporary art forms. The rich mixture of painters, sculptors, dancers, and composers, conducting classes simultaneously in the same building and then, after classes, gathering together over lunch or coffee, offered each of them an unusual chance to talk with and observe artists in other disciplines and to attend lectures by scholars outside the arts. For example, sculptor Seymour Lipton considered Morris Cohen's lectures in legal philosophy at the New School profoundly important to his own ideas. The most fruitful instance of interdisciplinary influence occurred between the composers and dancers. Henry Cowell and Aaron Copland each collaborated with Doris Humphrey on several occasions as did Paul Boepple.

Moreover, the intermingling of Americans, Europeans, and Latin Americans enlarged the cultural horizons of the entire institution. The cosmopolitan character of the New School artists can be seen in Seeger's annual international dance and music festival, Copland's interest in Latin American music, and the influence of European abstract art on New School painters and sculptors. The school's cultural diversity might in part explain its artists' resistance to nationalistic art, something that distinguished them from many other American artists in the thirties. Thomas Hart Benton's "regionalism" did not become strident until after he had left the New School and New York. And even though both Doris Humphrey and Aaron Copland composed "American" works in the thirties, they were both quite explicit in their commitment to art as an "international" and democratic enterprise: their content may have been "American," but their form was "modern."[88]

Art, for them, meant much more than a fine painting or a moving musical composition. It was even more than a way of life. As artistic humanists, they believed that the meaning of human existence rested in human artfulness. Horace Kallen, who regularly taught esthetic theory at the New School, expressed well this almost religious reverence toward artistic creativity in his two-volume study of western notions of beauty, *Art and Freedom,* published in 1942.[89] Without art, wrote Kallen, human freedom and dignity simply could not exist. Artfulness was the essence of "liberal humanism," declared Kallen. "Of man's ways before God, art is the bravest, the truest." Humans use nature to "create beauty," and in so doing affirm their freedom. "If humanity is destroyed in the process," prophesied Kallen, "still God has won no final victory. For God's victory cannot be that men should die, but that man should surrender, that he should repent his ways and submit his soul to the omnipresent yoke. In that way man maintains his ways, that science as art and art as science flourish in his spirit, then though death be his destiny, he conquers Fate and defeats God. He has not yielded his humanity; and his humanism stands untaken. In its deepest, its broadest sense, Art thus conquering Fate, conforms Nature to man, sets a bound to God's power and advances a frontier of freedom against the compulsions of the cosmos."[90]

For Kallen, art, science, and social science were substantially committed to the same enterprise: human liberation. Since its founding, the New School had espoused a broadly conceived form of democratic humanism similar to Kallen's. Much as James Robinson and Kallen's own mentor, philosopher William James, had done, the New School as a whole understood scientific knowledge and artistic creativity in explicitly humanistic and egalitarian terms. Science, art, and democratic politics were the means by which they believed the world would be reconstructed. So wholeheartedly had the New School embraced the arts that social research, for a time, seemed to have disappeared. The New School in the last half of the 1920s and in the early 1930s continued to offer an impressive selection of lecture courses in the social sciences, often by internationally prominent scholars, especially in psychology and psychoanalysis. But even as Alvin Johnson trumpeted the school's success, he realized that he had not succeeded in his efforts to reestablish a research program. Until 1933, its contribution to the arts not withstanding, the New School maintained its commitment to social research in its name alone.

4

ALVIN JOHNSON AND
THE ENCYCLOPEDIA OF
THE SOCIAL SCIENCES

DURING THE YEARS AFTER THE REORGANIZATION OF 1922, the New School relinquished its place at the forefront of social science research, and instead, under Alvin Johnson, concentrated on adult education and the fine arts. The success of the building program allowed the New School to strengthen these programs and, eventually, to reestablish itself as a research institute. In the 1930s it once again became a significant center for social research. Indeed, in the 1930s and 1940s, few other American institutions could match the social science faculty of the New School.

The reestablishment of social research at the New School occurred in two stages. The first stage began in 1927, when the Social Science Research Council appointed Alvin Johnson to the post of associate editor of the *Encyclopedia of the Social Sciences*. Through this work, Johnson became familiar with the major European social scientists, many of whom shared Johnson's political commitments, if not his philosophical premises. Johnson in turn used his editorship to popularize his own reformist ideas, which were strongly influenced by John Dewey's "instrumentalism." The second stage began in 1933, when many of the same social scientists Johnson had come to know in the course of his work on the *Encyclopedia* were expelled from their teaching and research positions in Germany. Johnson, then completing his editorial duties for the *Encyclopedia*, seized the opportunity to recruit the most distinguished of these refugee social scientists for the New School. In the process he created an autonomous "University in Exile," which in 1935 became the Graduate Faculty of the New School.

The contacts Johnson made as editor of the *Encyclopedia* were immediately manifest in the New School's course offerings. In addition to the "regulars," Harry Elmer Barnes, Leo Wolman, philosopher Joseph Jastrow, anthropologist Alexander Goldenweiser, and Horace Kallen, with special lectures by John Dewey and Franz Boas, the New School, in 1927, also boasted courses by Gaetano Salvemini, who had resigned his professorship of modern history at the University of Florence in 1925 to protest Mussolini's unconstitutional actions, Fritz Wittels, a student of Freud's and author of numerous books on psychiatry, Henry Brailsford, editor of the *New Leader* in London, and Vilhjalmur Stefansson, a pioneer in Arctic anthropology and an explorer. The move from Chelsea temporarily interrupted this upsurge, but the opening of the new building in 1930 resulted in a renewed upswing in additions to the permanent faculty. In 1930 New York University philosopher Sidney Hook and City College philosopher Morris Cohen joined Kallen to make the New School's evening lectures on philosophy unmatched in breadth in the United States. Moreover, Walton Hamilton, from the Yale Law School, Columbia historian Carlton P. Hayes, philosopher-theologian Felix Adler, Felix Frankfurter, British political commentator Harold Laski, and natural historian Julian Huxley, along with Jastrow, Barnes, and Wittels provided a wide variety of social science courses. Johnson, clearly, had utilized his position as editor of the *Encyclopedia of the Social Sciences* to enhance the New School's coffers. But since only Kallen and Wittels held permanent appointments, the New School still could not, truthfully, claim to be a permanent center of social research.[1]

The *Encyclopedia*, though, had a more direct impact on the New School as several members of the editorial staff taught regularly at the New School, including sociologist Bernard Stern, policy specialist Elizabeth Todd, philosopher Joseph Ratner, and political scientist Max Lerner. Lerner served as managing editor of the *Encyclopedia*, Ratner, Todd, and Stern as assistant editors.[2] Additionally, three of the central contributors to the *Encyclopedia*—Horace Kallen, Sidney Hook, and Morris Cohen—formed a cadre of lecturers in philosophy at the New School who, during the 1930s and 1940s, with Dewey, were the principal exponents of philosophical pragmatism in the United States. Finally, the idea of the *Encyclopedia* itself had initially come from New

School anthropologist Alexander Goldenweiser. Indeed, the *Encyclopedia*, when completed, could be seen as an extension of the spirit and mission of Alvin Johnson and the New School. In many ways it stands as the crowning testament to the ideas which in 1917 had led to the formation of the New School.[3]

Johnson's selection as associate editor of the *Encyclopedia of the Social Sciences* was in fact more fortuitous than purposeful. Edwin Seligman, the project editor, had intended to edit the encyclopedia himself, but soon realized that he lacked the editorial and administrative skills necessary for such an undertaking. Seligman offered the position of assistant editor to several individuals, but no one would accept the enormous burden of editing the projected ten-volume, eight-million word, interdisciplinary venture.[4] In desperation Seligman turned to Johnson, as he had once before when as chairman of the Committee of Fifteen he had asked Johnson to compile the report on prostitution.[5] Although Johnson was already occupied with his building program at the New School, he leapt at the opportunity. The *Encyclopedia* paralleled his interests at the New School, and, as it turned out, Seligman's conception of the *Encyclopedia* coincided almost exactly with Johnson's own views of the social sciences.

The initial idea for an encylopedia had come, not from Seligman, but from Alexander Goldenweiser, a student of Franz Boas at Columbia, who taught anthropology at the New School through the 1920s. In 1923 Goldenweiser organized a conference at the New School, which petitioned the American Sociological Society to sponsor an encyclopedia for the social sciences. Goldenweiser conceived of the encyclopedia as a logical extension of the New School's effort to integrate the social science disciplines and foster social change. Goldenweiser enlisted the support of six learned societies, which together set up a committee to explore the feasibility of an interdisciplinary encyclopedia. In 1926 the Social Science Research Council lent its support to the project and in 1927 it chose Seligman as editor.[6] Seligman secured financial support from the Laura Spelman Rockefeller and Russell Sage foundations, and also negotiated a contract with the Macmillan Company to publish the encyclopedia. In 1927 he traveled to Europe, where he gained the enthusiastic backing of European scholars. Having resolved the political problems and arranged the financial details, Seligman set to work, only to realize that he needed help. By hiring Johnson, Seligman in effect turned the project back over to the New School, where it had all begun.[7]

Seligman and Johnson comprised an ideal editorial team. Seligman, the genteel German Jew and elder statesman of American economists, easily assumed the role of benign but helpful father to the younger, brash, and decidedly ungenteel Johnson. Seligman fought all the battles with Macmillan, the foundations, and scholarly societies while Johnson supplied the energy and vision. Throughout their eight-year editorial partnership, the two men rarely disagreed on important points and their differences were for the most part limited to matters of funding and production schedules. When the final volume appeared in 1935, each man insisted that the other deserved full credit for the success.[8] In truth it was Johnson's encyclopedia, but without Seligman's backing and prestige the project could never have been completed.

Both Seligman and Johnson had wanted an encyclopedia that transcended the specialized concerns of the individual social science disciplines and presented material in an nontechnical manner.[9] As such they intended the *Encyclopedia*, in Seligman's words, to provide a "synopsis of the progress that has been made in the various fields of social science, in the broadest sense of the term." Here scholars could find reliable summaries, up-to-date bibliographies, and cross-references to subjects both inside and outside their own disciplines. Scholarly researchers would be given easy access to related work in other fields, and lay readers would find facts and theories on a variety of topics of general interest. Finally, Seligman and Johnson hoped that the *Encyclopedia* would establish "amid the welter and confusion of modern thought . . . a center of authoritative knowledge for the creation of a sounder and more enlightened public opinion on the major questions which lie at the foundation of social progress and world development."[10]

To accomplish these goals Seligman and Johnson agreed that the *Encyclopedia* had to be extensive, integrated, reliable, and accessible. They assured extensive coverage by including ten social science organizations as cosponsors, each of which provided two advisors to the *Encyclopedia*'s staff.[11] In addition, Seligman and Johnson set up a board of "advisory editors" consisting of seventeen Americans and eleven Europeans from England, France, Germany, Italy, and Switzerland.[12] An American board of directors oversaw the work of these various editors. The board included thirteen academic and nine lay members.[13] Although none of these individuals played a direct role in day-to-day editorial policy, Johnson frequently consulted them on questions of coverage and the appropriateness of particular topics and solicited their suggestions for prospective contributors. Johnson seems to have appreciated and utilized these advisors, although he never felt bound by anyone else's advice, even Seligman's.[14]

As editor of the *Encyclopedia of the Social Sciences*, Johnson brought together the work of a generation of western scholars. Like the New School, the *Encyclopedia* did not advocate a single, dogmatic point of view. Johnson allowed a wide variety of individual, methodological, and philosophical differences, treating each position with scholarly respect. Even so, the ideas of John Dewey and other American instrumentalists profoundly shaped the *Encyclopedia*, as they had the New School itself.

The *Encyclopedia* documented several significant changes in American life. It marked the coming of age of American social scientists who were unafraid to compare their work with that of Europeans and who had, indeed, initiated and shaped the definitive encyclopedia of the social sciences. Further, the *Encyclopedia* adopted an explicitly secular outlook that made religion a subject for investigation, not a source of normative values and cosmic purpose. Critical inquiry, rather than Christian belief, was its organizing principle. Reflecting the influence of American pragmatists, the *Encyclopedia* defined the sciences as rigorous methods of verifying propositions. Underlying its contents and organization were the assumptions Johnson brought to his work: the persisting relevance of cultural diversity, the natural and creative character of the mind, the plasticity of human behavior, the insignificance of racial differences, and the superiority of constitutional democracy to other political forms.

Although most of these ideas had been manifest in American society since the late nineteenth century, it was not until after World War I that all of these values became generally accepted among American intellectuals. As the official publication of the Social Science Research Council, carrying the sponsorship of scholarly organizations, the *Encyclopedia* enshrined these beliefs as unquestionable and authoritative.[15] Its dissemination into nearly every school, college, and public library in the country helped to popularize the ideas and values inherent in its creation and fulfillment.[16] Alvin Johnson considered these values fundamental to a democratic and cosmopolitan culture. He and the other regular lecturers at the New School had long before rejected the Christian, nationalistic, and free market values that Nicholas Murray Butler and other American university presidents of the time affirmed as the cornerstones of American civilization.[17]

Johnson assured his agenda for the *Encyclopedia* by recruiting for his editorial staff young scholars fresh from graduate school, such as sociologist Bernard Stern, economist Solomon Kuznets, and political scientists Ida Craven and Max Lerner. Both Craven and Lerner had completed their graduate work at the nontraditional and interdisciplinary Brookings School. Kuznets had worked under Wesley Mitchell at Columbia. Stern, too, had done his graduate work at Columbia.[18] Johnson rejected Seligman's inclination to "farm out" particular fields of inquiry to distinguished scholars, who would in turn distribute individual topics to other scholars. Johnson feared that such a policy would lead to partisan distortions and "cliqueism." Instead, he identified several individuals in a field and asked each one to write on a particular topic and to recommend others for related topics. This allowed Johnson the freedom to determine the author of each article and to distribute contributions throughout the scholarly community as he saw fit. As a rule, he allowed only one contribution from a single author to appear in each volume. By calling on so many authors, Johnson encouraged scholars to contribute work at nominal fees simply for the prestige, even as he gave informed readers the means to recognize individual bias in the articles. Moreover, by publicly revealing contributors, Johnson forestalled charges that the *Encyclopedia* had been written by a small group of insiders. The extensive list of contributors that appeared at the front of each volume effectively demonstrated the inclusive character of the *Encyclopedia*. Almost every significant American social scientist appeared at least once.[19]

Johnson achieved integration by personally overseeing the entire process, by choosing broadly trained—but young—social scientists as assistant editors, and by instituting elaborate editorial procedures. By refusing to subcontract articles, Johnson guaranteed that the *Encyclopedia* would bear his imprint. Likewise, his choice of young assistant editors allowed him to avoid any intellectual challenge to his authority. For the most part, the editorial staff idolized Johnson and labored faithfully to carry out his wishes.[20]

Johnson's procedure was to assign to a general field one of his assistant editors, who then combed all the relevant professional journals, monographs, and textbooks, compiling a list of topics and potential contributors. Each assistant editor filed his or her findings and cross-checked them with the other assistant editors. The entire staff then met with Johnson to decide which topics to include, how to develop the subject, and the desired length. Next, an assistant editor outlined each topic, and Johnson selected an appropriate scholar.[21] The assistant editor then sent the potential contributor an outline, along with a brief pamphlet that specified the expectations of the staff. The directions emphasized that the topic was to be developed with a "definite social science reference," directed to the perspective of "social sciences as a group, rather than that of the special field in which the article falls."[22] Once an article was received, an assistant editor read it, gave it a rough editing, and passed it on for Lerner's approval. If Lerner, the managing editor, found it acceptable, it was sent to Johnson for approval and final editing. If either Lerner or Johnson disapproved of the article, the assistant editor sent it back to the contributor for revisions.[23]

Thus, although Johnson allowed contributors to freely develop the content of their articles, he made certain they conformed to carefully established formal and intellectual guidelines. Since he knew a contributor's point of view before he assigned an article, to a considerable extent Johnson determined the content as well. The system proved remarkably effective. Virtually all contributors eagerly accepted Johnson's invitation, and most complied with his directions.[24] As a result, even though the *Encyclopedia* included articles by an enormous number of scholars from a wide variety of fields, Johnson managed to keep the enterprise under control.

Many of the factors that gave the *Encyclopedia* breadth and integration also assured its reliability. Frequent staff meetings, Lerner's oversight of the entire process, and Johnson's final reading helped to weed out errors and avoid embarrassing deletions. The interdisciplinary training of the editors meant that no single person staked out an exclusive claim to a particular field. Every topic came within the purview of the whole editorial staff, each of whom knew something about nearly every topic. This was especially true of Johnson himself, who seemed almost omniscient to some of the young editors. In the rare instance when no one on the staff felt competent to edit an article Johnson sought outside advice.[25] A tribute to the effectiveness of the editorial procedures as well as the abilities of the staff was that no reviewer of the *Encyclopedia* criticized its accuracy or accused it of political bias.[26]

The real test of the *Encyclopedia*, though, was its usability. Seligman and Johnson not only wanted school and public libraries to purchase it, they hoped that scholars in all fields would consider it an indispensable reference. To facilitate its use they adopted the simplest structure possible: alphabetical order. All readers had to do was to look up their subjects as they would in a dictionary. To further aid researchers the last volume of the *Encyclopedia* contained a topical index, an author-title index, and a subject index. The first volume included a 349-page introductory essay, which traced the history of the social sciences from classical times through their modern development in the various western nations. The articles themselves fell into three categories: short pieces of 500 to 800 words, extended essays of up to 20,000 words, and biographical sketches of deceased major figures in the social sciences. Finally, Johnson gave considerable attention to layout, design, type, and binding. He wanted an attractive, easy-to-use, and durable format. When Macmillan balked at his concerns, Johnson pressured Seligman to support him, and in the end Johnson for the most part had his way.[27]

All in all, Johnson, Seligman, and the *Encyclopedia* staff were successful in meeting their goals. Reviewers praised the *Encyclopedia's* objectivity and reliability, its coverage and integration, and its usability. At the time it was generally conceded to be the most important American scholarly publication since World War I. Most predicted that it would have a significant impact on American scholarship and public understanding. Later reviewers have compared it favorably with its successor, the *International Encyclopedia of the Social Sciences* (1968), for its inclusion of pieces by a relatively large number of radical and iconoclastic scholars.[28]

Johnson went to great lengths to assure that a wide spectrum of opinions was represented in the *Encyclopedia* and that no social issue was glossed over. In the classic tradition of encyclopedia editing, which evoked the heritage of the Enlightenment, Johnson did not hesitate to advocate change. He gladly assigned labor scholar John R. Commons the topic of price stabilization and German sociologist Werner Sombart the essay on capitalism, even as he offered conservative Austrian economist Joseph Schumpeter several biographical articles and German neo-Kantian philosopher Ernst Cassirer the sections on Immanuel Kant. On the more important of these issues, Johnson either agreed with the authors he had chosen or could trust their opinions; on the relatively unimportant subjects he tolerated even greater differences. In contrast, he invariably assigned topics addressed to important normative and methodological issues to close friends, such as philosophers Morris Cohen, John Dewey, Horace Kallen, and Sidney Hook, or to persons who shared his political views, such as Harold Laski, Charles Beard, Wesley Mitchell, Elizabeth Todd, or Carl Becker. The overwhelming bulk of the articles were, of course, technical and apolitical. Johnson distributed these randomly throughout the social science community, giving every scholar of significance a chance to participate. He operated the *Encyclopedia* very much as he might have run a passenger train. As long as he determined the schedule, chose the cars, and controlled the switches, the passengers were a matter of indifference. Indeed, even the editorial staff were ultimately free to act only as Johnson directed. Nevertheless, Johnson's tolerance, the scope of his learning, and his rigorous professional standards made the entire operation both balanced and eclectic.[29]

One reason for this was that Johnson himself sincerely believed in the efficacy of scientific methods when applied to social issues. His endorsement of a form of scientific objectivity did not, however, mean that he failed to take personal beliefs seriously. He openly expressed his own opinions and believed that social scientists should use their knowledge to help transform society according to their most deeply held values. Even so, he agreed that all cognitive beliefs, his own included, should be treated as hypotheses, not foregone conclusions. As director of the New School, Johnson was equally sensitive to diverse opinions. He expressed this attitude forcefully in the 1933 New School Catalog as he responded directly to Hitler's suppression of academic freedom in Germany. The catalog read: "As an institution the New School follows a settled policy of neutrality with respect to political and religious and social party grouping. It does not inquire whether a lecturer's private views are conservative, liberal or radical; orthodox or agnostic; aristocratic or proletarian. Neither does it undertake to restrict in any way the lecturer's freedom of utterance. The New School considers that it has fulfilled its obligation when it has assured itself of the scholarly competence and teaching capacity of its instructors."

To his own satisfaction, the ideas of constitutional democracy, economic planning, individual liberty, cultural pluralism, and scientific methodology—not to mention "instrumental" social science and objectivity itself—were themselves defensible propositions. Johnson was never satisfied to assert a belief, not even his belief in the efficacy of science and the scientific method. Beliefs must also be demonstrated, and in the *Encyclopedia* Johnson entrusted this task to City College philosopher Morris Cohen.

Cohen's 6,000-word essay, "Scientific Method," was one of the most influential articles in the entire *Encyclopedia*, considered by American social scientists in the 1930s and 1940s to be the standard brief on behalf of social science methodology.[30] Cohen defined science, not as a body of knowledge, but as a technique by which researchers could test the validity of their beliefs or hypotheses. Scientific research required a commitment to logical principles that could translate the phenomena of sensory perception into theories and hypotheses. Cohen argued that the inductive–deductive process of doubt, testing, and analysis was infinitely more difficult in the social sciences than in the physical sciences. Human behavior was as often affected by cultural factors as by the physical environment, and it therefore lacked the simple causal chains characteristic of noncultural phenomena. Moreover, social experiments were difficult if not impossible to repeat, and researchers faced almost insurmountable obstacles when they tried to isolate variables to determine causes. Finally, humans, unlike noncultural phenomena, constantly changed their characters and thus their behavior. As human beliefs and knowledge changed, so did the roots of behavior.

For these reasons, Cohen discounted the likelihood of discovering social laws comparable to the structural uniformities so useful to physical scientists. Social scientists could expect no more than insight into human behavior, yet the rewards of discovery were worth the effort. "Free doubt and free inquiry," affirmed Cohen, "naturally go together with freedom from paralyzing fear or awe of authority." Although social scientists could not provide certain answers, they enabled "large numbers to walk with a surer step. By analyzing the possibilities of any step or plan," wrote Cohen, "it becomes possible to anticipate the future and adjust oneself to it in advance." He concluded with cautious optimism: "Scientific method thus minimizes the shock of novelty and the uncertainty of life, so that man can frame policies of action and moral judgment fit for a wider outlook than those of immediate physical stimulus or organic response."[31]

Sidney Hook's article on determinism and Horace Kallen's on pragmatism echoed in somewhat more optimistic terms Cohen's endorsement of scientific methodology. Hook, who taught philosophy at New York University, attacked what he considered simplistic critiques of determinism. "Determinism in one form or another," he wrote, "is the theoretical presupposition of all intelligent social activity." No social regulation could be undertaken without the acknowledgment that in some sense human behavior was determined by circumstances. All people in their daily lives counted on others to act in predictable ways, and this alone indicated that it was absurd to deny the legitimacy of some level of determinism. Owing to the imperfect and tentative character of even the most reliable knowledge, however, humans could never hope to know enough to predict the future with absolute certainty. Even seemingly invariable physical laws were at best highly reliable predictions or no more than "something we hope to be true."[32] Prediction in the social sciences was much riskier.

Thus, Hook showed little patience for the crude behaviorism characteristic of the work of psychologist John Watson. According to Hook, Watson not only assumed the total plasticity of individuals, but also ignored the historical character of human culture. Although Hook rejected any suggestion of racial determinism, he acknowledged that humans lived within certain biological limitations both as individuals and as a species. He believed that most of the observable differences between individuals and social groups were the results of cultural factors. But, argued Hook, human culture was not a timeless, uncaused cause. Culture itself underwent continuous change, driven by the multitude of factors that arose from the interaction of biologically complex individuals and their even more complex physical and social environment. This knowledge should not divert social scientists from seeking causes, wrote Hook, but it should temper their claims to "scientific truth."

Horace Kallen brought the influence of the New School directly into the *Encyclopedia* in his article on pragmatism, a philosophical approach that would come to be known as the school's stock-in-trade through World War II. He began by endorsing the arguments of Hook and Cohen, defining their perspective as "pragmatic." Pragmatism, wrote Kallen, was an attitude toward reality, not a body of beliefs. Pragmatists accepted the "plurality and diversity of things and thoughts, the primacy of change, movement and activity, the genuineness of novelty and belief in immediate experiences as the court of last resort in validating ideas." According to Kallen, pragmatists rejected all efforts to set up any system of belief as final, unchanging, and eternally valid. Rather, they asserted that all beliefs were relative to their particular contexts. From a pragmatic perspective, all ideas had to be judged by their consequences, and a belief was true only if it resulted in predictable ends. "Pragmatism dissolves dogmas into beliefs," he concluded, "eternities and necessities into change and chance, conclusions and finalities into processes." For those who demanded infallible certainty and security, pragmatism afforded small comfort. Reality was, Kallen acknowledged, "too tentative, pluralist, temporal and relativist."[33]

This pragmatic conception of reality informed the writing throughout the *Encyclopedia*. The introduction, on the history of social science, was intended to demonstrate the development of a more and more scientific approach to social science. Edwin Seligman, in the preface, balanced and refined this point of view by emphasizing that social science could be understood only within its particular historical context: social science not only had changed through time, but also varied from one culture to another.[34] Johnson carried these ideas through into the body of the *Encyclopedia*, insisting that contributors place their subjects in historical perspective. Johnson and Seligman hoped that, in describing the historical and cultural framework which characterized all beliefs, including those of social scientists, they might help their readers, not only to transcend their own individual pasts, but their national, cultural, and class assumptions as well. With the tools of historic analysis, people would examine their own beliefs with some detachment, and thereby better appreciate and understand other people's beliefs.

This perspective can be seen most clearly in John Dewey's essay, "Human Nature." In it Dewey insisted that the age-old dispute between the advocates of nurture and nature, environment and heredity, distorted the character of human life. Human beliefs, like the human species itself, were natural in origin, and human nurture and development were themselves natural phenomena. Human beings embodied in common a number of permanent features, including physiognomy, linguistic skills, and analytical minds. But under certain conditions these features might fail to develop or might undergo significant change. Some individuals apparently possessed greater physical and mental aptitudes than others, according to Dewey, but he also believed that most important human differences were largely the consequences of environmental rather than genetic causes.[35]

Dewey's recognition of both genetic and environmental factors in human development led to several conclusions. As members of a genetically defined species, all humans possessed the ability to communicate, to think critically, to make intelligent, goal-directed choices, to grow socially and culturally, and to acquire the verbal and manual skills requisite for a productive life. Dewey, Kallen, Boas, Malinowski, Hooton, and Goldenweiser all rejected any suggestion that inherited differences, whether racial, sexual, or intellectual, were sufficient to justify discriminatory policies. Whether the topic was "Segregation," "Race," "Man," "Feminism," "Anti-Semitism," or "Race Conflict," the *Encyclopedia* affirmed the natural equality of humans and the desirability of equal opportunity.[36]

Dewey and the others also shared a belief, evident in the contributions, that human beings possessed a type of consciousness that enabled them to make choices. Such a consciousness allowed people both the means to shape their environment and, through their linguistic skills, to act cooperatively. With language, humans could communicate, organize activities, and develop common goals. With cooperative intelligence, they could impart purpose to nature and thereby improve the human condition.[37] Such attitudes, however, raised serious questions. If social scientists were to provide the knowledge that people needed to effect social change, on what moral authority were those changes to be made? According to whose values?

Alvin Johnson found his answer to these questions in liberal democracy, and he entrusted its defense in the *Encyclopedia* to his friend and frequent lecturer at the New School, British political theorist Harold Laski.[38] Laski argued that the idea of equality was central to the concept of democracy. Equality did not give the majority a right to force individuals to conform to a common mode. Rather, he suggested, a democratic society should strive for equality of treatment. He argued that as long as political authority rested on any basis other than popular consent, the right of individuals to pursue happiness would be thwarted. "The only way to respond to the wants of the individual," wrote Laski, "is to associate him with the process of authority. . . . Modern democratic theory is built upon the notion that the only way of responding to the wants of total experience in modern communities is to give that experience the free opportunity of expression; and the only way to give it that freedom is to offer it in its various aspects the responsibility of sharing in power." Popularly elected officials, chosen by free elections conducted in an environment of open debate, according to Laski, were the only legitimate agents of public policy.[39]

To the writers of the *Encyclopedia,* democracy—like the scientific method—was a process, not a particular program. Each was based on an unwavering faith in the ability of informed individuals to make farsighted, moral choices and a belief that, in the long term, agreement among people would outweigh disagreement. To be valid, the process had to be open-ended, and the flow of relevant information and opinion to the public had to be unimpeded.[40]

Johnson's deference to the twin authorities of scientific inquiry and liberal democracy may seem difficult to distinguish from a religionist's deference to a god, a Marxist's to historical necessity, or a neoclassicist's to natural law. Sidney Hook, expressing sentiments with which Johnson concurred, pointed out that there was nothing unscientific about holding values or even cherishing one value above all others.[41] After all, scientists, like all other people, deferred to values other than empirical truthfulness. For Hook, the difference between his own commitment to free inquiry and majoritarian democracy and a Christian's commitment to revealed truth or a Marxist's to historical necessity was that he allowed his beliefs to be critically scrutinized and publicly challenged. When all was said and done, he agreed to defer momentarily to majoritarian or scientific opinion, even when he believed that it was wrong, as long as he had the right and opportunity to continue to discuss the issue and as long as majorities were not allowed to use their power to destroy and impoverish minorities. Although Hook placed great confidence in scientists and majorities to act intelligently and morally, he did not consider them infallible; neither, of course, did he resort to what he considered the specious authorities of God, natural law, revealed truth, or historical necessity to defend his beliefs. Such, he believed, were the ploys of weak or dogmatic minds.

Neither Hook, Cohen, Kallen, Johnson, nor Dewey expected or even looked forward to moral and ethical consensus. Debate and controversy seemed to them essential elements of a truly vital political community. Believing that social progress could best be secured by a questioning and critical social environment and that scientific methods themselves rested on doubt and skepticism, they enthusiastically endorsed political structures that encouraged dissent and tolerated a wide diversity of opinion. The relative merit of particular values, they argued, could best be determined in an intellectually free community.[42] They considered the fight over issues almost as important as the issues themselves. For this reason, as intellectuals they refused to be walled in by the conventions of academic life. They insisted on carrying their arguments and opinions into public places, where they could be heard and acted upon. Their contributions to the *Encyclopedia of the Social Sciences* and their participation in the New School exemplified this trait.

Between them, Cohen, Kallen, and Hook made versions of pragmatism the unofficial philosophy of the New School, and the school's unofficial sponsorship of the *Encyclopedia of the Social Sciences* reinforced its advocacy.[43] Together with Dewey, these three comprised the core of a distinguished group of New York philosophers who dominated American philosophy between the world wars.[44] If the Harvard philosophy department of William James, George Santayana, Josiah Royce, and Hugo Münsterberg represented a "Golden Age" of American philosophy before World War I, then Cohen, Kallen, Hook, and Dewey, all of whom lectured regularly at the New School, would comprise a "Sterling Age." The Harvard philosophers were more contemplative, genteel, Protestant—and according to Santayana—more provincial than their successors. The New York pragmatists were more activist, more cosmopolitan, and, except for Dewey, Jewish. The first had their roots in the culture of nineteenth-century New England; the second came from the more heterogenous culture of twentieth-century New York City.

Despite these differences, their similar philosophical commitments drew the two together. Dewey openly acknowledged his debt to Harvard pragmatism; Cohen and Kallen had received their doctorates from Harvard. Hook studied first under Cohen at City College and then with Dewey at Columbia. Pragmatism could accommodate the young Jewish intellectuals who were entering the academic community in America in the 1930s, and it had more to offer these young scholars, both culturally and intellectually. No longer did an individual have to be a Christian to be an American philosopher, as had been the case when Kallen and Cohen had tried to find jobs after leaving Harvard prior to World War I.[45] Despite Cohen's unimpeachable credentials as a philosopher, City College had at first refused to allow him to teach philosophy. Instead, the college assigned him to the mathematics department. Only at Cohen's insistence and after the strenuous efforts of the head of the philosophy department, Harry Overstreet, did City College in 1911 allow Cohen to teach philosophy, the first Russian Jew to do so in the United States. Kallen suffered a similar fate until, also in 1911, he secured a position in the philosophy department at the University of Wisconsin.[46]

A survey of lecturers at the New School during the 1920s and 1930s confirms the link between pragmatism and Jewish entry into American academic life. Fully half of the regular lecturers at the New School were Jewish. Besides Hook, Cohen, and Kallen, they included Ernest Nagel, Joseph Jastrow, Fritz Wittels, Harold Laski, Albert Mayer, Waldo Frank, Aaron Copland, Charles Abrams, Franz Boas, Alexander Goldenweiser, Felix Frankfurter, and Max Lerner. This list does not include the largely Jewish Graduate Faculty, which was established in 1933.[47] Moreover, the New School acted as a rallying point for Jewish activities. Kallen actively supported the efforts of American Zionists and recruited for the New School a number of Jewish philanthropists including Jacob Billikopf and Julian Mack.[48] Morris Cohen, who throughout the 1920s had strenuously opposed Kallen's Zionism as contrary to a secular philosophy, nonetheless in 1933 established at the New School the Conference on Jewish Relations to help educate the public on the international threat of anti-Semitism.[49] Most dramatically, the New School, alone among American academic institutions, aggressively recruited those European intellectuals, most of whom were Jewish, who had been forced to flee Hitler.[50]

The lectures that Kallen, Cohen, and Hook gave at the New School soon became legendary: they established the school as the platform for pragmatism in the 1930s and 1940s.[51] On Monday evenings Cohen regularly rode down from Washington Heights to deliver his lectures on scientific method and on the philosophy of law, history, and science.[52] Hook walked over from nearby New York University to lecture on Marxism and human freedom. Kallen, a regular faculty member of the New School, lectured on the history of philosophy, psychology, and esthetics.

Kallen's best-known lectures were on the topic of "cultural pluralism," a concept he developed in part through the influence of William James and Franz Boas. Even as Cohen and Hook had insisted that scientific methods, intellectual freedom, and constitutional limitations were necessary features of a democratic culture, Kallen went one step further as he declared that cultural pluralism was possible only in a democratic society. Democratic institutions, he argued, encouraged attitudes that liberated individuals and guided them "into a fellowship of freedom and cooperation." Americans had only two choices, according to Kallen, "Kultural Klux Klan or Cultural Pluralism."[53] He argued that democracy entailed, "not the elimination of differences, but the perfection and conservation of differences. It aims, through union, not at uniformity, but at variety, at a one out of many . . . and a many out of one. It involves . . . a give and take between racially different types, and a mutual respect and mutual cooperation based on mutual understanding."[54] For Kallen, pluralism provided the cultural basis for an "experimental" democracy that respected individual rights and diverse cultural values. Kallen's pluralistic democracy was in effect a limited democracy of tolerance and compromise.

On a personal level, democratic pluralism offered Kallen the freedom to be Jewish. He found the absence of an established and orthodox culture in the United States exhilarating. For the first time since ancient times, he declared, Jews stood on equal terms with other cultural and ethnic groups. Although devoutly secular in his own Judaism, Kallen entertained no antagonism to those who were religious. Barrett Wendell's literature course on puritanism at Harvard had convinced Kallen of the sincerity of Christian belief. At the same time he was astonished and angered by the intolerance of Harvard Christians. He never forgot Harvard's refusal to accept him and his roommate, Louis Brandeis, on their own terms, as Jews. It was not enough for Harvard to admit Jews or even offer to refine them into Harvard gentlemen; Harvard and the United States should acknowledge the equal validity of Judaism.[55] For this reason, Kallen argued, not as an atheist but as a Jew, that religious freedom and human equality required a secular national culture. "Secularism cannot be freedom from religion." he asserted, "it must be freedom from coercion and exploitation by a particular religion. Secularism is the freedom to be different. . . . Secularism is the Will of God."[56]

Kallen's loyalty to cultural diversity also showed itself in his love for the city, and especially New York City. To him, New York was the paradigm of the secular, pluralistic democracy he envisioned for the United States as a whole.[57] His affirmation of New York was shared by many at the New School, and pervaded the *Encyclopedia of the Social Sciences* as well. Johnson and others entertained a strong belief in social progress which they saw realized in the process of urbanization that had taken place in the West since the late Middle Ages. Their attitude was articulated in the *Encyclopedia* by William B. Munro, a pioneer in American urban studies and professor at California Institute of Technology, whom Johnson had chosen to write the essay on the city: "In all ages, from ancient Egypt to modern America," wrote Munro, "the highest development of human mentality, initiative and achievement has been in urban communities." He continued, "With the city came the division of labor and possibilities for economic surplus, hence wealth, leisure, education, intellectual advance and the development of the arts and sciences."[58]

Further, the city created a special frame of mind, whether in ancient Athens, renaissance Florence, or contemporary New York. In the city individuals found themselves cut off from the soil, their native culture, and social restraints. Urban life invariably led not simply to individualistic behavior, wrote Max Boehm of the Institut für Granz-und

Auslandstudien in Berlin, but to a particular kind of individualism that he called "cosmopolitanism." Boehm, in his article, defined "cosmopolitans" as those individuals who substituted for attachments to their homeland "an analogous relationship toward the whole world." The world at large became a greater and more important homeland. Besides individualism and internationalism, he identified cosmopolitans by their attraction to rationalistic philosophies, secular interpretations of reality, and a tolerance for cultural and racial differences. Cosmopolitans accepted the cultural relativism of statements like "when in Rome do as the Romans." Boehm traced contemporary western cosmopolitanism to the eighteenth-century Enlightenment and acknowledged it as antithetical to the nationalism that had subsequently prevailed in Europe and the United States.[59]

Boehm himself exhibited profound ambivalence toward cosmopolitanism. He distrusted cosmopolitans' internationalism, their easy tolerance, and their often misplaced optimism. Nonetheless, without realizing it, he identified an unifying feature of both the *Encyclopedia* and the New School. Even the differences between Harvard pragmatists and the later New York pragmatists can in part be traced to the differences between Cambridge and Manhatten.[60] Horace Kallen, for example, who found the environment at Harvard uncomfortable, also rejected his hometown of Boston and his professorship at the University of Wisconsin for the sake of a hand-to-mouth, catch-as-catch-can appointment at the New School. In a 1964 interview, Kallen spoke frankly about his reasons for leaving Wisconsin. To him it seemed culturally backward, pro-German, illiberal, and anti-Jewish.[61] Alvin Johnson had undergone a similar peregrination that also ended in New York, but in the meantime he had passed through Bryn Mawr, the University of Nebraska, the University of Texas, the University of Chicago, Stanford, and Cornell. He came back to New York as editor of the *New Republic,* and finally settled down permanently as director of the New School. Only in New York did he find other like-minded people who loved the city, enjoyed intellectual controversy, gloried in the city's racial and cultural heterogeneity, and appreciated the virtually unlimited opportunities that New York City provided.[62]

Whatever else Johnson, Kallen, Hook, and Cohen may have shared with Clara Mayer, Aaron Copland, and Doris Humphrey, they were all cosmopolitan in outlook. But they did more than cast their lot with New York. As intellectuals and artists, they worked to reshape American culture consistent with the values and behavior that they identified with New York. It seems no coincidence that Charles Abrams—the pioneering dean of urban studies in the United States, immigrated from Poland as a child, lived in Greenwich Village, and as an attorney attended night courses at the New School—in 1939 set up at the New School the first urban studies program in the United States. Abrams's books, *The Revolution in Land* (1939), *The Future of Housing* (1946), and *Forbidden Neighbors* (1955), which revolutionized housing policy in the United States, grew out of his lectures at the New School. Abrams hoped that, through a far-sighted housing policy the federal government would open up opportunities for all Americans who wanted to live in cities to do so. He envisioned cities that were safe, livable, and accessible for everyone, much as New York had been for him.[63]

The New School social scientists made explicit in their writings many of the impulses that New School artists had been expressing throughout the 1920s and 1930s. Rosenfeld, Copland, Martin, and Humphrey considered modern music and dance ideally to be secular, urban, and democratic. Similarly, the New School painters, sculptors, and photographers affirmed the city at a time when many other American artists were turning to rural and traditional themes. Berenice Abbott's photographic essays on New York and Greenwich Village celebrated the busy diversity of urban life in contrast to the work of her professional contemporaries Ansel Adams, Dorothea Lange, and Walker Evans. In his 1923 lectures at the New School, Lewis Mumford—at Johnson's specific invitation—virtually invented the city as a subject for serious scholarly study and thereby issued the challenge that New School social scientists took up in the next decade. Whether they came from small-town America or abroad, whether Jewish immigrants or wealthy New Yorkers, whether social scientists or artists, at the New School they found an opportunity to express themselves in a cosmopolitan and self-consciously egalitarian environment. For them, America was New York.[64]

Such was their creativity that they, along with countless other Americans of their generation from similar backgrounds, very nearly redefined American culture. In 1930, when the first volume of the *Encyclopedia of the Social Sciences* appeared, American society remained largely nativist in outlook. Racial segregation still enjoyed constitutional sanction. Only a few critics took seriously modern dance, painting, and music. Barely a handful of intellectuals identified with sexual egalitarianism. And the idea of an effective international government seemed as dead as Woodrow Wilson. At the New School, though, and in the pages of the *Encyclopedia of the Social Sciences,* Alvin Johnson actively promoted racial and religous tolerance, modern art, sexual equality, and internationalism. Most of the individuals associated with the New School accepted such ideas implicitly and assumed that other Americans would come to accept them as well. In retrospect, the most remarkable aspect of their attitude was not their optimism or their naiveté, but their prophetic vision. Within two decades, these values had become so generally accepted by American intellectuals that in educated circles they had almost become conventional. Such cosmopolitan and democratic commitments made the New School an ideal environment for those German scholars who had to flee from Hitler, and who had themselves affirmed values similar to those dominant at the New School.

5

FOUNDING
A UNIVERSITY
FOR EXILES

IN THE SPRING OF 1933, the New School was primarily an experimental institution devoted to adult education and modern art, with a full-time faculty of only four or five members. Alvin Johnson had held the post of director for just over a decade, and his efforts had given the school a building designed to serve its needs precisely and a lecture program that was the envy of major universities. He had restored the school to financial solvency and had built for it a formidable reputation for academic excellence. In the arts, in philosophy, in the social sciences, the New School was at the heart of the movements that were making New York a vital capital of intellectual life in the 1920s and early 1930s. Still, in spite of these successes, Johnson had not abandoned his hope that he would one day be able to reestablish scholarly research at the New School.

In April of that year, as the Nazis expelled Jewish and socialist scholars from their university positions, Johnson saw his opportunity. Within six months, he had raised enough money to bring a dozen, and later a score, of the most distinguished of these refugees to the New School. To accommodate them he established a self-governing research institute within the New School which he called the University in Exile.

In a single stroke, Johnson transplanted a school of German social science to the United States and fulfilled his own pledge, made more than ten years earlier, to make the New School a center for social science research.

At the New School these displaced European scholars found a building and an institution ready-made for their use. Free of anti-Semitism, modernist in outlook, and politically committed to democratic values, the New School offered them an extraordinarily congenial environment, perhaps unique in the United States. In Alvin Johnson, the refugees found a trustworthy and steadfast friend and protector; in the refugees Johnson found the fulfillment of his vision for the New School. For the next twelve years Johnson presided over one of the most extraordinary groups of intellectuals and artists in the western world. At 66 West Twelfth Street social scientists, philosophers, and artists from throughout Europe and the Americas grappled with what they considered the fundamental issues confronting modern society. Free from political as well as traditional disciplinary constraints, the New School salvaged from the tragedy of 1933 a great intellectual treasure.[1]

In spite of the urgency of the situation and the speed with which Johnson had to work, the plans for the University in Exile were made with considerable care. A self-governing faculty had been one of the ideals of the founders of the New School, an ideal they had reluctantly abandoned because of its impracticality; its inclusion in the plan for the research institute was a sign both of Johnson's commitment to the idea and of his faith in it. He was true to the vision of the founders, as well, in his effort to assemble an intellectually coherent community of scholars. He recruited the core of his new faculty from a select group of German scientific institutes. He chose the rest of the immigrant faculty from among the dozens of European social scientists who lost their positions, first in Italy and Germany, and then in Austria, France, and Belgium. Most important, Johnson recognized immediately that his work on behalf of these scholars would have to go far beyond the mere creation of a place for them in the United States: cajoling the Rockefeller Foundation, hounding the German embassy and the Department of Immigration, and pleading with American Jewish philanthropists for sufficient funding were all part of his effort.

The New School's response to Hitler's expulsion of Jewish and socialist intellectuals from the universities and the civil service was but part of a larger western rescue effort. Even so, the New School responded differently, both in its timing and in its commitment of resources. From 1933 to 1944, between 1,000 and 2,000 European intellectuals settled in the United States. Of these, 178 received appointments to the various divisions of the New School, more than to any other American institution. Moreover, thirty social scientists—and social scientists were by far the smallest category of refugee intellectuals allowed to enter the United States—found permanent positions at the University in Exile and, later, the Graduate Faculty. Even the Rockefeller Foundation, whose abundant resources allowed it to play a central role in western rescue efforts, failed to match the enthusiastic and unequivocal commitment of the New School to refugee scholars.

For most Americans, the plight of the "dismissed professors" was distant and abstract. The Depression was of more immediate concern. There were not enough jobs for Americans, let alone jobs for European refugees. This was as true in American colleges and universities as in the society at large. Moreover, a nativistic and anti-Jewish prejudice was widespread, even in American academies. Such resentments were fed by the predictable defensiveness of American intellectuals toward European intellectuals, who often acted condescendingly toward American scholarship. This was the case in the social sciences, where refugee European social scientists were given a decidedly reserved reception by their American colleagues. The New School was the exception. Not only did it accept a relatively large number of scholars and artists, it welcomed them warmly. In fact, Johnson's failure to sustain a permanent faculty at the New School after 1922 may have worked to the refugees' advantage. At the New School no established group opposed their recruitment, nor were they under any compulsion to blend in or to become Americanized.

The original twelve refugees, who arrived in 1933 and 1934, gave the University in Exile its distinctive stamp. Eleven were German and one Italian; eleven were men and one a woman. These were the individuals, out of hundreds of candidates, whom Johnson and the Rockefeller Foundation had agreed to rescue. Despite great diversity in perspective, discipline, and personality, these twelve represented a reasonably coherent intellectual position. They were nearly all social democrats; their scholarship was empirically oriented. In part, their affinities were a consequence of the Nazi purge itself. As "enemies of the state," they were fervently antifascist and almost all were Jewish.

If Johnson and the Rockefeller Foundation were able to agree on particular individuals, however, they disagreed on their reasons for choosing them. The Rockefeller Foundation believed that it was aiding scholars who had broken with the German metaphysical tradition to pursue a "modern" or empirical social science, while Johnson hoped to find a faculty that would go beyond empirical research to address contemporary political and philosophical issues.[2]

Until World War I, the German university system had remained virtually unchanged from the time of the unification of Germany under the Prussian monarchy in 1870. Bismarck had allowed the universities to remain largely self-governing, but he had insisted that they support the policies of the state and avoid all politically sensitive issues. The professorial class, the academic equivalent of the German aristocracy, monopolized the university's resources and dictated university policy. Many professors found refuge in an esoteric philosophical idealism, which often denigrated the materialism of modern culture and scorned the findings of modern science. Thus, although the universities trained the middle classes, they did so in the way that the army trained the lower classes: to serve an aristocratic state. The German universities exhibited all the social and racial prejudices of the rulers of Germany, systematically excluding political radicals and discriminating against Jews. Claims of scientific objectivity and professionalism were often no more than elaborate rationalizations of national loyalty and racial prejudice.[3]

World War I, the Russian Revolution, and the dissolution of the Hohenzollern monarchy altered the German universities, and the Weimar Republic created the conditions that led to their liberalization. The government lifted official restrictions against Jews and socialists, and the faculties acquired more control over appointments and promotions. Yet, as in many other Weimar institutions, those who controlled the universities before 1919 often continued to control them afterward. Jews and socialists thus gained only limited access to the faculties, and as of 1930 only six socialists held full professorships in the entire German university system. These included Emil Lederer at Berlin and Karl Mannheim and Adolph Lowe at Frankfurt. Equally revealing, fewer than 8 percent of the professoriate were Jews, and most of these were in medicine, with almost no representation in the humanities and social sciencies.[4] The emergence in the 1920s of right-wing, nationalist student organizations jeopardized the nascent faculty autonomy, as these groups pressured willing administrators to appoint only "safe" candidates. Although change had occurred, it was not fundamental.[5] Distinguished Jewish and socialist scholars only rarely secured chairs in the universities; most were relegated to new universities like the Berlin Hochschule für Politik or the Kiel Institut. The "modernist" faction, as Fritz Ringer has called it, remained very much apart from the university world of the "Mandarins."[6]

Alvin Johnson first became acquainted with the world of German academics in the mid-1920s, when he went to Europe to find contributors for the *Encyclopedia of the Social Sciences*. Seeking European scholars who shared his own moral and political views, he found himself attracted to the work of "social" economists Emil Lederer and

Karl Mannheim, psychologist Max Wertheimer, and economist Adolph Lowe.[7] Johnson and his colleagues on the *Encyclopedia* understood that the work of these European social scientists was at odds with the dominant institutional tendencies in Europe as well as in the United States.[8] As Johnson looked to John Dewey for philosophical guidance, so Lederer, Mannheim, Lowe, and Wertheimer looked to Max Weber and, more distantly, to the Kantian philosophical tradition. They, like Johnson, were eager to see social science applied to some of the more perplexing social and political problems of the day and were skeptical of the movement toward academic specialization that was breeding political conservatism and moral irresponsibility around them.[9]

Private organizations such as the Carnegie Foundation, the Carl Schurz Foundation, and the Rockefeller Foundation had also cultivated contacts in the German university system. All had supported academic programs in Germany in the late 1920s, hoping to encourage German scholars to regain the place in the western intellectual community that they had lost with World War I.[10] The Rockefeller Foundation, beginning in 1928, particularly encouraged grant applications from German institutes engaged in international political and social research. They focused on places like the Kiel Institute, which specialized in business-cycle theory, economic research, and economic forecasting; the Institut für Sozial und Staatwissenschaften, which under the direction of Max Weber's brother, Alfred, studied the general economic conditions of Europe; the agricultural Institut für Marktforschung in Berlin, directed by Karl Brandt, which worked on Prussian land reform and its effect on regional and national prices; and the Frankfurter Gesellschaft für Konjunkturforschung, which also specialized in business-cycle theory. In sociology and political science the Rockefeller Foundation had identified (though not yet funded) sociologist Karl Mannheim's seminar at Frankfurt; the Institut für Volkriecht, led by legal theorists Hans Kelsen and Erich Hula at Cologne; and the Hochschule für Politik in Berlin, Germany's newest university, created in 1920 under the auspices of the Weimar government, where sociologist Hans Speier and political scientist Hans Simons had appointments.[11] The Rockefeller Foundation had intentionally selected German universities and institutes that emphasized empirical research and applied social science, seeking to encourage the empirical "minority" within the German university system.[12] The minority they had identified included many of the same individuals Johnson selected in 1933 as prospective members of the University in Exile.[13]

The advisors to the Rockefeller Foundation seem not to have recognized that the people they identified as value-free empiricists did indeed have significant political commitments. These political commitments were often at odds with the foundation's aim to promote the spirit of "Anglo–American empiricism," which they hoped would correct the idealism that in the foundation's view continued to dominate German social science.[14] Paradoxically, then, the very persons whom the foundation had considered "neutral" empiricists and who later came to the New School were themselves rebels against the positivism which had so angered the first founders of the New School in 1917.

Unlike the Rockefeller Foundation, Alvin Johnson realized from his first contacts with these scholars that many of them were more akin to the activist intellectuals who lectured and taught at the New School than to mainstream American social scientists. Although these German social scientists all adopted empirical methods, they also raised ethical questions about the nature of politics and society, much as Veblen, Dewey, Robinson, and Beard were doing. Those who came to Johnson's attention consciously directed their research toward the most serious problems of the Weimar Republic. As social scientists and as politicians, they hoped to create a more democratic Germany. As the Rockefeller representative Tracy Kittridge finally realized in March 1933, "Many of the leaders in this field are Jews or social democrats, or worse."[15] For Johnson, these qualities, as much as their adherence to the methods of empirical social science, made them appealing.

Johnson, as an economist and associate editor of the *New Republic*, had followed the political and economic situation in Europe for some time. He had first visited Europe in 1919 as a correspondent for the *New Republic*, although he had remained in England the entire time. Particularly concerned with European economic reconstruction, he had hoped that state planning might soften the impact of the business cycle and perhaps even provide some redress for the social inequalities that persisted in Europe. These changes might in turn open the way for more democratic political structures and ameliorate the rabid nationalism that plagued Europe. Although he was somewhat skeptical of President Wilson and his wartime promises, he nonetheless hoped that Wilson could fulfill them. Johnson returned to Europe in 1924, this time to witness the German economic crisis, caused by runaway inflation and exorbitant reparation payments. Bernard Baruch, Hoover's economic trouble-shooter, told Johnson, "Pack you toothbrush; we're going to Europe."[16] The next day, according to Johnson, he and Baruch left New York for Germany. On this trip, Johnson met some of the future contributors to the *Encyclopedia of the Social Sciences*. More important, he established a friendship with Emil Lederer at the University of Heidelberg.

On this second visit, his first to postwar Germany, Johnson's eyes were opened to a much larger and more precarious world.[17] He confronted monarchists, socialists, communists, and what to him seemed exotic, Old World Jews. He saw an economy on the verge of total collapse and a government besieged by an armed and violent opposition. Wherever he looked he found potential collapse. Germany's working class lived in abject poverty, often shunted off to "Potemkin villages" on the outskirts of industrial cities, and expressed open contempt for the socialist Weimar government. The instability of postwar German politics made it impossible for the government to implement state planning, respond effectively to spiraling unemployment, or control the runaway inflation. Pessimistically, Johnson concluded that "the forces of democracy will soon be displaced, probably by monarchists."[18] As Baruch's companion, Johnson gained access to a wide spectrum of German intellectuals and policymakers, particularly social democrats.

Back in the United States, Johnson kept these people in mind.[19] In 1927, when he accepted the editorship of the *Encyclopedia of the Social Sciences* and was looking for contributors, Johnson turned to these individuals for recommendations. In 1932, when he returned to Germany, he renewed his contacts with these old and beleaguered friends. By then the political situation had become desperate: breadlines were common and unemployment and economic stagnation had paralyzed the economy.[20] After this second trip, Johnson became restless. With major work on the *Encyclopedia* completed, he could no longer avoid the New School's mounting financial problems which had been exacerbated by the Depression. Compared with the situation in Germany, however, these problems seemed small. Johnson wrote a few articles for the *Yale Review,* outlined a series of short stories, and raked leaves on his lawn overlooking the Hudson River in Nyack. Roosevelt's election in 1932 left him perplexed.[21] He believed that the Depression required forceful governmental intervention to restore the economy, yet he doubted that Roosevelt was up to the task. Mistrustful of the president-elect's aristocratic bearing and his insistence on a balanced federal budget, Johnson was also disturbed by the narrow parochialism of Roosevelt's closest advisors. Concerned for his friends in Germany, he gained small comfort from the Democratic administration's "America first" policy.[22]

Even before Hitler's ascension to power in late January of 1933, Johnson realized that Germany had become "the land of the Nazis."[23] Yet neither he nor anyone else was quite prepared for what followed. With the burning of the Reichstag at the end of February and the anti-Jewish boycott in the first week of April, a few Americans sensed that Hitler was not simply interested in the restoration of the old conservative order. By early April, those with direct access to Germany had come to believe that Hitler intended a revolution.[24] Still, even for those who recognized Hitler's radical intentions, it was not clear what could be done in response. The dismissal on April 6, 1933, of all "non-Aryan" professors produced in the United States a much more indignant reaction than had the anti-Jewish boycott of the previous week or even the Enabling Acts of February and March, which had suspended the constitution. For Germans, though, the earlier actions had served notice of the Nazi regime's radical intent. Hans Speier, who was not himself a Jew, recalled that from the moment of the April 1 boycott he understood that his days in Germany were numbered and that the Nazi revolution would inevitably lead to war.[25]

On March 29 Tracy Kittridge, an associate in the Paris office of the Rockefeller Foundation, wrote, "It is my impression that while the State Department may be correct in announcing that the stage of persecution of Jews—meaning physical insults—is over, the more serious stage of discrimination has already begun."[26] Kittridge's telegram arrived in New York on the same day that the Nazis proclaimed the following:

> APRIL 6, 1933 MAINTENANCE OF SAFETY AND ORDER. The Minister of the Interior—Commissariat of the Reich—has ordained through the proclamation of April 5, 1933, No. 34953, that all members of the Jewish race (without regard to denominational affiliation) in the civil service, in community corporate activities, other lawful public bodies, as well as those employed on teaching staffs of private schools, are to be discharged from duty until further notice.[27]

The announcement instantaneously created almost 500 vacancies in German universities. Moreover, it sanctioned a witch hunt by pro-Nazi German students, who set out to find all "non-Aryans" still employed in schools or the civil service who were being protected by "disloyal" administrators. It also set into motion the process of "intellectual rescue."

By mid-May 1933 individuals and organizations in the United States, England, France, Turkey, and Palestine had compiled lists of those who had been dismissed from the German university system. Independently, both the Rockefeller Foundation and Johnson responded to the purge. Daniel O'Brien, assistant director in the medical services division of the Paris office of the Rockefeller Foundation, traveled extensively in Germany following the April 6 decree. In his interviews with Rockefeller contacts on German medical faculties, which had suffered the highest percentage of Jewish dismissals, he noted fear, despair, and shock on the part of medical personnel. He concluded his report by saying that "the state of revolution is a real one in Germany.

The Nazi Party is in complete power." Nonetheless, O'Brien recommended caution and patience. "I am inclined to feel the period of party suppression is likely to be a relatively short one," and "it is well to sit by and wait for a period of weeks or months."[28]

Johnson, however, decided that effective action could not be delayed. Two days after O'Brien's report to the Rockefeller Foundation, Johnson wrote to his confidante and future New School colleague, Agnes deLima, "I have another scheme in mind. Among the German professors who are being ousted, many are my personal friends. I'm setting out to find money, if I can, to get ten or a dozen of them to the U.S. to set up a German university in exile."[29] Within a week of his letter to deLima, Johnson enlisted the support of Edwin Seligman.[30] Believing that Seligman's name would give him entrée to Jewish philanthropic organizations and individuals, Johnson asked him to write what came to be known as "The Letter." On April 24, Johnson asked for help to create a "University in Exile" from the debris of the German purges. The letter concluded, "It must be done promptly. The world is quick to forgive invasions of academic liberty. It long ago forgave Mussolini. I shall never forgive Hitler. . . ."[31] Johnson asked for $120,000 over a two-year period to finance fifteen scholars at salaries of $4,000 per year. His plan was simple. Get the money first and the scholars second. He already had indications from his contacts on the *Encyclopedia* that many distinguished German scholars, under the right conditions, wished to come to the United States.

Three weeks later, on May 13, Johnson informed the *New York Times* that he intended to form a "University in Exile."[32] Paraphrasing the Seligman letter, Johnson indicated that he had some money in hand, but that most was yet to be raised. This, however, was misleading. Before the *New York Times* announcement was made, a wealthy Jewish businessman, Hiram Halle, who had made his fortune in petroleum refining and finance, had pledged the entire sum that Johnson required. Halle, who wanted to remain anonymous, had been "captivated" by Johnson's idea; he found the notion of a University in Exile irresistible.[33]

Johnson kept Halle's gift a secret to avoid scaring off additional contributors, and with good reason. Except for Halle, Johnson had found few willing donors. Before receiving Halle's donation in mid-May, he had collected only between $7,000 and $15,000.[34] Addressing mainly Jewish groups and individuals, Johnson encountered a conservative and tentative response that discouraged but did not surprise him. Earlier, when left-wing Jewish groups had attempted to organize a boycott against German products sold in the United States, the two leading voices of American Jewry had refused to participate. Both the American Jewish Congress and B'nai Brith argued that to participate in such a boycott would only confirm in anti-Jewish minds the existence of an international Jewish conspiracy.[35] With the exception of the Jewish Labor Council, most American Jewish groups agreed with the Rockefeller Foundation's assessment that the storm would blow over. Fearful of feeding Nazi propaganda and equally fearful of inciting American anti-Semitism, organized American Jewry all but ignored Johnson's call for "immediate" help.[36]

With Halle's backing but without the support of major Jewish organizations, Johnson went ahead with his plan. By early June, when Halle's gift was announced, Johnson had already taken steps to clear the way for his institute.[37] "The District of Columbia," Johnson later wrote, "will agree to charter almost anything"—even a nonexistent university.[38] Johnson realized that a charter, dubious or not, would be essential if he were to attract a European faculty.[39]

He had also held extended conversations with officials in the German embassy. "I'm going to shake those bastards until they let my professors go," he wrote deLima.[40] This proved unnecessary, since German policy at that time encouraged emigration of German Jews. In fact, Johnson might well have saved his annoyance for the United States. From officials in the Departments of Labor and Immigration, he learned that nonquota visas could be obtained only if two conditions were met. First, a job had to exist for the applicant. Second, the applicant had to have worked within that same occupation for two years prior to immigrating. In 1933 these conditions were not difficult to satisfy, but in the late thirties these regulations would become a serious barrier to immigration. All that remained was to go to Berlin and establish contact with his old friend Emil Lederer. In late May Johnson assigned Edwin Mimms, one of his assistants on the *Encyclopedia*, to this task.[41]

On May 23 a group of American educators and scientists, including Alvin Johnson, met to discuss the problem that Johnson single-handedly had been working on since the first week of April.[42] Convened by Stephen Duggan, the director of the Institute of International Education, an organization that promoted educational exchange between Europe and the United States, the group included representatives from the Rockefeller Foundation and several individual philanthropists. Edward R. Murrow served as the secretary of the group which established itself as the Emergency Committee in Aid of Displaced German Scholars. The committee agreed to find as many places as possible for dismissed European professors within the American university system. They would then act as a clearinghouse to match the scholars with the available openings. Further, the committee agreed to give preference to already distinguished scholars with productive years ahead of them between the ages of thirty-five and fifty-five.[43]

To finance this effort, the Rockefeller Foundation agreed to match dollar for dollar whatever funds the committee could raise from other sources. Earlier in May the foundation had created an emergency fund of $140,000 for all scholarly fields, with $50,000 allocated for the social sciences. They made this money available to the Emergency Committee. The committee in effect acted for the Rockefeller Foundation while the foundation itself remained behind the scenes.[44] Between 1933 and 1945, the committee saved some 600 European scholars and provided crucial funding for the efforts of the New School. It was not always an easy partnership—Johnson and the officers of the Rockefeller Foundation had profoundly different ideas about the rescue work—but, in the interest of refugee relief, both parties did their best to put their disputes aside.[45]

One of the first disagreements arose over the character of the Nazi movement. Johnson, whose evaluation of Germany had been shaped by his visits, believed that "democracy" as understood by Americans stood little chance against the antidemocratic tendencies of many Germans. Although Hitler exceeded his worst fears, Johnson always believed that the Nazis were much more than an aberration that would quickly burn itself out. For this reason, Johnson thought it likely that refugee relief would be a long-term proposition and recognized the need to establish permanent positions in the United States for these refugees. In contrast, the Emergency Committee, acting for the Rockefeller Foundation (as did the Assistance Council in Britain and the Comité des Savants in France), operated on the assumption that the Nazi excesses were only temporary.[46] Permanent relief and long-term programs were, in their estimation, unnecessary. As late as 1935, when the Nazi regime showed no signs of weakness or moderation, the Rockefeller Foundation considered its program complete and the emergency largely over.[47]

Part of the explanation for the attitude of the Rockefeller Foundation lay in its earlier efforts to reshape the German universities. Having provided funds for the "Americanization" of German research, at least in the social sciences, the officers at the foundation wished to safeguard their investment.[48] The foundation saw an opportunity to Americanize the German refugee scholars even further by dispersing them even temporarily, throughout the United States. The New School's preference to concentrate a core of social scientists in one institution seemed to the Rockefeller Foundation antithetical to their purposes. A University in Exile would encourage Europeans to remain European. Johnson, on his side, wished to preserve their European character because he believed that American social science needed a strong dose of European rationalism to save it from what he considered its increasingly irrelevant and implicitly conservative positivism. The Rockefeller Foundation wished to salvage the most empirical segment of German social science and, once in the United States, reshape it along the lines of mainstream American social science that Johnson and the New School rejected.

The ambivalence of the Rockefeller Foundation toward Jews, an attitude that Alvin Johnson in no way shared, also characterized the difference between the two rescue efforts. Rockefeller officers in the social sciences voiced their concern: "The conspicuous outcry against the German lack of liberalism finds itself faced on sober consideration with the fact that if too many Jews are introduced into the American university we shall run a surprising good chance of creating an uncontrollable amount of precisely the same sort of illiberal attitude here."[49] Or, as the director of the foundation, Raymond Fosdick, wrote to John D. Rockefeller II in December 1938, "We have reached the saturation point."[50] Put plainly, German Jewish scholars threatened to destroy the anti-Jewish quota system then maintained by many American universities. The Rockefeller Foundation feared that such a "saturation," transforming the gentlemen's agreement of fixed quotas for Jewish students and faculty, might provoke a virulent strain of anti-Semitism.

The officers of the Rockefeller Foundation were, in fact, reacting to the uncomfortable reality of American academic life. In the 1930s American universities and colleges systematically discriminated against Jews, thereby compounding the difficulty of placing refugees in a time of economic depression, When Johnson wrote to a colleague in psychology at Harvard concerning the possibility of setting up the University in Exile, he was told in reply that such a scheme "to resettle Jews" within American faculties did not have a "Chinaman's chance." Another colleague informed Johnson and the Emergency Committee that, if they were interested in finding "first rate" scholars, they were after the wrong group. Those Germans dismissed in April were Jews or social democrats, whose work was inferior anyway.[51]

One of the most dramatic cases of the prevalent reluctance to employ Jews involved the economist Hans Neisser, a Jew and a social democrat. While on the faculty at the Kiel Institute, Neisser had been described by Austrian economist Joseph Schumpeter as one of the most brilliant economic minds of his generation.[52] In 1933 Neisser was the only German Jew to secure a position on the faculty of the University of Pennsylvania. Seven years later, Neisser was still untenured; Pennsylvania let him go because he "couldn't get along with anyone." Neisser joined the Graduate Faculty of the New School in 1940 and remained at the New School until he retired in the early 1970s. Neisser, who developed models of income distribution in the early 1940s, was a pioneer in econometrics. His scholarship made significant contributions in both economics and phenomenology over his lifetime.[53]

Time and again, the Rockefeller Foundation, trying to find positions for the scholars it sponsored, confronted this problem and the related problem of American political conservatism. Individuals whom the foundation had supported during the 1920s and then rescued at great expense could find no place in established American universities. As much as the foundation wished to scatter their refugees across the United States, the fact remained that, in many cases, only the New School welcomed them. At the New School, neither their Jewishness nor their democratic socialism made them uncongenial. Johnson valued the efforts of individuals like Neisser to explore the philosophical and political issues raised by social science research. He shared their skepticism toward conventional social science as well as their determination to uphold the values of liberal democracy.

Alvin Johnson and the Emergency Committee were not the only participants in the rescue work. More than 100 German scholars found positions as a result of Jewish and British efforts at Hebrew University and a few other institutions in Palestine. The entire Warburg Institute, its staff and library, was transferred from Germany to London in 1933 and 1934, and the Institute for Advanced Studies was created at Princeton University, in part to provide positions for distinguished European intellectuals.[54] Even so, the Rockefeller Foundation, by subsidizing international groups such as the Emergency Committee, provided 50 percent of the funding for all rescue efforts. But in the social sciences the New School stood apart. Of the 157 German social scientists dismissed or forced to resign from 1933 to 1939, the New School provided faculty positions for thirty of them, and from 1933 to 1935 the New School spent 50 percent more than the Rockefeller Foundation for assistance in the form of salaries to social scientists. As Johnson wrote in 1944 to his friend and board member George Bacon, "It follows naturally that immediately upon the expulsion of Jewish and liberal professors from their chairs in Europe, we had to proceed to make places for as many of them as we could."[55]

Taking stock in late May, Johnson was no doubt pleased that he had indeed succeeded in making places for European scholars. To gather the scholars themselves, however, he realized that he needed a coordinator in Germany, a role that he hoped to assign to his friend Emil Lederer, professor of economics at the University of Berlin. He believed that Lederer would be capable of recruiting a faculty for the University in Exile much as he had coordinated German contributions to the *Encyclopedia for the Social Sciences*. Johnson wrote, "As Max Weber was the most dynamic figure in German social science, I chose for my group leader Lederer. He, while not a slavish disciple of Weber, was deeply influenced by his thought."[56] This dedication to Weber—and the political beliefs it bespoke—put Lederer at the center of an informal network of Germany's foremost intellectuals.

Johnson's choice of Lederer was an insightful one. Lederer was well known among the German socialists who throughout the twenties had worked to liberalize and democratize German society.[57] These socialists, many of them Jewish, were directly affected by the April Decrees.[58] When approached by Johnson, then, Lederer was in a position to act not only for himself but on behalf of his political and professional colleagues as well. These included sociologist Hans Speier; economist Adolph Lowe; Prussian state administrator Hans Staudinger; economists Gerhard Colm, Jacob Marschak, and Hans Neisser; philosopher and diplomat Kurt Riezler; political scientist Arnold Brecht; and sociologist Albert Salomon. As professor of economics at the University of Berlin, Lederer had been at the center of a group of social democrats then active in the German capital. At his home, throughout the twenties, social democratic politicians and intellectuals had gathered to discuss policy and strategy. Staudinger and Speier were particularly close to Lederer. Staudinger, who served first as Prussian minister of commerce and then as a social democratic delegate to the Reichstag, was the scholar-politician of the group. Speier was Lederer's assistant.

A second, related group clustered around Adolph Lowe, first at the Kiel Institute of World Economics and then at the University of Frankfurt. Lowe and Staudinger had become close friends in the early twenties, when they had worked together as government economics experts charged with dealing with postwar inflation. In the mid-twenties, Lowe received an appointment as chief of the statistical section of the Kiel Institute. There he collaborated with the institute's director Bernard Harms and recruited Gerhard Colm, Hans Neisser, and Jacob Marschak to work for the institute. In 1932 Kurt Riezler brought Lowe to the University of Frankfurt, where he joined Karl Mannheim in sociology.

Many of these scholars had established ties with the Rockefeller Foundation during the years before 1933. Yet, in the face of the April Decrees—during the months before Johnson was able to put his plan into action—the foundation was slow to respond to their plight. As early as 1931, the Rockefeller Foundation had recognized Lowe's department of international statistical economics at Kiel as a "pioneering" effort in business-cycle research comparable to Wesley Mitchell's National Bureau of Economic Research. In 1932 and 1933 the foundation invested some $45,000 in the institute's operation and was on good terms with the director, Bernard Harms, who retained Neisser and Colm even after the April Decrees despite their "obvious" Jewish origins.[59] Harms defended his action on the grounds that they were not listed on the May 6 dismissal order which enumerated the specific individuals to whom the April Decrees applied. At first Harms resisted the pressure of the local Nazi organization, which demanded that Neisser and Colm be fired. Undaunted, the Nazis raided the institute and physically removed Neisser and Colm. Despite such acts, the Rockefeller officer in Paris wrote to his superior in New York, "In the meantime it would be most unfortunate if our support were withdrawn. If we get out now the Nazis will think we were in it for political reasons."[60] The foundation's ambivalence was complicated by the anti-Semitism of many of its own staff, who in private sympathized with the Nazis. A letter of May 16, written by the Paris representative, makes those sympathies clear: "We should not forget that during the past 15 years the Jewish liberal element has been definitely favored in Germany, and they have ... attained to a situation which inevitably produced a reaction."[61]

In fact, both Emil Lederer and Jacob Marschak had gone to the Rockefeller Foundation with proposals to move its schools out of Germany. Marschak, a member of the faculty at the Kiel Institute, was described by his foundation sponsors as the "foremost mathematical economist in Germany."[62] On May 4 he traveled to Paris to propose to the Rockefeller Foundation that the foundation transfer the work it sponsored at Kiel and at Heidelberg to Geneva. Unknown to Marschak, Lederer had offered a similar suggestion. He proposed that the institutions sponsored by the foundation be reorganized outside Germany in a "new working arrangement."[63] Committed to its policy of "sit-and-wait," however, the foundation responded to neither suggestion, leaving Lederer and Marschak at the mercy of the Nazis. Within a short time the Nazis had singled out the Kiel Institute for its socialist and Jewish sympathies and had forced Bernard Harms, its director, to resign.

Some of the scholars who eventually found their way to the New School engineered their own escapes during the terrifying days after the April boycott. For example, Adolph Lowe and his wife had kept two suitcases packed in their apartment for several months. With rumors circulating that the arrest, dismissal, and imprisonment of Jews was imminent, Lowe expected the worst.[64] He had hoped that his friendship with Marxist theorist Max Horkheimer would spare him and his family. Horkheimer, a childhood friend, had entrusted Lowe with the administration of the Frankfurt Institute for Social Research when its members went abroad in mid-1932. Lowe, an activist who felt obliged to remain as long as possible in Germany, had elected at that time to stay. As a "religious" socialist and militant social democrat, Lowe was closely associated with theologian Paul Tillich, also at Frankfurt, and Eduard Heimann, an economic theorist.

On the morning of April 2, only hours after the anti-Jewish boycott had begun, Lowe found a notice in the *Frankfurter Zeitung* that announced that on April 3 all Jews were to turn in their passports. He went directly home and, after three hours of discussion with his wife, took the seven a.m. train to Geneva. Horkheimer met him there and subsequently offered Lowe a position at the Frankfurt Institute in Geneva. "It was only then," Lowe recalled, "that I experienced the sense of being a refugee."[65] Sustained by a small savings account, the generosity of the Salvation Army in Berne, and three months' "severance" pay, Lowe instead chose to negotiate for an academic post in either England or the United States.

Lowe's friend Hans Staudinger found himself in an even more precarious situation. Staudinger, like Lowe a decorated veteran of World War I and an active social democrat, was imprisoned by the Nazis for nearly six weeks. Aside from his activities as a social democratic representative to the Reichstag, Staudinger had also served as the leader of the Young Socialists, a clandestine group whose members had pledged in the event of political persecution to continue their work underground. In April, Staudinger and his group were discovered and arrested by the Gestapo. After the intervention of the Belgian government, Nazi officials released Staudinger on the condition that he leave Germany within six months and that he not communicate with any of his political colleagues lest they be placed in prison.[66] Unable to return to his home at Hamburg, Staudinger used Lederer's Berlin home as a safe house. When Edwin Mimms, Johnson's emissary, arrived at Lederer's house, Staudinger answered the door.

Mimms had arrived in Berlin with Johnson's plans for the University in Exile and, most probably, with a contract for Lederer to sign. He had undoubtedly expected to be able to enlist the help of Lederer immediately and set to work. Unfortunately, however, both he and Johnson had underestimated the state of panic that prevailed in Germany. Lederer had already left for England. Given Lederer's London address, Mimms thanked Staudinger and set out for England. There he explained Johnson's scheme to Lederer, who though interested would not commit himself. Instead, he offered to visit New York to inspect the school and discuss details personally with Johnson. Mimms and Lederer booked passage to New York. In New York, Johnson and Lederer quickly came to terms and settled on a preliminary list of faculty.

In late June, Johnson accompanied Lederer to London, where they spent nearly a month interviewing prospective faculty members.[67] Besides Lederer, Johnson hoped to appoint Lowe, Marschak, and Karl Mannheim.[68] Moreover, he knew the work of the agricultural economist Karl Brandt and the economists associated with the Kiel Institute, Colm and Neisser. Economic theory, sociology, and empirical research were to be the mainstays of the new institution. But Johnson wanted nothing to do with what he called "simple academics." In Lowe and Lederer, Johnson hoped to acquire scholars who were political activists. In Hans Staudinger and Arnold Brecht, also on the lists, he hoped to obtain politicians who were scholars.[69]

The Nazi regime was still in its early days, however, and several of Johnson's scholars were reluctant to abandon the Old World for the New. Marschak and Lowe, who believed that the regime would crumble in a relatively short time, preferred to find positions in England, and in August they succeeded in doing so. Karl Mannheim likewise preferred to remain in England. Johnson seemed almost relieved at Mannheim's decision, since Mannheim had insisted that the New School create a school of social thought that revolved around his own ideas. In Johnson's words, Mannheim wanted to be "the whole show."[70] Johnson clearly disliked his attitude, but he could not resist someone of Mannheim's prestige. Johnson's correspondence with Agnes deLima shows that he was surprised by such defections: "I expected these Germans to come and say da! da! Instead they are shopping. But I'll not be discouraged."[71]

As of July 1933, then, all Johnson had was Lederer's personal commitment. He and Lederer still had to locate, recruit, and arrange passage for the others on their list. Lederer did not wish to return to Germany, and Johnson lacked the language proficiency necessary for elaborate negotiations. At this point Hans Speier agreed to help. Speier had worked in Berlin at the Hochschule für Politik, a newly created school that depended on trade union support, and as Lederer's assistant at the University and on the *Archiv für Sozialwissenschaft und Sozialpolitik*.[72] In early April, Speier and his wife had lost their positions in Berlin, Speier for his connection with Lederer and the Hochschule and his wife, a doctor, because she was Jewish. With no money or prospects, Speier went to Lederer's house in early June. Like Mimms, he found Staudinger instead.[73]

Staudinger, along with Arnold Brecht, the most politically engaged of those who came to the New School, urged Speier to leave Germany immediately. He told Speier to go to Holland and to carry no names with him.[74] Speier, however, discomfited by the prospect of exile while his wife was expecting a child, chose the seclusion of a small town on the North Sea. Then, one morning in July, he noticed a mailman bicycling furiously toward him with a telegram. Lederer asked him to come to London. The next day, leaving his wife at the *pension,* he flew to London.[75] Speier eagerly accepted Lederer's offer to join the new faculty, as did Albert Salomon, sociologist at Cologne and part of Lederer's network.[76]

Back in Berlin, Speier contacted Karl Brandt, who insisted on a meeting in a hotel lobby—complete with prearranged signals—to assure that Speier was not a Nazi *agent provocateur.*[77] Brandt, tall and blond, a "double Aryan," signed on the spot, as did Frieda Wunderlich, the only woman on the original University in Exile faculty. Wunderlich was a political activist, though not a social democrat. An expert on social legislation, she edited *Sozial Praxis* and was a member of the Prussian parliament, where she knew both Brecht and Staudinger.[78] Arnold Brecht, meanwhile, was ensconced in a house his family owned on an obscure and inaccessible island off the northern coast. To reach him, Speier chartered a mail plane and flew through hazardous conditions to offer Brecht a contract to the New School.[79] His job completed, Speier returned to London, delivered the contracts to Johnson, and joined his wife in Berlin.

In the space of a few weeks, Johnson and Lederer had organized a faculty in social and political science that represented, according to the Rockefeller Foundation, the very best of German social science. Essentially, they had drawn their faculty from Lederer's intellectual and political network, which included political activists and research-oriented academics. As liberals, socialists, and Jews, they symbolized the democratic and pluralistic commitments of the Weimar Republic. Still, they had always been a minority in Germany and in the university system. The Nazi revolution was systematically dismantling everything they had accomplished following the war. Germany no longer offered them a future, and so the New School became for them more than a temporary refuge. It provided them the means to continue their work. In New York, at the University in Exile of the New School, the ideals of the Weimar Republic lived on.

The faculty that came together in September 1933 had been drawn for the most part from three universities: Frankfurt University, with its municipal connections and independent board of trustees; the Kiel Institute for World Economics, established in 1911 as a research institute; and the Berlin Hochschule, a municipal university. All but two of the original faculty were either economists, political scientists, or sociologists. Gerhard Colm, Karl Brandt, and Eduard Heimann, from Hamburg, taught economics; Hans Speier, Albert Salomon, and Karl Mayer, sociology; and Arnold Brecht and Frieda Wunderlich, political science. The remaining two were Max Wertheimer, philosopher, psychologist, and founder of "gestalt" psychology, and his close friend, musicologist Erich von Hornbostle, who died in 1934 before assuming his teaching duties. Wertheimer fit in comfortably with his social science colleagues and, together with Horace Kallen, formed the graduate program in philosophy and psychology at the New School.[80]

Beyond these original appointments, Johnson recruited two additional Rockefeller scholars, Italian political scientist Max Ascoli and Austrian Erich Hula, an authority on international law. Ascoli had at first sought an appointment at Columbia, but when negotiations broke down he accepted Johnson's offer at the New School. Hula originally rejected Johnson's offer altogether, deciding instead to return to Austria to work against fascism. Johnson persuaded the Rockefeller Foundation to appoint Hans Simons, a founder of the Berlin Hochschule and a Weimar diplomat, in Hula's place. In 1934 Johnson added Alfred Kahler, a student of Lowe's at Kiel; Fritz Lehman, a financial expert at Cologne; Arthur Feiler, a financial editor for the *Frankfurter Zeitung*; and Hans Staudinger. These appointments completed the faculty of the University in Exile. Within the year, Johnson formally merged the University in Exile with the New School and renamed it the Graduate Faculty for Social and Political Science of the New School.

In spite of its newly formalized status, however, the work of the University in Exile was not yet complete. In 1938 the Nazi takeover of Austria led to a second wave of refugees and Alvin Johnson found room for several of them at the New School. These included Erich Hula in political science, Felix Kaufmann in philosophy, and Ernst Karl Winter, also a political scientist and a vice mayor of Vienna.[81] Philosopher and diplomat Kurt Riezler, phenomenologist Alfred Schutz, and political philosopher Leo Strauss also arrived in 1938. When Gerhard Colm left in 1939, Johnson replaced him with Jacob Marschak and Hans Neisser. With the arrival of Adolph Lowe, who had been let go from his position at Manchester in 1940 for being a "naturalized alien," the "Kiel Group" had reassembled itself nearly intact at the New School. Johnson exploited the "new emergency" in Austria to secure additional support from the Emergency Committee.

The Europeans who came to the New School left behind their countries, their cultures, often their families, and most of their material possessions. Faced with the loss of their way of life and professional standing and recognizing that far worse lay ahead, they understood the futility and danger of remaining under Nazi authority. This was especially true of the second wave, some of whom had left their homes once already to take refuge in Austria. Unlike most other immigrants to the United States, they did not come to America as young people to seek a better life. They came in mid-career, forced to abandon successful and comfortable lives. By 1938, most of the paths of emigration had been closed; all their hopes depended on reaching the United States, and many had to escape to do so. Erich Hula's ordeal exemplified the experience of these refugees.

In 1933 Hula had returned to Vienna from Cologne to work for the municipal Chamber of Labor as it attempted to reform the city's political and constitutional structures.[82] In March 1938, fearing that the end of Austrian independence was near, Hula, supported by a wealthy Viennese businessman and close friend, agreed to travel to England and to publicize Austria's plight. Many Austrians still imagined that, if properly informed, England would refuse to appease Hitler further. But even as Hula worked out the details of his visit he concluded that it was too late. Instead, he accepted money from his friend to finance his own escape. Hula later recalled the evening of March 10, 1938, as the "worst night of my life." Austrian Nazis demonstrated by torchlight as he made his way home through the streets of Vienna. The next day Hula and his wife, Anne Marie, a native of Cologne, took the train to Prague. At the Czech border their escape was abruptly interrupted. Nazis ordered all passengers off the train. Only Hula and his wife, who had received new passports when visiting Chicago in 1932, were allowed to continue. They bluffed their way through by insisting that they were Austrian citizens currently living in the United States. A week later a similar incident occurred in Paris as Gestapo agents nearly arrested them at the airport. In September, after six weeks of such close calls, the Hulas arrived in New York. When notified of Hula's presence, Johnson remarked to a friend, "The fool who turned us down in 1933 is available again."[83] Johnson personally went to Ellis Island to greet the Hulas and expedite their entry procedures.

Johnson handled these tasks with good humor, enjoying the irony that he, a midwesterner and child of immigrants, was now the guardian for these cultivated but bewildered Europeans. He found housing for them, helped with their correspondence, and made them feel at home at the New School. He reshaped the New School itself to allow the Europeans to continue their scholarship and teaching and gave them control of academic activities within what became the Graduate Faculty. The Europeans looked to him as their friend and protector.[84] He, in turn, fondly described the New School to friends as "my university." His birthday became an institutional holiday. The faculty used it as an opportunity to express to him their appreciation and affection. As he once candidly explained, "I have the most self-governing faculty in existence. But as one of them puts it, 'We are completely self-governing, and Dr. Johnson decides everything.'"[85]

Still, Johnson's belief in the principles of faculty autonomy and academic freedom was sincere. He considered the Graduate Faculty a "free university," profoundly different from the German universities and such American universities as Columbia, where the faculty suffered from the capriciousness of its president, its board, and the state government. To assure academic freedom, Johnson granted the faculty control over its own organization, the curriculum, and its procedures for appointments and promotion. The faculty elected its own dean, was exempt from censorship by the administration, and was free to participate in politics with no restrictions. There was only one self-imposed limitation. All faculty were required to endorse the principles of academic freedom and political democracy as understood by the New School. No member of the faculty, read the faculty charter, can be a member of any group or political party which asserts the right to dictate in matters of conscience or scientific opinion.[86]

In matters of administration, however, Johnson maintained his right to run things as he saw fit. For example, in 1935 he concluded that the Graduate Faculty needed a separate and independent board of trustees. In his judgment, the New School board contained too many people who saw the school exclusively as an institution for adult education. In his most grandiose moments, Johnson envisioned the Graduate Faculty as the institution most likely to provide a sound theoretical basis for a "cosmopolitan and democratic" culture. To fulfill this destiny, the faculty needed freedom from the constraints of the school as a whole. Drawing on sympathetic friends—such as Charles Beard, Cornell historian Carl Becker, economist William McChesney Martin, and jurist Felix Frankfurter—Johnson created a separate board for the Graduate Faculty which provided him the freedom to direct its future as he wished. By the 1940s, however, when the two boards included so many of the same members that they were really indistinguishable, Johnson merged the two groups into one board with authority over all divisions of the school.[87]

Even though Johnson did not dictate on academic matters, he took steps to create an intellectual community among the faculty. He hoped at the same time to insure that his European faculty did not become just another isolated foreign enclave in New York City.[88] In the first year of the Graduate Faculty's existence Johnson organized the General Seminar, an interdisciplinary group in which all members participated. He simultaneously founded *Social Research*, a scholarly journal that published the work of the General Seminar in English.[89] From 1933 to 1937, the General Seminar consisted of about twelve scholars and after 1938 of between eighteen and twenty-five. The seminar, which met on a weekly basis over the course of a year, explored a single theme chosen by the faculty. Graduate students and outside faculty frequently attended and participated in the seminar. In the 1930s seminar themes included "America and Europe," "Political and Economic Democracy," and "Power in the United States."

The General Seminar quickly emerged as the intellectual forum of the Graduate Faculty, serving as a focus for new ideas and as a stimulus for interdisciplinary discussion. Despite the presence of several brilliant and opinionated individuals, the General Seminar drew the Graduate Faculty together around common political and intellectual concerns. The success of the seminar inspired several faculty members to join a second seminar, on the methodology of the social sciences, that met from 1933 to 1943. In that seminar, Max Wertheimer—the group's leader—consciously sought to relate the political concerns of the General Seminar to more fundamental philosophical issues of epistemology and value.[90]

Social Research, the school's quarterly publication, served as an adjunct to the two seminars. Johnson had conceived of such a journal years before, but now it seemed essential for the continuing scholarly vitality of the Europeans. He described *Social Research* as a "journal of social and political science" that presented the Graduate Faculty as a coherent group to the American academic community at large. In Johnson's words, "*Social Research* was an instrument in maintaining the collective spirit of the continental scholars comprising our faculty."[91] Unlike most American scholarly journals, *Social Research* was explicit about its policy of presenting a collective point of view. As editors, Lederer and Speier brought to *Social Research* the expertise and commitment that had characterized their work on the *Archiv*. Johnson appointed Elizabeth Todd, a former assistant editor of the *Encyclopedia of the Social Sciences*, to be the managing editor. Thus *Social Research* brought together in a single journal the personnel and the views of two of the most important positions within western social science: the Weberianism of the *Archiv* and the instrumentalism of the *Encyclopedia of the Social Sciences*.

Johnson insisted that Speier, as editor, and Todd, as managing editor, maintain strict control over the content and style of the articles in *Social Research*. Their task was to see that the journal represented the collective concerns of the Graduate Faculty and, more difficult, that those concerns were expressed in clear and intelligible English. To meet publishing deadlines Todd worked long hours, often late into the night and on weekends, to translate "gymnasium" English into what Johnson called "American."[92] Todd's efforts often upset European contributors, who felt that her straightforward style lacked the technical jargon appropriate for scholarly work. But Johnson stood firm behind

Todd's decisions; he recognized that stylistic clarity was nearly as important as scholarly content if his European social scientists were to influence American scholarship.

Johnson empowered Speier to edit all contributions to insure that they faithfully reflected the collective ideas of the faculty. Here, too, problems of personality and principle arose. This time the complaints came not from the Europeans but from Horace Kallen. When Speier told Kallen to revise a particular paragraph, Kallen protested to Johnson, accusing Speier of censorship and violation of academic freedom. Johnson responded by calling Kallen a "lone wolf," but he managed to quiet his charges of censorship.[93] Still, Kallen and other American scholars who lectured regularly in the Adult Education Division, such as Sidney Hook and Max Lerner, resented what they saw as the "Germanization" of the New School. Johnson, however, refused to back down. He later characterized his administrative techniques with one of his homey stories: "You know the middle western way of reconciling tom-cats. Put them together in a gunny sack and hang it on a branch to sway for a few hours in the wind. It works."[94]

By 1939 Johnson could justifiably look back with pride on his work. The Graduate Faculty claimed a prestigious and productive faculty of European political and social scientists, many of whom would otherwise have seen their scholarly lives terminated in mid-career. Johnson had responded to a tragic situation in a resourceful and timely manner in an effort matched by few others in the United States. No other American institution had offered so many refugee European intellectuals such a congenial environment. At the New School they were made to feel comfortable and were given the means to continue their work and the opportunity to communicate with American scholars. Moreover, Johnson for the most part allowed them to govern their own affairs. Here at the New School, as they looked back on their own pasts, they sought to explain what had happened to their dreams of social reconstruction, dreams that had seemed so promising in 1918. Reluctantly, they concluded that Hitler's emergence in Germany and Mussolini's in Italy were the consequence of an excess of democracy. Unhappily, it seemed, democracy and "totalitarianism" were inextricably linked.

6

THE POLITICS OF
DISILLUSIONMENT,
1933–1945

FOR THE FIRST YEARS OF THEIR TENURE, the emigré scholars at the New School concentrated their energies on the most important issue of their era: the nature of German and Italian fascism.[1] As sociologists, economists, and political scientists, they searched for its causes and dedicated themselves to finding its cure. They examined their own pasts and looked about themselves with critical curiosity as the United States—like Weimar, progressive and democratic—seemed miraculously to escape fascism's ravages. The course of fascism in Europe and its unexplained failure to infect their new home was the pressing topic of their work as individuals and of their General Seminar.

As social democrats, these scholars were deeply critical of the weaknesses inherent in liberal political systems. Many had been profoundly disappointed in the Weimar government, which had never satisfactorily eliminated the inequities of German society due to the constraints imposed by parliamentary process. In their view, Weimar had fallen because of the fragility and inadequacy of its parliamentary democracy in a time of crisis. As they looked together beyond their consensus, with the added benefits of time and distance, many of these European social scientists modified the more utopian of their political beliefs. Although they reaffirmed the cosmopolitan values that they associated with the Enlightenment and championed the importance of tolerance, free discourse, reason, and a polity based on human plurality rather than cultural, national, or racial exclusivity, many of them came to the conclusion that Weimar's greatest failure had been its simple majoritarianism.[2] By the late 1930s, the consensus among the Graduate Faculty was that the political phenomenon to which they gave the name "totalitarianism," the dictatorships common to both fascism and communism, represented the promise of false egalitarianism.

Emil Lederer, dean of the University in Exile and then of the Graduate Faculty, prepared the way for this shift from democratic socialism to a version of democratic liberalism. Lederer had come to the New School from the University of Berlin, where he had received a professorship in 1931. Before that appointment, however, from 1910 to 1931, Lederer had taught at Heidelberg, a center of academic and political dissent until 1919. Here he had come to know the great social theorist Max Weber and his wife Marianne. During these years he had also established friendships with Karl Mannheim, Hans Speier, Carlo Mierendorff, and Hans Staudinger, a fellow member of the Young Socialists. Virtually all these scholars, Weber included, had heeded the call of the new Weimar Republic in 1919, some as political activists, and others as public officials.[3] Max Weber put aside the misgivings embodied in his famous image of the "iron cage," and participated in the writing of the Weimar constitution.[4] Emil Lederer joined the Weimar Socialization Commission, which advised the government on the nationalization of the German economy.

Max Weber, whose work had shown a generation of intellectuals that political action was crucial, died in 1920, when the programs of Weimar had barely gone into effect.[5] By 1931, when Lederer received his prestigious professorship at Berlin, he had established himself as Weber's successor. Indeed, Carlo Mierendorff, speaking in 1932 at Lederer's fiftieth birthday celebration, described him as the carrier of Weber's legacy and the intellectual and spiritual leader of Germany's postwar democratic left.[6]

For Lederer, democratic socialism had seemed to offer an ethical system capable of releasing humans from the bonds of economic and political oppression.[7] Intellectually eclectic, Lederer rejected the mechanistic Marxism that was characteristic of many contemporary socialists and saw in parliamentary Weimar the means to create a popularly based and, ultimately, classless society. But the combination of self-serving trade unionism, business cartelization, and conservative fiscal policy seemed to deflect Weimar's course and deflate Lederer's vision. As a result, he became a critic of Weimar policies and called for extensive centralized economic and social planning. Yet as a sociolo-gist—influenced by the ideas of Max Weber concerning the progressive rationalization of state authority and its tendency toward total con-trol—Lederer remained sensitive to the possible abuse of centralized state power. He believed that new social movements contained the potential to exploit that power and threaten the very bases of democratic life. Lederer thus tempered his socialist vision with an awareness that western democratic structures were extremely fragile and susceptible to hostile forces. By the late 1920s, he saw the failure of Weimar as a warning to the West as a whole.

Lederer's early scholarly work in the United States, which he published in the first issues of *Social Research,* outlined these tensions.[8] As an advocate of economic intervention and state planning, he declared, "We cannot rely solely on the operation of economic laws." Continued loyalty to anachronistic free market theories in the face of the Depression would lead only "to the quietude of a cemetery."[9] In reflecting on the Weimar debacle, Lederer concluded that it had been as much a political as an economic failure. Only resolute political deci-sions, based on informed understandings of society, could have "prevented the destruction of democratic guarantees."[10] Such leader-ship had to come from outside the normal democratic political process. Social scientists committed to the ideals of democracy had to transcend their scholarly preoccupations and provide the intellectual and ethical leadership necessary to create a humane and democratic society.[11] Lederer's commitments were shared by his colleagues in the University in Exile. During the 1930s Hans Speier, Hans Staudinger, Frieda Wunderlich, Max Ascoli, and Max Wertheimer reflected on the causes of fascism, and each agreed with Lederer that a socialist democracy untempered by certain social and political constraints was as likely to lead to a fascist counterrevolution as to a humane social transforma-tion.

In the late 1920s, Lederer had been highly critical of Weimar for failing to align the German middle class with the Republic. He was con-vinced that in European society, and particularly in Germany, the most important group was not factory workers, but the "new" salaried mid-dle class.[12] Lederer was assisted in his study of the new middle class by one of his colleagues, economist Jacob Marschak, and by his friend and assistant, Hans Speier. Their work not only established the crucial role of the "new," or salaried, middle class in the European political economy, but also provided the basis for their notion of "mass" politics.

Marschak, who was born in the Ukraine and educated in Kiev, joined the Mensheviks in 1919 and served briefly as minister of labor in the Georgian Republic. When the republic collapsed, Marschak came to Germany. He received his academic training at Berlin and then Heidelberg, where he met Lederer. He published his first formal papers in Germany in the 1920s. Forced to leave Germany in 1933, Marschak received an appointment as director of the Oxford Institute of Statistics. While in England he wrote several articles on the measurement of consumption, including an article on the theory of wages for the *Encyclopedia of the Social Sciences.* A pioneer econometrician, Marschak served as a member of the New School's Graduate Faculty from 1939 to 1943.[13]

Marschak was influenced by the thought of Max Weber but, like Lederer, he revised Weber's ideas in light of his experience of postwar Germany. In *Economy and Society* Weber had compared capitalist and socialist economies, claiming that socialist economics were inherently inefficient. Marschak disputed this claim. He shared Lederer's belief that the new middle class, not factory workers, was critical for a stable democracy. In *The New Middle Class*, Lederer and Marschak revised some of the myths of "scientific" socialism.[14] Throwing aside earlier Marxist predictions that the business cycle would inevitably create an expanding factory proletariat, they instead suggested that the war had destroyed the traditional social order and had accelerated the growth of a new social group. Industrial concentration and social dislocation had led to the disappearance of independent proprietors, the "old" middle class of artisans and land-owning peasantry. The newly emerged stratum of white-collar employees would counter the proletarianization of European society and inject a new and vital buffer between corporate owners and wage laborers.

Socialists, who viewed this "new" middle class as an extension of the working class, failed to take seriously their particular economic and political concerns. Consequently, the white-collar middle class was never successfully integrated into the Social Democratic Party.[15] Unable to establish a political alliance between blue- and white-collar workers, social democrats failed to create broad popular support for their program, and allowed white-collar workers to gravitate to anti-parliamentary parties. Lederer and Marschak had warned that the success of the Weimar Republic depended on its ability to understand and effectively respond to the new situation.[16]

Although Social Democrats largely ignored Lederer's and Marschak's plea, Hans Speier did not. Speier's study of white-collar workers, begun in Germany in 1931 and published in the United States in 1939, focused on the issue that he and his colleagues at the New School addressed throughout the 1930s: the meaning and origins of fascism and Nazism.[17] Like Lederer and Marschak, Speier saw no conflict between his political sympathy for social democracy and his intellectual responsibilities as a social scientist.

Born in Berlin in 1905, Speier was the youngest person Johnson recruited for the Graduate Faculty. He had received his academic training in postwar Germany and was sensitive to the intellectual currents of Weimar in ways that his older colleagues were not. He had studied under sociologist Karl Mannheim, philosopher Karl Jaspers, and Lederer.[18] Like others of his generation, Speier rejected the mechanistic interpretation of Marx, and was above all concerned with "consciousness" as a salient aspect of class.[19] Accordingly, Speier considered class consciousness to be less a response to simple material conditions than a manifestation of social status and prestige in the context of the larger social order.[20] Specifically, he defined the new middle class in terms of the social origins of its members and in terms of its perceived social antagonisms.[21] Speier accepted Lederer's and Marschak's assertion of the importance of the "new middle class," but rejected their insistence that it was becoming increasingly homogeneous.[22]

This was so because Speier understood Germany's social history as characterized by the disappearance of the proprietary middle class, and its replacement in the twentieth century by salaried employees. Yet this new middle class was not yet a single group as defined by conventional concepts of class. It included dispossessed, low-level bureaucratic functionaries, clerks, and relatively prosperous factory workers. It was only the vicissitudes of Weimar's troubled economy that put the new middle class under constant threat and in the process pushed these individuals to class consciousness.[23]

Speier denied that the affiliation of salaried employees with nationalist and then Nazi ideology was simply a rationalization of their perceived interests.[24] Rather, he suggested that the German Right spoke to these interests in ways that the new middle class found difficult to resist.[25] Speier insisted that Weimar's disintegration had in fact created a profound state of alienation, in which people had become socially undifferentiated atoms, a "mass" of individuals rather than a class.[26] Their only class-consciousness seemed to be a recognition of their precarious state, and thus of the general breakdown of social cohesion in Germany. Thus it was itself a symptom of the breakdown of the larger social order. The Nazis simply exploited the vulnerabilities of this new group.[27]

In his work Speier had accomplished several objectives. He had challenged the proposition of "scientific" Marxism, evoked a notion of mass or atomized society, and provided the basis for a broader historical interpretation of fascism. Weimar democracy had collapsed, he argued, because it had not responded adequately to the social

changes in German society. The ease with which the republic had suc-
cumbed to Nazism suggested to Speier a congenital defect in parliamentary democracy itself. Fascism for Speier was a consequence
of the "elitism" or rule of the masses, of the worst features of un-
restrained democracy gone awry. By the early 1940s, Speier interpreted Nazism as complete or "totalitarian" repression in which the
state, by virtue of a monopoly over politics, communication, and
culture, exercised total control. Hitler's promise of a society free of
class and racial conflict seemed a perverted realization of Speier's own
dream of social democracy.

In the years immediately preceding his death in 1939, Lederer too
addressed the relationship between fascism and his earlier work on the
new middle class. Lederer's last book, edited posthumously by Speier,
evoked for the first time the concept of "totalitarianism." Published in
1940, *The State of the Masses* identified the breakdown of social classes
as a critical feature in the emergence of fascism.[28] Drawing on Speier's
work, Lederer analyzed the social basis and theoretical implications of
fascism, both Italian and German. He incorporated ideas from Freud's
crowd psychology and argued that social groups and crowds were not
identical entities.[29] A social group was united by common ideology and
interests, and its composition was homogeneous.[30] The members of
political groups, however, whose interests often cut across class lines,
had an incentive to strive for a broader unity. As long as social or class
differences existed, according to Lederer, this tendency would produce
balance and diversity within political groups. The breakdown of
classes, however, created a mass of undifferentiated individuals whose
actions were governed not by reason but by emotion, creating crowds
or mobs that lacked class concerns and identity. Lederer noted that
such masses have only temporary existences since education, social
standards, and customs all work toward eliminating their irrational
behavior.[31]

Fascism, Lederer believed, depended on the unfortunate confluence
of the dissolution of a social order and the advent of political
democracy. The masses were entering politics at exactly the time that
rapid postwar changes were taking place in German and Italian society. This enabled fascists to transform socially uprooted groups of individuals into permanent, fascist mobs. Fascism had explored the
dissolution of discrete classes and created a unique revolutionary community based on race or folk, a classless society.[32] Using pseudo-
socialist methods, fascist governments practiced economic interven-
tionism, not to transform the working class, but to subdue it by appealing to "barest envy."[33] Fascism borrowed both the means and ends of
socialism, but in the name of slavery, not freedom.

The first home of the New School, in Chelsea. The campus was formed by six back-to-back mansions, three in a row.

The courtyard "campus." The several buildings contained classrooms, a lecture hall, faculty studies, seminar rooms, kitchen facilities, and faculty apartments. *(Courtesy of the New School for Social Research)*

The library/study room. *(H. Shobbrook Collins, courtesy of the New School for Social Research)*

Alvin S. Johnson in 1935 after he had successfully reorganized the New School, moved it to a new building in Greenwich Village, and established the University in Exile as the Graduate Faculty. *(Courtesy of the New School for Social Research)*

Left: Joseph Urban's architectural drawing of the Twelfth Street building. Its modernist design contrasts with the surrounding brownstones. *(Peter Juley, courtesy of the New School for Social Research)*

Below: Urban's expressionist rendering of the auditorium complements the horizontal lines of the exterior of the building. The details of the facade and auditorium were altered in the course of construction. *(Peter Juley, courtesy of the New School for Social Research)*

Joseph Urban's building as executed at 66 West Twelfth Street. Later renamed the Alvin Johnson Building, it remains today the visual symbol of the New School. *(Underwood and Underwood, courtesy of Southern Illinois University, Carbondale)*

Clement Orozco's and Thomas Hart Benton's murals became the showpieces of the Twelfth Street building. The upper photo is of Orozco's controversial portrait of Lenin and Stalin. *(Peter Juley, courtesy of the Smithsonian Institution)*

The lower photo is of Benton's famous cityscape; in the lower right-hand corner, Alvin Johnson and Thomas Benton toast their joint achievement. *(Peter Juley, courtesy of the Smithsonian Institution)*

University in Exile opens in New York. Faculty of dismissed or furloughed German professors at the New School for Social Research. *Left to right, seated:* Emil Lederer, Alvin Johnson, Frieda Wunderlich, and Karl Brandt. *Left to right, standing:* Hans Speier, Max Wertheimer, Arthur Feiler, Eduard Heimann, Gerhard Colm, and E. von Hornbostel. *(NYT Pictures)*

Alvin Johnson and philanthropist Hiram Halle, who provided the initial funding for the University in Exile. *(Maria Feiler, courtesy of the New School for Social Research)*

At the same garden party, which celebrated the opening of the Graduate Faculty in 1936, are *(from left to right)* Karl Mayer, Kurt Riezler, and Hans Speier *(bottom)*. *(Marie Feiler, courtesy of the New School for Social Research)*

1943 press conference announcing the formation of the Ecole Libre des Hautes Etudes. In the foreground, seated at table, is Henri Bonnet. Other participants, in the background, are Alvin Johnson (presiding), Jacques Maritain, and Boris Mirkine-Guetzvevitch. *(Ralph Crane, Black Star, courtesy of the New School for Social Research)*

Meeting of the Graduate Faculty in 1946 soon after Alvin Johnson retired. Bryn Hovde, Johnson's successor as president of the New School, presides. *(Joe Covello, Black Star, Courtesy of the New School for Social Research)*

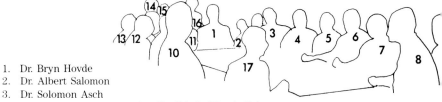

1. Dr. Bryn Hovde
2. Dr. Albert Salomon
3. Dr. Solomon Asch
4. Dr. Hans Neisser
5. Dr. Mary Henle
6. Dr. Abba Lerner
7. Dr. Adolph Lowe
8. Dr. Eduard Heimann
9. Dr. Carl Mayer
10. Dr. Horace Kallen
11. Dr. Frieda Wunderlich
12. Dr. Erich Hula
13. Clara Mayer
14. Dr. Hans Staudinger
15. Dr. Arnold Brecht
16. Dr. Kurt Riezler
17. Dr. Julie Mayer

To Lederer the implications were ominous. Not only was Marx's prophecy dubious—that class conflict would one day produce a classless society—but its fulfillment spelled disaster. The absence of social classes meant the end of human liberty. "The social classes," he said, "are the main productive agents [of creativity] and their influence is decisive."[34] "Social struggle is the great agent of life and what we might term progress."[35] To avoid the tyranny of fascism, socialism would have to adopt many of the values of classical liberalism. Socialism had to foster individualism, accept class differences, and abandon the ideal of community of a homogeneous mass. The difference between "socialism" and "liberalism," argued Lederer, was not that socialists did not care about individual freedom, but that they believed that collective action was the best means to secure freedom. In a democratic society, he continued, the transformation from a capitalist to a socialist economy must come about through the economic intervention of a benign state acting in the interests of the working and middle classes.[36]

When he had first come to the United States in 1933 Lederer had viewed liberalism and socialism as fundamentally different political positions, but by 1939 the differences no longer seemed significant. He had come to see that the classless, communitarian ideology of fascism resembled, if not communism, then Stalinism. By liberalizing socialist ideals, by abandoning the ideal of the classless utopia, Lederer was able to isolate the "essence" of fascism as antiliberal, anti-Enlightenment, and antidemocratic.

Hans Staudinger had met Emil Lederer in Heidelberg in 1911 or 1912, when both were members of a "secret" socialist society. In 1933 Lederer recommended Staudinger for a position at the New School. At the time, Staudinger was in prison undergoing a series of interviews by the Gestapo intended to persuade him to collaborate with the Nazis. Staudinger had attracted the attention of the Nazis because of his impressive record in the federal and state bureaucracy. First as the personal adjutant of the reichminister of economics and subsequently as a state secretary in Prussia, Staudinger had gained a national reputation as an efficient and successful civil servant. His ability to combine a bureaucratic career with socialist political activity testified to his political adroitness and personal charm. He was, in his own words, "a scientist operating in the political theater."[37] Born in 1889 into a Protestant family, Staudinger was the son of the philosopher Franz Staudinger, an economist, teacher, and "ethical" socialist who knew personally both August Bebel and Ferdinand Tönnies. Staudinger's own thought owed much to Tönnies's work, *Gemeinschaft und Gesellschaft*, and his lifelong belief in a socialist community was an intellectual and emotional commitment to Tönnies's ideal. At ninety, Staudinger still insisted, "I was always a socialist, one of the few who has the ideal of men living together in harmony, the best way possible, a real community."[38]

As a young intellectual, from his earliest days at Heidelberg, Staudinger had taken an active part in the debate over the "social question." He had concluded that the "scientific" Marxist prediction of the "withering away of the state" was a false prophecy. At the same time, he clung to a belief that the working class might create its own community as a result of its cultural autonomy and creativity. At Heidelberg, in his doctoral thesis, "The Individual and Community," Staudinger developed the ideas that shaped the remainder of his life.[39] Demonstrating, through an analysis of the history of musical societies, the progressive disintegration and then re-creation of a cultural community, Staudinger offered the optimistic prospect that the working class contained the seeds of a new community. The original artisan community, which dated back to the Middle Ages, had been destroyed by the factory system and the extension of market economy that replaced collective concern with individual greed. Staudinger suggested, however, that the factory workers of his day had begun to reject the "artificial," "bourgeois," and "mechanical" social relationships of the marketplace in favor of organic, communal ones.[40]

Staudinger believed that the emergence of musical societies among factory workers indicated that the masses, when liberated, might truly create. His analysis rested on his understanding of the liberating and creative possibility of leisure time, itself the consequence of economic transformation. Staudinger considered the modern, "rational" world, which Weber had found ambiguous, both positive and necessary. The individualism that informed capitalism had, paradoxically, created a structurally collectivized society, which would in turn give rise to a communitarian culture that repudiated the excessive individualism of bourgeois capitalism. Staudinger predicted that the working class would, as a result, emerge with a renewed sense of its collectivity. Revolution no longer seemed necessary for a socialist transformation. In Weber and Tönnies, in change and community, Staudinger had found the historical and theoretical perspectives for his social democratic commitments.

During World War I Staudinger was wounded and twice decorated. Following the armistice he received an appointment as *Geheimrat* in the Weimar Ministry of Economics. An active social democrat, he nevertheless retained his position in the federal bureaucracy until 1927. In these years Staudinger supported the policies of Walther Rathenau. Staudinger, with Rathenau and his long-time friend Adolph Lowe, argued that a socialist economy could be built within the existing economic structures. Instead of taking over the means of production, the state should act as a public entrepreneur through economic planning and resource allocation, assuming responsibility for economic growth and social equality without destroying the market economy.[41]

By 1927 Staudinger found his social democratic affiliations had become a liability in Weimar's increasingly conservative political climate. Resigning from the federal government, Staudinger secured a state secretaryship in the social democratic Prussian state government of Otto Braun. Attached to the Ministry of Trade and Commerce, Staudinger coordinated the energy industry of Prussia. He consolidated electrical companies, reduced prices, spurred rural electrification, and nationalized the production of potash, iron ore, coal, and electricity. In 1931 he and several colleagues protested the Bruening government's deflationary policies, calling instead for a wide-ranging program of reform. Although the German government did not adopt these proposals, in 1931 and 1932 the Prussian state government, under Staudinger's guidance, stimulated consumption and reduced unemployment by using profits from state industry to finance public works programs, which in turn provided employment and income for the unemployed.[42] In July 1932, German Prime Minister Franz von Papen ended Braun's efforts to transform private cartels into state enterprises by dissolving the Prussian government. Subsequent economic studies have substantiated Staudinger's later claim that his state-as-entrepreneur policy, *planwirtschaft,* had stimulated economic recovery prior to von Papen's action.[43] Arnold Brecht, Staudinger's colleague in the Braun government and later at the New School, successfully challenged von Papen's "coup" before the German Supreme Court. Staudinger, however, resigned from the government and declared his candidacy for the Reichstag as a Social Democrat from Hamburg.

Staudinger embraced the general slogan of his party, "Hitler means war," when he won a seat in the Reichstag. Almost overnight he moved from the confines of the Prussian ministry into the hectic and violent world of German politics. His adherence to the program of continued and, if necessary, clandestine socialist activity gained his reelection in November and brought the enmity of the opposition Nazi and Communist parties. He narrowly escaped an assassination attempt in early 1933, when an assistant warned him that communist squads were waiting for him to cross the Elbe by ferry that evening.[44] Within weeks of Hitler's appointment as chancellor, the Nazis arrested Staudinger at a meeting of his illegal, underground socialist group. At that time, in April 1933, Staudinger had been entrusted with more than a million marks, which he had raised from the Berlin banker Otto Jeidels. Jeidels, who may have represented the *Centralverein,* a German Jewish organization, had given the money specifically to aid the Social Democratic Party in exposing the anti-Semitism of the National Socialists.[45]

Of the thirty-six persons in their clandestine group, all but one were arrested in 1933 by the Reich police, but only Staudinger was charged with treason and threatened with hanging. After six weeks of intermittent beatings, solitary confinement, and secret messages to his lawyer and wife, Staudinger found out that his million marks were safe and he would soon be released. In response to his wife's efforts, the King of Belgium, for whom Staudinger had worked as a consultant, intervened and in June 1933 the Nazi government permitted him to leave.[46]

Staudinger later recalled that he had seemed almost alone in interpreting Nazi political doctrine as embodying the ideological pronouncements contained in *Mein Kampf.* His socialist colleagues, like Rudolf Hilferding, regarded the book as "monstrous drivel" and could not bring themselves to read it, while Jewish friends, especially anti-Zionists, refused his appeal for an anti-Nazi, antiracist fund in the Social Democratic Party. Staudinger, however, realized early that the "crackpot" and his "motley gang" were neither opportunists nor ad hoc radicals. Rather, they took the racist ideology of *Mein Kampf* seriously and meant to fulfill its ideological goals. "You have to know Hitler. I knew him. I hated him. Yet he was powerful": so, in a 1978 interview, Hans Staudinger explained the terrible but consistent vision of his political enemy.[47] The outbreak of war in 1939, the Russian invasion of 1941, and even the "Final Solution" itself were the logical developments of the ideas set forth in *Mein Kampf.*

Staudinger's experience with Nazism, and his conviction that Nazi ideology had permeated German society in general, inspired his work in the years after coming to the New School. In 1938 Staudinger worked with Alvin Johnson and one of his assistants, Werner Pese, on a translation of *Mein Kampf.* Two years later he published an analysis of the economy of the Third Reich, "The Future of Totalitarian Barter Trade Economy," in *Social Research.*[48] In 1941, again assisted by Pese, Staudinger wrote *The Inner Nazi,* in which he identified the relationship between Nazi ideology and Hitler's wartime strategy. Only recently discovered and published, *The Inner Nazi* is an interpretation of Hitler's political power by a contemporary observer.[49] In contrast to Franz Neumann's 1944 classic study, *Behemoth,* Staudinger argued that Hitler's ideology, far more powerfully than German society, determined the evolution of the Nazi state. At the same time he acknowledged that Nazi economic policy merely extended the neomercantilist practices which he and other state planners had developed between 1923 and 1933. Staudinger admitted that the "state-as-entrepreneur" policy, both before and after 1933, had opened the way for total state economic and then political domination.[50] Using strategies of price-fixing and production allocations to shift output from consumer goods to heavy armaments, the Nazis created a perversely European economic *Gleichschaltung* that made possible political hegemony. Ideological in purpose, Nazi economic policy, Staudinger insisted, was neither profitable in economic terms nor rational in Weberian terms. Indeed, it undercut the political and economic power of capitalist-industrialists as a class. Between 1920 and 1945 political ideology—not market or class forces—destroyed the traditional social order in Germany and created an egalitarian state.

Staudinger established the crucial role of racist ideology, identified the state as the monopolistic entrepreneur engaged in economic and political domination, and described the intimate relationship between Nazi theory and practice. His most important proposition, however, was that Nazism and fascism were attempts to re-create a community: in his terms, a racial community whose hatred and power were the absolute antithesis of the socialist community that he had hoped would replace bourgeois capitalism. As a young man he had embraced the idea of a democratic, socialist community; as a political refugee he discovered that the Nazis had utilized socialist means and rhetoric to pervert the dream of human community into a racist nightmare.

Staudinger submitted his manuscript to Alvin Johnson for publication in *Social Research*. After reading the manuscript, Johnson reported that he had become "magnetized" by the manuscript and was ready to devote the entire next issue of *Social Research* to its publication. Staudinger was pleased yet puzzled—pleased at Johnson's enthusiasm, puzzled at the attraction Johnson had described. Johnson—hardly a naive man—tried to explain that while he understood Staudinger's conception of Hitler and the Nazis as truly evil, he also felt strangely drawn by the power of Hitler's argument. For the first time he understood the incredible appeal of the Nazi movement. Staudinger remembers his own shock: "The Nazis were our enemy. We hated them. It could not be permitted that my book might somehow gain that enemy admiration." Staudinger recalls that Johnson insisted that the manuscript be published in *Social Research* even after Staudinger had decided that to do so would be wrong. Finally, Staudinger took the manuscript home and placed it on a shelf, where it remained for thirty-five years.[51]

Briefly in the mid-1940s, and permanently in the 1950s, Hans Staudinger succeeded Emil Lederer as the dean of the Graduate Faculty. After Lederer's death, many on the Graduate Faculty looked to him for personal guidance. Staudinger's personality was forceful and yet generous. Few could withstand his charm. Many of his close friends were also his academic rivals, and they felt the sting of his humor and opposition. Max Ascoli, later editor of the *Reporter,* was a gifted journalist and dapper dresser. Regularly, in the heat of argument, Staudinger would twist the buttons off Ascoli's suit jacket and, as he made his points, drop the buttons, one by one, loudly into one of the ashtrays on Ascoli's desk.[52] Ascoli forgave Staudinger's indiscretions because they shared an intense emotional and intellectual obsession with fascism: it had not only driven them into exile, but had destroyed their vision of a democratic Europe.

Unlike Staudinger, who considered himself a socialist, Ascoli had always called himself a liberal. He harbored few illusions about the possibility of an egalitarian community, nor did he think one desirable. Despite his misgivings concerning the mass democratization of western society, Ascoli, like his colleagues, accepted the change as irresistible and irreversible. He defined his task as finding a means to check the tyrannical tendencies within democratic society without destroying popularly based government. "Fascism was the product of democratic decay," wrote Ascoli in 1938, "a parasitic growth on the democratic structure."[53]

Ascoli joined the University in Exile in late 1933. Like his German colleagues, he had encountered fascism firsthand, but his acquaintance with the Italian version gave him an even longer experience with fascist political development. Born in 1898, Ascoli was an Italian Jew graced by both learning and wealth. Trained in the philosophy of law, he had studied literature and philosophy, the latter with Italy's great intellectual, Benedetto Croce. Croce, also a liberal, had become convinced that the search for transcendent values had been "eclipsed by the discovery of historical consciousness."[54] His contention that human freedom was embodied in historical change offered a philosophical means by which to break free from the deterministic thought of nineteenth-century positivism and Marxism. Ascoli perceived, however, that Croce's alternative, in the face of Mussolini's accession to power, offered only intellectual quietism as an antidote for political engagement. Croce's silence in the wake of Mussolini's "official" murder of his most vocal opponent, Giacomo Matteotti in 1926 earned him Mussolini's tolerance and Ascoli's contempt.[55] In 1928, Mussolini forced university professors to sign an oath of loyalty to the regime and the Duce, and on April 30, 1928, Mussolini placed Ascoli, one of eighteen professors who refused to renounce their opposition, under "protective custody" pending his exile.[56]

Ascoli interpreted fascism as the triumph of the irrational potential within mass democracy. Mussolini was able to make his power complete because the Italian political parties had failed to recognize the emergence of new social groups. Ascoli considered the "rise of the masses" to be as much a political as an economic phenomenon, to which political leaders had not adequately responded. Political parties, led in part by intellectuals, failed to educate their new constituents to the process of parliamentary democracy. Thus Italy had the forms of parliamentary democracy, but not its essential free and participatory spirit. This created a political vacuum. Into this gap, between state and society, strode Mussolini and his Black Shirts and eliminated the democratic state. In sum, wrote Ascoli, fascism was a "political technocracy: by eliminating democratic restraints, and scorning democratic ideals, the instruments of modern democracy could be made to perform revolutionary work."[57] The fascist state in turn created a new individual, declared Ascoli, who was "a close relative of the large masses ... he has no conscience, he is human energy without humanity, just as fascism is democracy without freedom."[58]

Max Ascoli further described fascism as an assault on the state apparatus by the unpolitical. While the German National Socialists emphasized the collapse of a social order to justify the imposition of a fascist political order, Ascoli suggested that the reverse had occurred in Italy. There, the breakdown of the political system was itself the consequence of an intellectual failure. Croce had taught his generation, argued Ascoli, to appreciate beauty and human creativity. He had neglected, however, to teach Italians to distinguish right from wrong.[59] As a consequence, intellectuals lacked the moral basis on which to make the political judgments necessary to defend democratic institutions. Fascism, argued Ascoli, exploited the apathy of intellectuals toward politics. If fascism was inevitable, it was so because Italian intellectuals had fatalistically believed that all history was determined. Their historical relativism had confused rather than educated the public. Croce's idealism, while attacking mechanistic positivism, offered no useful answers to Italy's political tragedy. Rejecting the distinction that Croce maintained between ideas and matter, values and politics, Ascoli declared that intellectuals had to reclaim their rightful political place. They had to provide the intellectual leadership necessary to create a liberalized democracy that respected both individual rights and constitutional limitations.[60] Their guidance alone could prevent the democratic masses from abusing the power of the modern state.

In response to what he considered the defects of Crocean intellectualism, Ascoli defended liberal democracy through his writing and actions.[61] He and other of his colleagues at the New School argued that their exile was itself a political act, but Ascoli extended those commitments. He took an active role in politics after the entry of the United States into the war. He transformed the Graduate Faculty's research efforts into a quasi-governmental research organization, the Institute for World Affairs, and also lobbied Italian-American groups to repudiate Mussolini. In 1949 Ascoli resigned from the Graduate Faculty to devote his energy to publishing a political journal, the *Reporter*. In the 1950s the *Reporter* became, along with the *New Republic*, an outspoken advocate of American anticommunism. For Ascoli, the tensions of contemporary politics, caused by the rise of mass participation, could be resolved only by an affirmation of traditional liberal values. Unrestricted democracy could only become totalitarian. American society represented for him the bastion of western liberty, and as such it had to be defended at all costs.[62]

Like Ascoli, Frieda Wunderlich was also preoccupied by the problem of political responsibility, believing as he did that democratization had opened the door to fascist success. For Wunderlich, however, it was less a consequence of a defect of democracy than a failure of public policy. Socialists in Germany, she argued, had become victims of their own ideology. Born in 1889 in Berlin, Wunderlich was a social historian and a prominent expert on social policy. A teacher at the Vocational Institute in Berlin, she also edited *Sozial Praxis* and served as a representative to the Berlin City Council, as a member of the Prussian State Parliament, and as a judge on the Prussian Supreme Court of Social Welfare.[63] At the New School, with Ascoli and economist Eduard Heimann, she taught a course entitled "Bolshevism, Socialism, and Fascism." Although never given to sweeping theoretical statements, Wunderlich gradually accepted many of the theoretical presuppositions that informed the model of totalitarianism that Lederer and Speier proposed.

Wunderlich cared most about finding the means to ameliorate the social problems of her day. Her concern for the conditions of working people, women, and children, and for the problems of poverty, alcoholism, and prostitution manifested themselves in the public responsibilities she had assumed in Germany. She contended that governments, not Hans Staudinger's "organized economy," could best solve economic inequities and that the state had an obligation to act on behalf of the socially disadvantaged. To be effective, however, it had to do so with care and discrimination. She was less concerned with large social schemes than with appropriate policies to meet specific problems. Wunderlich was not attracted to political parties or ideologies.[64] She believed that social progress could be achieved only through gradual and deliberate changes sanctioned by the public as a whole. A parliamentary democrat but not a social democrat, Wunderlich understood social science and social policy as pragmatic instruments of public compassion and justice.[65] She wished to find a nonideological alternative to both state socialism and free market liberalism.[66] Educated in philosophy, political science, and economics, she, of all the European emigrés, was perhaps closest to the position of Alvin Johnson and the founders of the New School.

Forced to relinquish her public responsibilities, Wunderlich, as an exile, resumed her scholarly studies. She asked: How did Weimar Germany, with its glorious declaration of political and social democracy, pave the way for Nazism? Why did the Republic fail? Like Lederer and Speier, Wunderlich believed that the answer lay in the social changes that had occurred between 1905 and 1929. An older Germany had disappeared, and a new one had replaced it. The new Germany was dominated by a salaried middle class, emancipated women, and factory laborers. Yet, Wunderlich argued, Weimar society was also dominated by a "materialistic" philosophy, replete with contradictions and misunderstandings. In addition, it was fully as bureaucratic as imperial Germany. The Weimar policy of increased social insurance, which created social guarantees to prevent the pauperization of the working classes, also created an army of permanently unemployed. The government had intended these social security adjustments to provide short-term relief for the able-bodied during lulls in the business cycle and permanent relief only for the truly disabled. Such policies had not anticipated the massive economic stagnation that pervaded the 1918–1930 era.[67] Socialist policy, Wunderlich argued, had thereby prevented the revolutionary situation that Marxists had predicted. The long-range effect of these bureaucratic measures nevertheless proved disastrous.[68]

Wunderlich criticized the manner in which the Weimar social welfare system had been administered. Rather than democratize the system by transferring control to neighborhood and community councils, Weimar simply took over the prewar governmental bureaucracies. The welfare system showed little concern for the individual. Instead, it dealt with the destitute as abstract social problems. The Depression of 1932 overwhelmed the system; it proved to be completely unable to provide even minimal relief. Having failed to establish any rapport or public trust, the welfare system came to be seen by those it served as insensitive and bureaucratic. Rather than win public support for the government, the welfare system had alienated its own constituents. "In 1932," wrote Wunderlich, "there was nothing left of the proud ideals of 1918."[69]

In this situation, Wunderlich suggested, Nazi rhetoric provided psychic compensation to Germany's unemployed. Left adrift by the economy, individuals salved their damaged self-esteem by identifying vicariously with national greatness. "The heroic ideals of a non-bourgeois life were combined with a longing to be protected within the group, to be obedient and submissive to the new community."[70] In identifying Nazism as a search for a new community that was both racially pure and anti-Semitic, Wunderlich focused less on the working class than on Germany's middle classes. She argued that the most serious mistake of Weimar social democrats was not their failure to respond to the "new" middle class of salaried employees, but their almost complete lack of concern for the old middle class of independent tradespeople, farmers, and small property owners who had been most hurt by the structural changes in the economy. Threatened by proletarianization, their impoverishment made them easy prey for radical politicians. "The shattering of bourgeois life," declared Wunderlich, "shook the German people like an earthquake."[71] This had occurred not simply because of rapid economic expansion but because the Social Democratic Party had been caught in its own contradictions. The remnants of the old propertied middle classes, those most attached to values of hard work and individual status, formed the backbone of the Nazi Party. "Too late the Socialists realized," wrote Wunderlich, "that they had neglected to win the group which according to Marxist philosophy should have disintegrated and turned socialist, but did not."[72] Political failure and ideological blindness resulted in policies that created the conditions in which Nazism flourished. But Wunderlich saw a deeper and more troubling problem. Nazism was also a counterrevolution.

As a scholar, Wunderlich was one of the first social scientists to give serious attention to the role and status of women in industrial economies. She observed that, after a hundred years of struggle for equal rights and cultural emancipation, women in Nazi Germany found themselves restored to the traditional position of guardian of children, church, and kitchen. Their earlier efforts to achieve equality had been accelerated by the wartime mobilization, during which women had made unprecedented gains in employment. Yet in the 1920s, as the government put more emphasis on public works to stimulate the faltering economy, employers and unions forced women out of factories and salaried positions to provide jobs for men. The situation became even worse after 1933 as National Socialists idealized and propagandized the image of women as wives and mothers.[73] Wunderlich described this as a "revolution," an overturning of values. Nazism, in its appeal to the old middle class, created a society that embodied the traditional patriarchal ideals of its most ardent supporters.[74] Nazism raised to a norm what Weimar policymakers had considered social problems and had tried unsuccessfully to ameliorate.

Wunderlich argued that Weimar's mixed economy, combining state and private ownership, was especially vulnerable to such an occurrence. Weimar's combination of a strong and entrenched bureaucracy with a relatively weak parliamentary tradition produced a form of state socialism that was easily perverted.[75] Nazism built on the edifice of democracy and socialism to create a totalitarian state crushing the parliamentary democracy that had preceded it. The Republic had used socialism in the name of freedom; National Socialism used it for the sake of a totalitarian state whose aim was the suppression of freedom. Forced to choose between equality and liberty, Wunderlich chose liberty. In her words, "Nazism reveals, just as Russian Bolshevism, that socialism has no value in itself. Such values as it may have derive solely from the ethical ideal with which it is connected."[76] Nazi ideology transformed Weimar egalitarianism into a "totalitarian" state as it eliminated all individual autonomy and liberty. Its equality, she argued, was finally the "equality of slavery." Wunderlich, like her New School colleagues, identified radical egalitarianism as the root of totalitarianism.

While the members of the Graduate Faculty concurred that "totalitarianism" was related to the democratization of European politics, their theories of causation differed. They bridged these differences by adopting the epistemological ideas of gestalt psychologist Max Wertheimer. Wertheimer's seminar on the methodology of the social sciences complemented the work of the General Seminar, and from 1933 to 1943 the entire Graduate Faculty participated in it. Wertheimer was one of the Graduate Faculty's great creative teaching talents and authentic characters, yet he was not widely known beyond the school. His manifesto on gestalt psychology, written in 1924, was not translated until 1943. Moreover, his only book, *Productive Thinking*, was published two years after his death through the efforts of Clara Mayer. In *Productive Thinking*, a sort of scientific poem to the principles of gestalt or wholeness, Wertheimer examined the philosophical implications of gestalt psychology as he related the mind to experience and the individual to society and nature. Trained as an experimental psychologist, throughout his life Wertheimer sought to transcend the limits of his training without abandoning his belief in the validity of empirical verification. Influenced by the rationalism of Kant and Spinoza, he tried to create an empirically verifiable alternative to what he called "associationist" psychology.

Two ideas led Wertheimer initially to question the validity of empiricist psychology, which dominated German science at the turn of the century: Ernst Mach's work in theoretical physics and field theory and psychologist Christian von Ehrenfels's paper "On Gestalt Qualities."[77] Mach suggested that while particles were important physical phenomena, they were nevertheless part of a larger field, or whole, whose property had to be understood as something other than the sum of the phenomena contained therein. Von Ehrenfels took Mach's insight a step further by identifying form, or gestalt, as a quality that presented itself to the mind as distinct from sensation. Gestalt qualities remained the same even when their sensate components were altered. Ehrenfels's famous illustration of a melody remains the most effective illumination of this insight. Ordered in a fixed relationship, six tones remain the same and are recognized as such even when the key is changed. What remains is the relationship, and the relationship is itself the melody. A tune is recognized not for its discrete sounds but because of its formal, or gestalt, qualities.[78] Influenced by Mach's and Ehrenfels's work, Wertheimer and his two collaborators Kurt Koffka and Wolfgang Köhler concluded that the experiments they had run to investigate apparent perceptual movement could be understood only when psychologists abandoned associationist theories and stressed instead the underlying unity of formal or structural relationships.[79]

Koffka and Köhler spent the rest of their careers working out the scientific basis of gestalt psychology. Each came to the United States—Koffka in the late 1920s and Köhler in 1935—and each taught for a time at the Graduate Faculty of the New School. Köhler developed the hypothesis of isomorphism, in which he argued for the existence of a fundamental correspondence between the order of the physical world and the way in which the human mind ordered perceptual events.[80] Each followed the same law of regularity and simplicity, or a fundamental tendency to parsimony. Köhler, however, refrained from the study of "thought" per se, and instead focused on the brain, thus leaving to Wertheimer the wider social and political implications of gestalt theory.

When he published his first papers, in 1912, Max Wertheimer was thirty-two years old. Born of a German-speaking Jewish family in Prague in 1880, he began his formal studies with Ehrenfels. Wertheimer continued his work in philosophy and psychology at the University of Berlin and then at Marburg where he received his Ph.D. in 1904. Subsequently, he taught at the University of Frankfurt. There he met his lifelong friend, musicologist Erich von Hornbostle, with whom he worked during World War I on a direction finder, called playfully the "Wertbostle." As the relatively unpublished dean of a nonconformist school of psychology, Wertheimer did not receive a full professorship at

Frankfurt until 1929, at the age of forty-nine, and he held it for only four years. Between 1933 and his death in 1943 Wertheimer taught philosophy and psychology at the New School. Since his English was always rough, he used the piano, as he had in Germany, to punctuate his classroom discussions.

In 1924 Wertheimer published a short paper on gestalt theory. In it he explored the philosophical implications of his experimental work. He insisted that gestalt theory demonstrated how structures, or the properties of whole systems, determined the parts. In his words, "The basic thesis of gestalt theory is that there are contexts in which what is happening in the whole cannot be deduced from the characteristics of the separate pieces, but conversely what happens to a part of the whole is, in clearcut cases, determined by the laws of the inner structure of its whole."[81] Wertheimer extended his argument far beyond the issue of perception as he argued that all aspects of human life, including consciousness, exhibited gestalt qualities which could be usefully examined by a gestalt method. The gestalt method of "seeing," he claimed, unraveled a reality which had been hitherto hidden.

Wertheimer declared that knowledge of such things as democracy, truth, ethics, or freedom necessitated a distinction between form and essence. The truth of the moment, he argued, was not the same thing as the "Truth," democracy was not simply majority rule but "a whole attitude toward life," and freedom was not the absence of restraints but a quality indicative of the whole social and political context.[82] The truth, or ethical norms, could be identified only by looking at events in the "right way," that is, grasping the sense or spirit of the whole context of the idea or norm.[83] The "correct form" of seeing, or what Wertheimer called "productive thinking," was itself an application of gestalt theory to questions of creativity as well as politics.[84]

Drawing on his previous experimental work, he proposed a "new" scientific method by which to interpret the meaning of consciousness and the structural unity of external reality. It would enable the mind to grasp the structural wholeness of a given problem and understand its gestalt quality. Using problems drawn from mathematics, Wertheimer distinguished between what he called "add-summative" processes of calculation in which the solution was the consequence of a series of cumulative steps, and "productive thinking," in which the relationships inherent in the problem determined its solution. In this manner, Wertheimer hoped to demonstrate the difference between the acquired methods of western logic and the inherent human ability to perceive structural wholes.[85] He believed that gestalt thinking was scientific in that it required an act of "centering" by which the observer was able to "forget" about the "self in thinking." Only the transition from a naive to a critical method produced a correspondence between mental perception and phenomenal reality.[86]

In the 1930s Wertheimer drew upon his gestalt theory to address questions of truth, democracy, ethics, and freedom.[87] In 1933, shortly after Hitler's appointment as chancellor but well before the university purges in April, Wertheimer heard a segment of one of Hitler's radio speeches. After listening for several minutes he snapped off the receiver, called his family together, and announced that they were to leave Germany that day. He had understood Hitler's gestalt. Wertheimer did not need to wait for the April Decrees to know that his days in Germany were over. He and his family moved to Marienbad, Czechoslovakia, where several months later Lederer and Johnson contacted them.[88]

Wertheimer's "liberal-democratic" commitments were similar to those of his social democratic colleagues on the Graduate Faculty. Posing his questions in epistemological terms, Wertheimer argued that formal democracy, or popular control, had been an illusion in postwar Germany. Weimar Germany had only superficially embraced democratic values. The failure of the Weimar Republic was neither a failure of "liberalism" as he understood it nor of "democracy." Yet by introducing majoritarian forms and rhetoric it had opened the door to disaster. The Nazis, through a combination of electoral participation and violence, had replaced the democratic forms of Weimar with a thoroughgoing totalitarianism that had no regard for individual or minority rights or even legal due process.

Lederer, Speier, Staudinger, Wunderlich, Ascoli, and Wertheimer had all found in Nazism a perversion of their most cherished ideals. A classless society for Lederer now evoked images of the unchained, deracinated masses. For Staudinger a social community had been metamorphosed into a racial one. Democracy ultimately revealed to Speier and Ascoli the shadow of a tyrannical human mass, and Wunderlich saw egalitarianism used to reaffirm traditional and patriarchal values. They all agreed that the deepest cause of the German tragedy was social change, not a crisis in "modernist" values. Wunderlich and Ascoli went one step further by blaming many of the problems on the political process itself. They all agreed, however, that fascism was a "modern" phenomenon at odds with the liberal ideals that were at the center of their own humanist commitments. Their common abhorrence of "totalitarian" government brought them to recognize their mutal adherence to "liberal" democratic values. After World War I, Wunderlich and Ascoli had rejected the utopianism of the social democrats even as the social democrats had dismissed them as hopelessly entrapped by "bourgeois" liberalism. Now their earlier partisan differences seemed insignificant when compared to their shared commitment to a constitutionally circumscribed democracy.

By the outbreak of World War II, the Graduate Faculty had established its identity as a center for social thought. The New School emigrés had provided American intellectuals with the basis for a postwar ideological consensus that identified Nazism and communism as variations of totalitarianism. By conceiving of totalitarianism as the antithesis of individual liberty and parliamentary democracy, the members of the Graduate Faculty merged socialist and liberal perspectives into a defense of American constitutional democracy. In so doing, however, they knowingly compromised the ideals they themselves had embraced as young intellectuals. Only later did one of their colleagues, Adolph Lowe, dissent. The problem of fascism, Lowe observed, was not that Europe had been too democratic, but that it had not been democratic enough. Lowe's point was telling. Totalitarianism, as the Graduate Faculty defined it, had succeeded in precisely those countries which prior to 1914 had had the least experience with parliamentary democracy. But facts alone, even when offered by a friend and colleague, could not shake the profound disillusionment of these European scholars. The ideas and attitudes of Speier, Staudinger, Lederer, Ascoli, Wunderlich, and Wertheimer defined the intellectual concerns of the New School through the 1950s; their postwar reassessments of socialism and democracy lead a number of American intellectuals to redefine American liberalism in the largely negative terms of antitotalitarianism. For the members of the Graduate Faculty, the horror of 1933 had destroyed the idealism of 1918. In 1918 these intellectuals had seen themselves as a vanguard. By the late 1930s they considered themselves a rear guard, committed to a desperate defense of Enlightenment humanism.

7

THE SECOND REFUGEE WAVE

IN THE 1940S THE NEW SCHOOL ATTRACTED a remarkable array of intellectuals. Having formulated a theoretical link between fascism and totalitarianism, the members of the Graduate Faculty viewed the renewal of world war in 1939 as a confirmation of their most dire predictions. Fascism was at war with liberal humanism, symptomatic, they believed, of the crisis of modern society. At the same time the war created a crisis within the institution. Although all agreed that Hitler and fascism had to be defeated at all costs, the prospect of Allied military victory raised the more problematic issue of historical responsibility and postwar reconstruction. Moreover, Hitler's invasion of Poland in 1939 and France in 1940 brought to the New School a new wave of European refugees, who, although antifascist, had not participated in the founding of the Graduate Faculty and therefore did not necessarily share the emotional bonds and political commitments of the original circle.

The New School, by once again assuming a leading role in the rescue of these scholars, unintentionally transformed itself from a small and homogeneous institution into a much larger, multifaceted university. By 1942 the New School included, in addition to the Adult

Division and the Graduate Faculty, the newly created Institute of
World Affairs presided over by Max Ascoli and Adolph Lowe, the self-
governing French and Belgian Ecole Libre des Hautes Etudes, as well
as Erwin Piscator's Dramatic Workshop, which had begun in 1940.
Although these additions brought a new diversity to the school,
perhaps bringing it closer than at any other time to the ideals of its
founders, they also cost a great deal. The individuals who joined the
New School after 1940 challenged the liberal-democratic consensus
established in the 1930s, for within the various divisions of the New
School were individuals of widely divergent political and philosophical
views. Their antifascist united front lasted only until 1945, when the
political tensions that came to characterize the Cold War divided the
faculty itself.

As it had in the early 1930s, the New School represented the major
American effort to accommodate the influx of refugee intellectuals that
arrived at the end of the decade. Genuinely humanitarian action on
Johnson's part once again coincided with the needs of the New School
and the Graduate Faculty. The Institute of World Affairs, the Ecole
Libre des Hautes Etudes, and the Dramatic Workshop were designed
to meet the needs of the second refugee wave and to allow the New
School to participate in the war effort itself. They also helped to com-
pensate the school for the loss of wartime student enrollments. As in
earlier American rescues, Alvin Johnson played a central role, and he
again found willing allies at the Rockefeller Foundation and the
Emergency Rescue Committee. Even before the fall of France both
Johnson and the new director of the social sciences at the Rockefeller
Foundation, Joseph Willets, recognized that a new emergency was
upon them.[1] Willets's presence appears to have influenced the foundation's response to the emergency. A Quaker and long-time friend of
Wesley Mitchell, Willets had been professor of economics at the Whar-
ton School at the University of Pennsylvania. He not only looked
favorably on the New School's efforts, but was free of the genteel anti-
Semitism that characterized many of his predecessors at the
Rockefeller Foundation.[2]

Willets was well aware of the problems Johnson and the foundation
had encountered in trying to place Jewish scholars from the first wave
of refugees in American universities. He must, then, have been relieved
to learn from Tracy Kittridge, who had remained in charge of the
Rockefeller European operations, that the new wave of exiled scholars
would include a smaller percentage of Jews. Kittridge felt that it would
now be much easier to find positions for these intellectuals than it had
been in the early 1930s.[3] Willets insisted that the foundation act immediately, but soon discovered that his concern was not shared by the

foundation as a whole. And, to his surprise, the problem of anti-Semitism persisted. One member of the board wrote, "We must recognize that the saturation point was reached two years ago with regard to the number of Jews in America."[4] Still committed to the effort, Willets needed a plan. "Night seems to be settling down on the people who have given the finest meaning to the word culture," he wrote. "But what shall we do?"[5] As in 1933, Alvin Johnson was prepared. When he arrived at the Rockefeller Foundation offices on July 9, 1940, he suggested two strategies.[6] First, the New School and the Emergency Rescue Committee should, with Rockefeller funding, find positions for 100 refugee scholars of the "first rank." Then, if they could not find positions in American universities, or if such positions were not available immediately, the New School would offer to employ them all as research assistants. The New School agreed to sponsor as many refugee scholars as the foundation would fund. As before, the Emergency Rescue Committee provided resources as well as contacts to facilitate the rescue and resettlement.[7]

Willets described Johnson's plan as "aggressive and ingenious." He agreed to provide $400,000 for salaries, another $100,000 for transportation, and $65,000 to the New School to cover administration costs. Willets instructed Alexander Makinsky, the Rockefeller agent in France—and, after June 20, in Lisbon—to assist designated refugees in obtaining passage to the United States. In addition, the Emergency Committee maintained its office in France under the direction of Varian Fry.[8] Johnson and the New School assumed responsibility for all other details, which included negotiating with foreign governments and the State Department and screening eligible candidates. The foundation again wished to remain behind the scenes.

Johnson's second request was more self-serving, but not without merit. Echoing the suggestion that Marschak and Lederer had made in April 1933, he proposed that the Kiel Institute, with its members scattered throughout England and the United States, be reassembled as the Institute of World Affairs at the Graduate Faculty. It would be organized under the direction of economist Adolph Lowe. Such an institute, funded by an injection of money by the Rockefeller Foundation, would solve the school's ongoing financial dilemmas, which had once again reached crisis proportions in 1940. Willets, aware that the New School faced possible foreclosure proceedings, did not believe that the foundation should "bail him [Johnson] out."[9] Consequently, Johnson temporarily abandoned his scheme to reestablish the Kiel Institute, and the Rockefeller Foundation agreed instead to support Lowe's appointment as head of a small research program on totalitarian government and economics.[10]

By late July 1940, the money and machinery for the second rescue was in place. With Makinsky and Fry in Europe, the New School developed an internal administration run from Johnson's office to handle the rescue. Else Staudinger, who held a doctorate in economics from Heidelberg, created the American Council for Emigrés in the Professions (ACEP) to coordinate the rescue effort. By early September, through good fortune, connections, bribery, heroism, and fortitude, the first group of scholars, most of them from France, arrived in Lisbon. Henri Grégoire, a Belgian classicist who joined the New School's Ecole Libre des Hautes Etudes, reported to Makinsky's Lisbon office that he had left his New School "contract" somewhere in Marseilles. It had taken Grégoire nineteen hours to clear the border between Spain and Portugal. He had seen and then lost contact with the Russian-born political scientist Boris Mirkine-Guetzévitch while on his way from Paris.[11]

Grégoire's absent-mindedness was all but insignificant among the problems that beset the organizers of the rescue program. Of the 100 scholars whom the program supported, only about fifty were located and ultimately brought to the United States. Twenty-three of these found positions at the New School, within the newly organized Institute of World Affairs or the Ecole Libre des Hautes Etudes. After the New School, Columbia and Yale appointed the largest number of Rockefeller refugees from this second wave; Columbia offered three appointments and Yale two.[12]

Most of those who found their way out of occupied Europe did so between September 1940 and December 1941, before the entry of the United States and the North African landings in 1942 made escape virtually impossible. Not only were the escape routes themselves closed, but the opportunities for asylum in the United States were severely limited. The attitude of key State Department personnel toward refugee intellectuals became even more intolerant than it had been during the 1939–1940 period. Most who escaped in that fifteen-month period came from France, through Spain and Portugal or Morocco and the West Indies, to New York. Two examples illustrate the difficulties of escape: Boris Mirkine-Guetzévitch, who successfully made it through, and historian Marc Bloch, who did not.

In September 1940 when Grégoire encountered Mirkine, the Russian-born political scientist had already been dismissed from his teaching position in Paris. As director of the French Institute on Human Rights in the 1930s, Mirkine had monitored international human rights violations, especially in the Soviet Union, Italy, and Nazi Germany. Since he was a former Menshevik and a Francophile, the Nazis considered him especially offensive. Through his connections with physicist Jean Perrin, a Nobel laureate who had helped found the Comité de Secours to help German Jews in 1933, Mirkine contacted Varian Fry in Paris.[13] Fry passed the news of Mirkine's dismissal on to the Rockefeller Foundation in New York, and they consulted Johnson.[14] At the New School Else Staudinger assembled Mirkine's folder, obtained references from American scholars in his field, and with Johnson's approval included his name in an October list of candidates for consideration by the Rockefeller Foundation. Contracts were sent out, and Mirkine informed Johnson that the Spanish and Portuguese consuls at Marseilles would issue the necessary transit visas to enable him to travel from France to Lisbon.[15] Simultaneously, the American consul at Marseilles granted entry visas to Mirkine, his wife, and their young daughter as they qualified for admission to the United States as nonquota immigrants. Mirkine's New School contract guaranteed him a position in the same field in which he had worked during the two previous years. In Lisbon Makinsky gave Mirkine his travel stipend, purchased his tickets, and negotiated reservations for an exact date of departure.

To finance the first leg of his journey from Paris to Marseilles and then to Lisbon, Mirkine sold on the black market $15,000 worth of gold for $8,000.[16] Varian Fry assisted him with this. Fry reported to the foundation that the cost of escaping occupied Europe had increased dramatically in recent months. In a business involving anyone from "bishops to gangsters," Fry wrote, "a passport complete with valid Spanish, Portuguese and exit visas would range today in the neighborhood of 120,000 frs."[17] Mirkine arrived in Marseilles at the end of November 1940. He had purchased the necessary transit and exit visas, but on December 7 he wrote to Makinsky in Lisbon that the American consul had refused to authorize his American papers. Makinsky told Mirkine that his New School status made the granting of visas a mere formality and telegraphed Johnson in New York to confirm the arrangements.[18]

On January 20 Mirkine and his family were still trapped in France, urging Makinsky to use his influence with the Ministry of Justice. Finally, on February 7, two and a half months after his arrival in Marseilles, Mirkine reached Lisbon.[19] Five weeks later, on March 16, six months after leaving Paris, he obtained reservations on an American Export Lines ship and also on the Pan-American Clipper only to find that he would have to refuse these reservations because of State Department delays. After February 1, the State Department instructed American carriers to give priority to American citizens for "repatriation" and to place all alien immigration "personnel" on waiting lists.[20] With his papers finally in order, Mirkine successfully booked passage on a Portuguese ship by paying a 25 percent surcharge. Despite his frustratingly difficult wait, Mirkine finally escaped occupied Europe and arrived safely in the United States after a journey of almost seven months.

Marc Bloch, historian at the Sorbonne, editor and founder of the *Annales,* and veteran of World War I, had been recommended to Johnson by Leland Waldo of the American Philosophical Society.[21] Bloch had written to several friends in the United States in the summer of 1940 requesting assistance in leaving France. As a Jew, a decorated soldier, and a socialist, Bloch had been barred from his position at the Sorbonne, which, in any event, the Nazis closed entirely in early November. Moving south, near Lyons, Bloch found himself in a difficult situation. His mother, who was in her eighties, and two of his six children, who were over the age of eighteen, required exceptional nonquota visas. Johnson and Staudinger nevertheless assembled the usual documentation, issued a contract, and informed Bloch of his appointment.[22] Bloch was aware of the visa difficulties that might impede his departure and voiced misgivings about leaving his elderly mother in Vichy France. At the time he was writing his memoir of the 1940 debacle, published posthumously as *Strange Defeat,* and had already been in touch with members of the French Resistance.

His mother's death in the spring of 1941 allowed Bloch to accept the New School appointment, and he so informed Johnson. But despite the best efforts of Johnson and Staudinger, the State Department denied nonquota visas for Bloch's two elder children.[23] In March 1941, Bloch learned through the consul at Lyons that in accordance with the new immigration regulations he would immediately be granted visas for three of his children with the promise of additional visas in June.[24] Learning of the difficulties in obtaining transit visas through Spain and Portugal, Bloch believed that he could book passage via Martinique for New York.[25] In June, however, the State Department announced new regulations. Visas were not given to those refugees who left any immediate family members behind in occupied Europe. As potential hostages their presence might be used, the State Department argued, to compromise the immigrant in the United States.[26] Caught in the diplomatic morass and confusion created by the State Department, Bloch chose to remain in France.[27] Within a year he had joined the Resistance forces operating in the south and was captured and executed by the Gestapo in June 1944, just weeks after the Normandy landings.

The stories of Marc Bloch and Boris Mirkine-Guetzévitch illustrate the enormous turmoil surrounding the migration that followed the fall of France. There were only two tightly constricted escape routes, which ran from the south of France to Morocco or Lisbon. All other exits were closed. Homeless and penniless, refugees grasped at their only hope for escape. With no explanation, the various national authorities either turned them back, shunted them off to refugee centers, or, miraculously, allowed some to escape. In Lisbon, Makinsky felt that these obstructions were in part intentional and sanctioned by the State Department. His suspicions were shared by most of the refugee community. Fry expressed his own bewilderment and anger. Writing to the Emergency Rescue Committee, he complained of being "in the dark" concerning State Department regulations and bitterly blamed it for the agonizingly slow process. Fry accused the American embassy in Vichy of lethargy and hostility toward those who requested exit visas. Specifically, he identified the First Secretary as an anti-Semite and a snob. As for the others, he wrote that "they have no more interest in the refugees than they have in Chinese coolies." Fry concluded, "86% of the persons whose names we have cabled you are still waiting for an answer. I wish you would get someone with the proper background to take the State Department by the scruff of its neck and the seat of its pants and shake it until all visas fall out of its pockets."[28]

No one accepted Fry's challenge and the State Department continued to frustrate and stall rescue efforts. A fundamental disagreement existed within the Roosevelt administration between those who agreed with Willets and Johnson that the refugees would be invaluable acquisitions and those who agreed with Breckinridge Long, a Roosevelt appointee, who virtually controlled the avenues of escape. Long argued that the refugees' presence created a national security risk.[29] The debate was largely determined by Long, who managed to thwart the efforts of those seeking relaxed quotas. An old politico who had guided Roosevelt's floor fight at the 1932 Democratic convention, Long had then been rewarded with the ambassadorship to Italy. A well-known and vocal bigot, he had for several years courted and flattered Mussolini. Although Long was quietly recalled from Rome because of a drinking problem, Roosevelt then appointed him head of a new division created by the State Department to deal with the "refugee question." From 1940 to 1942, as chief of the Special War Problems Division, Long, together with his long-time associate Avra Warren, whom he had appointed head of the Visa Section, dictated the award of visas. Like others of his ilk, Long continued to believe that communism and international Jewry were intimately linked.[30]

At Long's direction, only 15 of the 567 aliens who applied for visas in France were accepted in July and August 1940. Pressure from individuals within and without the State Department momentarily eased the restrictions during January and February of 1941, the period when

Mirkine slipped through. It appears that Johnson's friendship with economist Adolf Berle, then assistant secretary of state, helped expedite Mirkine's case, his application being one of only six that received favorable attention in early January 1941. Thereafter, through July 1941, a calculated confusion reigned. As one observer has pointed out, "Delay was the order of the day as consuls, aware of the unsympathetic attitude of their superiors, outdid themselves in an effort to build up a good record."[31] Fewer than 20 percent of those who applied for visas in 1940 and 1941 were approved. In that context, the New School's success rate of more than 50 percent was remarkable, no doubt a consequence of Rockefeller influence. On July 15, 1941, the refugee "problem" solved itself when the State Department ordered all its consulates in occupied Europe closed.

In early 1942, Johnson, Hans Staudinger, and Makinsky met with State Department officials in Washington. Johnson, having complained of departmental "high jinks," requested the meeting. They spent the day testifying before a governmental panel comprised of representatives from the FBI, the Visa Division, Naval Intelligence, and the Department of the Army.[32] After a day of answering questions concerning the purpose of the New School and the refugee scholars, Makinsky and Johnson concluded that the State Department and the intelligence services were hostile to the newly arrived emigrés and to the New School as well. Johnson had to defend himself against charges of heading a "Communist outfit."[33] The hostility stemmed from both programmatic and ideological sources. Many in the government argued that social scientists were neither necessary nor particularly useful to the war effort. Warren and others wanted to admit only those scientists whose technical knowledge could contribute to winning the war. Moreover, Warren and his colleagues in the Visa Division were anxious to preserve good relations with Vichy France. They wished to exclude not only potential political "activists" but indeed anyone who promised to be politically engaged. They regarded the creation of the Gaullist Ecole Libre at the New School, in particular, as dangerous to American policy. In their eyes the New School had acted contrary to American policy on the refugee question. Johnson had not simply tried to save as many intellectuals as possible, but had in almost all cases selected intellectuals with strong antifascist and social democratic commitments.[34]

For their efforts, Johnson and the Rockefeller Foundation were accused of rescuing and harboring "commies," "Jews," and "sex perverts." Some of their critics even cited reports of the New York State Legislature's old Lusk Committee, which had investigated the New School in the early 1920s for having been mentioned in the columns of the *Daily Worker.*[35] While Johnson and Raymond Fosdick of the Rockefeller Foundation firmly rebutted the "crackpot" accusations, Johnson acted to place the New School above suspicion as he rewrote the New School's charter.[36] The original charter had disassociated the New School from any political activity that inhibited the pursuit of the truth. With similar intentions the Graduate Faculty had adopted the motto of Heidelberg University, "To the Living Spirit," although it did so by a vote of 6 to 4 in executive committee.[37] Then, in July 1940, the Graduate Faculty in anticipation of a new charter endorsed two statements. The first disqualified for a faculty appointment any "communist or fellow traveler." The second affirmed the faculty's appreciation of the United States as the "citadel of liberalism." The changes Johnson made in the charter were in accordance with these two statements.

The Graduate Faculty's strong support for this anticommunist position is not surprising. As social democrats, many had been bitter opponents of the Communist Party in Germany and Italy, a hostility Johnson himself came to share.[38] Yet, their adoption of an anticommunist clause as early as 1940 indicates the extent to which Johnson, the New School, the Graduate Faculty, and the wider public had become sensitive to the charge of radicalism. It may also reveal the degree to which many members of the Graduate Faculty, and especially the Germans and Italians, had come to think of themselves as Americans. For the French and Belgians, fascism seemed a foreign imposition, something to be dealt with as a military problem. But for Italians, Germans, and even Austrians, fascism—and indeed totalitarianism—seemed a manifestation of the instability of their own societies: its triumph tended to alienate them from European civilization itself.[39] Military defeat alone was insufficient to deal successfully with an evil that permeated their European culture. Ardent in their loyalty to the United States, they may well have begun even then to equate that loyalty with the anticommunism that soon washed over American society in general.

Other changes that were taking place at the New School showed that the refugee scholars were settling in and beginning to feel a real commitment toward the school and its intellectual community.[40] When the outbreak of war in Europe brought American and European social scientists together in their concern over the threat of fascism, the members of the Graduate Faculty determined to use their experience to reach out to their American colleagues. Breaking away from their exclusively European orientation and methodology, they established a series of thematic seminars that focused on current policy issues. These seminars allowed the Graduate Faculty to continue to pursue the question of the viability of democracy in Germany.

THE INSTITUTE OF WORLD AFFAIRS

In 1941 economist Eduard Heimann and political scientist Erich Hula joined sociologists Karl Mayer and Albert Salomon and philosophers Kurt Riezler, Leo Strauss, Horace Kallen, and Felix Kaufmann in an effort to look more deeply into the questions raised in the seminars. They called themselves the Study Group on Germany and organized themselves along the lines of the policy committees that had existed in the Kiel Institute.[41] Alvin Johnson, who, with Lederer, had hoped since 1933 to reestablish the renowned institute, gave them every encouragement. The study group met regularly for nearly nine months to examine what they called the "German problem."[42] The practical approach that they borrowed from the Kiel model also characterized the Peace Research Project, another policy committee that flourished at the New School during these years, and became institutionalized in the Institute of World Affairs, which grew out of the two policy groups in 1942.

The study group agreed to address the question of German national character, and its members presented papers which, despite their diversity, dealt with the historical and philosophical implications of the "crisis of European liberalism." Relatively unconcerned with the exact means by which Hitler had come to power, they asked instead whether or not Hitler and Nazism should be understood as something intrinsic to the German national character. Despite numerous disagreements, they concluded that by 1929 there had remained no practical political alternative to National Socialism.[43] There were factions within the groups, Adolph Lowe and Eduard Heimann arguing that German society was fundamentally antagonistic to liberal doctrines and Horace Kallen and Kurt Riezler claiming that the spirit of German liberalism, which had shown itself during the Enlightenment, had been crushed by historical events.[44] Taken together, however, both interpretations pointed to the triumph of illiberalism in Germany after 1870. In this sense, both factions agreed that even in 1919 the prospect for liberal democracy in Germany had been grim.[45]

Felix Kaufmann, an Austrian philosopher who had written extensively on the philosopher Edmund Husserl, addressed these issues from a different perspective, taking issue with Horace Kallen's assertion that democracy could thrive only where there was a tradition of liberal politics. In his reexamination of Dewey's *German Philosophy and Politics,* Kaufmann discussed the ways in which he thought American philosophers, particularly Dewey and Santayana, had unfairly treated the tradition of German idealism. Kaufmann defended Kant's philosophical and ethical positions against Dewey, who had argued that, in distinguishing between those things which could be known scientifically and those things which could not, Kant had created a "Metaphysical Conceit."[46] This conceit, Dewey contended, encouraged German authoritarianism and mysticism. Kaufmann, however, held that this type of uncharitable reading of Kant was responsible for the mistaken linking of German illiberal political development and the apolitical attitude of academic idealism. Kaufmann instead argued that Kant was the embodiment of the German Enlightenment, the philosopher of reason.[47] Properly understood, Kant had said that, although ethical judgments were subject to critical discussion and evaluation, individuals were in the final analysis responsible for their own actions. Kaufmann dissented from a purely cultural/historical explanation of Nazism, refusing to write off the German heritage as unredeemably authoritarian. The difference between Kallen and his party and Kaufmann was that Kallen believed that Anglo–American democratic culture was the only viable model and Kaufmann continued to uphold the integrity of the German intellectual tradition.

Just as significant as these differences of opinion was the changing character of the faculty's work. With the outbreak of war, the Graduate Faculty received a number of grants for work designed to meet specific policy goals, most of them related to postwar German reconstruction. The work that resulted was practical and policy oriented rather than theoretical, reflecting the interests of Max Ascoli, who raised the money and supervised faculty research until 1942. In the late 1930s and early 1940s, Ascoli had worked with antifascist Italian-American organizations to mobilize opposition to Mussolini.[48] In July 1941, Nelson Rockefeller invited him to travel in Latin America as an American ambassador to the Italian communities to work against their profascist leanings. In Ascoli's words, "Essentially, it means to sell the United States to the wops ... being myself a wop and deeply devoted and grateful to this country."[49] Ascoli also undertook the initial planning for the Institute of World Affairs. He arranged for help from the Frankfurt Institute, wrote grant proposals to the Rockefeller and Rosenwald family foundations, and convinced Johnson to bring Adolph Lowe from England to head the institute.[50] In early 1942, when Lowe took over the directorship of the school's research projects from Max Ascoli, he inherited a talented but intellectually disparate group of international scholars, and a program whose finances were in shambles. In addition to the Study Group, he also found the Peace

Research Project, a collective program organized two years earlier by sociologist Hans Speier and psychologist Ernst Kris. By 1942 they had already received funding to study the communications of democratic societies.[51] Later in the year, Lowe reorganized both projects under the auspices of the Institute of World Affairs.

Speier and Kris, through an examination of German, British, and Soviet radio broadcasting, developed a theory of mass communication and a social psychology of totalitarianism.[52] They argued that totalitarianism was a perverted form of democracy, and that totalitarian communication was itself a "post-democratic" phenomenon based on mass participation and predicated on "a contempt for man as a reasonable being."[53] Lacking any sense of autonomy or social obligation, the masses in totalitarian states were susceptible to the magical appeal of mass communication, slogans, rumors, and propaganda.[54] Democratic societies, in contrast, were still dominated by social groups that, even in wartime, were sufficiently coherent and self-interested to resist political manipulation. A democratic citizenry continued to respond to logical arguments while totalitarian communication depended on emotionally laden propaganda to sustain the mass audience's essential irrationality. Indeed, totalitarianism undermined the very idea of rational communication.[55] Kris and Speier published their work in 1944 in a book entitled *German Radio Propaganda*. There, as others of the Graduate Faculty had done before, they treated totalitarianism and democracy both as manifestations of "modern mass culture." Beneath the surface of all democracies they saw the spectre of totalitarianism. Without appropriate constitutional limits, all democracies had the potential to become totalitarian.

Thanks to Rockefeller rescue efforts and the funding of the Doris Duke Foundation, the ongoing collective research of the Graduate Faculty was reorganized by Johnson and Lowe, in the winter of 1942–1943.[56] In announcing the formation of the new Institute of World Affairs in November 1943, Johnson described it as the American equivalent of the research-oriented Kiel Institute, which Lowe had also directed.[57] Johnson and Lowe wanted the institute to bridge the gap between the theoretical concerns of a European faculty and American notions of social science research. The primary duty of research, declared Johnson, was to understand human affairs that are "intelligible only in their organic unity."[58] Johnson called for interdisciplinary research, explaining that the institute would deal with strategic or policy questions in the context of long-range trends. Johnson left it to Lowe, however, to determine the specific research program of the institute.

In an eighty-page paper, Adolph Lowe outlined his own understanding of the world at mid-century. He saw the promise of a more coherent world community in the political and economic integration that seemed necessary in the wake of World War II. The most important step in that integration would be the reconstruction of postwar Germany, a process which would have a profound effect on German society and which would be shaped in large part by the United States. Lowe called for a systematic program of economic planning: Europe should not be abandoned to the blind and erratic forces of the marketplace.[59] Along with many of his colleagues, Lowe believed that the future of democracy depended on the control, if not the elimination, of drastic fluctuations in the business cycle. Only such planning could prevent a recurrence of 1933. Thus, even as the institute grappled with issues of international economic integration, it did so as a means of resolving the "German problem." As Johnson and Lowe declared, Germany at peace would be no less a problem than Germany at war.

Lowe's arguments were at odds with the sentiments of many of his colleagues on the Graduate Faculty. Lowe, like Kaufmann, hoped not only to find a "solution" to the German problem, but believed that such a solution held the key to both postwar reconstruction and to the restoration of a socialist democracy in Germany. Lowe's focus on specific economic and political problems was not based on the Graduate Faculty's identification of Nazism and communism as varieties of totalitarianism. However, as the institute came to include more and more recent refugees and as the projects themselves addressed an ever widening series of questions, the theoretical tensions between liberals and social democrats were pushed into the background.

In 1942 the Rockefeller Foundation commissioned the Graduate Faculty to conduct a study of Germany's position in postwar Europe. The project resulted in a series of papers, which examined such subjects as totalitarian methods of state intervention, women's place in the German labor force, the demise of small business in Germany, the decline of working-class living standards, and resource allocation under the Nazis.[60] The Institute of World Affairs took over the project and placed it under the direction of Arnold Brecht. Brecht assembled a research group that included Hans Simons, political scientist and future president of the New School, and a handful of graduate assistants including Werner Pese and Helmut Wagner.

Arnold Brecht was the most prominent Weimar public official on the Graduate Faculty. Born in 1884 and educated in jurisprudence, he, like his colleague Hans Staudinger, received the imperial title of *Geheimrat* in 1919. In 1921 he joined the Ministry of the Interior as the chief of the section on constitutional law. A political democrat and republican, but not a Social Democrat, Brecht possessed a deep-seated loyalty to German constitutionalism. In 1927, when the Social Democrats lost their membership in the Weimar coalition, conservatives purged Brecht from the federal bureaucracy and, like Staudinger, he readily found a position in the Prussian State Ministry as a delegate to the Reichstrat.[61]

Brecht's political moment came in 1932 when he brought, and subsequently won, a challenge in the German Supreme Court to von Papen's dismantling of the German federal-state system. Brecht considered von Papen's dismissal of Prussian ministers and their replacement by federal commissioners as the fatal blow to the Weimar constitution.[62] Hitler's ascension to power spoiled Brecht's constitutional victory. In March 1933, when Hitler addressed the Reichstrat, Brecht, alone, rose and lectured the Führer on the forms and procedures of parliamentary behavior. As a consequence he became an *unzuverlässig,* an undesirable. Brecht left Berlin on March 31, 1933.

Brecht and his colleagues in the German Research Project argued that a new Germany had to be created to avoid the most serious defects of the old. Brecht identified two sets of parallel problems. Given his own experience, he believed that a decentralized or federal Germany would have stalled National Socialism's rise to power. In a pilot study, he and his colleagues demonstrated that on a regional basis Nazism was much weaker than it had been nationally. Although the democratic coalition of Social Democrats, Republicans, and Centrists had never held a majority in Germany and lost all national significance after 1927, they continued to command regional majorities. Von Papen's "coup" had made it possible for the Nazis to overwhelm these local areas of democratic or republican electoral strength and to engage in a *politique du pire* with the Communists.[63] Yet, the pre-1932 federal structure of Germany was itself the product of a more fundamental constitutional problem. The rivalry between Prussia and the Reich, between one giant state and the rest of Germany, had created a political disequilibrium that threatened future stability. While Germany's political geography seemed to demand a federal structure to nurture its nascent democratic tendencies, Brecht believed that it should avoid simply returning to the historical pattern of a dominant Prussia lording it over smaller regional divisions. In this sense the Papen putsch of 1932 had eliminated an outmoded constitutional arrangement which had itself, in Brecht's eyes, threatened the reestablishment of constitutional democracy in Germany. By the end of the war Brecht had finished his work. His concern for the reestablishment of a democratic Germany and his painstaking research combined with practical political experience to produce a major work in applied social science.[64]

Erich Hula, an Austrian journalist and political scientist who had joined the New School in 1938, shared Brecht's more philosophical concerns. Born in Vienna at the turn of the century, Hula was a product of German high culture and Hapsburg cosmopolitanism. He received his doctorate of law at the University of Vienna, where he studied with Hans Kelsen. They later became colleagues at the University of Cologne. Like Max Ascoli, Hula had visited and studied in the United States before 1933 on a Rockefeller Fellowship and had become an expert in international law under Kelsen's guidance. When he lost his post at Cologne in 1933, Hula declined an offer from the New School and instead returned to Austria where he worked as a political journalist and secretary for the Chamber of Labor in Gratz and Vienna.[65] In 1938 Hula wrote an article for *Social Research* on the experiment of Austrian corporatism between 1934 and 1938. The article, strongly influenced by Hula's Catholic humanism, almost caused his colleagues at the New School to reject his candidacy for appointment. In the article Hula defended Austrian Chancellor Kurt von Schuschnigg, who in 1936 had virtually allied Austria with Nazi Germany. His "defense" puzzled members of the Graduate Faculty. When, however, they discovered that Hula had secretly aided several socialists in 1937 and 1938 and had planned to leave Vienna before the Nazi coup, the Graduate Faculty was satisfied with Hula's antifascist credentials.[66]

As it turned out, Hula's analysis of modern politics closely paralleled those of his colleagues at the New School. In his description of postwar Austrian politics Hula defined two sets of problems, one political and the other historical. Historically, the Austrian monarchy had maintained an uneasy equilibrium. As a multinational society, it had avoided the excesses of state sovereignty; as an aristocratic cosmopolitan culture, it had moderated the harshness of class conflict; and as a Catholic nation, it had never committed itself to a fully secularized notion of "positive" law. Austria had not undergone the same process of economic expansion and political integration that had characterized western Europe. Its tradition of cosmopolitan Catholicism offered an alternative to the traditions of formal political and economic liberalism, which Hula found unsatisfactory. He objected to an uncritical affirmation of the sanctity of private property, the sovereignty of the individual, and the inevitability of social conflict. Moreover, he rejected what he took to be the theoretical underpinnings of liberalism, scientific and legal positivism. Hula considered the Austrian attempt at pluralism, which had embraced ethnic diversity within a Catholic, corporate framework, a courageous effort to avoid the excesses of either formal liberalism or totalitarianism.[67] The dilemma for Hula was that, without an inherent liberal-democratic tradition, Austria had failed to resist Nazi influence and dominance. Unable to embrace social democracy, he agreed that totalitarianism and liberalism were the only choices available.

Hula challenged the assumptions that, in his opinion, informed the optimism of the years just following World War II. He rejected the tendency to universalize or treat as normative either democratic values or the findings of social science research. He argued that, as long as sovereign states existed, international law had to recognize national sovereignty and could not realistically be premised on its demise. Hula's frequent suggestion that natural law might serve as a source of authority was not contradicted by his own realization that he lived in a secular world. Personally, he may have preferred to return to a world community based on some version of natural law, but he offered no defense for natural law and, indeed, he thought it inappropriate to resort to private religious beliefs in public discourse. Unlike nineteenth-century Austria, the world at large did not share a common faith, let alone a common religion.

Hula and Brecht together upheld the Graduate Faculty's continuing preoccupation with the theoretical problems raised by the war. Each assumed that a return to prewar politics was impossible and undesirable. Like Speier and Kris, they also believed that democratic liberalism was the only viable alternative to totalitarianism, a conclusion with which their colleague Leo Strauss agreed. But even more than Hula and Brecht, Strauss rejected what he saw as the "amoral humanism" that characterized the various forms of democratic liberalism. The most systematic thinker of the second refugee wave, Strauss was also the most critical of western culture, which he identified as "modern liberalism."

LEO STRAUSS

Leo Strauss, who came to the Graduate Faculty in 1938, was for many at the New School "the Philosopher." Strauss denied that social science offered a way out of the "crisis in values," by which he meant the crisis of western liberal thought.[68] Rather, he argued, we must turn away from the social sciences altogether and return to classical philosophy. For Strauss the whole "modern project," which had begun in the seventeenth century, was so utterly suspect, so tragically flawed, that contemporary science—and hence social science—was beyond redemption. He labeled Max Weber "a noble nihilist" and Martin Heidegger, in Strauss's eyes the most important modern philosopher, a

National Socialist. The present had become so problematic for Strauss that only the insights of premodern, classical philosophy could illuminate the darkness.

Educated at a classical gymnasium, at the age of twenty-two Strauss earned his doctorate at Marburg. As the Weimar Republic entered its most precarious years, Strauss returned to the university, first to Freiburg and then to Giessen. There he met Hans Jonas and Hannah Arendt as fellow students of Martin Heidegger. Heidegger exerted a profound effect on Strauss's thought, which Strauss spent the remainder of his life trying to exorcise.[69] In the 1920s, Heidegger offered young German intellectuals a stimulating philosophic perspective. His *Sein und Zeit,* published in 1927, became essential reading for many postwar German intellectuals. On two basic grounds Heidegger radically criticized the western philosophical tradition and passed these two criticisms on to his students.[70] First, he repudiated modern technological society and its philosophical barrenness. Second, he suggested that the "modern crisis" was not simply modern, but a question that confronted humanity's very being or identity. Heidegger concluded that the entire tradition of western philosophy, from Plato and Socrates through Kant, was flawed. As such, to recover the "ontological" rather than the merely "logical" roots of philosophy, Heidegger proposed a return to pre-Socratic philosophy. To do so entailed a thorough reexamination of western philosophy, which raised anew the question of human identity, or, as he called it, *Dasein.* Heidegger proposed to erase western philosophers' "forgetfulness of being."[71] For Strauss, however, Heidegger's "Greek turn" represented an abandonment of the most precious discovery of the ancient philosophers: that reason as revealed in nature was the essential human attribute. Heidegger was correct, but he had gone too far. Strauss's own position derived from his qualified acceptance of Heidegger's "antimodernism."

As a professor of Jewish philosophy and as a Jew, Strauss had spent considerable time and intellectual energy studying both classical and medieval political theory. As a young German-Jewish intellectual, Strauss viewed the failure of Weimar less as a German tragedy than as a fatal weakness within liberal thought itself, a weakness which he associated with Spinoza. In 1932, just prior to his departure for England, Strauss developed this theme further. Writing for the *Archiv für Sozialwissenschaft und Sozialpolitik,* he examined the assumptions of "liberal" political theory within the context of the Weimar experience. Strauss concluded his essay by identifying Hobbes as the other key source of modern political theory. He wrote:

> The critique of liberalism . . . can only be completed when we succeed in gaining a horizon beyond liberalism. Within such a horizon Hobbes achieved the foundation of liberalism. A critique of liberalism is therefore possible only on the basis of an adequate understanding of Hobbes.[72]

No less than Spinoza, Hobbes had become in Strauss's eyes a formidable figure whose ideas dominated modern political thought.

In October 1932 Strauss "found himself" in Paris, thanks to a grant from the Rockefeller Foundation. Living on rue Saint Jacques, in the Latin quarter, Strauss participated in the life of the international intellectual community that had sought refuge in Paris. He conversed at length with French Catholic theologian Jacques Maritain about Thomism, with French philosopher Alexandre Koyré, who had just completed his work on Descartes and Galileo, and with the Russian emigré philosopher Alexandre Kojevisky, or Kojève, who was instrumental in the revival of Hegelian thought.[73] Strauss also maintained an extensive correspondence with Gershom Scholem, a philosopher of Jewish mysticism who had emigrated to Jerusalem, as had Strauss's colleague from Germany, Hans Jonas.[74] Then, early in 1934, Strauss traveled to England, where he completed his work on Hobbes.[75]

As he had done in an earlier study of Spinoza, Strauss ascribed Hobbes's development to the circumstances of his intellectual environment, especially his humanistic education, and to the impact of the new science that dominated seventeenth-century thought. Hobbes had searched for the best form of the state, not as the ancients had done—by reflecting on the reason inherent in humanity—but from the "experience of human life." Hobbes's experience was of course informed by the historical trends of the times, the most important of which was the rise of the bourgeoisie. As Strauss put it, "The genesis of Hobbes's political philosophy is nothing other than the progressive supplanting of aristocratic virtue by bourgeois virtue." Bourgeois virtue rested on the notion of the right of the individual to preserve his or her life. As a consequence, the modern, liberal state no longer sought to govern itself in accord with human nature or reason, but rather as the author of human nature through its own self-justifying laws. Strauss believed that Hobbes had made a decisive break with classical "rationalism," unwittingly preparing the way for the eventual abandonment of reason itself. The inability of liberal political theory to defend itself and the concomitant precariousness of European Jewry was the legacy of the seventeenth century's crisis of reason and faith. By 1935

Strauss had come to believe that the work of his teacher, Heidegger, was the logical culmination of that heritage.[76]

After publication of his book on Hobbes, Strauss actively sought an appointment in the United States. The Rockefeller Foundation and Harold Laski of the London School of Economics recommended Strauss to Alvin Johnson. No doubt Hans Speier, Strauss's friend in pre-Hitler Berlin, supported his appointment, which Johnson offered in 1938. At the Graduate Faculty, Strauss pursued his analysis of liberal theory. In 1941, *Social Research* published "Persecution and the Art of Writing," in which Strauss set forth his "methodology" of textual analysis.[77] In this seminal paper, Strauss not only argued for a method of textual analysis as the only effective means to uncover the "Truth" of ancient political philosophy, he also rejected his own earlier contextual interpretation of Spinoza and Hobbes.

The background of "Persecution and the Art of Writing" includes the tragic circumstances of Nazi victory. Strauss considered Nazism an extreme and almost irresistible form of liberalism. In "Persecution" Strauss hoped to establish the political nature of all "true" philosophy, by which he meant a purely private concern, a source of personal morality. In its private character, philosophy's goal becomes moral self-preservation: "the secret kingship of the philosopher" is the realm of the "perfect man [who] lives privately as a member of an imperfect society which he tries to humanize within the limits of the possible."[78]

Hence, Socrates—the philosopher and the stranger—lived a life of both contemplation and danger. To protect themselves, Strauss argued, all true philosophers have resorted to the device of esoteric (or concealed) and exoteric (or hidden) writing. Political or critical philosophers presented their truth on two levels, a pragmatic philosophy for the "vulgar multitude" and an idealized philosophy for other "philosophers." In this light, Strauss saw Spinoza as a champion not simply of rationalism, but of a secular atheism. According to Strauss, by appearing to question the very idea of revealed truth, Spinoza had made it impossible to affirm either the rational ideal of Athens or to return to a religious Jerusalem.[79] This dilemma haunted Strauss as he proceeded to his most important New School work.

Strauss began his study of natural-right theory, *Natural Right and History,* in the years immediately following the war. In it he traced the history of the idea of natural right from its origins to its eventual replacement by social science. According to Strauss, the birth of philosophy itself coincided with the discovery of nature, from which derived the concept of natural right or political philosophy. Strauss distinguished natural right from divine revelation: "If man knows by divine revelation what the right path is, he does not have to discover that path by unassisted efforts."[80] Philosophy was the unassisted search for the right path based on an understanding of nature's authority. Classical natural-right theory was the "idea of justice according to nature," or the search for ethical norms.[81] The tension between philosophy and what Strauss called "the city," between the possible and the actual, was what made philosophy a critical enterprise.[82]

As a historian of political philosophy, Strauss viewed the natural-rights tradition as fixed until its absorption into Christian theology by Aquinas. The modern form of natural-right theory, associated with Hobbes and Spinoza, "was a reaction to the absorption of natural right by theology." Thus, Strauss understood modern natural-right theory as a flawed attempt to restore classical theory. In exorcising the religious content imposed by Aquinas, Hobbes and Spinoza had also rejected its transhistorical assumptions in favor of a form of historicism. Classical natural-right theory was, in Strauss's terms, teleological, insofar as it presupposed a natural tendency toward perfection. The impact of nonteleological natural science in the seventeenth century made such an understanding of natural right impossible.[83] Hobbes was concerned not with how humans ought to live, but with how they actually lived. Under the impact of modern natural right, the individual and the actual, rather than the community and the possible, had become the subject of political philosophy.[84]

Strauss identified two critical moments, the first at the end of the eighteenth century and the second at the end of the nineteenth century, after which modern political philosophy was transformed into either social science or history. He saw the rise of descriptive social science as an attempt to recover the classical understanding of nature and reason. He also recognized, however, that what he understood as descriptive social science had been superseded by the work of Max Weber. Weberian epistemology suffered the same flaw that marred all other modern forms of naturalistic thought since Hobbes. Indeed, for Strauss, Weberian social science would inevitably reach a point "beyond which the scene is darkened by the shadow of Hitler."[85] Strauss insisted that what he called Weber's radical distinction between facts and values made it possible to speak of concentration camps but not cruelty.[86] Weber had insisted that social science could neither epistemologically nor methodologically validate ultimate values. Yet Weber, by insisting on the existence of the "hairbreadths" distance between scientific and philosophical inquiry, had in fact sought to preserve philosophy from the arrogance of modern science. Strauss interpreted Weber's most basic point, the subtle difference between facts and values, as a declaration of their radical distinction and the ultimate irrelevance of values.

This accusation became the lynchpin of Strauss's philosophical program. By characterizing Weber's thought as no more than a subtle form of positivism on the basis of Weber's "belief that there cannot be any genuine knowledge of the ought," Strauss stubbornly refused to face up to the enormous epistemological problems of his own natural-right theory.[87] All his disclaimers to the contrary, Strauss's notion of natural right was finally as theistic in spirit as Thomistic natural law. Strauss had simply driven the Christians out of his philosophical temple, but it was still more a temple than a secular polis. Strauss's natural-right theory rested on an act of faith on behalf of "scriptural" truth as revealed in philosophical texts. In his own way, Strauss represented a return to a form of scriptural fundamentalism, even as he claimed the mantle of philosophical rationalism.[88]

Strauss argued that fascism and the blindness of liberal thinkers to its meaning were the critical political problems of his age. In this, he was in agreement with his colleagues at the New School.[89] Yet Strauss's indictment was twofold. Political scientists had failed to comprehend fully the nature of modern tyranny. And although Germany had lost the war, German thought, by which Strauss meant history and science, had garnered the fruits of victory. By ignoring the teaching of the ancients, modern thinkers in their orientation to facts and context could not recognize evil when it was reborn.[90] It was necessary, declared Strauss, to return to a classical understanding of philosophical truth. Unlike his mentor Heidegger, Strauss returned to ancient philosophy not to detect the flaws in Socratic ideas, but to reconstitute those ideas as a means to understand the present.[91] In accepting the Platonic notion of political philosophy as a search for the "best regime" or society, Strauss also recognized that the best regime, the one in which the "best men rule," as a natural aristocracy, was not necessarily "practical."[92] Only by distinguishing between the real and ideal was Strauss able even qualifiedly to support liberal democracy, a regime of laws, and preferable only to the other practical alternatives.

Paradoxically, Strauss's qualified affirmation of liberal democracy and his indifference to the immediate historical causes of political dislocation were reminiscent of the tepid support that so many German intellectuals had offered the Weimar government.[93] Because the republic had not lived up to their idealized notions of an aristocratic order, many German conservatives had failed to resist Hitler actively. Strauss, like his mentor Heidegger, had affirmed a vision of politics so radical that he had become a critic of the very political order whose ideals he affirmed. Strauss seemed unable to put aside his own quest for purity in order to undertake the practical task of publicly defending an imperfect, but decent, political community. In rejecting as illegitimate the fundamental premises of democratic liberalism—individual rights, collective well-being, positive law, and explicit popular consent— Strauss in effect invited politicians to be guided only by some mysterious, private notion of wisdom and virtue as defined by "true" philosophers. Strauss, like so many other interwar German thinkers, seemed incapable of placing his Weimar experiences in balanced perspective. Tested in the crucible of Weimar, liberalism and social science alike had failed. Each, having adopted a standard of relative or contextual truth, failed to offer westerners a system of absolute values.

1945–1950

After the war, the Graduate Faculty continued to inquire into the sources of totalitarianism, but many shifted their research interests from the "German problem" to American culture. Could the United States, and by implication western Europe, sustain a liberal-democratic political order which would not degenerate into totalitarianism? To answer this question, the institute undertook its largest collective research enterprise, the Leisure Time Project, conducted between 1947 and 1950. Paralleling the research of sociologist David Reisman and critical theorist Theodor Adorno and under the direction of Hans Staudinger, the Leisure Time Project investigated the "role of culture vis-à-vis the masses" at a time when formal culture in the West was becoming "democratized."[94] Adolph Lowe had originally proposed a study of the leisure activities of ethnic minorities, but Staudinger convinced him that such a study could be extended to determine the cultural basis of class consciousness among factory workers. Staudinger believed that factory workers had created a culture within the context of a capitalist economy that was collective and communal rather than individualistic and competitive. He argued that "culture founded on a high degree of individualism . . . was destined to be only an historical episode."[95] He hoped to demonstrate his claims by developing questionnaires that provided objective evidence of working-class attitudes about enjoyment and satisfaction. "The cultural pattern of our society has undergone changes," wrote Staudinger. "What we cannot understand yet is [their] direction. . . . These changes are revolutionary, and the transition to mass culture is still in flux."[96]

After two years of research, which included pilot studies, questionnaires, and several Master's theses, Staudinger announced the tentative results: first, the cultural activity of factory workers was largely determined by their workplaces, and, second, family and religious values were much less influential than were an individual's peers.

Staudinger also found that workers derived little satisfaction from their leisure activities because of the nature of factory work itself. Staudinger concluded reluctantly, "We live increasingly unreflective lives, determined externally."[97] Staudinger decided not to publish the findings of the project, according to his account, not because of its methodological shortcomings, which were significant, but because of his own political commitments. The conclusions seemed to undercut his socialist faith in a human community of autonomous critical individuals.

The Leisure Time Project was discontinued in 1950. Had it been completed, it would have been the last of the institute's studies, but that place went instead to a project conducted by Alfred Kahler and Ernst Hamburger. The book they produced, *Education for an Industrial Age,* dealt with the relationship between mass education, democracy, and industrialization.[98] An economist, Kahler was the only member of the Graduate Faculty whose family were factory workers. Before assuming his scholarly career, Kahler himself had been a locksmith and had entered the Berlin Hochschule für Politik without the benefit of a gymnasium degree. In Breslau in the 1920s Ernst Hamburger, at that time a factory worker, had organized a study group with several friends as a kind of informal version of what was known in the United States as adult education.[99] In 1933 Hamburger left Germany for France, where Mirkine-Guetzévitch befriended him and gave him a position on the journal *Cahiers de la Presse.* Interned in 1940, Hamburger made his way to the United States where Mirkine brought him to the institute and helped secure him a position as a research assistant.

In their joint study, Kahler and Hamburger asked: What kind of education is possible and desirable in an industrial democracy? They argued in favor of a universal system of education, from elementary to advanced levels, which integrated vocational skills with the liberal arts. Industrial society was based on work, and education should prepare students to participate as workers. At the same time a democratic society required a moral and intellectually mature citizenry. Pure liberal arts, with its prejudice against vocationalism, was by implication a genteel education, a residue of nineteenth-century, middle-class pretensions. It was an abstract luxury which an industrial democracy could no longer afford. An industrial society could not leave the acquisition of essential skills to chance or to an inferior system of education. Kahler and Hamburger argued that "a sound vocational education does not prevent . . . a balanced education. It does not compete with the goals of a truly humanistic education: on the contrary, it embodies some of the latter's oldest and soundest principles . . . the integration of education with the actual social process."[100]

When contrasted with such conclusions, Staudinger's project and his decision not to publish its findings are vivid evidence of the dilemma that rent the Institute of World Affairs. The research of Staudinger, a committed socialist, revealed his growing distrust of popular culture, an attitude shared by Brecht, Hula, and Strauss, but not by Lowe, Kaufmann, Kahler, and Hamburger. Given the diversity of the faculty after 1940, the totalitarian model—with its implicit antidemocratic assumptions—simply could not provide a basis for long-term policy research at the New School. Although it operated throughout the 1940s, the Institute of World Affairs could not recapture the coherence and focus of the Graduate Faculty of the 1930s.

After the war, the bonds that held the institute together were loosened even further, as many faculty members received offers from other schools. In 1949 Adolph Lowe was invited to return to Germany, to participate in the revival of Weber's journal, the *Archiv,* and to help revive the intellectual life at Heidelberg and Frankfurt. Lowe examined the new Germany but found that it was dominated by liberal economic practices abhorrent to his notions of state planning, riddled with people associated with the Third Reich, and still confirmed in its belief that Germany was the "center of the universe."[101] Lowe, along with Speier, Brecht, Colm, and Simons returned to Europe in the late 1940s as consultants, but none found West Germany sufficiently congenial to forsake their new American identities. In Lowe's eyes especially, the defects of the past had not been effaced by the war. The German problem remained, and the Germans at the New School were still alienated from their homeland.

Although most of the emigré scholars stayed at the New School, by 1950 the work of the institute was over. Speier, Strauss, and Ascoli left the Graduate Faculty for other academic and intellectual pursuits and Brecht and Riezler returned to more formal philosophical and theoretical work. Finally, in 1950, Lowe requested that he be allowed to return to teaching and writing, although he agreed to supervise the institute's posthumous publication of Karl Mannheim's writings. Staudinger, who served as the dean of the Graduate Faculty, took over as director of the institute, which became the research division of the Graduate Faculty. In 1950 the research division itself was terminated.

Lowe's and Johnson's dream of reconstituting the Kiel Institute had never been realized in the Institute of World Affairs, although its mission to apply social science to real social problems had inspired much useful work, including pioneering efforts in econometrics by Hans Neisser and Franco Modigliani. Its projects had been overshadowed by work at other American institutions.[102] It had never had a budget to match those of other American think-tanks, such as the Rand

Corporation, and when it lost its independent funding in the 1950s it was forced to close. As a consequence, many of its most productive members took up once more their study of the formal problems of epistemology. At the same time, the pressures that had produced the New School's anticommunist clause had not gone away, and the turn from policy analysis to more philosophical concerns and narrow academic issues may well be seen as a prudent move in the face of McCarthyism. The New School did not escape claims that it harbored socialists and communists, but reorganization helped to deflect some of those claims and made the school less vulnerable. Perhaps by circumstance, perhaps by intent, but certainly ironically, the New School moved away from its more practical involvement with the problems of mass democracy just as those problems were threatening the cultural and political life of the United States.

8

THE FREE FRENCH
IN NEW YORK

In 1942, while Ascoli, Johnson, and Lowe were reorganizing the research activities of the Graduate Faculty into the Institute of World Affairs, several refugee scholars from Vichy France were setting up their own academy in exile in New York. Like the institute, the Ecole Libre des Hautes Etudes was sponsored by the New School, but it was from the beginning much more autonomous, an institution designed to serve the needs of scholars who saw themselves as temporary visitors in the United States. Although it shared the dedication to academic freedom that characterized the rest of the New School, it always understood itself as an instrument of French domestic politics. Its faculty members continued to view themselves as French, never losing their faith in French culture or in French democracy. They had no desire to become Americans. For them, New York and the New School were only a temporary refuge, where they could continue their scholarship and work toward the overthrow of the Vichy government. At the end of the war, virtually the entire faculty returned to France. Still, their preoccupation with French politics notwithstanding, the faculty of the Ecole Libre participated actively in the intellectual life of the New School during the war years. Like the School's American and German members, the French believed that as social scientists they were obligated to explore the philosophical and epistemological questions that the rise of fascism had made so urgent.

For many French scholars in New York, the establishment of the Ecole Libre brought an end to a period of extraordinary confusion and alienation. France's defeat in June 1940 had dramatically challenged the French intellectual community. The collaboration of Marshal Pétain with Hitler, although discrediting the French Right, confirmed fascism's continuing fascination to a significant part of the French populace. Recognizing that they were in danger, some French intellectuals fled the occupied zone and found refuge in the south. Others tried to leave but, because of legal obstacles or family ties, were forced to remain in France at great personal risk.[1] Still others, many of them Jewish or socialists, managed—despite the enormous difficulties involved in obtaining entry visas, finding passage, and securing employment—to escape France. Many of them made their way across the Atlantic to New York, some with the assistance of Alvin Johnson and the Rockefeller Foundation. These refugees from Vichy, as well as a number of French-speaking Belgian and Russian emigrés, joined the French nationals who had been stranded in the United States by the war. For these French-speaking men and women, America became both a place of exile and a sanctuary. Prior to 1942, however, they lacked cohesion and direction as a group. They were refugees committed to the resistance to Nazism but unable to help.

The idea for a Free French university came from the French exile community in London and New York. Its inspiration was both political and intellectual. Gustave Cohen, a medievalist at the Sorbonne, theologian Jacques Maritain, who had been stranded in the United States in 1940, and historian Pierre Brodin of the Lycée Française conceived of a French-speaking university located in New York. Cohen, an organizer and orator, argued that such an institution would provide the French exile community a cultural and intellectual rallying point. Maritain, who believed that the European war, and consequently his exile, would be long, found the idea of a French university attractive. He saw it not only as an intellectual forum for the resistance, but also as an expression of French educational reform. He suggested to Cohen and Brodin that they use the Ecole Pratique des Hautes Etudes in Paris as a model to create a university that avoided the bureaucratic excesses of the French educational system.[2] Without realizing it, Maritain envisioned a French university committed to many of the same goals as the New School.

With Maritain's idea of the Ecole Libre, Cohen set to work. In the summer of 1941 he spoke to Johnson, who was at first unenthusiastic.

Johnson had already led the effort to rescue French scholars, and the New School had offered appointments to several French refugees; he wanted no further entanglements, particularly if they might entail additional financial obligations.[3] After a conversation with Max Ascoli, however, Johnson decided to pursue the idea. Johnson was always looking for ways to expand the New School, and Cohen had asked only for a few classrooms and institutional affiliation. Cohen persuaded Johnson and Ascoli that a French university would be inexpensive and might eventually serve as a magnet for Latin American scholars whose socialist affiliations placed their careers in jeopardy.[4] Johnson and Cohen also discussed the possibility of publishing a scholarly journal comparable to the German-dominated *Social Research*. By September 1941, Cohen had identified those French and French-speaking scholars in the United States who were willing to assist the project, which he tentatively called the Institut des Hautes Etudes Franco-Belges. In November Cohen excitedly called Pierre Brodin, "*Ca y' est*—that's it— I've done it!"[5]

Cohen's enthusiasm was justified. On February 12, 1942, the Ecole Libre des Hautes Etudes officially opened in the auditorium of Hunter College, uptown from its classrooms and offices in the Twelfth Street building in what the French came to call the New School's *quartier latin*. Two to three thousand listeners enthusiastically greeted speeches by Johnson, Cohen, who announced Charles DeGaulle's financial and political support, and the words of the Ecole Libre's first president, Henri Focillon, art historian at the Collège de France and Harvard. The prospectus of the Ecole Libre captured the euphoria of Franco-American good will as it declared: "The project ... intends to be a substantial contribution to the progress of studies and to the development of French 'culture' in the U.S.A. under the protectorate of the Greatest Republic and of the Greatest City in the world."[6] Cohen had negotiated an arrangement that allowed the Ecole Libre to operate as part of the New School but to govern most of its affairs autonomously. It had its own board of directors and administrators, and its faculty members were free to hold appointments at other American institutions, such as the Graduate Faculty. It was a fortuitous arrangement for both parties, the Ecole Libre gaining the facilities and support of the New School, and the New School enhancing its reputation as a gathering place for European intellectuals.

In the Ecole Libre's first semester, ten professors taught more than 300 students in forty courses. By May this had swollen to sixty-five instructors in five divisions: Letters, Law and Politics, Sciences, Oriental Languages and Philology, and Latin American Studies. Almost 1,000 students enrolled in more than 200 courses. The faculty described the courses as equal to those taught at the Sorbonne or the Collège de France. This claim was supported by such courses as Roman Jacobson's "Linguistique générale," Henri Bonnet's "Problèmes d'organization internationale," Claude Lévi-Strauss's "Ethnographie générale," Georges Gurvitch's "La Sociologie française," and Raoul Aglion's "Droit comparé."[7]

Before the Ecole Libre had even opened its doors in 1942, its board of directors announced plans to publish a French-language scholarly journal, *Renaissance,* which appeared three times. Johnson had originally envisioned the journal as serving a specific end. "Such a periodical," he wrote, "like *Social Research,* would hold aloof from propaganda, but as representing the liberal ideas that have been built up through the ages it could be more effective for our national purposes than any straight propaganda."[8] The editors of *Renaissance* insisted that theirs was not a political journal and that they did not engage in politics. At the same time they rejected the notion of the Ecole Libre as an ivory tower of quietism. "We would," the editors declared, "be guilty of the treason of the intellectuals if we closed ourselves in the *templa serena* of philosophy and pure research."[9] They believed that noncommitment was virtually impossible for scholars who upheld the values of liberal humanism. They concluded, "If one considers politics to be taking a position against totalitarian slavery and tyranny or in joining the immense forces engaged in saving civilization, then we would engage in politics."[10]

Although the Ecole Libre's faculty had defined their role as politically engaged scholars, this did not answer the more practical question of what they could do to help overthrow the Vichy government. One answer came during the opening session at Hunter College, when it was announced that, three days earlier, on February 9, Charles DeGaulle had authorized the Ecole Libre to grant degrees as the University of France Libre. Such a designation meant that the Ecole Libre had become an arm of the Gaullist bloc of the French resistance. This alliance had come about not only through the energies and good will of Jacques Maritain, Gustave Cohen, and Alvin Johnson, but also as a consequence of political appointments and policies of the Gaullist factions in London and New York since the summer of 1940. After the defeat of France in 1940, the French community in the United States, particularly in New York, found itself divided among those who supported Vichy, those who were avowed Gaullists, and those who were anti-Vichy and also anti-Gaullist. The task that faced the Gaullists in the United States was twofold: first, to organize French support for DeGaulle; and second, to organize American public opinion against the Vichy government, which the United States had officially recognized.

Although the French exile community itself was not of primary concern to the Free French organization in London, DeGaulle recognized its strategic importance in shaping American policy toward France.

In June 1940 Alexander Koyré, who had been teaching philosophy of science in Cairo, made his way back to France to offer his services to the army. DeGaulle's representative encouraged him to return to Cairo and travel from there to the United States. Former Harvard philosopher George Santayana arranged for an entry visa for Koyré and his wife and wrote to Johnson urging a position for his friend at the New School. In early 1942, Koyré traveled to London and attempted once more to join the Free French army. The Gaullists told him that it was more important for him to "make propaganda" for France Libre. Almost forty years later, when asked if that was the most important aim of the Ecole Libre, his widow, Madame Koyré, acknowledged that it was not. Was it then secondary? "Oh no," she said smiling. "It was far too important to be secondary."[11]

While Koyré was shuttling back and forth from Cairo to Paris in the summer of 1940, Jacques Maritain received a letter from Charles DeGaulle. DeGaulle sought Maritain's advice on the appointment of a personal representative in New York. Maritain recommended Raoul Aglion.[12] When Aglion, a diplomat and legal expert who had also been in Cairo, arrived in New York in October 1940, he and his wife reported immediately to Maritain. Maritain, no doubt, expressed to Aglion his curious mixture of optimism and pessimism. He had prophesied a disastrous European "civil" war and yet was among the staunchest supporters of Charles DeGaulle. He also believed that America's moral and intellectual strength would eventually save France and Europe, suggesting that he in part accepted Pétain's notion that the French defeat had been caused by moral decay.[13] More important, Maritain provided Aglion with detailed information on the French exile community in New York.[14]

Aglion found a complex, even sectarian, situation. In 1940–1941 several groups had already organized the New York French community in an effort to influence American policy toward Vichy France. For example, in September 1940, a group called France Forever proclaimed its Gaullist intentions and loyalty in a newspaper of the same name. Several months later the journalist Genevieve Tabouis founded another group, Pour la Victoire, with enough funds to publish a newsletter.[15] Tabouis, a well-known radio personality, called the "Cassandra of the Republic" in the 1930s, was the paper's maverick inspiration. When Tabouis's Gaullist sympathies cooled in early 1942, she announced in *Pour la Victoire* that she now favored General Henri Giraud, who had taken power in North Africa, as the "savior" of France. *France*

Forever, however, remained in the Gaullist camp. For more than a year the Giraud–DeGaulle division in the anti-Vichy contingent dominated the internal political struggle in the French community. Consequently, many prominent French intellectuals and politicians in New York found it impossible to align either with the old-fashioned centralized nationalism of DeGaulle or the opportunist Giraud. The Gaullists were anxious to remedy this confusion. Toward that end, they had specifically authorized Aglion to encourage the creation of an institution like the Ecole Libre.

The Ecole Libre prospered in direct proportion to the success of the Gaullist faction of the resistance. After the American landings in North Africa in the fall of 1942 and the creation of the quasi-government or *Comité nationale* of DeGaulle, most French living abroad either declared their admiration for France Libre or remained silent. This enabled Aglion, now both a member of the faculty of the Ecole Libre and DeGaulle's personal representative, to encourage Gaullist support for the school with even greater success. By mid-1943, with its enrollment and course listings still growing, the Ecole Libre had become the focus of united Gaullism in New York.[16] This is not to say that the Ecole Libre was simply a Gaullist institution. When Henri Bonnet, an authority in international law, left in 1942 to join the Gaullist government in Algiers, the school was beset with political division. Most faculty members, although personally loyal to the positions of DeGaulle and the Resistance, were unwilling to politicize their classrooms directly. For many, their flight to the United States had been a consequence of their refusal to kowtow to political authorities. When the Gaullist "government" in Algiers passed the Crémieux Laws of 1943, which placed French education abroad under the control of the new "state," some protested against that attempt to reimpose the centralized structures of traditional France even before liberation. Jacques Maritain's reaction was indicative of the tensions that emerged in 1943–1944. Despite his willingness to support Gaullist policies generally, Maritain refused to take an ideological position. Nevertheless, when Lévi-Strauss, Koyré, and Mirkine, who made up the nucleus of the Gaullist group, formed a *comité républicain et démocratique* to discuss contemporary politics, Maritain agreed to sign the manifesto for reasons of solidarity.[17]

Such political solidarity, and even scholarly collaboration, was typical of the Ecole Libre throughout its existence. Although their research during these years lacked the collective focus that characterized the work of their German colleagues, the French and Belgian exiles at the Graduate Faculty acted more and more as a community. Their common mission was shaped by the shared experience of war and exile and reinforced by their common political commitment to the Gaullist Resistance. Many viewed themselves as the representatives and even the guardians of French culture. As a result, the publication and editorial policy of *Renaissance* became increasingly important. Contributors affirmed their loyalty to French traditions of liberty and their hostility to anything associated with Vichy. In Aglion's words, "The policy of the *revue* will be exactly that of the Ecole: *France Combattante.*"[18]

Edited jointly by Belgian classicist Henri Grégoire and Alexandre Koyré, *Renaissance* was subject to the same controversies and political divisions that characterized the French emigré community as a whole. Accepting the need for the appearance of unity within the Resistance, the editorial board agreed that no article would be accepted for publication without the unanimous approval of the board. This policy went unchallenged until January 1944, when, for what turned out to be the last issue of *Renaissance,* Henri Grégoire submitted a commentary for the regular political column, "Chronique Politique." A classicist, Belgian-French patriot, war veteran, and academic entrepreneur, Grégoire was also the single most difficult personality at the Ecole Libre. A political activist, he had edited the left-wing journal *Le Flambeau* during World War I and prided himself on his political acumen. In his commentary, Grégoire apparently challenged the current policies of the exiled French and Belgian governments. Lévi-Strauss requested that Grégoire read his commentary aloud to the board, which asked that he delete several politically controversial passages. Grégoire refused and threatened to resign. The board prevailed on him to remain, but when Grégoire threatened to publish his article without board approval, both Koyré and Lévi-Strauss resigned from the board.[19] Koyré and Lévi-Strauss—although committed to *Renaissance,* to the Ecole Libre, and to the notion of unity within the Resistance—could not accept anti-Gaullist policies. The nearness of victory now made the political divisions within the Resistance more significant than their unified opposition to the Vichy government.[20]

Even as the faculty members of the Ecole Libre were united in their opposition to Vichy, so they were unanimous in their loyalty to all things French. When the Ecole Libre was set up in 1942, Jacques Maritain was undoubtedly its most renowned personality. Yet, as scholars, Gustave Cohen, Henri Focillon, Alexandre Koyré, Boris Mirkine-Guetzévitch, and Roman Jacobson were Maritain's equals. These men, together with several dozen other French, Belgian, and Russian scholars, provided the Ecole Libre with one of the most distinguished faculties in the world. This remarkable group of French-speaking scholars continued to sustain the illusion that France and civilization

were virtually interchangeable terms. Cosmopolitan in their search for
the values and themes of human experience, they were parochial in that
they did so largely in terms of French history and culture. This was as
true of the Russian and Belgian scholars as of the French. Moreover,
the entire faculty, Gaullist or anti-Gaullist, Belgian, Russian, French,
Christian or Jew, upheld the viability of parliamentary democracy.
Although they variously labeled themselves liberals, democrats, and
socialists, they eschewed the communist Left as much as they did the
fascist Right. The French Revolution was their political touchstone,
and for them "reason," "liberty," and "humanity" were not empty
timeworn shibboleths.

These liberal humanists were characteristic of the interwar generation of French intellectuals.[21] Complacent in their belief in the superiority of French culture and a secularized form of Christianity, they were
frequently uncomfortable with the empirical orientation of the social
sciences and impatient with those who refused to equate "civilization"
with western traditions. Jacques Maritain was particularly forceful in
defending the Christian humanist position. Nonetheless, the Ecole
Libre also included several individuals who found such French traditions intellectually restrictive. Defining themselves as social scientists
as much as humanists, scholars such as Roman Jacobson and Claude
Lévi-Strauss studied human society with the same systematic rigor
that physical scientists studied natural phenomena. They and their
non-Christian colleagues also felt uncomfortable with the implicitly
Christian basis of French humanism. During the war, these differences
remained submerged and were hardly noticed. After the war, however,
French social scientists, among them Lévi-Strauss, challenged many of
the philosophical and cultural assumptions of western humanism even
as they affirmed its ideals.

Alexandre Koyré's work as a philosopher of science conformed to
the tradition of French humanism. Koyré studied the relationship between medieval and modern thought to determine the philosophical
continuities. His search for universals, a project common to the work of
many at the Ecole Libre, terminated not in Christianity, but in
idealism. Born in Russia, educated in France and in Switzerland (where
he studied with Edmund Husserl), Koyré returned to Russia in 1916,
having served two years in the French army. Late in 1918 he returned
to France after his Russian military unit, which fought on both sides
during the civil war, disbanded. In France, Koyré returned as well to
scholarship and to the task of establishing the medieval sources of
Cartesian thought.[22] Sympathetic to neo-Platonism and philosophical
idealism in general, he identified civilization with human reason. In
"Discovering Plato," an essay written in New York in 1945, he af-

firmed his belief in the necessity of political order, civil responsibility, and reason.[23] For him, the barbarism of Nazism was a horrible aberration which all civilized people were compelled to resist.

Similarly, as a literary historian, Gustave Cohen tried to delineate the differences between traditional and modern culture in order to determine their more fundamental continuities. Cohen was born in Brussels and educated in Bordeaux, Paris, Leipzig, and Amsterdam. He enjoyed a distinguished teaching career, first at the University of Strasbourg and then at the Sorbonne. Like his associates Lucien Febvre, Henri Pirenne, and Henri Focillon, Cohen tried to define the meaning of European and French culture.[24] In a two-volume history of French drama written between 1928 and 1932, he argued that French classical comedy had its roots in medieval religious expression.[25] Like Koyré, Cohen emphasized the intimate relationship between the sacred and the profane. This relationship, he argued, provided the genius of French culture and sustained its moral development. In December 1940, when the Vichy government closed his courses at the Sorbonne, Cohen accepted an invitation to teach at Yale which allowed him to reside in New York. A person of enormous energy, Cohen in 1943 completed his important synthesis of medieval culture, *La Grande Clarté de moyen age,* during the same period that he was helping to set up the Ecole Libre. In *La Grande Clarté,* Cohen argued that the label "Middle Ages" was itself misleading. Rather than an intellectually moribund period between antiquity and the Renaissance, medieval civilization, declared Cohen, was "the first modern era where we can witness the essential innovations of our age."[26]

Cohen's belief in the links between the spiritual values of medieval Christianity and the secularism of antiquity and the Renaissance was shared by his long-time colleague, art historian Henri Focillon. Focillon's reputation rested on his books on medieval art and the Renaissance humanist Benvenuto Cellini. In 1934, Focillon collaborated with Cohen and Henri Pirenne on a history of European civilization from the eleventh to the fifteenth century. Focillon and his coauthors traced the medieval origins of the literary, artistic, and social forces that culminated in the Renaissance, finding even here the crucial contribution of French civilization.[27] Prior to his appointment in 1941 as president of the Ecole Libre, Focillon had taught at the Sorbonne and at the Collège de France. His untimely death in 1943, just months after the first session of the Ecole Libre, deprived the institution of one of its most distinguished scholars.

Boris Mirkine-Guetzévitch shared with Focillon, Cohen, and Koyré a fundamentally liberal political perspective. He too looked to French culture for his understanding of the sources of western civilization. A

native of Russia, Mirkine-Guetzévitch, like Koyré, left Russia after the
civil war. Born in Kiev and educated in Petrograd, where he received his
doctorate of laws in 1914, Mirkine departed for France in 1919. Fervently committed to a liberal, parliamentary order, Mirkine was bitterly disappointed by the Russian Revolution. For him the French
Revolution stood for everything the Russian Revolution had forsaken:
reason, order, and liberty. Before the Terror, he argued, the French
Revolution had provided Europeans with an ideal political order. In his
studies of modern European law and government, Mirkine time after
time discovered the persisting influences of the French Revolution.
Without it, he declared, modern political democracy was inconceivable.
As editor of *Cahiers de la Presse,* a 1930s news digest, he had witnessed
the steady erosion of French political democracy in the last years of the
Third Republic, but had then found in DeGaulle the embodiment of the
ideals of liberty and order. In his courses at the Ecole Libre, he explicitly identified the Gaullist Resistance with the yet unfulfilled ideals of
1789.[28]

In the public eye no one at the Ecole Libre rivaled Jacques Maritain. In his writings he summed up both the strengths and limits of
French liberal humanism. In April 1940, just weeks before the German
invasion of France, the New School invited Maritain, then teaching at
Princeton, to lecture on the meaning of war. The New School's choice of
Maritain was interesting. After flirting with Catholic royalism and the
right-wing Action Française, Maritain in the 1930s emerged as a major
theologian. Born a Protestant, married to a Russian Jew, he converted
to Catholicism and studied philosophy with Henri Bergson in France
and then at Heidelberg, all prior to World War I. Between 1914 and
World War II he sought to relate the thought of Thomas Aquinas to
contemporary society.[29] Convinced by Aquinas's proofs of God's existence, Maritain explored the possibility of the transcendental nature
of existence. He argued that there had always existed an intelligence or
spirit that could comprehend all that was intelligible. If true, this
meant that the individual ego existed eternally in God. Maritain believed that the existence of a rational, transcendent being, in which all
humans shared to the extent of their rationality, provided a convincing
philosophical underpinning for a new Christian polity. Thus, although
he acknowledged fundamental differences between medieval and
modern society, he thought that they also possessed common impulses.

As a politically concerned theologian, Maritain wished to inject his
spiritual vision into what he considered an otherwise materialistic and
disoriented civilization.[30] In his 1940 New School address, he developed
several of the themes which he had touched on in his recently published
Le Crépuscule du civilization.[31] He argued that World War II was a

"war of civilization," which had been unleashed by the uncivilized, un-European, un-Christian Nazi "scourge" against all humanity. Maritain maintained that the war's justness and the obligation of all civilized people was clear cut and imperative. Citing the scholastic argument that a just war is one that is caused by the "warding off of evil," Maritain declared that only a just peace could be the outcome of such belligerency. A just peace depended not only on the victory of moral virtue, but on the political reformation of Europe as well. By calling for a new federal policy, Maritain proposed at the same time to march forward and backward, forward to a dream of a democratic United States of Europe, backward to a Christian Europe, free from the encumbrances of nationalism. Echoing the attitudes of many on the Graduate Faculty, Maritain identified the problem of Europe as the German problem. Yet he did not wish to stop here. A new Europe, he wrote in 1940, could succeed only to the extent that it solved its social as well as its political problems. He believed that social equality depended on the prior establishment of political democracy. In his New School speech, Maritain did not elaborate. Still, he raised the same question that many others had posed: By what authority could a democratic society be justified? As a Catholic, Maritain located his source not simply in the transcendence of God, but in God's word as well.

During 1943 and 1944, Maritain wrote *Christianity and Democracy* at the Ecole Libre.[32] His thesis was straightforward. The Christian gospel taught that the state had an obligation to serve humanity by maintaining law. Although ultimate authority rested in God, political authority derived from the people and therefore must serve the common good. Politicians were thereby morally obligated to create and preserve institutions that served all social classes as well as the human community. For Maritain, parliamentary democracy became a humanistic and religious imperative. Europe had failed to sustain a democratic community because, in his eyes, Europeans had misunderstood the democratic implication of their faith. In dividing their own historical understanding between traditional and modern, Christian and secular, they had divorced themselves from the spiritual foundations of democracy itself. Only by recognizing the inalienable relationship between personal freedom, democratic politics, and Christian teaching could Europeans reconstruct a just society. Maritain viewed Nazism and communism as totalitarian twins at war with the fundamental principles of Christian democracy. Yet he insisted that a new Christian democracy must in no way be a revised form of the liberal-capitalist democracy that had failed to establish a moral community, and paved the way for a totalitarian victory. Maritain saw in the United States the basis for such a democracy because only in

America had Christianity and democracy been understood as complementary and reinforcing values.[33]

Maritain's faith in the virtue of American democracy, although naive, had as its corollary his belief that totalitarianism was a historical and spiritual consequence of European failure.[34] Like many of his intellectual and political generation, he hoped to separate the spirit of eighteenth-century liberalism from its marketplace associations, even as he offered a Thomistic Christian democracy as an alternative to totalitarianism. In his closing statement at the New School in the spring of 1940 he declared:

> It is not enough to outlaw communism to be through with communism. Nothing will have been accomplished as long as men have not resolved . . . the principles made manifest by communism, and I believe that a social philosophy inspired by integral humanism is the only means whereby to resolve these problems.[35]

For liberal democracy to survive and thereby preserve civilized society, he argued, it must commit itself to waging war against all forms of totalitarianism. In this respect, throughout his tenure at the Ecole Libre, he engaged in politics, his claim that he wished to devote himself to "pure philosophical principles" notwithstanding. After the invasion of Normandy, Maritain cast aside all pretense of scholarship; within weeks of the liberation of Paris he had written to Algiers, requesting permission to return to France. In late 1944, DeGaulle appointed him as ambassador to the Vatican.

In the 1930s and 1940s the work of Maritain, Koyré, Cohen, Focillon, and Mirkine was original and compelling. At that time, the prestige of the Ecole Libre derived largely from the reputations of these men. Giants in their fields, they commanded the respect and, in Maritain's case, the awe of their generation. Yet by the early 1950s their ideas and scholarship had become dated. One problem was their insistence that explicit political and moral lessons could be learned from scholarly inquiry. As imposing as their research and learning often was, it usually only provided additional documentation for what they already believed to be true. Further, after the war their notion of "France as Civilization" seemed anachronistic to all but the most passionate francophile. Finally, their understanding of themselves as interpreters of the western humanistic heritage who sought to identify the continuities and verities of civilization made them resistant to the vocabularies and methodologies of the social sciences, which they viewed as a deterrent to understanding and communication. As a result, these eminent scholars of the interwar generation failed to com-

mand the continuing scholarly interest of the academic community and
of their two more experimental colleagues, linguist Roman Jacobson
and anthropologist Claude Lévi-Strauss.

Roman Jacobson was born and educated in Moscow, and it was
during his years at the university there that he organized the Moscow
Linguistic Circle. In his early work he challenged linguists to go beyond
their preoccupation with historical, etymological, and phonetic issues
and approach language holistically as a symbolic system. The narrowly
cultural approach of traditional linguistics had obstructed the view
that human languages exhibited similar structures, he argued. After
leaving Russia in 1920, Jacobson read the work of the French linguist
Ferdinand de Saussure and extrapolated from him a system to code the
constituent elements of a language. Jacobson also borrowed from
Saussure the distinction between speech, the flow of words, and the
structure of meaning or syntax. Jacobson postulated the existence of a
finite number of linguistic structures built on components, or
phonemes, which operated according to "general laws."

Between 1920 and 1939 Jacobson lived in Prague, where he extended his research and elaborated his linguistic theory.[36] In 1939 when
Hitler invaded Czechoslovakia Jacobson fled, staying briefly in
Sweden and then Norway before coming to the United States in June
1941. At the time of his appointment to the Ecole Libre, Jacobson was
the world's preeminent linguist. There, collaborating with Grégoire, he
produced definitive evidence that verified the authenticity of the Russian epic poem, *The Song of Igor.*[37] Because of his more cosmopolitan
orientation and the technical and non-nationalistic character of his
work, he, more than any other senior scholar at the Ecole Libre, successfully transcended the French particularism of the institution.
Jacobson searched for universal laws of human language, not continuities within European civilization. His research was not based on
political considerations nor was it bound by European parochialism.
The work he completed in the 1940s laid the groundwork for postwar
structuralism in linguistics and anthropology.

At the Ecole Libre, anthropologist Claude Lévi-Strauss found in
Jacobson the intellectual inspiration for his own work. Lévi-Strauss
was born in 1908 to a secular, Jewish, middle-class family. In 1931 he
received a doctorate in philosophy and a degree in law, but his early
writings were devoted to socialist politics, an interest he sustained
throughout the war.[38] Lévi-Strauss had been schooled in the positivist
tradition of Comte and Durkheim, a tradition that held empirical
science to be the culmination of knowledge. He was interested in the
philosophical concerns of Kant, but as a young man he found Marx,
Darwin, and Freud more compelling. The most significant influence on

his early intellectual development, however, was Durkheim whose concept of society as an integral system, susceptible to scientific inquiry, represented a major insight for Lévi-Strauss. Even so, Durkheim's tendency toward functionalism and his positivist notion that social phenomena could be understood in the same terms as biological data disturbed Lévi-Strauss.

Lévi-Strauss insisted that he became an anthropologist through a series of accidents.[39] The first occurred in 1935, when the University of São Paulo invited him to Brazil. The unforeseen opportunity to conduct anthropological field work in Brazil diverted him from a political career as a socialist. The second accident was France's defeat in 1940, which led to his flight to New York. There, at the Ecole Libre, he met Jacobson and through him discovered linguistics. While in New York, Lévi-Strauss also renewed his friendship with André Breton, who introduced him to a group of surrealist painters who shared his recently acquired interest in pre-Columbian art.[40]

While in Brazil, Lévi-Strauss had accumulated a vast collection of ethnographic data, but he found that he lacked the necessary interpretive framework. If nothing else, his training in philosophy convinced him that existing scientific epistemology was inadequate to the task of finding the unities of cultural life. As he later recounted, "I was a structuralist without knowing it."[41] At the Ecole Libre, he showed little interest in the work of the other faculty members except that of Jacobson. "There was," he said, "no school at the New School. Just Jacobson and me." Although this was true in the sense that the faculty shared no ideological or philosophical school of thought comparable to that of, for example, the Frankfurt School, there was at the New School a common commitment to social science, social change, and liberal-democratic politics. Moreover, at the New School, Lévi-Strauss enjoyed an almost unique opportunity to work with an international collection of social scientists in a variety of fields, including anthropologists Franz Boas, Margaret Mead, and Bronislaw Malinowski. As a young cultural anthropologist seeking to develop his transcultural theories, he found New York itself a rich field for investigation.

Lévi-Strauss turned to anthropology in part because he was dissatisfied with what he saw as a failure on the part of modern philosophers to move beyond the claims of twentieth-century positivists.[42] He resolved to bridge the gap between scientific knowledge and human meaning, but to do so he realized that he would have to go outside philosophy. He believed that structural analysis offered a means to explain otherwise disparate social facts through a new understanding of human thought and culture. His faith in the possibilities of structural analysis were based in turn on his belief that scientists could address

fundamental questions of human existence, or what he called "Being in
relation to itself,"[43] and thereby restore the apparent dichotomy between knowledge and metaphysics.[44]

On his arrival in New York, Lévi-Strauss offered his first course in
parenté, or kinship. He quickly followed this up with an explanatory
essay in *Renaissance.*[45] How, he asked, could the striking similarities in
the art of the ancient Chinese, the South American Indians, and the
Aborigines of Australia be accounted for? Traditional interpretation of
the phenomenon of split representation—a motif in which a three-
dimensional object is depicted on a plane or rounded surface split apart
as if it had been sliced at the rear with its two sides symmetrically
folded out to the viewer—had stressed either cultural contact or a common historical origin. Lévi-Strauss questioned the validity of such
theories, pointing out that similarities were manifest in representa-
tions made by people centuries and continents apart. Instead, he proposed a theory of psychological causes, or what he called the structural
analysis of forms. "Let us ask ourselves," he wrote, "if internal connections of a psychological or logical nature will allow ourselves to understand parallel occurrences."[46] He argued that split representation in
carvings, drawings, and facial tattooing represented a deep cultural
division, common to the societies that created the images. Its appearance in diverse settings was attributable, not to some mysterious
pattern of diffusion, but to deep-seated human needs. Was this, asked
Lévi-Strauss, a resort to a "magical connection"? He replied, "Perhaps; but magical connections, like optical illusions, exist only in men's
minds and we must resort to scientific investigation to explain these
causes."[47]

Shortly after the appearance of his article in *Renaissance,* Lévi-
Strauss published a short study on the role of the maternal uncle in kinship structures.[48] Again, he sought an explanation for what he called
the "chaos of discontinuity," caused by a reliance on historical con-
tingency to explain the existence of particular social phenomena—in
this case, the maternal uncle. Historical or diachronic analysis, he
declared, not only failed to account for the appearance of a thing in
disparate times and places, it also resulted in an "individualistic" and
"atomistic" interpretation.[49] Such interpretations tried to explain the
meaning of phenomena through their functions rather than their relationships. By using historical explanations, anthropologists had
isolated what they wished to know rather than inquiring about the
meaning of the phenomenon itself. Lévi-Strauss argued that it was inadequate merely to account for the existence of certain cultural-social
facts in diverse times and places; anthropologists must go beyond that
to the task of determining current meaning when the original function

no longer acted as a cause. Accounting for phenomena whose existences were maintained and "transmitted" unconsciously was the real challenge.

Perplexed, Lévi-Strauss turned to Roman Jacobson and the work of Ferdinand de Saussure. "No one," he recounted in a recent interview, "had ever bothered to mention Saussure to young French philosophers."[50] Under Jacobson's influence, Lévi-Strauss concluded that of all the cultural disciplines only linguistics could claim the status of a science. Empirically based, it seemed capable of explaining the "tenacious survival in contemporary vocabulary of relationships which have long since disappeared." In addition, linguists had already begun to experiment with holistic methods in their work.[51] Saussure and Jacobson both argued that the meaning of a particular linguistic fact was revealed only in its more general structural context, not in its own particular content. If the meaning of language derived from common linguistic relationships, then the way was open for the discovery of general laws. Within structural linguistics, Lévi-Strauss perceived a model for structural anthropology.

As Lévi-Strauss envisioned it, structural anthropology involved the scientific study of social relationships. Such a science could account for the persistence of those relationships in diverse times and places in the same way that structural linguistics explained the persistence of linguistic relationships. It allowed him to uncover the deeper, subconscious meaning of social relationships based on general laws of social life. To his mind, he had resolved the problem posed by the limits of knowledge that had been claimed by the positivists. Human society could be studied on a scientific basis because all humans shared common mental structures.

Still, epistemological problems remained. Structural anthropology, which required observers virtually to merge their consciousnesses with those of their subjects, invited subjectivity. Here, too, Lévi-Strauss turned to Jacobson, who had invoked a notion of economy or parsimony to referee between two competing and valid interpretations of the same "fact." Taken from physics, the so-called law of parsimony stated that the simpler explanation was the correct one. Given the nature of the social world, its appropriateness rested, in Lévi-Strauss's opinion, "upon the identity postulated between the laws of the universe and the laws of the human mind."[52] "I was struck by the usage that Jacobson made of the law of parsimony," he recalled. "This admittedly metaphysical idea that the mind can understand the world is a kind of philosophical hypothesis which is convenient to me."[53]

From his studies of split representation and maternal uncle, Lévi-Strauss moved on to broader inquiries about kinship, myth, and culture in general. But he did so with the structural insights he had forged in New York between 1941 and 1945. In anthropology, he had found answers to questions which his earlier philosophical work had denied. To know the human mind, in Lévi-Strauss's terms, meant a turn to the "epistemological attitude" of structuralism.[54] By the early 1950s, he concluded that all forms of social life were subject to explanations which he had originally applied only to language. This was, he wrote, because society is composed of "systems of behavior which represent the projection, on the level of conscious and socialized thought, of universal laws which regulate the unconscious activity of the mind."[55] Science, in this case anthropology, claimed to embrace what nineteenth-century positivists argued could not be known—the human mind. It did so through abstract models of unconscious human behavior, but models purportedly validated by empirical data. In Kantian terms, Lévi-Strauss attempted to synthesize the rational and empirical. Humans have knowledge of the structure of the world because they create categories with which to order it. Those categories "work" due to the assumed correspondence that exists between the mind and the world at large. While Lévi-Strauss denied that structuralism was a methodology in itself, it remained nonetheless a method by which to understand a world that humans had constructed.

In *Tristes Tropiques,* published in 1955, Lévi-Strauss reflected on the events that had brought him from France to Brazil and then to New York. The duty or "calling" of anthropology, he maintained, was to discover the common features contained in all human societies, to break down artificial distinctions between "primitive" and "advanced," and instead to evolve a model of human cultural experience. To this extent anthropology was ideally suited for scientific investigation. Anthropologists could study other cultures, yet remain detached, because they were not a part of those cultures. Other societies, he concluded, were not better than ours. Rather, they offered us a perspective on ourselves. But toward what end? There seemed little connection between the Lévi-Strauss who had begun his career seeking to reform politics through socialism and the anthropologist of the 1950s who sought to understand human consciousness through cultural anthropology. Lévi-Strauss himself believed that his anthropological work served the same ends as his socialist politics. We seek to know society, he maintained, in order to "distinguish those principles of social life which may be applied to the reform of our own customs . . . for our own society is the only one we can transform and yet not destroy."[56] In the 1940s Jacques Maritain, speaking from within French culture, had espoused a form of Christian democracy that he believed was universally applicable. As a Jew, Lévi-Strauss could not accept so parochial a humanism. His universe included all humans, Jews and Christians, nonwesterners and westerners, primitive and technologically advanced. Social science, particularly anthropology, seemed to him a more productive enterprise than a postwar politics that understood the universe in terms of its own narrowly restrictive traditions.[57] Social science and comparative anthropology seemed to him well suited to the task of creating a new and genuinely humanistic French society.

Lévi-Strauss's faith in the potential of social science was shared by a remarkable number of his colleagues at the New School, European and American. Lévi-Strauss occasionally saw but rarely chatted with his colleague Max Wertheimer, who along with Karl Koffka and Wolfgang Köhler, had "discovered" gestalt psychology. Wertheimer, like Lévi-Strauss, postulated the structural unity of the physical world, attacked the atomistic tendencies of behavioristic experimentalism, held to a version of the law of parsimony, and claimed that scientists could know the physical world because the human mind corresponded to the laws that it imposed upon the universe. Curiously, Wertheimer and Lévi-Strauss did not know one another. Yet there remains a strong affinity between structural anthropology and gestalt psychology.[58] The coincidence in the same building of two distinct disciplines both devoted to a similar understanding of the human mind seems more than simply fortuitous. Characteristically, Lévi-Strauss found such a coincidence unremarkable. It was, after all, to him "structurally" predictable.

In 1944 Lévi-Strauss ended his work in New York. In June of that year, Allied landings in Normandy opened the way for the return home of the French and Belgian exiles at the Ecole Libre. DeGaulle's *Comité nationale* had become the provisional government of France. In the winter of 1944–1945 the French government recalled Lévi-Strauss, who had recently been elected secretary-general of the Ecole Libre, to consult on the future of the school. The government also asked him to assume the position of *conseiller culturel* in New York. At the same time, the faculty of the Ecole Libre found itself divided between those who wanted the school to continue as a French cultural outpost in the New World and those who felt that with the end of the war there was no further need for a French university in the United States.[59]

In France, Lévi-Strauss, who was personally more concerned with postwar recovery than with the future of the school, proposed that the government establish a French–American foundation that incorporated the Ecole Libre into a wide-ranging kind of Alliance Française. When his idea failed to gain support, he returned to New York in the spring of 1945, with orders to close the school. The government withdrew its annual $70,000 subsidy, and the New School, facing financial problems of its own, refused to come to the aid of the Ecole Libre. Threatened with extinction, the Ecole Libre began searching for affordable space of its own, and set to work at negotiating a new agreement with the French government and redefining its relationship with the New School.

In 1946, the school momentarily appeared to have solved its dilemma. Henri Bonnet, then French ambassador to Washington, and Bryne Hovde, newly appointed president of the New School, initialed an agreement whereby France would provide between $50,000 and $75,000 to establish an international division at the New School. As *conseiller culturel*, Lévi-Strauss approved the release of these funds.[60] A problem arose, however, because the new leadership of the Ecole Libre consisted of the same individuals who, in late 1943, had protested the establishment of the Crémieux Laws that had centralized French education. This time they were equally unwilling to cede their autonomy, even to the New School. Pierre Brodin, who became director of the Ecole Libre in late 1946, wanted an independent school, and several of his colleagues, including Henri Peyre, Grégoire, and Ernst Hamburger, agreed.[61] In the winter of 1946, the Ecole Libre refused the New School's plan, turned down the money from the French government, and charted its own, independent course. On a modest scale, it has continued to function as an agent of French culture in New York.

In a sense, both groups were correct. The Ecole Libre had been created as a cultural and intellectual center for French refugees and an advocate of a free, antifascist France. Peace had made this work unnecessary, as Brodin and Lévi-Strauss both understood. Lévi-Strauss, whose interest lay with the new French government, saw that its purposes would best be served by the creation of a new French university, under governmental sponsorship, which would replace the Ecole Libre. In contrast, Brodin wanted to redefine the Ecole Libre as a truly independent institution, free from government control and overseen by its own autonomous board of trustees. In any case, the heroic era of the Ecole Libre had ended with the defeat of Germany, when its most distinguished scholars returned home to help reconstruct a democratic France.

POLITICS ON STAGE
Piscator and the Dramatic Workshop

THE DRAMATIC WORKSHOP, ESTABLISHED IN 1940, was the last of the three new divisions organized at the New School during the war years. Totally unlike the other two divisions and very different from the research-oriented New School as a whole, the Dramatic Workshop nonetheless brought a new form of public recognition to the school. Led by the world-renowned German dramatist Erwin Piscator, the workshop sought to link "serious" American drama to the politically informed theatre of Weimar Germany. In Germany, Piscator, a member of the German Communist Party, had been repeatedly accused of allowing his politics to compromise his art. At the New School, however, he avoided any explicit identification between his Marxist beliefs and his dramatic productions; if anything, the politics implicit in his New York productions were those of democratic humanism, similar to that of Alvin Johnson. Piscator's presence and tenure at the New School—he stayed more than ten years—are evidence that the school was willing to tolerate political radicals during the era of the "united front," following Germany's invasion of Russia. It was not until after the war, when the Cold War had shifted the attention of the American public to the perceived threat of communism, that the New School decided for a variety of reasons—Piscator's politics among them—to close the Dramatic Workshop.

Erwin Piscator and his wife Maria Ley arrived in New York during the winter of 1939. A refugee from Hitler's Germany and from Stalin's Russia, Piscator hoped to begin anew his effort to create an avant-garde, politically informed, and popular theatre. Discovering on his arrival that the State Department would not issue him a visa as a theatrical director, he realized that he would have to identify himself as a teacher and verify it by securing a full-time teaching position. Piscator cabled friends in Europe to send him certification that he had taught at the Deutsche Volkshochschule and had lectured on drama during the previous two years in Paris. In May, with these documents in hand and carrying letters of introduction from physicist Albert Einstein, German dramatist Max Reinhardt, and novelist Sinclair Lewis, Piscator presented himself to Alvin Johnson.[1] Johnson was then working to consolidate the various theatre activities of the New School into a single department with the prospect of forming a drama division. Theresa Helburn, then director of the Group Theatre, had already organized a playwriting workshop to be offered the following winter. When Piscator appeared, Johnson immediately recognized the opportunity that a person of his distinction and experience offered the New School.

In Piscator, Johnson had found someone whose dreams and ambitions exceeded even his own. Piscator hoped to make the New School the creative center of American theatre. He envisioned a "dramatic workshop" that prepared students for professional careers through laboratory courses, lectures on theatrical history, and professional public performances. Moreover, he hoped to integrate students' dramatic studies with the other activities at the New School by requiring courses in economics, contemporary politics, sociology, philosophy, and art. Dramatic Workshop students would study not only the theatre but the modern world as well. He would bring to the New York stage, declared Piscator, the "theatre of commitment" by restoring to contemporary drama the communal purpose and moral seriousness of classical drama.[2]

In the most general terms Johnson shared Piscator's vision. Piscator's determination to break with conventional theatre coincided with the purposes of the New School, just as his determination to use drama to encourage commitment to peace, democracy, justice, and freedom paralleled the New School's notion of a morally informed social science. Still, Johnson was disturbed by Piscator's reputation as a radical, and also by his determination to use the theatre as a vehicle for political discourse.[3] Piscator had outlined his method for doing precisely that in his classic work, *Political Theatre*. In 1937, in a letter to a friend and fellow Weimar radical, Felix Gassbarra, he had declared, "I can only work against bourgeois society, I can never work with it or through it."[4]

At the New School Piscator not only had to work with and through "bourgeois" society, he had to soften the rough political edge of his drama as well. Johnson willingly accepted the lapsed Weimar communist as a fellow modernist, but he had no sympathy for the ideological extremism that had, in Johnson's view, contributed to the destruction of the Weimar Republic. He believed that Piscator could make a valuable contribution to the New School, but he wanted him to conduct himself as a part of a larger, more pluralistic, modernist tradition. As he lectured Piscator, "Every successful rebellion becomes at long last a tradition. In the chain of history, each link of tradition has been forged by a rebel of the previous period."[5] Johnson could accept Piscator as an intellectual or artistic rebel who helped forge a new tradition, but not as a political rebel committed to destroy the state.

Piscator had dedicated his life to the theatre from early adulthood. Born in 1893 in Ulm, Germany, Piscator grew up in Hesse-Nassau, the child of a Protestant merchant family. In 1913 he entered the University of Munich, where he studied theatre history with Arthur Kutscher, one of the most innovative minds in German theatre at the time. As a student, Piscator played bit parts in the Bavarian Court Theatre. Drafted into the army in 1915, Piscator served in the infantry on the Ypres front. At the same time he wrote scripts for the army theatre units and published several antiwar poems in the radical magazine *Die Aktion*. While at home on sick leave, in 1917, Piscator met poet and publisher Wieland Herzfelde who introduced him to the Spartacist Party. On his return to active duty, Piscator joined the army theatre unit as an actor where he remained until the Armistice in 1918. Following his discharge, Piscator and Herzfelde went to Berlin where, with Herzfelde's brother John Heartfield and painter George Grosz, they participated briefly in the Berlin dadaist circle and joined the revolutionary Spartacist Party. All of Piscator's later work as a dramatist was shaped by his intense experience of the events surrounding World War I: the destruction of the war, the promise offered by the Russian Revolution, and the cultural radicalism embodied in dada and "expressionism."[6]

For all Germans World War I was traumatic. It marked the eclipse of German power, ended the monarchy, and ushered in an era of unprecedented political violence. For Piscator and other radicals, the war had demonstrated the utter bankruptcy of bourgeois society. The Kaiser, capitalism, and bourgeois culture appeared to be integral parts of a dehumanizing and exploitative conspiracy against humanity. In 1915 in the trenches at Ypres, Piscator wrote: "How did these people—bricklayers, butchers, and the like—dare to act as the minions of militarism, as N.C.O.'s and Corporals, how could they boast about their treatment of those timid souls who retreated like snails into their shells at the first contact, those who knew only too well why their bodies were decked out in carnival colors: because they might die in them? ... Oh, the system is fine, and the torture clearly works: the yoke sets firmly on everybody's neck, yet they need only realize that together they make up the State, that they constitute the power, that without them, the State is a torso without limbs, round and smooth as a billiard ball."[7] Yet Piscator also believed that without leadership the masses would never awaken to assume rightful control over their own lives. In his opinion, the "revolution" would have to be as much cultural as political. Without new art forms, themselves expressions of the potential of individual freedom, humanity would lack the vision necessary to create a just and permanently peaceful society.

In 1919 communism and expressionism offered Piscator two very different alternatives. Communism, as articulated by its German party and as manifested in the Russian Revolution, promised to destroy class structures, end the economic inequities perpetrated by a market economy, and transcend the national rivalries that seemed to lead inexorably to militarism and war. Dadaism shared its rejection of all things bourgeois, but in the context of a total apolitical nihilism. For Piscator, politics could serve culture by freeing it from the bonds of bourgeois values while art could communicate the values of a new social order. Piscator agreed with the Dadaists' repudiation of bourgeois life and art, but he rejected their indifference to politics. He asked postwar artists and writers to utilize the "expressionism" of dada and the politics of communism to create a new, more relevant art capable of provoking social change.

Expressionists, through stylized gestures and dramatic symbols, sought to transmit emotional messages to their audiences. Expressionist dramatists were concerned primarily with their impact on audiences rather than with the perfection of the production itself. Piscator believed that expressionism, conveying the message of communism, offered the formula for a new "political" theatre. He agreed with his friend Bertholt Brecht, who asked rhetorically: "How can the theatre be entertaining and instructive at the same time? How can it be taken out of the hands of the intellectual drug traffic and become a place offering real experiences rather than illusions? How can the unliberated and unknowing man of our century with his thirst for knowledge and freedom, the tortured and the heroic, misused and inventive man of our terrible and great century, himself changeable and yet able to change the world, how can he be given a theater which will help him to be master of the world?"[8]

In the 1920s Piscator and Brecht, along with other Berlin radicals, had revolutionized the German theatre. Brecht's plays and Piscator's dramaturgic innovations created a new dramatic genre, expressionist in imagery and communist in politics, which they called "epic theatre."[9] However, while the war, dada, and the Communist Party acted as important reference points throughout Piscator's life, they did not alone define his work as a dramatist. Temperamentally, Piscator seemed unable to rest on past accomplishments or accepted answers. He could not resist the temptation to alter, improvise, and change. Minutes before the opening curtain came up on a new play Piscator was at work making changes. Several times he even delayed openings an hour or more to introduce last-minute alterations that required rehearsals and set changes. So, too, his restless creativity could not long accept the simplistic view of society and politics offered by the Communist Party.[10]

The compulsion to improve even his best production was consistent with Piscator's understanding of his role as a dramatist. He saw 1919 as the year one. It marked the end of the older "bourgeois capitalist" order and the beginning of a "modernist communist" society. His task was to explore and discover new forms of dramatic expression reflective of the technical and collective reality of the emerging social order. He imagined himself to be a scientist of drama whose discoveries provided new data for inventive and socially committed dramatists. He believed that "epic drama," like previous dramatic traditions, would take years, if not generations, to define itself. Even so, as it became evident that he was constructing a tradition rather than ushering in a revolution, Piscator's German productions gradually became less overtly political and more artful and philosophical.[11]

Piscator's maturation as a dramatist was apparent in the 1920s. In the Communist Party's Proletariches Theatre, Piscator introduced "agitprop" drama to German audiences. Agitprop—short for "agitation and propaganda"—consisted of short skits presented to party audiences and designed to communicate political messages to uneducated workers, mobilizing them to political action. The "plays" featured stylized characters representing political personalities or symbolized social classes. The scripts were little more than a collection of party slogans. Agitprop performances, largely impromptu affairs, were mounted in labor halls and beer halls or wherever an opportunity presented itself. Actors had to respond to their particular audience as they addressed current political issues. Beyond its propaganda func-

By the late 1940s the evening courses at the New School had become an integral feature of the cultural life of many New Yorkers. *(Courtesy of the New School for Social Research)*

Top: Max Lerner's lectures on politics in the early 1950s regularly filled the New School auditorium to overflowing. *(Kosti Ruohomaa, Black Star; courtesy of the New School for Social Research)*

Above: Horace Kallen's courses in philosophy, psychology, and esthetics remained a mainstay of the adult education program until his retirement in the early 1960s. *(Kosti Ruohomaa, Black Star; courtesy of the New School for Social Research)*

Right: Chaim Gross at work with a sculpture student in the early 1950s. *(Peter Moore, courtesy of the New School for Social Research)*

The 1947 opening of *Lysistrata* at the President Theatre in the theatre district represented a high point in Piscator's tenure in New York. Shortly after, President Hovde notified Piscator that the New School would terminate its sponsorship of the Dramatic Workshop. *(A.J. Balcomb, courtesy of the Erwin Piscator Papers, Morris Library, Southern Illinois University at Carbondale)*

Scene from Robert Penn Warren's 1948 adaptation of his novel *All the King's Men* for production by Piscator. Warren joined the board of directors of the Dramatic Workshop after its disassociation from the New School. *(Courtesy of the Erwin Piscator Papers, Morris Library, Southern Illinois University at Carbondale)*

In 1944 the twenty-fifth celebration of the founding of the New School brought together the surviving founders. *From left to right:* Horace Kallen, Alice Belknap Hawkes, Alvin Johnson, Agnes Leach, Florence Corliss Lamont, Frances Hand, and Wesley Mitchell. *(Fred Stein, Black Star; courtesy of the New School for Social Research)*

In 1949 Alvin Johnson is honored with some of the "women of the New School" to whom he often had turned to save the school in its moments of financial distress. *From left to right:* philanthropist Edith Rosenwald Stern, Alvin Johnson, advisory board member Eleanor Roosevelt, and chair of the New School Associates, Edith Wise Sommerich. *(J. Griffith Davis; courtesy of the New School for Social Research)*

Hans Staudinger and Adolph Lowe, lifelong friends and colleagues, were key figures in the prominence of the Graduate Faculty in the 1950s. *(Fred Stein, Black Star; courtesy of the New School for Social Research)*

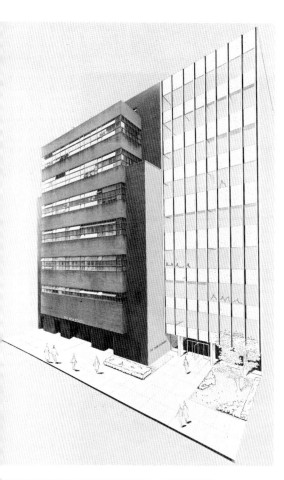

Left: Architectural drawing of the 1956 Kaplan addition to 66 West Twelfth Street. *(Architectural drawing by Mayer and Whittlesey; courtesy of the New School for Social Research)*

Below: Together with the List Building that adjoined it from Eleventh Street, the new addition formed a courtyard campus. *(Peter Moore, courtesy of the New School for Social Research)*

In the late 1950s Thomas Hart Benton returned to the New School to restore his murals, which were sold in the mid-1980s. *(Courtesy of the New School for Social Research)*

Hannah Arendt presiding over her graduate seminar in spring 1968. At Arendt's immediate left is Jerome Kohn, currently director of the Graduate Faculty Master of Arts in Liberal Studies Program. *(Peter Moore, courtesy of the New School for Social Research)*

1968 Student strike. Police guard the former Lane Department Store building on the corner of Fifth Avenue and Fourteenth Street, which had been renovated to house the Graduate Faculty. (Benedict J. Fernandez, courtesy of the New School for Social Research)

tion, agitprop allowed Piscator to apply expressionist ideas to dramatic productions. He dispensed with elaborate scripts, replaced discrete acts with a sequence of scenes, encouraged actors to converse directly with the audience, reduced scenery to suggestive symbols, and used a narrator to keep the audience informed of the larger political significance of the sketches. Piscator's agitprop provided German dramatists with a number of new techniques. Dramatists were no longer tied to the picture-frame stage—to any stage, for that matter—or to elaborate naturalistic staging, or to the conventional relationship between actors and audiences. His agitprop plays became stock items in the German Communist Party's propaganda program, and in the United States inspired the Federal Theatre's "Living Newspaper." But Piscator himself soon found the narrow propaganda of agitprop artistically limiting.[12]

Coincidentally, in 1924 the party decided to participate in the German elections. For this, it needed propaganda devices that appealed to a wider public. It commissioned Piscator to direct a series of propaganda revues similar to the popular Berlin cabaret sketches that the dadaists had performed. Piscator produced two revues, *The Red Revue* (1924) and *Despite All* (1925), which played to packed houses. Drawing on his agitprop experience, Piscator transformed the largely frivolous and ribald cabaret performances into serious and entertaining political theatre. Each revue lasted approximately two hours and included about a dozen different acts. Piscator tied together newsreels, dramatic episodes, music, dance, and striptease acts with a running dialogue between two narrators. Each performance culminated in a "Parade of the Proletariat," in which the entire cast led the audience in a rousing rendition of the *International.* Although the revues proved highly successful, attracting large audiences and critical acclaim, they did not fully satisfy Piscator's desire for serious drama. In 1924, when Piscator received an offer from the Volksbuhn, a major Berlin theatre organization, he accepted it eagerly. Invited initially to substitute for another director, in 1925 Piscator obtained a regular position at the Volksbuhn.[13]

The Volksbuhn Theatre depended on a popular membership of about 140,000. Its subscribers attended quality theatre and paid only modest prices. Its organizers envisioned the theatre serving two different functions: to bring high art to the masses and to provide a socially committed theatre. Piscator saw his appointment as an opportunity to present serious new drama to a wider audience. As he later wrote, "In its most fruitful periods the theatre was deeply involved with the community ... today the fate of the theatre ... must align itself with the needs and requirements and tribulations of the masses.''[14] Through the Volksbuhn he finally reached an audience which extended well beyond the Communist Party, and at the same time he gained access to one of the most technically sophisticated theatre houses in Germany. Piscator made good use of his opportunity.

Between 1925 and 1927 Piscator directed six plays for the Volksbuhn. He experimented with the theatre's revolving stages, introduced documentary films, often using several projectors at once, and employed political cartoons by radical artist George Grosz. He rewrote scripts and adapted classics to conform to his own political tastes, frequently eliminating extensive dialogue, using symbolic acting instead. Establishing himself as Berlin's most exciting and innovative director, his plays became political events in themselves, as he urged his audiences to carry the revolution to the streets.

Piscator's overt politicization of the stage proved too much for the Volksbuhn's largely conventional board of governors. They dismissed him in early 1927.[15] Piscator's dismissal paralleled a growing political conservatism throughout Germany; the free-wheeling days of Weimar were coming to a close. Undaunted, he turned adversity into opportunity. In late 1926 Ludwig Katzenellenborgen, a wealthy Berlin brewer, had offered him 400,000 marks to set up a theatre company and had even suggested the possibility of constructing a theatre building according to Piscator's specifications. Piscator leased the Nollendorplatz Theatre which, with characteristic aplomb, he renamed the Piscatorbuhn. At the same time he commissioned Bauhaus architect Walter Gropius to design a "total theatre" to accommodate the equipment for Piscator's elaborate technical effects. He also organized a drama collective, the Studio, which was associated with the Piscatorbuhn, to train actors and playwrights in his "objective" methods. Piscator's close friend Felix Gassbarra headed the Studio; among its members were such radical artists as Brecht, Walter Mehring, Hans Eisler, Erich Muhsam, and Franz Jung.

At the Piscatorbuhn, Piscator directed and produced more than a dozen plays, most notably Ernst Toller's *Hoppla, We Live;* Brecht's *In the Thicket of the State;* and an adaptation of Jaroslav Hašek's *Adventures of the Good Soldier Schweik.* Piscator continued to stage politically provocative drama and also to experiment with such special effects as simultaneous stages, puppets, agitprop choruses, narrators, and newsreel documentary. He encouraged audience involvement and occasionally enlivened his productions with specially commissioned musical compositions by Hans Eisler and Kurt Weill. Technically and dramatically, Piscator's adaptation of *Good Soldier Schweik* was by all accounts his finest production. In *Schweik* he effectively placed an appealing character, played by the popular actor Max Pallenberg, with a setting that included a treadmill, Grosz cartoons, puppets, music, film, and elaborate lighting.

Despite the success of some of his productions Piscator ran into financial and political troubles. From 1929 to 1931, of all the plays he managed to stage only one—Carl Crede's *Paragraph 218*, a satire of the German law outlawing abortion—proved financially successful. Moreover, after the emergence of National Socialism as a potent force in German politics in 1929, Piscator could no longer expect authorities to stop with mere disapproval of his work. In 1931, anticipating the worse, he accepted an invitation to work in the Soviet Union, the only nation likely to welcome his Marxist theatre. His departure brought to a close an extraordinarily creative period of his career. Perhaps recognizing that he had achieved a distinctive new form of dramatic art, Piscator published *The Political Theatre*, a crystallization of his ideas.[16]

Piscator insisted that drama must come to terms with serious human concerns. It should reject the theatre of personal emotions and melodrama and instead assume its proper social and didactic responsibilities. Piscator asserted that in its role as a moral institution the theatre should confront audiences with the political and social "reality" of their times. He wanted dramatists to place events and personalities in historical context and to interpret their political significance. Contemporary drama, obsessed with personality and personal relations, was not only frivolous and superficial, it distracted audiences from the political and historical forces determining individual choices. He asked dramatists to relate the personal and episodic events of daily existence to the more fundamental realities of class and social conflict. Piscator's statement that art is good only "when it comes directly to grips with life, when it is created out of the raw contrasts from which life is formed," echoed a long-standing tradition of German drama.[17]

As a Marxist, Piscator believed that a true understanding of the "forces of history" had enabled him to cut through the "illusions" of immediate experience and grapple with fundamental social and economic truth. "The theatre was no longer trying to appeal to the audiences' emotions alone," he wrote, "was no longer speculating on their emotional responsiveness—it consciously appealed to their intellect. No longer mere elan, enthusiasm, rapture, but enlightenment, knowledge and clarity were to be put across."[18] Still, Piscator was frequently less interested in provoking his audience to critical thought than in committing them to "historical facts" as he presented them. Confident in his vision, he sought to create the dramatic forms that would enable him to communicate those facts to his audiences.

Piscator has been unfavorably contrasted to Brecht, whose "epic drama" represented a new dramatic form. Piscator believed that such remarks were unfair. He considered mechanical devices necessary to the creation of a drama that dealt with the historical and political context of life, that expressed the *weltanschauung* of its age so that audiences would no longer be immobilized by the cacophony and seeming chaos of modern life.[19] Actors and dialogue alone could not bring the larger, transpersonal world into the theatre without becoming purely symbolic and abstract. Such reification drained drama of its vitality. Good drama depended on the ability of the audience to identify with the specifics of the play and the personalities of the actors. To make it relevant, Piscator introduced context into drama without destroying the texture that made it entertaining and believable.

Piscator succeeded in creating a larger-than-life drama through imaginative and undisguised use of narrators and special effects. Among his most successful efforts in this regard were the narrators in the Red Revues, who related the various acts of the revue to one another and created a coherent and unified performance; the background newsreels in *Rasputin,* which juxtaposed the carnage of World War I with the Czar's on-stage detachment from the war; and the treadmill in *Schweik,* which carried the personable and bewildered Schweik relentlessly to his historically determined fate. Piscator not only used films and machinery to present different but related events simultaneously; he also used them as symbols for the twentieth century itself. His unabashed use of technical effects in the theatre forced audiences to confront the mechanical reality of their own society and its implications.[20]

Early critics of Piscator also charged that, whatever the political or historical merits of epic drama, it was bad theatre. It failed to hold audiences' attention and, above all, it did not entertain. Only the most politically committed or witless, they charged, would be attracted to epic drama. Piscator responded to such criticism with his notion of total theatre which required wholly new theatres and effects. The building that Gropius designed for him in 1927, but which was never constructed, employed the latest theatrical technology, including film projectors, revolving stages, and sophisticated lighting and sound systems. Piscator's goal was to surround his audience with the production itself, monopolizing their attention. He instructed Gropius to arrange the seating so that the audience could not distance themselves from the stage or from other members of the audience. Gropius accomplished this by placing sound speakers throughout the auditorium, making all of the walls and even the ceiling usable as projection screens, and constructing multiple stages, including one that could be moved to the center of the auditorium.[21]

Together, these features deemphasized the importance of center stage. Action occurred anywhere in the theatre. Piscator frequently placed actors among the audience; these actors addressed remarks to the actors on stage, who in turn answered the "voices from the audience." Gropius arranged the seating so that everyone in the theatre looked at other members of the audience as well as at the action on stage. These visual relationships merged the audience into a mass, making individual detachment difficult. Piscator intended these "total effects" to integrate the audience by denying them the spatial and social distance necessary to resist theatrical effects.

Piscator did not stop here. His concepts of epic drama and total theatre required a drastic change in the training of actors, directors, and playwrights in what Piscator called the "objective style." To provide this training Piscator organized the Studio in 1927. Epic drama required actors who could compete with machinery, special effects, simultaneous action, and plays which did not depend on personality development or elaborate dialogue. Piscator asked for an "unsentimental, impersonal, mathematical style of action which harmonized with the machinery."[22] The Studio, established to teach this so-called objective style, trained actors in gymnastics and dance so that through ritualized movements they could express the less conscious forces of society and history. The plays themselves deemphasized psychological development and relied on special effects, symbolic acting, and narrators to sustain dramatic movement and maintain interest.

Piscator's total theatre, or epic drama, was openly anti-intellectual and anti-individualistic. He wished to provoke his audience into political action, not philosophical contemplation. His political commitments, combined with the volatile climate of Weimar Germany, obscured for him what in retrospect appears overly manipulative. Weimar affected Piscator in much the same manner that he wanted his total theatre to affect audiences. Brecht later recalled that Piscator's were "the most vitally alive productions in the lively theatrical centre of Berlin, which between revolution, inflation, stabilization and collapse ... exactly mirrored their environment in cool, controlled and passionately shaped pictures ... his plays and productions of the time, though frequently problematic in hindsight, correspond to the era and its people. They set us on the stage and formulated our emotions and opinions ... their significance: substantiation and suppression, challenge and critical examination."[23]

Piscator's most creative period ended in 1931. Financial problems and the rapidly deteriorating political situation in Germany convinced Piscator in 1931 that he must leave. The International Worker's Aid (IAH), a communist organization established in 1921 to support in-

tellectuals and artists in the West, invited Piscator to Moscow to produce several films. He spent his first three years making *The Revolt of
the Fishermen,* based on a novella by Anna Seghers. By the time he had
completed the film the political climate in Russia had changed, and the
film was poorly received by party officials. Frustrated in these efforts
he turned his energies toward the establishment of a professional
theatre in Engels, a town in the German-speaking Volga Republic.
Piscator envisioned a theatre comparable to the German state theatres
comprised of German refugees such as himself, Brecht, Eisler, and
Friedrich Wolff, and Theodor Plivier. But, like everything that he tried
in Russia, the Volga project bogged down. Cosmopolitan German
refugees, their political radicalism notwithstanding, found the provincial backwardness of Engels singularly unattractive; the Volga Germans reciprocated by treating the German-speaking outsiders with
hostility and resentment; and Soviet authorities were themselves
preoccupied with Stalin's by now sweeping purges.[24]

Soon after, Piscator was made director of the Soviet-sponsored International Association of Revolutionary Theaters (MORT), for which
he received an office with a staff of fifteen. Under his direction, MORT
became a clearinghouse for all avant-garde and antifascist theatre in
Russia. As president of MORT Piscator first met Americans Harold
Clurman, Cheryl Crawford, Stella Adler, and Lee Strasberg of the
radical Group Theatre, who apart from their political interests had
come to the Soviet Union to see firsthand the famed "method acting"
of Constantine Stanislavski. In July 1936 Piscator left Russia, ostensibly to attend the "united front" Reassemblement Universel de la
Paix in Belgium. In truth, he had already decided not to return to the
Soviet Union. By 1936 the ominous intent of the proponents of
"socialist realism" to root out all avant-garde art had become clear.
Piscator's own work had been attacked as "formalistic" and "vulgarly
sociological." More serious, rumors abounded of the suppression and
even execution of those who had failed to conform to the new Stalinist
guidelines. Ironically, the Soviet Union had become more dangerous for
German communists than Nazi Germany.

For the next two years Piscator lived in Paris, working on several
different projects. His only success during these years was his mar-
riage to Maria Ley, a wealthy widow who had danced professionally for
the great German dramatist Max Reinhardt. For the rest of his life,
Piscator received Ley's unfailing support, both personal and financial,
as he desperately tried to reestablish himself as a dramatist. Finally, in
late 1938, the Piscators secured a temporary visa and sailed to New
York. Their choice proved doubly fortunate: they left Europe only

months before the outbreak of war and in New York found a sanctuary where Piscator could rethink his ideas and revive his career as a dramatist.

Unlike the theatre community of Berlin in the 1920s, the theatrical establishment in New York was largely apolitical. Here Piscator's political views were a decided liability. Facing as great a challenge as he had encountered since his years as a young director in Berlin, Piscator was indeed obliged to start over again, although not quite from scratch. At the New School and among members of the Group Theatre, whom he had first met in Moscow, he was highly regarded. And, however demoralizing the previous decade, Piscator had confronted the implications of his own radicalism. In New York, Piscator reexamined his ideas in an institutional and cultural context quite different from Weimar Germany. On the surface his twelve-year stay in New York seemed a lull in his career. This is true only with regard to his public reputation. At the New School, as director of the Dramatic Workshop, Piscator learned as much as he taught. His tenure at the New School prepared him for a postwar resurgence that drew as much from his work during the 1940s as from his more radical period in Weimar.

The Dramatic Workshop was organized in 1939 and offered its first courses in the spring of 1940. Ostensibly a two-year drama school that advertised itself as a "link between academic education and a professional" career, the Dramatic Workshop was in fact the umbrella organization for all of Piscator's multifarious enterprises while in New York. Besides the academic program, the Dramatic Workshop sponsored three semiprofessional, off-Broadway theatres, a children's theatre run by Maria Ley, several summer theatres, drama critic John Gassner's March of Drama lecture-performance series, radio and film workshops, and a subscription repertory theatre. It also instigated numerous civic and philanthropic activities, such as the 1943 "Rally of Hope" at Madison Square Garden on behalf of Jewish war orphans and several united front, antifascist assemblies.[25]

Because Piscator's work in New York lacked the revolutionary rhetoric and elaborate technical effects of his Weimar years, some have underestimated this phase of his career. Yet, measured by the number and range of productions, his New York work was prodigious. The most complete account of Piscator's productions lists about 450 New York productions compared with a lifetime total of only 600. That is, nearly 75 percent of his productions occurred in New York between 1939 and 1951. Granted, many of these New York credits represent student productions and other presentations of the Dramatic Workshop which Piscator did not himself direct. And the list itself was compiled largely

from the Piscator material at Southern Illinois University, which
documents almost exclusively his New York years. Nevertheless, this
era seems to have been the busiest and most varied in his life.[26]

Alvin Johnson allowed Piscator to run the Dramatic Workshop
pretty much as he saw fit, as long as it lived within its means and
neither interfered with other activities at the New School nor embarrassed it. Johnson explained to Piscator in 1941 that he was free to
teach his ideas of epic drama and put on modest theatrical productions,
but he had to tone down, if not eliminate entirely, his specifically Marxist rhetoric. He could advocate a "universal theatre," insist on the
moral responsibilities of dramatists, and emphasize the economic and
social context of his epic productions. But there was to be no talk of a
"revolutionary" or "proletarian" theatre or even explicit criticism of
"capitalism" or "bourgeois democracy." Moreover, the New School's
own economic constraints severely limited Piscator's theatrical
possibilities.[27]

While the Dramatic Workshop was much more than a school, it was
less than a drama company. And, though it resembled in many ways his
earlier Studio in its training functions, the Dramatic Workshop's lack
of full autonomy limited Piscator's creative freedom. Indeed,
throughout his stay in New York, Piscator played down his radical past
and instead identified himself with the broad spectrum of the Left.
Shorn of their raw communist rhetoric, Piscator's productions remained "political" only in the same "concerned" sense that the New
School was itself political. As Johnson instructed Piscator in a letter:
"There is not in the potential of America today a revolutionary earthquake. There are too many tremors some of them frightening. But our
crust is too fluid and too adjustible [sic] for the great dramatic over-
turn." Johnson continued, "The New School . . . recognizes that it lives
in the world of tremors, not overwhelming earthquakes. It means to
take part in the rise of the common man, by tremors, because there will
be nothing else in America. It recognizes this obstruction and that this
obstruction must be cut away; that summed up through generations
this means a revolution. It has no sympathy with the starry eyed nin-
compoops who hope to inaugurate in America processes that were vital
in tsarist Russia or in Kaiserlich or post-Kaiserlich Germany. A big
earthquake is a wonderful generator of drama." Asked Johnson, "Can
you generate drama on tremors? This is your problem, my dear
Piscator."[28]

Without "earthquakes," Piscator's drama lost much of its danger
and excitement. Still, the tremorous nature of American society forced
him to see himself as part of a larger leftist constituency and to trans-

cend his sectarian past. In a 1942 magazine article, "The Theater for the Future," Piscator associated his theatre with the "progressive forces" of his time. He wrote, "The Epic Theater demonstrates life. It pretends to be theater but in the highest sense is the representation of ideas, rather than private relationships. The Epic Theater aims to supplement the emotional appeal of its new style with intellectual content, to particularize the symbolic, and also restore a simple, classic beauty which the Expressionists mistakenly cast aside as petty when they reacted from the old style of theater. . . . In the future theater will no longer try to catch the audience on the initial level of realistic presentation." Piscator wrote, "Instead it will assume a poetic force for mass audiences, which hitherto it has exercised mainly for the happy few. . . . The task of the future theater in this country will be to place the technical resources of modern invention at the service of this great unconscious, poetic mass-mind." Piscator concluded, "It will be housed in appropriately designed buildings, and will be supported by a critical and earnest public. It will be the child of reason, keeping its own festal beauty—a rounded world with its terrors and joys, and with a whole company of merry and sorrowful fools from Aeschylus to our own time. . . . It will attain a new maturity, a synthesis of the arts, and will be an incomparable instrument for the expression of all human experience and thought."[29] Such sentiment can be seen as a cynical effort on Piscator's part to carry out party directions and represent himself as part of the antifascist and democratic Left. But after leaving Russia Piscator seems to have let his party membership lapse, and his refusal after 1947 to return to East Germany despite generous government offers confirms the sincerity of his remarks. Perhaps most important, his subsequent work in the United States and Germany conformed to these universalist ideals.

At the New School Piscator made few close friends. Students and colleagues alike found "the director" difficult to work with, and few could accept uncritically all of his ideas on the theatre. In spite of this, he attracted an extraordinarily talented and ambitious group of students to his program and hired an extremely capable staff to teach them.[30] His faculty was recruited from among the existing teachers at the New School (Sidney Kaufman and Paul Zucker), members of the Group Theatre (Theresa Helburn, Harold Clurman, Eleanor Fitzgerald, John Gassner, Stella Adler, and Lee Strasberg), and old Weimar associates (Hans Eisler, Mordecai Goralik, Erich Leinsdorf, and Carl Zuckermayer). Piscator himself oversaw the directing seminar, which served as the core of the curriculum. Stella Adler, and later Lee Strasberg, handled the acting program; Maria Ley headed dancing and gymnastics. Hans Eisler directed stage music and composition. Sidney Kaufman managed radio and film, and Theresa Helburn coordinated playwriting.

Students were required to take a prescribed program. The first term included courses in theatre research, acting, voice and speech, dance, the history of dramatic styles, and rehearsal. In the second term students concentrated on their chosen areas of specialization and were additionally encouraged to enroll in evening academic courses at the New School. In the second year students participated in the "Laboratory," a general seminar made up of faculty and second-year students. The members of the seminar discussed specific problems and ideas and planned school productions. Despite the heavy academic load, students spent the majority of their time working in actual productions. Piscator insisted that students could not become dramatists without writing, producing, directing, and performing their own plays. Moreover, through these student productions the Dramatic Workshop became more than a school. It became an experimental theatre.[31]

Not satisfied with student productions alone, Piscator organized the Studio Theatre and later the President and Rooftop theatres, for plays in which he used both students and professional actors. Piscator hoped that these productions would provide him access to Broadway and the opportunity to reestablish himself as a major dramatist. Although some tension existed between Piscator's own ambitions and the Dramatic Workshop's function as a school, for the most part his ambitions were shared, not only by Alvin Johnson, but by the students themselves. They too wanted to reach the legitimate theatre, and many enrolled in the Dramatic Workshop because it had advertised itself as a link between the amateur and professional stage. And indeed a surprising number of Dramatic Workshop students later distinguished themselves in the theatre. The most prominent were playwrights Tennessee Williams and Philip Yordan and actors Marlon Brando, Walter Matthau, Rod Steiger, Shelley Winters, Tony Curtis, Harry Belafonte, Elaine Stritch, Ben Gazzara, and Michael Conrad. Nearly all of them considered themselves "Piscator students," just as faculty colleagues acknowledged the influence that Piscator had on their work.[32]

Although Piscator's energy and vision sustained the Dramatic Workshop, his notion of epic drama did not become an orthodoxy for faculty and students. Stella Adler and Lee Strasberg were influenced by Piscator's theory of objective acting only in the most general way. In their workshops they taught Stanislavski's method acting, which stressed a form of psychological preparation that allowed actors to "become" the characters they were playing. It is hard to imagine a method more at odds with Piscator's objective acting, and yet neither

Adler nor Strasberg noted any tension between themselves and Piscator.[33] Similarly, John Gassner and Theresa Helburn never felt any obligation to indoctrinate their students with the ideas of epic theatre. Rather, drawing on their own work with the Group Theatre, they argued in favor of an American dramatic idiom informed by European ideas but which addressed American social issues.[34] Even Maria Ley's ideas on dance, which resembled Piscator's objective method, owed almost nothing to Piscator. She was instead a disciple of the Swiss dance theorist Emile Dalcroz who had insisted that dance movements embody the precision of mathematics. Paul Boepple had introduced the Dalcroz method at the New School in the early 1930s. Ley took over these courses when they were incorporated into the Dramatic Workshop as she continued the Dalcroz tradition at the New School.[35]

In short, the Dramatic Workshop embraced a variety of modern approaches which shared a disenchantment with traditional dramatic forms as well as with the commercialized drama epitomized by Broadway. Instead of an orthodoxy, they each advocated a dramatic form that took itself seriously as art and which embraced a "realism" that confronted audiences with contemporary life, a theatre of provocation and commitment, not diversion and escapism. "Realism and contemporary intent alone can give us a living theatre," insisted Gassner.[36] Broadly leftist in politics and modernist in expression, the Dramatic Workshop offered students far more than epic drama and objective acting. Yet in several respects the Dramatic Workshop adhered to Piscator's notion of the theatre. It taught students to think in terms of the "total" production as it required them to study all facets of the theatre as well as philosophy, history, and sociology. It sought to create a "people's theatre" that reached beyond a small circle of theatrical devotees. Its pluralistic modernism and its humane commitment coincided with the goals that the New School had affirmed since its establishment in 1918.

Piscator organized three separate theatres in New York: the Studio Theatre, located in the New School's Twelfth Street building (1940-1944); the President Theatre on Forty-eighth Street in the theatre district (1945-1951); and the Rooftop Theatre on Houston Street in the Lower East Side (1947-1950). The Studio Theatre, located in the New School's auditorium, sponsored various Dramatic Workshop productions during the early 1940s. Designed by Joseph Urban in the style of the Viennese Secession, the New School auditorium captured the expressionist mood of Piscator's productions. It nevertheless served poorly as a theatre, and was particularly ill equipped to accommodate Piscator's elaborate technical effects. In spite of this, Piscator was ambitious to make the Studio Theatre more than a

theatrical laboratory for avant-garde plays and new dramatic techniques. He saw it as a "doorway to Broadway," in which professional
actors and writers could present truly professional performances.
Piscator promoted each major Studio Theatre production and invited
the New York drama critics to judge the plays by professional standards.[37]

Despite an uneven record, the Studio Theatre fulfilled many of its
stated aims. It performed the first professional productions of two
unknown American playwrights, Philip Yordan and Frank Gabrielson.
Through adaptations by Ferdinand Bruckner and Klaburn, it introduced some of the more interesting developments of the contemporary
European stage. And finally, Piscator's own epic productions offered
New York audiences a clear alternative to Broadway. Whatever their
technical and artistic shortcomings, the productions at the Studio
represented serious and experimental drama. After the demise of the
Group Theatre and the Federal Theatre project in the late thirties, the
Studio Theatre stood virtually alone in its offering of critical, contemporary drama.[38]

In 1942, with the production of Daniel James's *Winter Soldiers*, the
Studio Theatre's professional dramatic productions came to an end,
ironically a victim of its own success. In 1940 the Dramatic Workshop
had negotiated an agreement with the theatrical unions, which allowed
union members to accept roles in Studio productions without pay with
the understanding that these performances would remain experimental
and would not compete with Broadway shows. After *Winter Soldiers*,
Actors Equity terminated the agreement, claiming that the Studio
Theatre had become a "professional" theatre and had thereby violated
the earlier understanding. After protracted negotiations and Piscator's
failure to raise the $20,000 subsidy necessary to continue Studio pro-
ductions at union scale, the Studio Theatre ended its dramatic productions except for a special performance of Bruckner's adaptation of
Lessing's *Nathan the Wise* in 1944.[39] Deeply disappointed, Piscator
nonetheless continued the work of the Dramatic Workshop and kept
alive the idea of the Studio Theatre by sponsoring a number of theatre-
related activities. These included a panel discussion on Brecht's drama,
John Gassner's lecture series on "The Comedy of Social Criticism," a
United Front symposium in which Brecht participated entitled "Free
World Unity Through Creative Art," and an international dance
festival organized by Maria Ley. As it turned out, union opposition was
only the beginning of Piscator's problems.

From the inception of the Dramatic Workshop, other segments of
the New School had resented its presence. Drama classes competed
with other courses for classroom space. The Studio Theatre's rehear-

sals and productions monopolized the auditorium. Many believed that a professional drama school had no place in an institution devoted to adult education. Drama students were young, boisterous, and, to some, rude. Moreover, in a time of financial stringency, many believed that the Dramatic Workshop drained resources needed for other activities. Finally, there is some evidence that the more conservative German social democrats on the Graduate Faculty, most notably Hans Simons, sought to use the issue of fire regulations to rid the New School of what they considered a political undesirable.[40]

Alvin Johnson, with Clara Mayer's support, defused the situation. In 1944, in response to mounting criticism, Johnson authorized a formal evaluation of the Dramatic Workship and its relationship to the New School. The report concluded that the Dramatic Workship attracted students to the New School as a whole and that its productions provided the school a great deal of favorable, free publicity.[41] Even its financial drain on the New School was nominal; its annual deficit had dropped from around $10,000 in 1941 to only $1,400 in 1944. In contrast, the entire New School ran a deficit of about $180,000 in 1944, of which nearly 60 percent was attributable to the Graduate Faculty. At the same time enrollments at the Dramatic Workshop had increased from eight full-time students to over sixty, even as the number of students attending its evening lecture courses had grown from 50 to nearly 400. This growth had occurred at a time when enrollments in the remainder of the New School had declined.[42] The report argued that the Dramatic Workshop's program was not an undue burden on the New School's resources, and that in fact its purpose was congruent with the New School's educational mission. The Dramatic Workshop complemented the New School's fine arts program and attracted adult students to the school's courses; in addition, dramatic productions enlivened the creative life of the school.

Still, Johnson and Mayer realized that as long as the Dramatic Workshop shared the Twelfth Street facilities of the New School, the tension between it and the remainder of the New School was likely to increase. They, like Piscator, believed that the Dramatic Workshop should expand both as a dramatic school and as a producer of serious drama. After postponing any final decision for one year, they solved the problem by acquiring the small but fully equipped President Theatre on Forty-eighth Street in the theatre district. At this new facility, Piscator could conduct the Dramatic Workshop out of sight of the remainder of the New School. But his critics had served him a warning. If in the future the Dramatic Workshop appeared financially unsound, the New School would likely end its sponsorship.[43]

The move uptown in 1945 coincided with other major changes in the Dramatic Workshop. First of all, Alvin Johnson, Piscator's friend and benefactor, retired as active director of the New School and Bryn Hovde replaced him as president of the New School. Second, with the end of the war in sight, Congress passed the GI Bill, which among other things offered war veterans generous educational benefits.[44] In 1946 the Dramatic Workshop for the first time found itself in the enviable position of being flooded with tuition-paying students, momentarily making it one of the largest dramatic schools in the country. To take advantage of the opportunity, the Dramatic Workshop had to conform to the Veterans Administration's accreditation requirements. Piscator recruited Paul Ransom, a recent graduate of the Yale Drama School, as director of academic activities. Ransom hired new staff, including speech instructor Minnie Rutkoff, enlarged the curriculum, and set up attendance and grading guidelines consistent with the GI Bill. Simultaneously, the Dramatic Workshop, under the auspices of the New School's bachelor of arts program, offered a bachelor of drama degree for students with two years of college credit who completed their undergraduate education at the Dramatic Workshop and the New School.[45]

At first, the GI Bill seemed the answer to all of Piscator's problems. It made the Dramatic Workshop economically independent, and therefore less vulnerable to critics at the New School. The flood of applications from ex-GIs allowed Piscator to be selective in admissions, since he now had a large pool of students whose scholarships were already funded. These "GI scholarships" also provided Piscator leverage to enforce course and attendance requirements and standards of behavior, a task that had been difficult for him when the Dramatic Workshop needed tuition-paying students more than they needed the Dramatic Workshop. As the most active drama school in New York, the Dramatic Workshop could legitimately claim that it served as a bridge to Broadway. Its location in the theatre district heightened this image for prospective students, as did the enormous success of its alumni Marlon Brando and Tennessee Williams in the 1947–48 production of *A Streetcar Named Desire*. The GI Bill also enabled Piscator to hire administrators to handle academic and student-related activities. Free from administrative responsibilities, Piscator devoted his time to teaching and directing student productions. At the same time he established a preferred relationship with Hovde, who adopted the Dramatic Workshop as his special project. Exhilarated by the turn of events, Piscator sponsored summer theatres in Southold and Great Neck, New York, and Charleston, South Carolina, and commissioned original plays for the President Theatre. It seemed that, after all, he might fulfill his dream of becoming a major figure of the New York stage.[46]

The President Theatre had to operate under the same constraints that the theatrical unions had imposed on the Studio Theatre. This meant that Piscator's productions had to be staffed entirely by union personnel, including ticket sellers, musicians, and stage hands—at an estimated cost of $20,000 to $30,000 per production—or they had to be all-student productions, without advertisements or ticket sales at a box office. With the increase in the number and quality of students, this did not prove an undue handicap. Piscator simply emphasized the teaching function of his productions and enrolled his subscription audience as adult education students. This had the unforeseen advantage of creating an audience that attended a wide range of Dramatic Workshop activities, including Gassner's March of Drama lecture-productions, Ley's dance performances, and various symposia and lectures on modern drama, as well as four or five full-scale plays per year. Piscator offered his audiences at the President Theatre an array of postwar drama unparalleled in New York. His productions included an adaptation of Jean-Paul Sartre's *The Flies,* Armand Salacrou's *Nights of Wrath,* Robert Penn Warren's own adaptation specifically for the Dramatic Workshop of *All the King's Men,* Wolfgang Borchert's *Outside the Door,* and John Matthews's *Scapegoat,* an adaptation of Kafka's *Trial.* Although the small President Theatre, with seating for only 300, limited Piscator's technical efforts, its intimate size was ideally suited for audiences who had come to discuss as well as view the various Dramatic Workshop productions.[47]

Encouraged by the success of the Dramatic Workshop and the President Theatre, in 1947 Piscator leased the Rooftop Theatre on Houston Street and Second Avenue. The Rooftop Theatre was situated atop the Yiddish National Theatre in what had once been Minsky's Burlesque House. The 800-seat theatre provided space for larger student productions and offered Piscator the opportunity to establish a "people's" theatre in New York. At the Rooftop Theatre the Dramatic Workshop offered subscribers a repertory of almost thirty plays that had earlier been performed at the President. As at the President, these were exclusively student productions and a large part of the repertory was taken directly from Gassner's popular March of Drama series, which presented a history of drama through lectures followed by illustrative plays. These plays included works by Aristophanes, Shakespeare, Molière, Goethe, Strindberg, Hauptmann, Ibsen, Chekhov, Costeau, Pirandello, Toller, Brecht, O'Neill, Hellman, Anderson, and Odets. The audience consisted of students from the Dramatic

Workshop and the New School Adult Education Division, school teachers, high school students, and union members.[48] Despite the success of the Rooftop and President productions and the enlarged enrollment of the Dramatic Workshop, Piscator once again found that his ambitions had outstripped his resources. This time, his critics were not to be denied.

The Dramatic Workshop's difficulties began in late 1946, when it was mentioned in a *New York Times* article on the lax administration of GI Bill benefits to drama schools.[49] Apparently a number of Dramatic Workshop students had complained to the *Times* reporter that their teachers often failed to meet classes, take attendance, and check class assignments; they also described the disorganized character of some classes and the school as a whole. These reports led Hovde to authorize an in-house investigation, which coincided with a drop in veteran applications.[50] With the number of veterans eligible for education benefits declining after 1947, the Dramatic Workshop found itself with a diminishing base of support at the very time that Piscator had expanded the school's activities and responsibilities.

These administrative and financial problems were compounded by a shift in the nation's political climate with the onset of the Cold War. Its long-standing association with political radicals made the New School the subject of several anticommunist inquiries. These came to a head in the summer of 1947, when the House Un-American Activities Committee subpoenaed German composer and former instructor at the New School Hans Eisler to testify.[51] Eisler readily admitted his past communist affiliations, but explained that he had allowed his party membership to expire in the 1930s and, in any event, had never engaged in any subversive activity.[52] Following his hearing Eisler voluntarily left the United States and returned to East Germany, later to be joined by Brecht.

At the time of Eisler's interrogation his brother Gerhard had been arrested on charges that he was head of a Soviet spy ring. When questioned by newspaper reporters, Johnson acknowledged that Hans Eisler had taught at the New School from 1936 to 1942 and had been associated with the Dramatic Workshop, but that he had taught music, not communism. Johnson denied that he or the New School had been aware of Eisler's communist affiliations and referred reporters to the statement in the New School's constitution that read, "No member can be a member of any political party or group which asserts the right to dictate in matters of science or scientific opinion." Privately, though, in a letter to Joseph Urban's widow, Johnson admitted that he had known of Eisler's past affiliations, but had seen no problem in his teaching at the New School as long as he did not use his classroom to indoctrinate students. Indeed, the New School had always prided itself on its un-compromising commitment to academic freedom. In a letter to the faculty and students earlier in the year, Johnson had ridiculed the cur-rent "red scare" as "anti-radical ghost dancing."[53]

In less than a year, however, as the era of the United Front ended and the Cold War accelerated, such libertarianism became inexpedient. Hovde and Johnson himself became outspoken critics of the Soviet Union and its American "fellow travelers." In a speech to Americans for Intellectual Freedom at Freedom House entitled "The Soviet Threat to Man's Artistic Freedom," Hovde placed the New School at the forefront of the postwar anticommunist movement.[54] Piscator found himself threatened not only by American anticommunism generally, but by the New School itself. The very people who in the past had shielded Piscator from his critics had themselves now enlisted in the anticommunist crusade. Like his close friends Eisler and Brecht, Piscator had no place to turn. The most frustrating aspect of his situa-tion was that everyone at the New School carefully avoided any men-tion of his communism. Instead, criticism was couched in terms of sloppy administration and financial irresponsibility.[55] It is little wonder that Piscator at this time chose to present an adaptation of Kafka's *The Trial*.

An examination of the sequence of events that led to the Dramatic Workshop's disassociation from the New School reveal that Piscator was justified in his claims that Hovde and the New School board never gave him a clear account of their intentions. In October 1946, Hovde in-formed Piscator that the board of trustees had "voted to continue the present relationship for another two years," or until June 30, 1949. In a private meeting with Piscator, Hovde apparently explained that this resolution was not intended as a threat by the board to terminate its relationship with the Dramatic Workshop. Rather, Piscator should see it as a vote of confidence that provided the New School the time to study the possibility of making the Dramatic Workshop a permanent part of the New School. If in 1949 such a relationship seemed inad-visable, Hovde promised to work out a plan for the orderly reorganiza-tion of the Dramatic Workshop as an independent institution.[56]

A year later, in December 1947, shortly after the Eisler incident, Henry Wendriner, who was director of finance for the Dramatic Workshop and apparently ignorant of any change of sentiment at the New School, echoed Hovde's encouraging assessment. In his annual report Wendriner informed Piscator that enrollments had rebounded, that the Dramatic Workshop had presented critically successful pro-ductions, and that the school had developed an effective administra-tion. Far from anticipating trouble, Wendriner optimistically looked foward, not to retrenchment and disassociation, but to expansion of the workshop's program and continuation of its relationship with the New School. According to Wendriner, the situation had never looked brighter.[57] Then, with no warning, came the board's decision in February 1948 to sever the Dramatic Workshop from the New School, effective June 1, 1948.

Stunned, Piscator protested to Hovde that the board, without consulting him, had reneged on its commitment to sponsor the Dramatic Workshop through June 1949. And, contrary to Hovde's explicit promise, it had made no provision for the orderly transition of the Dramatic Workshop to an independent status. Piscator reminded Hovde that as a consequence of the board's earlier assurances he had leased the theatres and instructional buildings through June 1949 and had offered several members of the faculty similar contractual extensions.[58] Apparently responding to the force of Piscator's arguments and their legal implications, Hovde backed off. In a compromise offer, Hovde agreed to continue to support the Dramatic Workshop through June 1949 and facilitate its transition to an independent school of drama.[59] Piscator in turn agreed to take immediate steps to set up a separate board, seek independent certification from the New York State Board of Regents, and secure funding to cover existing debts.[60]

The tie between the New School and the Dramatic Workshop officially broken, Piscator's relations with Hovde and Johnson improved dramatically. In a warm letter, Johnson wished Piscator well, complimented him on his accomplishments, and even agreed to serve on the new independent board, although Johnson insisted throughout that Piscator had brought his troubles on himself through financial mismanagement.[61] In February 1949, Piscator publicly announced the reorganization of the Dramatic Workshop as an independent institution. Besides Piscator and Johnson, the board included playwright Elmer Rice, Ben W. Huebsch of Viking Press, John Gassner, and Robert Penn Warren.[62] For almost three years the Dramatic Workshop carried on much as it had in the past. It could not, however, survive for long. Piscator failed to attract the financial support the school needed, and the New York Board of Regents rejected the Dramatic Workshop's application for certification. In addition, the United States Immigration Department refused Piscator's application for citizenship. In June 1950, Alvin Johnson resigned as president of the board, severing the New School's last tie to the Dramatic Workshop.[63]

Piscator persisted in his efforts until October 1951, when, fearing that Joseph McCarthy would summon him to appear before the Senate Un-American Activities Committee, he left New York for West Germany. Maria Ley remained behind in New York City, keeping the

Dramatic Workshop alive for another two years. For the next fifteen years Piscator led a revitalized West German theatre. By the 1960s he had become an inspiration for a remarkable generation of young German playwrights and writers, including Peter Weiss, Hinar Kipphardt, Rolf Hochhuth, Tancred Dorst, and Günter Grass. Piscator died in 1966 at the very time his work was finally receiving the critical recognition in the United States he had so long desired.[64]

From 1939 to 1951 Piscator presented to New York audiences a panorama of exciting drama. He had kept alive the idea of an experimental and politically committed theatre during the 1940s and had demonstrated the feasibility of vital off-Broadway productions. For a decade the Dramatic Workshop had been the most important source of contemporary European drama in the United States. Piscator confirmed for people like Marlon Brando, Lee Strasberg, Tennessee Williams, Stella Adler, and John Gassner that drama was a serious art with serious moral responsibilities. He imparted to them the best of the German dramatic tradition that he exemplified. Although it is difficult to document Piscator's influence on American drama, nearly all who worked with him attested to his importance. As for the New School itself, the presence of people like Erwin Piscator and Hans Eisler may well have kept the school from adopting the intolerant attitudes of the Cold War earlier than it did. During the 1940s the New School's affirmation of academic freedom was not an empty and meaningless slogan. It was a declaration of principle, a declaration that guided the actions and policies of the school. This of course changed in the late 1940s at the New School and elsewhere, but it remained a standard and precedent which the New School could return to in less troubled times.

10

A RETURN TO
SOCIAL THEORY
The Graduate Faculty,
1945–1960

STUDENTS ENROLLING AT THE NEW SCHOOL'S GRADUATE FACULTY in the years immediately following World War II found themselves in strange, if unexotic, quarters. The New School's modern building, constructed fifteen years earlier, had undergone what Alvin Johnson called "significant modifications." Temporary offices, makeshift classrooms, and cluttered corridors accommodated students, faculty, administrators, and programs. The sounds of telephones and typewriters rattled through the crowded, hive-like series of rooms and cubicles that now filled Joseph Urban's once spacious interiors. Each weekday evening several thousand New Yorkers poured in fresh from their daytime jobs at Macy's, Best's, or even Merrill Lynch. And as they rode one of the New School's three chronically lethargic elevators, they might have jostled and even exchanged words with a middle-aged man or woman distinguished by a foreign accent and a mannered civility.

"When I went to spend an evening with one of my professors at the Graduate Faculty—and mind you that didn't even occur during the first two or three years—I encountered not free flowing sociability, but an intense, formal, European intellectual and political agenda."[1] As Robert Heilbroner and students of the University in Exile recalled their graduate professors, they often used the word "intense." Whether in the crowded offices of Adolph Lowe, Alfred Schutz, or Kurt Riezler, or in the art-deco apartment buildings of Manhattan's West Side, American graduate students encountered and in some cases even came to know their European mentors. Meanwhile, they—the members of the Graduate Faculty and "their" administrators, the Hanses, Simons and Staudinger—struggled to educate a new generation of American graduate students in the subtleties of continental epistemology.

During these years, from 1945 to 1960, the Graduate Faculty emerged as the most vital component of the New School. Many of its "legendary" members had decided after the war to remain at the school, and their vigorous classroom personalities punctuated its intellectual life. No longer merely exiles or foreigners, Alfred Schutz, Adolph Lowe, Kurt Riezler, Albert Salomon, Frieda Wunderlich, Karl Mayer, Erich Hula, Hans Simons, and Arnold Brecht had become nationally recognized scholars. More than at any other time in its history, the New School in the 1950s was immersed in serious intellectual dialogue. The exile generation at the Graduate Faculty, then in their last decade of active teaching and scholarship, returned to the debate over the ideas of Max Weber that had informed their own graduate work. On West Twelfth Street in New York, these now elderly Europeans once more confronted the old debate between fact and value, science and politics, as a very new postwar world emerged around them. To their young American graduate students these discussions were fresh and provocative, particularly when contrasted to the increasingly technical and specialized preoccupations of most other American graduate schools. The presence of the emigré scholars kept alive a tradition of humanistic inquiry in which the pursuit of knowledge was a moral and political commitment as well as an intellectual odyssey. Their presence helped to fill the unique educational space which the New School had cut out for itself.

Alvin Johnson officially retired as president of the New School in 1945. Despite his retirement, however, he continued to effectively control the school. His successor, Bryn Hovde, resigned in 1949 after it had become clear that he could not work effectively with Clara Mayer, who had been dean of the Fine Arts and Adult Divisions since the early 1940s. The board appointed Hans Simons, dean of the School of Politics and one of the original faculty of the University in Exile, as the new president. Three years later the board elevated Hans Staudinger to the position of permanent dean of the Graduate Faculty. Simons, Staudinger, and Mayer worked with Johnson as they had over the last two to three decades, to oversee the growth and development of the Graduate Faculty in the critical decade of the 1950s.

At the same time that power was shifting in the New School administration, the faculty directed its own activities away from public policy research and back to classroom teaching and publication. They turned increasingly to theoretical and philosophical concerns rather than to the vicissitudes of contemporary life. Still, as the scholarly stature and output of the school increased, members of the faculty occasionally voiced concern over the new-found academic respectability and acceptability. They questioned the growth of centralized administrative authority at the school and lamented the passing of democratic self-governance. At the same time, they appreciated such amenities as group health insurance and regular sabbaticals which stability and institutionalization afforded. They worried that the national trend toward bureaucratizing education—from which their own school was not immune—would allow academic recognition to go to the merely industrious and conventional rather than to the creative scholar. And, as the faculty became more established and secure, the intimacy and interdependence bred of marginality and difference waned and their ranks began to break. Leo Strauss and Hans Speier accepted offers elsewhere, Strauss at Chicago and Speier with the Rand Corporation. Others—Adolph Lowe, Kurt Riezler, and Erich Hula—received but rejected similar invitations from the University of Chicago.

Still, among the European scholars at the New School a sense of an academic community persisted. With the exception of Max Ascoli and Kurt Riezler, who had independent sources of income, the faculty remained financially and psychologically dependent on the school and on Alvin Johnson. With salaries continuing at a modest level, some were forced to accept assistance from anonymous private benefactors, whose generosity had been inspired by Johnson's still considerable gifts of persuasion.[2] Most of the original members of the Graduate Faculty continued to rely on one another for company and occasional help, despite political and philosophical disagreements. They lived within walking distance of each other, either in the Washington Heights section of Manhattan or in the adjoining suburban area of Riverdale in the Bronx. They shared subway rides downtown, often ate together in the New School cafeteria, and attended each other's family celebrations.[3] When Albert Salomon moved from Riverdale—which reminded him of the Rhineland—to Manhattan's Upper West Side, others felt that he had rejected the exile community in favor of a more conventional Jewish-American life.[4] For most of the emigré faculty, the New School remained the focus of their personal and professional lives.

The consolidation of the Graduate Faculty in the 1950s itself depended on significant changes that had occurred during Hovde's brief tenure. The death of Max Wertheimer in 1943 had left the

Graduate Faculty, and especially its psychology department, with a vacancy that could not easily be filled. Wertheimer, who along with Kallen had straddled both philosophy and psychology, was succeeded by Solomon Asch and Rudolf Arnheim, both of whom were given part-time appointments, and by Mary Henle, who joined the faculty on a full-time basis. Asch extended Wertheimer's theories into the field of social psychology by applying gestalt ideas to the interrelationship of the individual and society. Arnheim, who taught courses in the late 1940s and 1950s at the Graduate Faculty and in the fine arts department, widened gestalt psychology to include esthetics. His work in art and perception followed Wertheimer's original intentions and Köhler's notion of correspondence. Of all Wertheimer's followers, Arnheim alone pursued the theoretical implications of gestalt psychology and maintained its scientific place in the discipline.[5]

Mary Henle, a graduate student of Köhler's at Swarthmore, had completed her doctoral work at the New School. After receiving her appointment she devoted much of her career to publicizing and promoting gestalt psychology. In addition to her studies of cognitive processes, Henle wrote extensively on the history of the gestalt movement. She remains at the New School as emeritus professor of psychology.

When Henle, Asch, and Arnheim received their appointments to the Graduate Faculty, the psychology "division" was still dominated by Wertheimer's gestalt psychology and, through Kallen and his younger colleague Reuben Abel, the pragmatism of James and Dewey. The appointments of Arnheim and Asch and the occasional teaching of Köhler created the need for an experimental laboratory, which was established in the early 1950s. In the mid-1950s, when the psychology department gained its "independence" from philosophy, several American-trained psychologists of behavioralist and empiricist orientation were brought onto the faculty. With the addition of Joseph Greenbaum, who became dean of the Graduate Faculty in the mid-1960s, and Leon Festinger, the psychology department altered its more philosophical focus. Henle remained the guardian of the gestalt faith, but American clinical and experimental work came to dominate.

In 1949, the faculty of the New School suffered a second loss when Leo Strauss left for the University of Chicago. A scholar whose expertise crossed the barriers of academic disciplines, he had regularly offered his courses on the history of political philosophy in the political science department and his seminar on Spinoza as part of the philosophy curriculum. Strauss had been at the center of an interdisciplinary and conservative minority at the school, and his departure left that group without its center and deprived the New School of one of its critical voices. Like Wertheimer, Strauss was difficult to replace.

Karl Löwith, a philosopher, who had studied under Heidegger, lectured for a short time. He was succeeded by Eugen Kullmann, a younger German scholar, who taught philosophy at the school for many years, but never received a permanent appointment. Howard White, Strauss's first graduate student at the New School, eventually replaced Strauss. White, like Henle, was an American, and he had married the daughter of Strauss's colleague and friend Kurt Riezler. As the first "Straussian," White devoted his career to an exposition of the classical political ideas in sixteenth-century English thought, especially of Shakespeare and Bacon.[6]

By 1950 the coming and going of the faculty ceased, and the institution commenced a decade-long period of stability. With the loss of Wertheimer and Strauss, other faculty members came to the fore, first Arnold Brecht and Kurt Riezler and then Alfred Schutz and Adolph Lowe. Their shared interest in the work of Max Weber helped establish a reputation for the New School as the preeminent American center for the study of social theory. This was true even as both European and American social science prepared to abandon the signposts that the members of the Graduate Faculty had blazed along the path of "continental" epistemological investigation. The allure of empiricism, on the one hand, and neo-Marxism, on the other, would prove finally too strong for the New School's intellectual tradition. Still, for a time, between 1950 and the early 1960s, the Graduate Faculty made the work of Max Weber the source of its intellectual dialogue, and influenced a small but significant group of younger American scholars.

In the mid-1950s Arnold Brecht abandoned his earlier policy interests to work on his most important book, *Political Theory: The Foundations of Twentieth Century Thought.*[7] In that study Brecht explored Weber's distinction between science and ethics and suggested that, although political scientists could describe the actual state of affairs in the world, they had lost the moral authority to confront that reality. This "crisis of democratic thought," Brecht argued, was a consequence of the profound effect Weber's thought had had on modern political theory.

Brecht's judgment was echoed by Kurt Riezler, who had joined the Graduate Faculty in 1938 after an active career in German politics. Riezler had served in the cabinet of Chancellor Bethmann Hollweg during World War I and had participated in the scheme that allowed Lenin's famous sealed boxcar to cross Germany in 1917 to Russia. In the 1960s the publication of his secret World War I diaries became the single most important source for the historiographical explosion that culminated in Fritz Fischer's landmark book, *Germany's Aims in the First World War.* Shortly after World War I, Riezler accepted a post as curator of the University of Frankfurt where he played a part in assembling a distinguished faculty that included Adolph Lowe, Karl Mannheim, Paul Tillich, and Max Wertheimer. Like Strauss, Riezler had been profoundly affected by Heidegger.[8] Believing that philosophy had lost track of its original agenda and had abandoned ontology, Riezler sought a "true" philosophy in the thought of Parmenides and Aristotle.

In April 1933 Riezler was arrested briefly by the Nazis and relieved of his post at the university. As a well-known diplomat, he was soon released and permitted to draw his pension while he wrote his work on Parmenides. In late 1938 he contacted the Kreisau Circle, the aristocratic anti-Nazi faction, and shortly after departed for New York.[9] Little is known of his further political activities, save that his conservative stance echoed the position he had taken as early as 1913. His "Greek turn" represented a search for a philosophical system of absolutes that he could affirm in the light of the disintegrating effects of the contemporary world. His books *Physics and Reality* and *Man: Mutable and Immutable* identified in terms of the history of science the same demarcation between modern and classical that Strauss had postulated in political philosophy. His last work, *On Man*, premised a loss of direction in modern thought that stood in contrast with ancient philosophy's grasp of the whole.[10]

Riezler's pessimism was not shared by all his colleagues. Occasionally the faculty's intellectual disagreements, particularly over the meaning and significance of the social sciences, severely tested the bonds forged by their common refugee status. For example, when Leo Strauss published his first English critique of Weber, Staudinger marched into his office and declared, "You have stabbed me," and swore never again to speak to Strauss. Days later they met again and embraced. "You know," said Staudinger, "we loved each other."[11]

Few members of the Graduate Faculty had been Max Weber's student, but all were agreed that he was the most important German thinker in their lifetimes. As an empirical social scientist and as an intellectual concerned with the theoretical problems of the social sciences, Weber had set the terms of debate for German social scientists in the first half of the twentieth century. He, more than any other German thinker of his generation, wrestled with questions of objectivity, the relationship between nature and society, and the possible tensions between scientific knowledge and political action. The richness of his writing and the complexity of his thought invited controversy. Not only were Weber's heirs divided over the correctness of his position in a given area of inquiry, but they often fought for recognition as the definitive interpreter of his position.

The factors that account for the intensity of the debates at the New School extended to the Graduate Faculty's European experiences. For those who came to the Graduate Faculty in the 1930s the events following World War I had been shattering. Even prior to 1933 many had been conscious of what they perceived as the inadequacy of modern thought. They believed that the political failures of conventional liberal and socialist policies had stemmed from intellectual and theoretical shortcomings. Germany in particular had failed to solve the riddle of "modernization." There may have been a German nation, but there remained several different German societies: traditional, modern, and transitional. The failure of social scientists to explain or resolve the problems of postwar Germany seemed to many to have opened the door to Nazism. The political failures of the Weimar Republic, in the face of resurgent nationalism and enormous social and economic tensions, raised doubts concerning the viability of liberal politics and the integrity and usefulness of empirical social science.

Adolph Lowe, a German economist, and Alfred Schutz, an Austrian philosopher, shared these concerns. In the 1950s they emerged as the Graduate Faculty's dominant thinkers and most influential teachers. In the late 1940s, Lowe and Schutz agreed to present a joint seminar on the meaning of the social sciences. Robert Heilbroner, then a graduate student in economics at the New School, recalled that the intellectual atmosphere was charged with expectation, yet the result was disappointing. Lowe, a philosophical economist, and Schutz, a philosopher of sociology, talked "past one another." Each hoped to integrate the ideas of Weber, Kant, and American pragmatism into his own perspective, but in the end they spoke of very different things. Schutz was concerned with the speculative meaning of contemporary social science and Lowe was interested in the application of social science to public policy. The differences between them were intrinsic to the debate over Weber which surfaced at the Graduate Faculty in the fifties.

Alfred Schutz was a member of the emigré generation, but he had come to the New School by his own circuitous route. He was born in 1889 in Vienna, the only child of an assimilated Jewish family. He received a classical education and, after serving in the Austrian army during the last year of World War I, completed a doctorate in law and politics at the University of Vienna. Schutz then joined the legal department of Reitler and Company, a private banking house in Vienna. Between 1922 and 1932, in his spare time, he wrote his *Der sinnhafte Aufbau der sozialen welt,* later published in English as *The Phenomenology of the Social World.*

In that remarkable book, widely acclaimed for its enterprise and density, Schutz attempted to provide the "interpretative sociology" of Weber with a sound philosophical justification. As Kant had sustained the authority of Newtonian science, so Schutz hoped to resolve what he understood as the crucial question of the social sciences. In his words, "the theme of all sciences of the social world is to constitute an objective meaning out of subjective meaning contexts."[12] If the Kantian question was, How is a pure science of nature possible?, then Schutz tried to go "beyond Kant" to give the social sciences a philosophical grounding that came to grips with the issues raised by the philosophy of Edmund Husserl.[13]

Schutz rejected those perspectives that limited scientific inquiry to a strict reliance on empirical data as he affirmed the spirit of Kantian, rationalist philosophy. In the words of Schutz's student, Thomas Luckmann, phenomenological sociology represented "a return to the things that Kant said you can't know about."[14] Schutz searched for an epistemological basis for a science of humanity by grappling with the questions that positivists said could not be answered. Yet he also believed that social scientists had to do more than simply find their own methodology; they had to liberate themselves from the natural sciences as well. He argued that Weber had only partially accomplished this latter task. Weber was not a philosopher, and Schutz considered his thought internally confused and naive. By making explicit Weber's philosophical assumptions, Schutz hoped both to save the central validity of Weber's work from the vague concept of *Verstehen*, or "understanding," and to identify the means by which knowledge could be obtained both empirically and "from essential insight."[15]

At the New School Schutz rejoined his Viennese colleagues Felix Kaufmann and Erich Hula, whom he had known since the early 1920s. In Vienna Schutz and Kaufmann had belonged to an informal intellectual circle dominated by Ludwig von Mises which read extensively in the works of Henri Bergson and Edmund Husserl.[16] Rejecting the more formal positive law tradition of Hans Kelsen as well as the logical positivism of Marburg philosopher Paul Natorp, Schutz turned to Kaufmann. In turn, Kaufmann urged Schutz to read Husserl's *Logical Investigations*. At first, Schutz found Husserl unacceptable. Only later, after studying Bergson did he find in Husserl's "Crisis of European Philosophy" what he had been looking for, a clear statement of the idea of "intersubjectivity."[17]

"In fact Schutz once told me," related Maurice Natanson, "that he started his life as a neo-Kantian."[18] Schutz insisted that social facts were never simply facts, but formulations of the mental activity of the observer. This contradicted the arguments of such positivists as Rudolph Carnap, who declared that observers could know only what had been perceived.[19] Such subjective phenomena as motive and values, which accompanied behavior, were aspects of the scientifically insignificant world of essences. For positivists like Carnap, since mental phenomena had no ontological standing, only the empirically knowable was real. Bergson, and then Husserl, led Schutz to question these apparent limitations and insist that social scientists might give priority to issues of meaning. In the *Phenomenology of the Social World* Schutz tried to reconcile the goal of sociology, "to see the world of social facts with an unbiased eye and to classify these facts," with the task of philosophical psychology, to understand the intended meaning of the individual.[20]

Schutz was careful to distinguish what he called intersubjectivity from some mysterious notion of universal consciousness found in the German metaphysical tradition. And he argued that we achieve consciousness of phenomena, of their essences, through acts of mental attention. This required a "bracketing" or a willful suspension of belief in the external world of appearances in order to peer beneath existence toward essence.[21] This "phenomenological consciousness" or awareness was a form of seeing, a means of access to the world of essences.

For social scientists, particularly sociologists, the problem was how to obtain a scientific or critical form of understanding which objectively rendered the other's point of view.[22] According to Schutz, whereas the natural sciences provided a formal system by which to classify an objective and empirically identifiable reality, "the theme of the social sciences is to constitute an objective meaning out of subjective meaning contexts."[23] This could be accomplished through the application of ideal-types, which involved the creation of artificial models, indeed "utopias," whose function was to explain, not predict.[24] Thus Schutz believed that the meaning of the sensory world—distinct from its behavior—could best be understood by the phenomenological method, a method appropriate for the social sciences.[25]

Schutz dedicated *The Phenomenology of the Social World* to Husserl, whom he had never met. After reading the manuscript, Husserl offered Schutz an academic post at Freiburg but Schutz refused. His decision was critical not only to his philosophy but to his life. Had he become a professional scholar in 1932, it is unlikely that he would have been identified by Alvin Johnson or any other rescue agency. As a Jew his academic career would have been terminated in 1933 or 1938. As a banker, however, he survived. During his first years in New York, Schutz's European connections served him well.

In 1939, Viennese economist Friedrich Hayek, the editor of *Economica*, asked Schutz to contribute a critical review of Talcott Parsons's recently published study of European sociology.[26] Schutz used the opportunity to write an extended essay, which occasioned his first English expression of his own work. Two years later his important essay "William James: Concept of the Stream of Thought" appeared in the first journal devoted to phenomenological philosophy. These two papers provided what one student of Schutz has called his moment of intellectual Americanization; more appropriately, however, they may be seen as a part of a gradual evolution in Schutz's thought and expression.[27] His introduction to American intellectual life coincided with a change in his writing style. His ideas, which had been obscured by the technical density of his early writings, were not significantly changed, but emerged with a new clarity after 1939.

In his critical review of Parsons's *Theory of Social Action*, Schutz stressed the special character of social science and the role of the observer. By discounting the role of the observer, declared Schutz, Parsons had ignored the important difference between the social and natural sciences and adopted what Schutz considered a naive form of naturalism.

Parsons responded to Schutz's phenomenological method by questioning its epistemological validity. What were the means, he asked, by which such an operation could be judged as adequate, given the intent to disclose the subjective and essential meaning rather than the objective and observational? Schutz had employed the "postulate of adequacy," a criterion of universal applicability in which the model created must not only correspond to action in the sensory world but be "reasonable" and "understandable" to all human actors. Schutz, in effect, resorted to an argument of rationalist clarity as proof of the adequacy of his ideas.[28]

Although his encounter with Parsons brought Schutz into conflict with mainstream American social science, his reading of William James convinced him that he had found an American counterpart to Husserl. Concerned not to reduce James to Husserl, "one to the other," Schutz realized that they both shared a common "concern for consciousness." Furthermore, James's "stream of thought" paralleled Husserl's attack on positivism. James and Husserl together, for Schutz, represented a total rejection of "the atomism prevailing in the psychology of Locke, Hume or J. S. Mill."[29] Schutz, like Wertheimer and Lévi-Strauss, sought to define the human mind in terms strikingly different from the prevailing naturalistic assumptions of positive empiricism. The task, argued Schutz, was for the thinking, subjective "I" to know over time the empirical "me." This was accomplished through phenomenological reduction, which "makes accessible the stream of consciousness in itself."[30] James, who had been engaged in a similar effort, provided Schutz an American response to Parsons and an American equivalent to continental phenomenology's notion of consciousness.[31] Far from "Americanizing" his thought, Schutz's reading of Parsons and then James reinforced his phenomenological approach. He identified Talcott Parsons's thought as but a variation of positivism and claimed William James as an American, rationalist ally.

In identifying James, and later George Herbert Mead, as American counterparts to Husserl and Bergson, Schutz acquired an American vocabulary that expressed the rationalism of Husserl. He replaced his distinction between "naive" and "critical" with the more familiar American terms of "common sense" and "scientific." In the mid-1950s Schutz wrote that "common sense knowledge of everyday life is sufficient for coming to terms with fellow men . . . in short with social reality."[32] Moreover, knowledge of this reality depended on the "mental construct" appropriate to a particular "level" of organization. But scientific knowledge, or phenomenological investigation that yielded meaningful explanatory understanding, had to be thought of as operating on a "second level," or "second degree." To reach this level—to set aside social reality and become observers—social scientists used ideal-types, models, or puppets, whose value lay in the realm of understanding, not prediction. "This is what Max Weber understood by his famous postulate of subjective interpretation," wrote Schutz, which "has to be understood in the sense that all scientific explanation of the social world can and for certain purposes must refer to the subjective meaning of the actions of human beings from which social reality originates."[33] Selectively drawing on continental rationalism and American psychology, Schutz sought to create a philosophical foundation for Weber's sociology of ideal-types. In the wake of nineteenth-century positivism, he too wished to reunite science and philosophy.[34] Phenomenology was Schutz's defense of rationalism against the scientism of positivists such as Carnap and the subjectivism of intuitionists such as Dilthey. To this extent Schutz and Weber, as well as James and Dewey, were involved in a common enterprise.

Adolph Lowe shared Schutz's determination to expand the epistemological basis of the social sciences, but, unlike Schutz, he applied these weighty concerns to practical and theoretical economics. His career spanned fifty years and two continents, but his work retained throughout a remarkable consistency. In a variety of ways, he sought the means by which to attain the moral good of a free economy. Lowe was a critic of contemporary capitalism and of "positive" economics; his understanding of the origins of the English political economy led him to propose state control or intervention to reorder economic structures. Yet his hope had been that, although "necessary," such intervention will be but a temporary technical restoration of the political and moral goals of freedom.

Lowe, who taught at the New School between 1940 and 1978, first gained academic prominence in 1931 when he earned an appointment at the University of Frankfurt. A municipal institution, Frankfurt was not subject to centralized control and was therefore able to offer a haven to Jewish scholars, even during the conservative counterattack against Weimar "cosmopolitanism" of the late 1920s.[35] In addition to Mannheim, Tillich, and Wertheimer, the Frankfurt faculty also included the "critical theorists" Max Horkheimer, Theodor Adorno, and Friedrich Pollock of the Institute for Social Research. These Frankfurt scholars maintained their common intellectual ground even in the face of their diaspora after 1933. At the New School Adolph Lowe, an "economic philosopher," sustained the Frankfurt agenda.[36]

A socialist and a Jew, Adolph Lowe had anticipated little of his future career. Lowe was educated in the law; his student days belonged to the era of the imperial university prior to the outbreak of World War I.[37] In 1915 he entered the army, joining his unit just before its assault on Verdun. Fortunately for Lowe a precautionary medical exam revealed a heart irregularity, and Lowe was sent to the rear. His company was destroyed at Verdun. Lowe very likely owed his life to the medical exam which, as it turned out years later, had been a misdiagnosis. Lowe was perfectly healthy, a condition he has sustained into his nineties.[38] Transferred to Ludendorff's command, Lowe helped prepare plans for postwar demobilization. He served on the Socialization Commission, which sought to nationalize the German economy, and then joined the Ministry of Economics, where he first met Hans Staudinger.

By 1922 Lowe, like Staudinger, was convinced that only state intervention in the business cycle could bring about economic equality without endangering economic growth. Never an advocate of bureaucratic allocations of labor, resources, and production, Lowe believed that through capital investment the state could at one time direct economic growth and control the business cycle. Lowe claimed that economic planning could control the market without displacing it. His ideas and research closely paralleled those of Wesley Mitchell in the United States, and his notion of the "state as entrepreneur" was shared by Staudinger. After 1924, Lowe and Staudinger faced concerted conservative opposition to their ideas. Lowe left the government in 1926 to accept an academic post at the Kiel Institute; Staudinger moved into the Prussian state government.

Lowe's academic reputation derived from his position at Kiel as the director of a group of young socialist economists who had proposed unorthodox responses to the depression. Lowe, Hans Neisser, Gerhard

Colm, and Jacob Marschak worked together there to prepare a series of policy papers based on extensive research designed to counter the deflationary effects of Chancellor Brüning's fiscal retrenchment. As head of the statistical research division, Lowe directed the work in international economics, focusing on international business cycles. Working with Colm and Neisser, Lowe's team completed two volumes of reports that dealt with the "structural changes of the world economy."[39]

Lowe and his colleagues identified the global nature of the economic fluctuations that characterized the emergence of a world economy. They tried to determine how the German government could alleviate the destabilizing effects of such cycles on the national economy. Lowe's group developed the methods of measurement which are now called econometrics. These "political economists" expected their work to be used to shape governmental economic policy, but by 1931, when Lowe left the institute to assume a professorship in theoretical economics at Frankfurt, only the socialist-dominated Prussian state government of Otto Braun showed any interest in the group's work.[40]

In the 1920s, Lowe had been drawn to Paul Tillich's and Eduard Heimann's notion of religious socialism. Lowe first met Tillich in 1919 and had worked closely with Heimann, a theoretical economist, on the Socialization Commission in 1919 and 1920.[41] Both Tillich and Heimann wished to restore the intellectual rapport between socialism and theology. Heimann, echoing the neo-Kantian socialists, argued that traditional liberalism had abandoned its earliest commitment to the freedom of humanity and now emphasized only a bourgeois form of individualism, shorn of its communal obligations. Similarly, Marxism with its emphasis on economic determinism was as materialistic as the bourgeois society that it proposed to replace. True socialism, argued Heimann, represented a fusion of the two great movements of cultural unity, liberalism and Christianity, which together could restore social community and political freedom. Heimann proposed a form of "economic democracy" in which the majority, by constitutional means, would transform society through an alliance between the working and middle classes.[42] He believed that a nationalized economy, directed from the top, had enormous authoritarian potential. As an assimilated Jew, he embraced the ethic of Christianity and had little difficulty with the label "Christian" socialism. Curiously, Paul Tillich, a Protestant theologian, preferred the term "religious" socialism, and Lowe, who never abandoned his own Jewish heritage, found Tillich's less sectarian position more attractive.

Tillich argued that socialism was religious insofar as it pursued the goal of social justice through the creation of a universal community. Echoing the ideas of Weber, Tillich believed that the emergence of bourgeois capitalism had been accompanied by a kind of "disenchantment with the world."[43] Originally united, bourgeois society and Christian humanism had become separated. As a result, bourgeois society was the "bearer of Christian humanism from its religious origins down to its profanely antireligious and anti-Christian realization."[44] In its rejection of socialism, declared Tillich, late capitalism abandoned *Karios*, or real and unconditional human concern, which served as the basis of religious sentiment. Religious socialism represented for Tillich a commitment to the ideal of a just society. Even as he affirmed "a thoroughly rationalized, democratic, constitutional state," Tillich insisted that such an order remained spiritually empty without the "eros" of religious commitment, without human concern.[45] Socialism became the means by which Tillich sought to reinvigorate the "spirit of religion" in western society.

Tillich and Heimann led Lowe to reject both conventional Marxism and trade union socialism as little more than varieties of bourgeois capitalism. Throughout his life Lowe believed that economic analysis, no matter how sophisticated, was finally only a means to a broader social philosophy. Convinced of the validity of the market concept, Lowe nevertheless believed that the political culture should be infused with the values of a religious socialism. Hitler's emergence denied Lowe the opportunity to apply his ideas to the German economy. In leaving Germany in 1933, Lowe also lost the intellectual community in which he had participated at Kiel and Frankfurt. Lowe and Mannheim emigrated to England; Tillich, Colm, Neisser, Heimann, and Marschak proceeded to New York. All but Tillich eventually received appointments at the New School. Colm and Marschak left the New School in the late 1930s, just before Lowe rejoined Neisser and Heimann in the Graduate Faculty.

In 1933 Lowe accepted an appointment to the economics faculty at the University of Manchester. He remained in England for seven years, continuing the work he had begun in Germany, though concentrating more on social philosophy than on business-cycle economics. Like his former colleagues, some of whom were already at the Graduate Faculty, Lowe was preoccupied by the triumph of Nazism in Germany. The two books he wrote during this period, *The Price of Liberty* (1935) and *Economics and Sociology* (1937), both addressed the failure of German democracy.[46] Lowe came to believe that the English model offered the only means to survive the present "social and spiritual crisis of western Europe."[47]

After England declared war on Germany in 1939, Lowe found that his naturalization did not guarantee his employment. Alvin Johnson came to his aid and, through Hans Staudinger, negotiated a Rockefeller appointment for Lowe as director of the yet unfunded Institute of World Affairs. Lowe turned his attention almost entirely to the institute, modeling it after the Kiel Institute and dedicating his next ten years to his administrative and teaching duties. He did not return to theoretical and philosophical issues until 1951.[48] Still, during this interval, Lowe examined four sets of interrelated problems: the nature and purpose of economic theory, the validity of inductive as opposed to deductive reasoning in economic analysis, the universal applicability of the laws of supply and demand, and the question of a "free" versus an "interventionist" economy.[49]

Lowe's path back to theoretical scholarship was a troubled and sometimes discouraging one. In New York he had never been able to revive the energy of the Kiel Institute and, two years after his resignation as chair, the New School dissolved the Institute of World Affairs. The problems of war and resettlement had been superseded by new international questions, which the Graduate Faculty chose not to address. Furthermore, the Graduate Faculty had steered itself in a new and cautious direction, emphasizing its role as an American university comprised of European teachers. Policy research became secondary to teaching and academic scholarship. Meanwhile, Lowe was failing to make progress in his own work. His critical evaluation of conventional economics in the name of a yet unformulated alternative had stalled. In the summer of 1948 Lowe returned to Germany for a visit. While walking through the Black Forest, he found his earlier moral concerns rekindled.[50] In the next few years Lowe produced, by his own calculations, 60,000 words that were never seen in print. By 1954 his mind had become "more or less clean."[51] This mental reconstruction opened the way for Lowe's magnum opus, *On Economic Knowledge,* a treatise on the epistemology and meaning of economic theory, published in 1965.

In *On Economic Knowledge,* Lowe proposed a radical response to what he understood as the crisis of industrial capitalism. With the triumph of technology the twentieth century had, Lowe argued, already ameliorated "Adam's curse" of scarcity.[52] Now economists should concern themselves with the relationship between the goal of creating material abundance and the means by which individuals acquire it. Classical theory provided an analysis of both economic "means" (Smith's injunction to follow enlightened self-interest) and "ends" (the wealth of nations); but classical thinkers assumed that all individuals behaved invariantly. That notion of an apparent conformity led economists to presume regular, continuous, and consistent reactions to market factors, and thus predictability. Smith's system, or political economy, accomplished exactly what his successors claimed theory could not do. It created an economic consciousness by announcing the goal of economic activity—bettering our condition—while claiming to have discovered those natural laws whose existence led inexorably to the fulfillment of the goal. Yet everywhere, Lowe noted, individual behavior diverged from the "lawful" end of optimization. Conventional theory could no longer convincingly explain, let alone predict, economic behavior.[53]

Lowe identified this as the crisis of contemporary economics and society. Whereas classical economics once proposed a goal, that end had come to be understood not as a choice but as fact. As a consequence, conventional theory not only took for granted the existence of fixed goals—actually, political decisions—but took as choices patterns of behavior that were themselves "caused" by those very decisions. By isolating economics from society, by maintaining the standard of prediction, and by denying its own role in creating consciousness, conventional theory had failed to provide a critical framework to examine economic policy. Lowe did not discard Smith's original intent to create the consciousness necessary to establish an economy of abundance. He wished to accomplish for the twentieth century what he believed Smith had for the eighteenth, to create a "spontaneous conformity" in which all members of a society shared the same economic goals.[54]

For Lowe the challenge was twofold: first, to restore externally the factors, or "controls," to insure a reasonable pattern of behavioral conformity of individuals as "decentralized" economic actors; and, second, to do so in the context of an economic theory appropriate to the circumstances of contemporary society.[55] Without controls, Lowe predicted that political leaders in the face of economic chaos would impose their will on society, destroying all semblance of economic and political liberty. Totalitarianism might well be the long-term price for the short-term luxury of an insufficiently guided marketplace.[56] Put differently, Lowe called for the formulation and articulation of a public policy of "controlled choices" to establish a consensus on economic goals. The creation of common economic ends through a democratic process would insure the subsequent conformity of behavior on the part of economic actors who were themselves guided by the means that economists had determined would achieve the publicly defined goals.

Economic theory, then, became a search for appropriate means of action, given the prior establishment of ends or goals. To define this process Lowe self-consciously employed analytical constructs drawn from Kant's *Critique of Practical Reason,* but he admitted that his ideas needed a "new logic." Although a logic based on cause–effect relationships, or what he called "mechanical structures," was appropriate for chemistry and physics, Lowe held that social-economic organizations required a "teleological" or "instrumental" analysis.[57] Lowe's concept borrowed heavily from the vocabulary of American pragmatism, particularly from Charles Sanders Peirce, in the same way that Schutz had found intellectual comfort in James.[58] Responding to his critics, he maintained that his purpose was not to undermine the scientific standing of economics but to restore it. In an age of postindustrial technology, the real illusion was the so-called order of the marketplace. As he explained in a letter to his student Robert Heilbroner, "Since society is unlikely to present us with a reality corresponding to our premises we must create such a reality."[59]

Instrumental analysis, designed by Lowe to reestablish the relationship between society and the economy, became political economy. Lowe believed that rational planning could connect the economic goals of society with the technical means of their achievement. Knowledge meant action, and in this respect Lowe remained loyal to the tradition of Marx and Weber. Nevertheless, Lowe found conventional Marxist economic analysis anachronistic.[60] Marxist economists had ignored the possibility of a political economics based on democratic procedures. Instead, they had elaborated a schema of crises based on the mechanical conception of the business cycle. Echoing the ideas of his old colleague and closest friend, Hans Staudinger, Lowe advocated a peaceful, rational, and democratic transition from capitalist to socialist economic organization.[61] Yet, outwardly, Lowe systematically refused to address the question of social organization. "I am," he said, "a Weberian to the extent that I believe that science can derive means suitable to given ends."[62] His fusion of Marx and Weber, of praxis and process, informed by Kantian distinctions between science and philosophy, did not propose to indicate the values by which Lowe felt society ought to choose. For him, such a question was essentially philosophical and political, not simply scientific.

In his subsequent work—specifically, *The Path of Economic Growth*, published in 1976—Lowe sought to provide firm empirical basis for his instrumental analysis. Ultimately, Lowe wanted to establish a just social community informed by Tillich's concept of ultimate concern. Given the actual condition of the economic system, however, Lowe believed that state control, planning, and economic intervention were necessary and appropriate. His affirmation of an ethical socialism represented a cast of mind that was both thoroughly analytic and yet idealistic, if not utopian. Like so many others at the New School, he sought a logical and scientifically valid alternative to what he believed was an uncritical and positivist social science. And like many pragmatists Lowe believed that experience or practice preceded theory. Yet like Schutz, he upheld a continental rationalist perspective, insisting that the human mind not only determined the character of investigation, but rendered final judgment as to its value as well.

Schutz and Lowe were not alone in this conviction among the members of the Graduate Faculty. They, along with Albert Salomon and Karl Mayer in the 1960s, and their students Peter Berger, Thomas Luckmann, Maurice Natanson, and Robert Heilbroner, found that the ideas and attitudes offered by a Weberian dialogue raised precisely for the social sciences the issues posed by the heritage of Kantian rationalism. In virtually any other American university in the 1950s Lowe or Schutz would have been isolated, culturally and intellectually. Under their influence, however, the New School became the center for phenomenological philosophy.

Schutz was joined, and then succeeded, by Aron Gurwitch and Dorian Cairns, who in the late 1950s and early 1960s made philosophy the Graduate Faculty's most distinguished department. The appointment of Hans Jonas in the mid-1950s and Hannah Arendt a decade later assured the department's continued prominence. Departmental distinction, however, entailed a significant price for the Graduate Faculty's goal of interdisciplinary synthesis. By 1959 the self-conscious superiority of the philosophy department was itself evidence that generalized study and interdisciplinary scholarship no longer distinguished the Graduate Faculty from other American universities. Nonetheless, even in the early 1960s the Graduate Faculty continued to affirm the principle, and to a degree even the substance, of interdisciplinary social theory. In fact, Schutz's success had to some extent depended on his close working relationship with two of his colleagues in sociology, Karl Mayer and Albert Salomon.

With Schutz, Mayer and Salomon made Weber's work the central concern of the Graduate Faculty, although as sociologists and teachers they brought different perspectives to the school. Each of them had studied sociology at Heidelberg, and both were charter members of the Graduate Faculty. Mayer had begun his teaching in the United States, but Salomon had served previously on the faculties at Cologne and the Berlin Hochschule. In addition, as part of Lederer's network, Salomon had edited the Social Democratic political review *Gesellschaft*. Salomon's sociological concerns reflected in part his political commitments, but they revealed as well a remarkable intellectual breadth. To see more clearly Weber's place in the history of sociology, particularly his relationship to Durkheim, Salomon was inspired to study not only Durkheim, but Balzac, contemporary Judaism, and Tocqueville as well.[63] Salomon, more than any other member of the Graduate Faculty, introduced Weber's work to American social scientists through his historical and theoretical articles in *Social Research*.[64]

Rejecting the conventional interpretation that Weber was a tormented intellectual, a modern prophet, preoccupied with the emptiness of modern life, Salomon instead emphasized Weber's dialogue with Marx.[65] Drawing on Weber's historical essays, particularly *The Protestant Ethic and the Spirit of Capitalism,* Salomon described Weber as interested in the realities of "everyday life." Weber had demonstrated the "fact" of contemporary rationalization, a process that erased the residues of religious prophecy and charisma.[66] In contrast to Marx, however, he saw the process of modernization as caused by individual social acts which were not inevitable. Salomon insisted that a fundamental tension existed in Weberian thought between freedom and history.[67] His interpretation of Weber stressed the gradual process of change that Weber had identified as characteristic of western historical development. As a socialist, Salomon used Weber's interpretation to justify the gradual transformation of capitalist society through political action. Like Lowe and Staudinger, he affirmed Weber's idea of rational transformation as a historically and politically valid alternative to Marxian revolution. Like Lederer and Mannheim, he turned to Weber, rather than Marx, for both his interpretation of society and his understanding of politics. Marx's vision of a classless society had no place within the "ruthless realism" of Weberian analysis.

As Salomon became more concerned with the evolution of "historical sociology," he began to look equally to the French tradition of Durkheim and then to Balzac and Tocqueville. Having found, however, that Weber's work in its later stages had become static and that the French tradition seemed suffused with a scientistic positivism, Salomon in his later years turned to Kant and Judaism.[68] As a sociologist, historian, and theorist, Salomon insisted that humans were both the architects and subjects of their own social order. This insistence on rational humanism led him to conclude that behind the variety of human expression lay some fundamentally unchanging quality, or essence, which he found best expressed in Judaism. As a Jew, Salomon reaffirmed the dignity of human freedom as embodied in Kantian ethics.[69]

Karl Mayer, the youngest of the Graduate Faculty's "Big Three" (as Jonas, Salomon, and Mayer came to be known to the postwar student generation), acted as the self-appointed guardian of Weber's work. Educated at Heidelberg, Mayer completed his thesis, entitled "Church and Sect," under the direction of Alfred Weber and Karl Jaspers.

Mayer's thesis elaborated the Weberian typology outlined in the *Protestant Ethic*.[70] His stature at the New School, however, rested on his reputation as a teacher. His courses on Weber and the sociology of religion remained staples in the sociology program for almost thirty years. Mayer's most significant contribution may have been his attention to historical sociology. His concern with religion led him to offer comprehensive courses in comparative history, one of which he called "Sociology of Modern Anti-Semitism."[71] By stressing the historical and sociological evolution of the interrelationship of ethnicity, society, and ideology in France, Germany, and the United States, Mayer anticipated the work of many American historians in the 1960s; his emphasis on comparative social-political history echoed Weber's earliest concern. By describing the avalanche of anti-Semitism as a consequence of the tensions of modernization, the discrepancy between a bourgeois and a lingering preindustrial world, Mayer incorporated Weber's richest historical investigation and made a genuine, if "silent," contribution.

Schutz, Salomon, and Mayer together comprised, in the 1950s, an important intellectual focus at the Graduate Faculty. If they did not produce an enduring intellectual synthesis, they did sustain the tradition of Weberian thought, which American social scientists had often ignored or distorted. Schutz hoped to reconcile Husserl and Weber so as to overcome the philosophical distinction between subject and object. Meanwhile, Salomon and Mayer, by focusing on Weber's historical investigation, for the most part ignored epistemological problems. Salomon sought to develop the relationship between Marx and Weber; Mayer insisted on the purity of Weber's ideas. For each, and for different reasons, Weber was the most important intellectual of the twentieth century, and together they made Weberian analysis a defining characteristic of the Graduate Faculty in the 1950s.

The 1950s were also years of significant student productivity. A generation of postwar graduate students, many of them veterans, turned to the New School as an alternative to mainstream American higher education. Although Strauss had taken most of his followers with him to the University of Chicago in the late 1940s, Schutz, Salomon, and Mayer taught a host of graduate students, some of whom became prominent academics in the 1960s.

Maurice Natanson, for example, who received his doctorate in philosophy at Nebraska, came to the New School in the early 1950s on a postdoctoral fellowship to study with Schutz. Under Schutz he received from the Graduate Faculty a Doctor of Social Science degree, one of the few people to earn this second doctorate. Under Schutz's guidance, Natanson undertook a study of the University of Chicago sociologist George Herbert Mead. According to Natanson, Mead's ideas had been taken over and distorted by behavioral sociologists.[72] Moreover, because Mead's work had been published from stenographic records of his lectures, replete with contradictions and repetitions, it invited controversy. Natanson argued that Mead had been influenced more by Husserl's phenomenological method than by positivism. Natanson's reinterpretation of Mead paralleled Schutz's work on James: to search out the epistemological assumptions of Mead by demonstrating pragmatism's close affinity to phenomenology.[73] Natanson viewed Mead's concern with consciousness, the relationship of subjective and objective meaning and the question of intersubjectivity, the consequence of a first-rate theorist's "unconscious" identification with phenomenology.[74] Natanson's approach typified the Graduate Faculty's concern with the relationship between theory and reality. According to Natanson, Mead accepted the notion that the "individual in his experience is continually creating a world which becomes real through his discovery."[75] Natanson's thesis that social reality was itself a human construction was shared by his fellow graduate students Peter Berger and Thomas Luckmann.

In the early 1960s Peter Berger and Thomas Luckmann, who later joined the sociology department of the Graduate Faculty, wrote an ambitious work on the sociology of knowledge, *The Social Construction of Reality*. Acknowledging the work of Weber, Durkheim, Marx, and Mannheim, it was largely a tribute to Alfred Schutz. Rather than delineate the relationships between ideas and society, Berger and Luckmann went to great pains to distinguish between ideas and knowledge. Knowledge was not the same as the ideas present in a given social context. Rather, it was the way in which people knew "reality in their everyday non- or pre-theoretical lives."[76] Accepting the assumption that the very notion of reality was itself a human creation, Berger and Luckmann insisted that sociologists could know a conscious reality that existed outside the limits of positivist, behavioralist, or functionalist descriptions.[77]

In maintaining that the sociology of knowledge ought to inform sociology, they sidestepped the problems that had preoccupied much of the theoretical work of the Graduate Faculty. Schutz had carefully differentiated between "naive" and "critical" knowledge, even as he had used observations about everyday or common-sense "knowledge" to substantiate his claims for a phenomenological, scientific, critical, or "bracketed" knowledge. By concentrating on the naive, everyday, or prescientific source of knowledge, Berger and Luckmann abandoned Schutz's phenomenological method. In many ways they returned to the work of Weber, which Schutz himself had spent a lifetime revising. As second-generation scholars at the New School, Berger, Luckmann, and Natanson carried forward the Graduate Faculty's preoccupation with the Weberian heritage. Well into the 1960s, their reading of Weber set the institution apart from the majority of American institutions. In this respect little had changed since 1933.

This conjuncture at the New School of European rationalists and American pragmatists was not accidental. The philosophical and moral impulses that had led to the founding of the New School in the first place had also informed Johnson's appointments to the Graduate Faculty. Whether Americans—Veblen, Robinson, Beard, Mitchell, and Kallen—or Europeans—Schutz, Lowe, Salomon, and Mayer—the New School had provided all of them a home. Throughout the twentieth century the New School had served as a refuge for critical and nonconformist social theorists, thriving it seemed on adversity, poverty, and experimentation. The challenge of the 1960s and 1970s would be to maintain the original spirit of inquiry at a time of financial success, physical expansion, and impending administrative and faculty retirements. Few at the Graduate Faculty in 1959 could have foretold that within four years the New School would lose virtually everyone who had made the school such an exciting institution in the 1950s. Some died, some retired, but nearly all had left the school for good.

11

NEW STUDENTS FOR A NEW ERA
Adult Education in the Postwar World

THE YEARS AFTER WORLD WAR II WERE GOOD YEARS for the New School as a whole, but they were boom years for the Adult Education Division. Adult education enrollments, which had dropped to a low of 1,300 in 1942, climbed to a staggering 4,500 in 1945, a level that remained fairly stable into the 1950s. Enrollment at the Graduate Faculty did not increase so dramatically, but the reputation of its scholars—particularly those in its philosophy department—drew both attention and students to the entire school. Despite changes in its leadership during the fifteen years from 1945 to 1960, the New School managed to absorb the influx of new students, recruit a faculty to teach them, and increase its physical plant to nearly three times its wartime size.

The most significant change of those fifteen years was the departure of Alvin Johnson. Since 1924, Johnson had made practically all the key decisions concerning the school, and the faculty, staff, and board were personally as well as professionally loyal to him. In 1932 he had conceived of the University in Exile. Later he had lent critical support to the Institute of World Affairs, the Ecole Libre, and the Dramatic Workshop. In 1943 he had proposed the Bachelor of Arts program for the New School and had lobbied the New York Board of Regents for its approval. In 1944, when he announced his plan to retire, it was not clear that the institution which had become so identified with his personality would survive. Johnson himself had no doubts. Although he had maintained a very personalized administration, he had also built an institution with a devoted board of trustees, a distinguished faculty, and a debt-free physical plant. Clara Mayer and Hans Simons were trusted and able administrators, experienced in running their sections of adult education. Furthermore, Johnson's successor, Bryn Hovde, was a midwesterner and a self-described "fighting liberal," cut in the mold of Johnson himself.[1]

On the surface, Hovde seemed perfect for the New School. He had received his doctorate from Iowa State University, had served as professor of history and political science at the University of Pittsburgh, had been technical secretary for UNESCO, and, just prior to his appointment as president of the New School, had headed the Division of Cultural Cooperation at the State Department.[2] His liberal politics, his international connections, his academic training, and his administrative experience all pointed to his suitability and success. Unfortunately, such was not the case, and Hovde's five years at the New School proved personally disastrous. His greatest weakness seems to have been his lack of political acumen. He took over an institution that was still run by two strong administrators, Mayer and Simons, experienced in academic in-fighting, who had no intention of taking orders from Hovde. Mayer not only enjoyed a strong base of support in the Adult Education Division, but had ready access to the board through her brother, Albert Mayer. Simons was a member of the board and served as the spokesman for the Graduate Faculty. And, most important of all, Johnson never actually retired. He accepted the title of president emeritus and then kept his office, received visitors, made suggestions, and engaged in institutional intrigue. While refusing to shoulder responsibilities, Johnson nonetheless continued to exercise informal influence.[3]

Hovde, in all fairness, occupied a difficult position. It is hard to imagine how he, a newcomer, could have succeeded in imposing his rule while old-timers like Johnson, Mayer, and Simons were still in place. At best a figurehead, he proved ineffective, even incompetent. Under his administration the New School went into serious debt, the Graduate Faculty lost several of its most distinguished members, including Hans Speier and Leo Strauss; the Ecole Libre disassociated itself from the New School; and the New School disassociated itself from the Dramatic Workshop. Most of this would have occurred in any case, but Hovde became a convenient scapegoat, whom few respected and most disliked. Realizing that things were coming apart, Hovde tried in early 1949 to gain control of the New School by getting rid of his chief nemesis, Alvin Johnson himself. Hovde asked Johnson to give up his office and go back to his home in Nyack. Apparently without protest, Johnson agreed, and then over the summer orchestrated Hovde's dismissal.[4] In September Hovde recognized all was lost and resigned. The following June the New School announced the appointment of Hans Simons as its president.[5]

Born in 1893 in Velbert, Germany, Simons had served in the German army during World War I and was decorated for valor. His father was foreign minister and chief justice of the Weimar Republic, and for a brief period held the position of acting president. In 1921 Simons received his doctorate from the University of Königsberg and during the 1920s held various minor administrative positions in the federal government. From 1924 to 1930 he served as director of the Hochschule für Politik in Berlin, which he helped to found. Blacklisted by the Nazis in 1933, Simons escaped from Germany in 1935 and joined the Graduate Faculty in New York. In 1940 he became an American citizen. Although he took a leave of absence from the New School in 1947 to help organize the occupation government and draft a constitution for West Germany, he returned to the United States after two years. Discouraged by the dim prospects for a democratic Germany and shaken by what he discovered had taken place under the Nazis, Simons reconfirmed his loyalty to his adopted country and assumed the presidency of the New School with eagerness.[6]

Hans Simons, who had always been popular at the New School, was an excellent choice to reunite the school after the divisive influence of Hovde. He had been a leader of the Graduate Faculty since soon after his arrival there, and was by all accounts an excellent teacher. His adult education lectures on international politics enjoyed consistently high enrollments, and as dean of the School of Politics and chair of the Faculty Council Simons proved himself an able academic leader. Most important, over fifteen years he had learned to work amiably with the faculty, the board, Clara Mayer, and Alvin Johnson. The New School knew what to expect from Simons, and Simons knew the source and limits of his power. A strong and decisive man, Simons recognized that, without the support of Johnson, Mayer, the board, and the faculty, he would not succeed. His only imaginable rival for the position was Clara Mayer, and there is no indication either that the board considered her or that she wanted the job. Certainly, the appointment of a woman to head the New School would at the time have appeared risky, and her lack of a doctorate may in itself have disqualified her practically, if not legally, for the presidency of an institution that awarded academic degrees.

With the presidency, Simons inherited serious financial problems from Hovde. The New School had accumulated a debt of several hundred thousand dollars over the past decade of expansion. The GI Bill, which had temporarily provided a boon for the Graduate Faculty, had ceased bringing in large numbers of students. Enrollments throughout the school, although not dropping precipitously, were declining. Furthermore, at a time when the New School could least afford to compete, many of its most prestigious faculty members were receiving offers to go elsewhere. Simons realized that a major effort to increase enrollments and revenues was needed. Whatever other strengths Simons possessed, his personal aloofness and German accent made him an ineffective fund-raiser. Recognizing this, he turned to Alvin Johnson with the daring proposal that what the New School needed, if it hoped to survive, was a new building. Johnson agreed to try to raise the money for the project.[7]

In 1955 the board announced a $2.5 million campaign to double the size of the West Twelfth Street building and add a four-story structure on West Eleventh Street. Together, the additions would triple the New School's building space. With pledges from the Mayer family, from Max Ascoli and the Rosenwald Foundation, and from philanthropists Marshall Field, Vera and Albert List, Jacob Kaplan, and Israel Rogosin, Simons began construction in 1956. The project was completed in 1959. The original building, designed by Joseph Urban, was renamed the Alvin Johnson Building, the Twelfth Street addition became the Kaplan Building, and the Eleventh Street structure was called the List Building. The new space provided room for library expansion, a larger fine arts program, classrooms, and, in the area between the Twelfth and Eleventh Street buildings, a "courtyard" campus. This complex of buildings, collectively known as 66 West Twelfth Street, formed what is today the Adult Education Division and administrative offices of the New School. (In 1967 the Graduate Faculty moved two blocks away to the corner of Fifth Avenue and Fourteenth Street.)[8]

The new buildings represented Simons's most substantial accomplishment as president. With the completion of the Twelfth Street addition in 1957, adult education enrollments soared, doubling within seven years.[9]

During the 1930s Alvin Johnson, anxious to keep the New School afloat, had used funds and faculty from the Adult Education Division and the Graduate Faculty to nourish and sustain each other. In 1941, members of the Graduate Faculty taught 75 percent of the adult education courses. As the emphasis in adult education changed back to arts and cultural enrichment, however, the participation of the Graduate Faculty in its offerings declined. By 1958, only about 9 percent of the adult courses offered were taught by members of the Graduate Faculty. In effect, the two divisions had become separate entities.[10]

The Adult Division had itself been divided, as well, when the board in 1943 reorganized the curriculum into the School of Politics and the School of Philosophy and the Liberal Arts. The "schools" were placed under the leadership of Hans Simons and Clara Mayer, respectively. This reorganization coincided with a swing away from the social sciences, a move that seems to have contributed to an upsurge in enrollments.[11] In 1945, the School of Philosophy and the Liberal Arts listed 131 of the 210 courses offered and enrolled two-thirds of the program's students. Another major change, made at about this time, was the establishment in 1944 of a B.A. program. Although ostensibly designed to take advantage of GI Bill benefits, its more lasting effect was to draw to the school students who, for one reason or another, wanted to resume their college educations or move on in their professional careers outside a conventional undergraduate institution.[12]

These changes were complete by the time Hans Simons took his leave of absence from the School of Politics in 1947. His successor as dean, the political theorist Saul Padover, inherited a position at the head of a thriving program. Padover, born in Detroit to Italian-Jewish parents, received his doctorate from the University of Chicago in 1932. During the war, he was decorated for his secret intelligence work with Max Ascoli, whom he had first met in 1938 when Ascoli had been in need of a translator. He then joined the Graduate Faculty, where he wrote books on Jefferson and on European politics; finally, in the 1970s, he edited the works of Karl Marx. He was an able successor to Simons as dean of the School of Politics, but remained there only until 1956, when he resigned to return to teaching and writing. Padover in turn was succeeded by Arthur Swift, who became a central figure in the institutional politics of the New School in the early 1960s.[13]

An examination of the adult education students and courses testifies to the continuty of the New School during the fifties. Most conspicuously, women continued to outnumber men in all divisions of the New School by about a two-to-one ratio, except in the Graduate Faculty, in which the ratio was reversed. There are several reasons why women so consistently found the New School appealing. The institution aggressively marketed itself to women. It always hired women to its faculty (particularly for its adult education courses) at a time when many institutions did not. Its evening schedule and convenient location in Greenwich Village, near major lines of public transportation, made it accessible to women. Perhaps even more important was the New School's flexible curriculum, which made it attractive to individuals reassessing their careers, a majority of whom were married women. It is not surprising that Gerda Lerner, the dean of American women historians, not only received her B.A. from the New School in 1963 while in her mid-forties, but in the early 1960s taught at the New School what may have been the first course on women's history offered in the United States. Lerner, like so many other New Yorkers, used the New School to facilitate her entry into a profession relatively late in life. The New School enabled its adult students to circumvent conventional patterns of professional education. It provided a ready-made network in New York City for virtually any profession outside the sciences, including business, law, publishing, government, the arts, and education.[14]

An examination of the adult education students in the 1950s shows that they closely resembled those of the 1920s and 1930s. The only significant shifts among the occupational groups were a steady rise in the percentage of housewives (from between 2 and 8 percent before the war to 14.7 percent after) and a decline in the percentage of nurses, psychologists, and social workers (from nearly 10 percent to only 5.7 percent). It seems clear that increasing numbers of housewives found further education at the New School more attractive after World War II. Nurses, psychologists, and social workers, on the other hand, were probably attracted to more rigorous professional programs offered elsewhere.[15]

Educationally, the students showed no significant change in academic preparation. A slightly higher percentage had attended some college but not graduated (about 22 percent before 1945 and nearly 30 percent in the 1950s), but the percentage who had received bachelor's and advanced degrees remained at about 55 percent and 16 percent, respectively. The geographical distribution also changed little. In the 1950s about half of the students came from Manhattan, 15 percent from Brooklyn, 8 percent from the Bronx, 13.4 percent from Queens and Long Island, 3.2 percent from Westchester County, and 7.5 percent from New Jersey. The remaining 2 percent came from Staten Island, Pennsylvania, Connecticut, and New York State. The only detectable change in geographical distribution was a slow decline in students from Brooklyn and the Bronx, offset by a comparable increase from Westchester County, Queens, and Long Island. These shifts seem to have reflected population shifts within the New York metropolitan area rather than changes in the student body at the New School. On the whole, New School students remained mostly female, relatively well educated, often Jewish, and from the more affluent boroughs of New York, a profile that would have applied equally well to the students of the 1920s and 1930s.[16]

Similarly, those who lectured at the New School in the 1950s resembled the lecturers of the previous decades. They were an extraordinary and eclectic group. In some cases they were the same people. Although women had always lectured at the New School, the percentage of women lecturers increased steadily from about 5 percent in the 1920s to 9 percent in the 1930s, to 15 percent in the 1940s, 20 percent in the 1950s, and 25 percent in 1960.[17] Most lecturers taught courses in the arts, literature, psychology, and current events. Most would have identified themselves as politically liberal or progressive, although there were exceptions, such as conservative political commentators Peter Vierick and Russell Kirk. Whatever lecturers' political persuasions, however, they were almost all secular humanists. In the Art Division Berenice Abbott, Stuart Davis, and Peggy Bacon continued to offer courses as they had in the thirties and forties. Also in the Art Division, art historian Meyer Schapiro lectured on modern art and gestalt psychologist Rudolph Arnheim taught the psychology of art. In the Adult Education Division political commentators Max Lerner and Hans Kohn, socialist advocate Norman Thomas, theologian Reinhold Neibuhr, and political theorist Hannah Arendt periodically lectured on contemporary politics; Sidney Hook and Ernest Nagel taught philosophy; Karen Horney and Erich Fromm offered courses in psychology; critic Alfred Kazin and poet Robert Frost taught writing and literature; Margaret Mead gave courses in anthropology; and Adolph Berle lectured on economics.[18] Like earlier lecturers, these people did not seem to have been attracted simply by the pay, although it was at times generous.[18]

In 1951 Rutgers anthropologist Ashley Montagu explained why he taught at the New School. His remarks echoed those expressed by other instructors.

> Students come to the New School of their own volition because they want to know. This is a blessing to the teacher in many ways. New School students are the best of all question askers. They not only ask questions, they also make contributions of their own to the learning and the teaching process. They feel free, and are encouraged to feel free, to bring their own experience and knowledge to bear upon the development of any point. In my classes I have often learned fundamental facts of greatest importance and in one or two cases I have persuaded students to publish in scientific journals, with much accruing benefit to the universe of knowledge. What more can a teacher say than that he learns from his students? Another reason I like teaching at the New School is the warmth prevailing everywhere. Other schools are free, but at the New School warmth is added, and that makes a great deal of difference. There is a humanity and a cordiality at the New School which is unique. One feels welcome and free,

and if there was a better practical demonstration of democracy in action than the New School I have yet to learn of it.[19]

The openness and tolerance of the New School which Montagu celebrated was seriously threatened by an episode of McCarthy-like anticommunism. At various times the New School had been accused of being "procommunist," or at the very least "socialist." From the New School's perspective this was ironic, since as an institution it had always gone to great lengths to avoid any explicit identification with the American Socialist Party, let alone the Communist Party. Moreover, since the mid-thirties Alvin Johnson, like much of the Graduate Faculty, had come to see communism as but a leftist variety of "totalitarianism." The charter of the Graduate Faculty expressly prohibited faculty members from belonging to any party or organization that dictated in matters of intellectual or scientific opinion. As a practical matter, this meant that the New School would not employ any member of the Communist or Nazi Party, and generally would treat with hostility zealots of any faith. For Johnson, "true believers" were the enemies of academic freedom. He accepted Beard's and Robinson's description of their conflict with President Butler at Columbia as a conflict between academic freedom and academic dogmatism. Butler, the Communist Party, the Ku Klux Klan, and the various legislative committees that sought to interdict "un-American activities" all seemed to Johnson to share an antagonism toward freedom of inquiry and expression. Confident in their own versions of the truth, Johnson believed, such persons were determined to impose them on everyone else.[20]

Johnson felt that the New School had consistently fought on the side of academic freedom. It had struggled against intolerance, bigotry, and totalitarianism, as exemplified in the New School's founding, its stand during the Red Scare of 1919, its rescue of the victims of Hitler and Mussolini, its open rejection of anti-Semitism, its early endorsement of black civil rights and female equality, its public opposition to fascism and communism, and, most of all, its unwavering defense of intellectual and artistic freedom. The New School, under Johnson's leadership, had found it relatively easy to separate itself from religious zealotry, fascism, racism, and anti-Semitism. The school's "leftist" commitments, however, which by 1950 amounted to little more than a critical attitude toward laissez-faire economic policy, a rejection of traditional Christian cultural values, and an affirmation of a form of scientific rationalism, were often shared by members of the Communist Party. Indeed, in the 1920s and 1930s the New School attracted as faculty members and students a number of individuals sympathetic to the Communist Party and the Soviet Union, some of whom were party members. These people saw no tension between intellectual honesty and party membership, even if Alvin Johnson and others at the New School disagreed.

All this said, Alvin Johnson was by temperament a tolerant individual. He believed that well-intentioned persons, those who shared his moral and political beliefs, would in the tolerant context of the New School be tolerant themselves. Moreover, within prescribed limits he enjoyed controversy and the free play of ideas. His unofficial guidelines for faculty appointments were that candidates currently belong to no secret organizations (such as the Communist Party, the Nazi Party, or the Ku Klux Klan) and that they not harangue their students. Beyond this, good teaching, intellectual precosity, and personal civility were Johnson's primary criteria for appointment. At various times he knowingly hired Marxists, among them Bernard Stern, Sidney Hook, Hans Eisler, and Erwin Piscator, after assuring himself that they were not party members.[21] Nevertheless, in 1940 Johnson had supported the Graduate Faculty's adoption of an explicitly anticommunist clause in its charter in response to the school's difficulty with the Department of State and Immigration. After 1947 Johnson's anticommunist rhetoric intensified, and in his private letters he acknowledged that he had been meeting regularly with FBI officials since the 1930s to report on the faculty. A Rockefeller Foundation memorandum indicated that Johnson had also monitored files of "enemy aliens" in the early 1940s for the federal district attorney. According to Sidney Hook, Johnson on at least one occasion "wanted to get rid of a Communist Party member" but "delegated it to Clara Mayer." Other evidence indicates that Johnson personally questioned individuals about whom he had doubts, and that he would never have tolerated someone who in his opinion was an ideologue.[22]

Even so, Johnson did not fire Hans Eisler, Erwin Piscator, or Bernard Stern. Their disavowal of party membership and their current conduct were sufficient for Johnson, although the circumstances of Piscator's departure from the New School are ambiguous. In any case, Johnson appears to have remained on the sidelines, and to this day Maria Ley believes that Johnson acted honorably toward her husband and the Dramatic Workshop. Moreover, as anticommunism became a means to discredit political opponents in the 1950s, Johnson, Kallen, Simons, Hook, and others at the New School came out against what they described as a "new witch hunt." Once again, the New School represented itself as a "fortress" of academic and artistic freedom.[23]

Ironically, just as the New School began to criticize publicly the anticommunist crusade of Senator Joseph McCarthy and others, it enmeshed itself in a self-destructive, anticommunist episode entirely of its own making. In 1951 the board of trustees, in response to scattered criticism, instructed the administration to hang a curtain over the portion of the Orozco murals that sympathetically portrayed Lenin and the Russian Revolution. They asked Simons, further, to remove the murals as soon as possible without damaging them. This action by the board soon caused the school untold embarrassment. New York newspapers wrote it up, Artists Equity protested, and a group of New School students petitioned the administration.[24]

The incident became a comedy of errors. First, despite the board's instructions, Simons realized that it would be impossible to remove the murals undamaged; they were frescoes, and the pigments of the paint were part of the plaster walls. Next, at the request of Alma Reed, Orozco's former agent, the Mexican government agreed to pay for the rehabilitation of the murals, a generous and diplomatically sensitive offer which the board refused to accept since it wanted them removed, not restored.[25] In addition, Johnson himself took enormous pride in the murals and had often used them as an example of the New School's atmosphere of tolerance and freedom, most recently in his autobiography, *Pioneer's Progress,* published in 1950.[26] Finally, under pressure, the board reached a compromise. It agreed that the murals, as an important work of art, should be preserved, and it affirmed that anyone had the right to examine the murals whenever they wished. But because the murals were on the wall of the cafeteria, they "violated the liberties of those who found them objectionable." Consequently, while the room was in use as a cafeteria or during any other public function, the board ordered that the curtain be drawn across the Soviet scene only.[27]

The compromise pleased no one. Those who had advocated the removal of the murals considered the school's vacillation tantamount to sympathy with the Russian Revolution and international communism.[28] Those who had criticized the veiling of the murals accused the administration of kowtowing to McCarthyism and succumbing to political paranoia. The New School's reputation had been sullied, they declared, and the continued presence of the curtain simply advertised its compromised condition. A "Student Mural Committee" insisted that "such an act of official suppression" represented nothing less than "a capitulation to the forces of darkness."[29] At the very time that McCarthy and his ilk had largely discredited themselves, the New School had managed to appear both cowardly and stupid. Later, with no fanfare or announcement, the curtain was removed.

As ludicrous as the affair now seems, there were serious issues involved and the veiling symbolized a momentary change at the New

School. In the early fifties painter Robert Gwathmey of the art department met with Clara Mayer in Central Park, where she questioned him about previous party membership. Stunned, Gwathmey recalls that he refused to answer but was so upset he immediately resigned from the New School.[30] In 1953 the board reviewed two other faculty members on suspicion of Communist Party connections, philosopher Harry Slochower and economist Karl Niebyl.[31] During these same years the administration also received inquiries from congressional and Senate committees, the FBI, and numerous individuals.[32] Attorney Clarence Mitchell of the New York law firm of Choate, Mitchell and Ely, after receiving a Graduate Faculty course catalog from Simons and an assurance that the school was not affiliated with the socialist Rand School, nonetheless suggested: "It would seem to me desirable for any new school in America to include at least a few good American names. This list reads like a collection of foreign Jews."[33] Although few critics of the murals had expressed such blatantly bigoted sentiments, the anticommunist atmosphere of the early 1950s had a demoralizing effect on the New School. This was compounded by slumping enrollments and continuing budget deficits, which increased the school's dependence on donors and thereby its vulnerability to outside political pressures. The malaise, though, proved short lived. In 1955, with the announcement of the new building program, the New School established a momentum that sustained it through the 1960s.

The construction of the Twelfth Street building in 1930 had given new impetus to the arts at the New School, and the building project of the 1950s had a similar result. The 1934 *New School Art Bulletin* read: "Art is no longer a thing apart, a serene escape from the social turmoil. It asserts its right to a share in the process of creating society. . . . There can be no mistaking the collective movement of art toward historical relevancy."[34] That humanistic affirmation of art as a form of rational inquiry and communication, an interpreter of modern life, was shared by most of the artists who taught at the New School. In the 1930s, Max Wertheimer's course, "The Psychology of Music and Art," had reinforced the New School's rationalistic and humanistic approach to artistic expression. After his death in 1943, Wertheimer's student Rudolf Arnheim carried these same concerns to students in his course. "Arts and the Psychology of Perception," which he taught at the New School through the 1960s. Artists and scholars who joined the art faculty during the 1940s and 1950s for the most part affirmed this humanistic perspective. These included sculptors Seymour Lipton and Chaim Gross and painters Robert Gwathmey, Julian Levi, and Louis Schanker who, together with Stuart Davis, Peggy Bacon, photographer Berenice Abbott, Camilo Egas, and sculptor José de Creeft, offered a humanistic, but no less modernist, alternative to the dominant abstract expressionism of the fifties as the New School, following World War II, emerged as an important center for the arts in New York City, even as its art faculty and students increased in number and professional influence.[35]

The writing program at the New School likewise enjoyed significant growth in the postwar years, although it too continued patterns established before the war. In 1927 Gorham Munson, a member of the Stieglitz circle, on impulse offered a writing workshop at the New School. Student response was so overwhelming that Johnson asked Munson to repeat the course. Over the next forty years Munson's writing workshop became legendary at the New School. His handbook for young writers, *The Written Word*, was derived from that course.[36] After the war, responding to student demand, the New School expanded its writing workshops, adding Charles Glicksberg, Don Wolfe, and Hiram Haydn as teachers. In conjunction with the workshops the school published *American Vanguard*, an anthology that included the best writings of the New School workshops and *New Voices: American Writing Today*, an anthology that drew largely on young New School writers. Munson, Haydn, Wolfe, and Glicksberg not only trained their students to write, but in many cases secured writing jobs for them and lobbied publishers on their behalf. From 1945 to 1960 students from the New School writing workshops published nearly a hundred novels and won numerous literary prizes. The most notable were William Styron, Mario Puzo, and Sigrid deLima, daughter of Agnes deLima, long-time director of public relations at the New School. Styron and deLima each won the prestigious Prix de Rome for their first novels.[37] In the early fifties the program had become so successful that critic Maxwell Geismar, writing in the *Nation*, asserted that "the New School has become the richest center of new fiction among all our colleges and universities."[38]

Music and dance at the New School did not prosper after the war as writing and the plastic arts did. After the thirties, the dance program never again achieved the stature of its heyday, when Doris Humphrey, Charles Weidman, and Hanya Holm had taught studio dance and John Martin had lectured on modern dance. The same was true of music. By 1935 Charles Seeger had left, and Ernst Toch, after teaching at the New School for two years, moved on to California. In 1942 Hans Eisler also went to California. Aaron Copland returned for an occasional lecture, but only Henry Cowell remained as a full-time faculty member.[39] The explanation may have had less to do with the New School itself than with other factors: California's emergence in the 1930s as the center of modern music in the United States, the expansion of music and dance in American universities, and the establishment of the Juilliard School as the preeminent American school for music and dance. After the 1930s modern music and dance may simply no longer have needed the fairly limited facilities and patronage that the New School offered. Whatever the explanation, the New School, under Cowell's direction, continued to offer a modest music program. It claimed at least one renowned composer, John Cage, who in the 1950s and early 1960s not only challenged virtually every conventional assumption then held by composers but influenced several important New York painters as well.[40]

Cage, like Cowell, was at odds with the American music establishment and with nearly everyone who taught at the New School in the 1950s. This is particularly evident when Cage is compared with his contemporary at the New School, sculptor Seymour Lipton, who did not believe that Cage's work qualified as art. Cage, inspired by the libertarianism of Henry David Thoreau, Walt Whitman, and his own mentor Henry Cowell, in turn considered Lipton an esthetic authoritarian who feared individual creativity.[41]

Cage grew up in Los Angeles and graduated from high school in 1912. He attended Pomona College for two years and then left to travel in Europe and the United States, pursuing various interests along the way. In 1933 he left California again to go to New York, where he planned to study under Henry Cowell at the New School. Cowell, after working with Cage for about a year, recommended that he return to California to work with Arnold Schoenberg. Cage studied off and on with Schoenberg over several years, spending the next decade moving from place to place, composing music, studying other artistic fields, and making a living at whatever happened to come his way. In 1948 he accepted a short-term teaching position at Black Mountain College, an experimental school near Asheville, North Carolina, where he organized his first artistic "happening."[42]

Apart from Cowell and Schoenberg, the most important influences on Cage appear to have been a series of lectures he attended on Zen, delivered by Professor Daisetz Suzuki at Columbia University in the early 1950s, and *I Ching*, a Chinese game of chance. In 1956, on a whim, Cage offered a class on modern music composition at the New School. Cage's course soon became a source of inspiration for several New York painters, including Al Hansen, Dick Higgins, George Brecht, and Allan Kaprow.[43] To this day Cage continues to teach occasionally at the New School. In his words, its "lack of academic rigor" makes it an ideal institution.[44]

By any conventional standard, Cage's compositions are not music at all. They exhibit neither structure, harmony, nor rhythm. By design they have no beginning, end, or middle. They begin when listeners start to listen and end when they cease to listen. Cage refuses to define music as anything more than "a continuity of sound" or "noise," which includes silences as well as whatever incidental noises listeners might hear, such as street sounds, private conversations, and rumblings in the heating system.[45] In 1952 Henry Cowell gave one of the clearest descriptions of Cage's music:

> To John Cage, a brief series of sounds, or even a single combination of them has come to seem complete in itself, and to constitute an audible "event." But he does not use the conventional organization of music, in which such events are related through planned rhythms, melodic, and harmonic succession to produce what we are accustomed to consider an organic musical development. Instead, since Cage conceives each musical "event" to be an entity in itself that does not require completion, he simply places them one after another and sees them related through their existence in space, where they are set in a planned order of time. Each "event" is an aggregate of materials of sound that cohere, making a tiny world of their own much as physical elements find themselves joined together in a meteorite. A work of Cage's therefore, might well be likened to a shower of meteors of sound.[46]

In the fifties Cage was attracted to the paintings of abstract expressionists, which like his own compositions seemed to be unstructured, with no end or beginning. In contrast, however, he rejected those painters who made Nietzschean-like claims to special artistic insight and who insisted that their works revealed their inner selves.[47] Cage dispensed with structure in an effort to eliminate all forms, hierarchies, and boundaries. He denied that either he or his work was in any sense special. They were but aspects of reality, valuable in themselves, but not more valuable than anything or anyone else. Indeed, art for Cage became an event or, as he called it, a "happening." Successful art, he argued, should "change ways of seeing [and hearing] to open up one's eyes to just seeing what there was to see" and one's ears to sounds.[48] As an artist, Cage did not try to create beautiful or precious artifacts; his goal was to expand his audience's sensory perception, to make them aware of themselves and their surroundings. His compositions simply existed. There was no harmony of sounds or forms. "If art was going to be of any use," he said, "it was . . . not with reference to itself but . . . to the people who used it, they would use it not in relation to art but . . . to their daily lives."[49]

Drawing on Zen, Cage understood art as purposeless play, an affirmation of life. He was not interested in bringing order out of chaos, interpreting reality for others, or creating esthetic ideals and sensibilities to inspire humanity to higher ends. He intentionally used chance to determine the exact character of his compositions, by that means removing his own values and judgments from the final product. He assembled the parts and determined the time and place, but he left the order and even the duration of his compositions to chance. He hoped that his use of chance would lead individuals to an insight into the community they shared with the remainder of nature, to suspend their sense of selfness and resign themselves to reality. Cage unequivocally rejected the assumptions of western rationalism as egotistical, coercive, and artificial, even as he affirmed egalitarianism and secularism.[50]

Although he was overtly apolitical, Cage nonetheless recognized the political implications of his notion of art. A remarkably consistent individual, Cage carried his anarchic view of art into life, or, perhaps more accurately, he carried his anarchic ethic of life into his art. In truth, he lived his art. He described himself as a "practical anarchist," which he defined as a person who lived as free as possible without provoking the police. He did not advocate the overthrow of the state or the dissolution of institutions. He acknowledged the importance of "organizing" the functions necessary for life (what he called the "utilities"), but insisted that music, play, and personal relations should be left to individual whim.[51] Divorced in 1945, he considered coercive all "relationships" that were unnecessary for life itself, even family relationships. His insistence on freedom without responsibility was one reason he so liked teaching at the New School. He could teach whatever he wanted. If his students did not enjoy it, they were free to leave. He owed them nothing even as he owed the New School nothing. The New School was a proper "utility," similar to the electric company. Cage could use it when he wished, for as long as he wished, so long as he paid his bills.[52]

Temperamentally and intellectually, few persons could be as different from one another as John Cage and Seymour Lipton. And yet both taught what they described as "modern art" at the New School, and for similar reasons. Modern art allowed both to express themselves freely, and the New School offered them the opportunity to share with others, on their own terms, their ideas on art. One of the premier American sculptors of the postwar generation, Lipton—far more than Cage—exemplified the values that had, by the 1950s, become embodied in the New School. Born in New York City in 1903, Lipton attended New York public schools, including City College. In 1927 he graduated from Columbia and in 1929 received his D.D.S., also from Columbia. In the early thirties Lipton gave up his career in dentistry and devoted himself full time to sculpture. He first exhibited at the radical John Reed Club. He described himself as a "Morris Cohen liberal and a Franklin Roosevelt Democrat," and his work in the thirties reflected those political commitments. Three of his best works were wood sculptures entitled *Lynched, Breadlines,* and *Revolutionary Front.* In 1940 Lipton taught his first course at the New School. Influenced by artists from the "School of Paris," who came to New York after 1940, Lipton moved away from representational and politically oriented art. By the early 1950s he had become known for his abstract, welded steel figures, in which he dealt symbolically with psychological, philosophical, and religious themes. His work is represented in many of the major American and European museum collections.[53]

For twenty-five years Lipton taught at the New School, an experience he described in an interview in 1981:

> I worked all day by myself, and I found it entertaining to be with a group of people who were intelligent, were able to ask intelligent questions . . . in the kind of situation that gave rise to polemics, to discussion, to search, to adventure. One of the big things that I found in teaching at the New School was that there was a kind of excitement in the method in which I addressed myself to the class. This is very important because I had no fixed syllabus. I had absolute free rein, nobody came in and told me what to do or how to teach and I made it absolutely clear I could never teach creativity.[54]

Although Lipton had established himself on his own as an important sculptor, it was through the New School that he found his most important patron, Vera List. According to Lipton, one night after class he called a student aside and recommended that he have his clay sculpture cast. The student replied that he could not afford it. Vera List, another student in the course, overheard the conversation and asked Lipton if the piece was good enough to warrant casting. Lipton assured her that it was. She then offered to pay the cost if the student would make a second casting for her. Surprised at her interest, Lipton asked if she could afford the $150 for the two castings. List answered that she could. His interest aroused, Lipton inquired if she had any art in her home. According to Lipton, List replied in a matter-of-fact way that she owned a Matisse, a small Cézanne, and a few pieces by other impressionists. "I realized from her manner of speech," recounted Lipton, "that she was telling the truth! She wasn't boasting. . . . I said, 'That's wonderful!' " Lipton later learned that Vera List's husband, Albert List, was president of RKO, and that she was a novice art collector.[55]

Later, when List asked Lipton if she could visit his studio, he replied, "Certainly! Anytime you want!" At his studio she chose one piece, asked to buy it, and then inquired about a larger piece. Lipton explained to her that the larger piece was not for sale because he hoped that a museum would acquire it. At this, List offered to buy the piece and present it to the Metropolitan Museum of Art. The Metropolitan readily agreed to accept it. In the process Lipton and the New School secured two generous patrons, Vera and Albert List. The Lists purchased several other sculptures from Lipton, promoted his work, and took an avid interest in the art program of the New School. In 1956 the Lists contributed money for the construction of the Eleventh Street building, which included an art gallery. In the 1960s Vera List served on the board of the New School and advised the art department. With Paul Mocsanyi, the director of the New School's art gallery, she transformed the New School into an important institution for New York art.[56]

Lipton's primary interest in the New School had always been intellectual. Even before he joined the art faculty he had attended lectures at the New School. He traces one of his most important insights to a lecture on legal philosophy given by Morris Cohen at the New School. The lecture led Lipton to read Cohen's *Reason and Nature* and *Logic and the Scientific Mind*, which Cohen had coauthored with Ernest Nagel. From Cohen, Lipton adopted a notion of "polarity." Human existence consisted of a multiplicity of tensions, between life and death, irrationality and rationality, sadism and eroticism, individualism and community, law and lawlessness, love and hatred, peace and war, philanthropy and misanthropy, creativity and destruction. All were equally real and equally human. For Lipton, courageous individuals, while embodying these potentials, resisted their own polarization. They sought an equilibrium that made possible both human survival and individuality.[57]

But artistic creativity, argued Lipton, went beyond the intellectual recognition of the human condition. "The rationalist in Cohen was great as far as it went, but it was a limiting force," declared Lipton. As a sculptor Lipton sought to draw intellectually on philosophy and history, but without the artist's creative encounter with materials and tools, he declared, "there is a loss of intensity of a single human soul, and it is my deep belief that the single human soul in the Jeffersonian sense is the final desiderata of mankind. If you lose that you lose everything." Lipton believed that art should be inventive, but that it should not be mere oddity. It should employ the "instruments of history," but should do so to further the ends of arts, "to help gouge out the forms necessary to present the peculiarities of what goes on in the blood of a single human being in the second half of the twentieth century."[58]

When asked about his opinion of John Cage's work, Lipton replied, "I didn't like Cage's work. ... I can't accept his preoccupation or propensity toward oddity and defiance of everything of the past, all the rules of the past, all the meaningfulness of the past, and throwing them out of the window and starting afresh. This kind of realism is not academic. It's anarchic, and it tends toward oddity and the bizarre, and it doesn't fulfill my feeling for certain human needs for organization, harmonic organization in some way."[59] Although Lipton had little use for Cage's "happenings," he did not think it inappropriate for Cage to teach at the New School. Lipton accepted Cage's nonsensical work as one of the polarities of reality. And as long as Cage did not seek to impose his esthetic on others, Lipton believed that Cage had the right to express it even as Lipton had the right to dismiss it.

Like Lipton, the New School was tolerant, if not approving, of John Cage's "practical anarchism." He was apolitical by their standards, and therefore inoffensive; and besides, he always attracted enough students to pay his salary. More important, the public recognition he brought to the New School strengthened its reputation as an avant-garde institution. Others at the New School may have thought that Cage was peculiar, but his particular kind of irrationality, his advocacy of a radical form of human freedom, was much more to their liking than a rationality dictated by a church or political party. Seymour Lipton—who believed that creativity existed within the bounds of logical thought and included a responsibility toward the rest of humanity—had more in common with those who had guided the New School, but John Cage still qualified for membership in the school's church of "liberalism."

For Alvin Johnson, Clara Mayer, Hans Simons, Seymour Lipton, and John Cage the New School at the end of the 1950s continued to stand for academic and personal freedom. The banner that Beard and Robinson had first raised by resigning from Columbia and founding the New School had been carried faithfully through another decade. Two new buildings had been constructed, enrollments were climbing steadily, and the school's broadly defined ideological legacy appeared secure. It seemed an appropriate time for those who had built and nurtured the New School for nearly four decades to turn over their responsibilities to the succeeding generation. But the hope for an orderly succession proved illusory. At the New School the troubled sixties began at the very start of the decade; the early 1960s proved to be the most traumatic period in the New School's crisis-ridden history.

12

THE CHANGING
OF THE GUARD

THROUGHOUT ITS FORTY-YEAR HISTORY, the New School had maintained a remarkable degree of intellectual and institutional cohesion. Despite, perhaps because of, chronic financial difficulties, both the Adult Division and the Graduate Faculty had remained true to the principles of their origins. For this reason, the 1960s were a particularly difficult time for the New School. Prosperity, popularity, and the expansion of programs and buildings all contributed to a loss of intimacy, if not of common purpose. Similarly, academic and administrative routine replaced what had been an integrated, if sometimes chaotic, internal spirit. As courses, departments, and divisions proliferated, the institution lost the personal qualities that Alvin Johnson and Clara Mayer had instilled and the sense of urgency that had informed the work of the original members of the Graduate Faculty. Still, some of the old character persisted. The appointments of Hans Jonas and Hannah Arendt in philosophy and Robert Heilbroner in economics insured the intellectual vitality of the Graduate Faculty in the 1960s, while the appointments of Jack Everett as president and Allen Austill as dean of the Adult Division reaffirmed the educational and moral commitments of Johnson and Mayer.

The changes of the 1960s, particularly those within the Graduate Faculty, stand in contrast with the stability of the 1950s. Then the Graduate Faculty's institutional solidity had provided the basis for its intellectual stature. Hans Simons, Clara Mayer, and Hans Staudinger together provided the institution's continuity. Staudinger's generous personality, political skills, and obvious competence made him an effective leader of the emigré faculty. For those who worried that the Graduate Faculty would come to resemble a conventional graduate school, there was the comfort of Adolph Lowe's explanation. "Departments at the Graduate Faculty exist only for administrative convenience."[1]

By late 1958, however, departmentalization and competition for students threatened to transform the once interdisciplinary and cooperative Graduate Faculty into a conventional American graduate school. Moreover, although other departments retained their theoretical orientation, economics and psychology at the New School had gradually become much more oriented toward experimental and quantitative research.[2] The turning point came a year later, in 1959, when Hans Simons announced his resignation as president. Staudinger, energetic as always but well past the normal age of retirement, followed suit. Their simultaneous departures ushered in a five-year period of institutional crisis, which reached a climax in Clara Mayer's forced resignation in 1960. Finally, in 1963, Alvin Johnson became, appropriately, the last to leave. In 1959, however, the pending presidential appointment was seen not so much as an opportunity to replace the old leadership as an issue within the current debate concerning the school's "essential" character.[3]

In the mid-1950s, several administrators had wanted to abandon the New School's experimental and political ethos and move it into the mainstream of American higher education. Arguing that the institution needed an endowment, they proposed that a regular B.A. degree program be established as part of a full-scale undergraduate college, complete with full-time, tenured faculty appointments and accreditation.[4] Hans Simons had already moved the school along these lines by expanding the physical plant, enlarging the faculty, and encouraging teachers in the Adult Division to hold their students to collegiate standards. He had done so, however, without fundamentally altering the unorthodox character of the school, always seeking the advice and support of Alvin Johnson, Clara Mayer, and Hans Staudinger.[5]

At the time of his retirement, Simons commissioned a series of reports, self-studies, and evaluations, all of which argued the need for change. In particular, several of these reports pointed to the increased tension that existed between the adult and graduate divisions. Some argued, for reasons that are not quite clear, that the Adult Division inappropriately subsidized the graduate program. Without actually calling for the dissolution of the Graduate Faculty, they nonetheless offered it as an "appropriate possibility." The Graduate Faculty responded aggressively by developing its program in a manner that emphasized the singular role of disciplinary departments.[6] The prolonged succession crisis led many on the Graduate Faculty to conclude that their institution could survive only by becoming more like other American graduate schools. The proponents of this position argued that only new appointments could renew the school. They also declared that Europe now had little to offer, either intellectually or politically. There could be no new University in Exile. Surprisingly, many of these arguments came from the Europeans themselves, but Adolph Lowe, for one, disagreed. If the Graduate Faculty were to be renewed, he stated, it would have to embrace an ideal of "enlightened" or "philosophical specialization." The contemporary world needed more than well-trained functionaries, insisted Lowe, echoing the pleas of James Robinson: it needed individuals with strong ethical commitments and broad philosophical horizons.[7]

Lowe's argument fell less on deaf than on deafened ears as the board in early 1960 announced the appointment of Abbot Kaplan of UCLA as the New School's fourth president. The faculty advisory committee—comprised of psychologist Rudolf Arnheim and biologist René Dubos, among others—had nominated Francis Horn, president of the University of Rhode Island, and natural historian Loren Eiseley of the University of Pennsylvania.[8] The board, however, chose Kaplan, whom it had imagined would be good for public relations. After only one day in office, Kaplan resigned, returning to accept the deanship of UCLA's Division of Theater Arts. Acting quickly, the board appointed Staudinger's successor as dean of the Graduate Faculty, Henry David, as the fifth president of the New School. David remained only two years, even though the board had clearly looked to him as a person who would bring continuity at a time of institutional embarrassment. A labor historian, David had taught at the City College of New York and then at Columbia University. He had also been director of the National Manpower Council, supervising an eight-volume study of human resources. As dean of the Graduate Faculty from 1959 to 1960, he had worked under Simons and Mayer. Noting Clara Mayer's personalized style of direction, David characterized the New School's administration as a "mom and pop operation," sorely in need of a rational and bureaucratic organization.[9] His first important act as president of the New School was to ask for Mayer's resignation as dean of the Adult Division.

Despite the protests of a large segment of the most prominent teachers in the Adult Division, including composer Henry Cowell, literary critic Alfred Kazin, and writers Kenneth Koch and Marion Rich, David replaced Mayer with William Birnbaum, a political sociologist who had earlier taught at the London School of Economics.[10] David sought to place the school on a more businesslike footing, strengthen and regularize its degree programs, and locate new sources of financial support. But, like Hovde before him, David misunderstood the New School. Mayer's firing proved disastrous. In one stroke the New School lost its most loyal administrator, the generous financial support of her family, the backing of its German-Jewish constituency, and the loyalty of much of its most effective faculty. By 1962 it was clear that David's attempt to "restructure" the New School along more conventional university lines might well destroy the school. Then, in the winter of 1962–1963, David convinced some members of the board that they should merge the New School with its neighbor, New York University.[11]

The board discussed the issue, framed by David in financial terms, only to find itself badly divided. David argued that the school would need $400,000 to remain intact and independent, but older members— Dorothy Hirshon, Vera List, Elinor Gimble, and David Levin—rejected David's suggestions outright. Johnson himself did not participate in the discussions, having been "banished" to his home in Nyack. For the first time in forty years, Johnson seems to have been denied a significant role in New School policy. The board continued to resist David's notion of a merger, but it did consider the possibility of eliminating the Graduate Faculty to solve the financial crisis.[12] Ultimately, however, the board expressed its lack of confidence in David's leadership.

In February 1963, shortly after his eighty-eighth birthday, Johnson decided to discuss the problem with his old colleague Hans Staudinger. Together, they worked out a strategy to "save the school" one more time. Staudinger and Johnson contacted Joseph Halle Schaffner, a partner in Hart, Schaffner and Marx and the nephew of Hiram Halle, who had provided the original funding for the University in Exile in 1933. Johnson convinced Schaffner to pledge a substantial portion of the $400,000 they estimated was needed to keep the New School intact and preempt any decision to sell or radically alter the institution.[13] With Schaffner's pledge in hand, the two old veterans approached other long-time New School supporters, many of whom David had either ignored or alienated by his methods. Within a matter of weeks, Johnson and Staudinger had secured pledges for the full $400,000. Working closely with allies on the board, Johnson and Staudinger then called a secret meeting to present their plan to the entire board.[14] Surprised and pleased, the board agreed to ask for David's resignation and announce a fund-raising campaign. Johnson and the board then quickly appointed a new president, Robert MacIver, a board member and distinguished Columbia social scientist who had retired from teaching in 1950, but who remained active in the field of public policy. MacIver, hand-picked by Johnson and committed to preserving both the adult and graduate divisions, agreed to serve as interim president.

By intent, MacIver's administration was temporary and transitional. The financial and administrative crisis solved, the New School entered the 1960s ready to ride the currents of prosperity. This was as true of the Graduate Faculty as of the school as a whole. By 1967 the Graduate Faculty had expanded so much that it had to abandon its quarters on Twelfth Street for a new building several blocks away on Fifth Avenue and Fourteenth Street. New appointments of Peter Berger, Thomas Luckmann, and Arthur Vidich in sociology; Hans Jonas, Aron Gurwitch, and Hannah Arendt in philosophy; Joseph Greenbaum and Leon Festinger in psychology; Robert Heilbroner in economics; Hans Morgenthau in political science; and the creation of a department of anthropology further testified to the Graduate Faculty's vitality.

There were departures, as well, in the course of the decade, and by 1970 few of the old guard remained. Adolph Lowe, Arnold Brecht, Erich Hula, Hans Neisser, Hans Speier, and Hans Staudinger continued to teach part time as professors emeriti, but they were no longer active forces in the Graduate Faculty. Despite the new appointments and the shift in emphasis from theoretical and philosophical interests to empirical research, however, Robert Heilbroner, Hans Jonas, and Hannah Arendt reaffirmed the faculty's traditional interest in philosophy and politics. Two of them, Jonas and Arendt, though relative· latecomers to the Graduate Faculty, were members of the University in Exile's original European emigré generation. Both had fled Germany in 1933, but neither joined the New School until considerably later, Jonas in 1953 and Arendt in 1967, although she had lectured in the Adult Division at various times in the 1950s. Heilbroner, born into a German-Jewish family in New York, had studied economics with Adolph Lowe. He joined the Graduate Faculty in 1968.

Jonas emigrated first from Germany to Palestine and then to Canada. Arendt fled initially to Paris, arriving in New York in 1940 after her forced internment in southern France. As refugees from Germany, Arendt and Jonas were preoccupied with defining the role, not just of intellectuals, but of German and Jewish intellectuals. Each joined the Graduate Faculty only after they had reached what they considered satisfactory conclusions. In Arendt's words, "When one is attacked as a Jew, one must defend oneself as a Jew."[15] Yet each had chosen to live in New York rather than in Israel. Moreover, unlike their friend and former fellow graduate student Leo Strauss, neither of them repudiated modern thought, nor did they alienate themselves from German liberalism. Although they made their Jewishness central to their identities, neither did so in explicitly religious terms. They both understood themselves as "moderns," and as such they utilized a post-Kantian vocabulary to analyze contemporary political and philosophical problems.

Arendt, who died in 1975, and Jonas, who continues to write and teach, first met in 1924 as philosophy students in Martin Heidegger's seminar at Marburg. For them, Heidegger had brought German philosophy "to life again."[16] They, along with many other young German intellectuals, flocked to him as the new master. Heidegger drew on both the neo-Kantian heritage of Marburg, represented by philosopher Heinrich Rickert, and the phenomenology of Edmund Husserl. Claiming that he had recovered philosophy's original and unique intent—to inquire into the ontology of being—Heidegger criticized the entire western philosophical tradition from Plato to Kant. He invited his students to follow him back to the roots of pre-Socratic philosophy to discover the hidden subterranean alternative to the western tradition. Heidegger's flirtation with Nazism in 1933–1934 led many of his students to reject his teachings entirely. For Arendt and Jonas, Heidegger's politics underlined the already deep tensions that existed in the 1920s between him and his Jewish students. Unlike their fellow student Leo Strauss, Arendt and Jonas devoted their subsequent careers to finding "modern" alternatives to Heidegger's philosophy. Throughout their careers, each of them debated the meaning and value of human knowledge and society. Despite great differences in their formal concerns, both Arendt and Jonas dealt with similar questions of ethics and judgment.

At the New School, from 1953 to 1975, Jonas explored the problems arising out of the conventional philosophical notion of consciousness. "When many years ago I turned to the study of Gnosticism," wrote Jonas recently, "I found that . . . Heidegger enabled me to see aspects of gnostic thought that had been missed before."[17] Jonas began his formal studies at the age of eighteen with Heidegger and the Protestant theologian Rudolf Bultman. Although Jonas wrote his dissertation on Augustine, as did Arendt, his philosophical reputation prior to the mid-1950s rested on his monumental, three-volume study of Gnosticism. Influenced by the idealism he found inherent in Kant, Husserl, and Heidegger, Jonas uncovered in early Christian Gnosticism a mirror for contemporary life. In studying the Gnostic "mind," Jonas postulated the existence of a dualism that so radically distinguished between the divine and the human that objective "norms" became impossible.[18] In their denial of objective ethical standards in favor of an inner truth, Gnostics seemed, to Jonas, to be remarkably like contemporary existentialists.[19] Jonas believed that modern philosophers should resist the "Gnostic" temptation to seek inner truth and search instead for a rationalist means to bridge the apparent chasm between human action and human knowledge. Such a division, Jonas believed, derived in part from the nihilism inherent in existentialism and in part from western philosophers' concern with consciousness.[20]

Between 1930 and 1952, Jonas published several books and dozens of scholarly papers. Still, he failed to receive a permanent university appointment. He spent almost a quarter of a century in political and intellectual exile. Born in 1903, Jonas entered the University of Marburg in 1922, completed his dissertation on Augustine in 1928, and soon after started work on his *habilitation,* a major scholarly work required to enter the academic profession in Germany. While at Marburg Jonas participated in several Zionist organizations, which he later characterized as middle class and middle of the road. In 1923 he interrupted his studies to spend eight months on a farming community in Palestine. He recalls thinking at the time that if he were forced to leave Germany permanently he would emigrate to Palestine. In the spring of 1933, Jonas left Germany for London. He had intended to go to Jerusalem, but determined first to finish his scholarly work at the British Museum. Three years later he left London for Palestine.

In Jerusalem, Jonas obtained a series of visiting teaching appointments at Hebrew University. Following the outbreak of anti-Jewish riots in 1936, Jonas joined the Zionist military organization, Hagganah. In 1940 he entered the Jewish Brigade of the British army as an artillery officer, a rank he also held in the Israeli army during the 1948 War of Independence. During the two years of demobilization, from 1946 to 1948, Jonas taught ancient history and classical languages at the British Consulate School, which closed when Israeli independence was declared in 1948.[21]

After a dozen years of only irregular academic appointments, Jonas decided to emigrate. He wrote to his old friend Leo Strauss for help. Strauss in turn contacted Else Staudinger, director of the American Committee for Exiles in the Professions. Staudinger wrote to her Canadian counterpart, who found Jonas a position at Carleton University in Ottawa. Jonas came from there to the New School for the summer of 1953, and was offered the chairmanship of the Graduate

Faculty's newly independent philosophy department a year later. It took another twelve months to obtain a visa from the State Department, but in 1955 Jonas finally joined the Graduate Faculty.[22]

By the time Jonas arrived at the New School he had determined to embark on a new project. Whereas his earlier work on Gnosticism had been influenced by Heidegger, his new work was critical of Heidegger's philosophical position. While serving in the army, Jonas recalled, it had all become clear. In the military, with no access to formal intellectual resources, but with an enormous amount of free time, he had reflected on the question of "being." He rejected the idealist tendency to understand human existence in terms of consciousness, an exclusively mental phenomenon.[23] Instead, Jonas called for a "philosophy of organism," which took into account all those attributes that made up a living being. Jonas believed that he had gone well beyond Heidegger's influence without abandoning the centrality of the idea of "being." If, Jonas argued, humans deal with their entire being, they confront the totality of human existence, physical as well as mental. The physical, animal part of human existence links humans to the world; it enmeshes us in "our material reality."[24] Jonas insisted that the dualism of German philosophy had artificially separated consciousness from matter. In his own work, he sought to provide a philosophical explanation for the unity of human consciousness and nature.

In 1959, to celebrate the twenty-fifth anniversary of the Graduate Faculty, Jonas delivered to a special session of the school's General Seminar an address entitled "The Practical Uses of Theory."[25] Jonas noted that no theory adequately explained the use of theory and, therefore, the place of philosophy within the realm of human activity. He believed that ethical norms had traditionally been derived from notions of divine authority and, subsequently, from the mutual processes of the self, the individual. Jonas, whose concerns were ontological, postulated a new "philosophy of life" to embrace human biology and consciousness and thereby "relocate the foundation of the ought from the ego of man to the nature of being in general."[26] The tendency among contemporary philosophers to separate ontology from ethics, argued Jonas, mirrored the dualism by which modern thinkers separated theory from application. By locating human consciousness in nature, he defined ontology as a search for ethics based on principles discoverable "in the nature of things."[27] He ranged far afield from the technical and epistemological questions that had preoccupied much of the Graduate Faculty, yet he also reaffirmed the institution's longstanding insistence that social scientists take seriously the moral implications of their work. Questions of judgment, he argued, are the most important questions, and may be properly understood only when human nature is itself more completely and wholly grasped.

Hannah Arendt also dealt with issues of ethics and judgment. Three years younger than Jonas, Arendt rejoined her old friend on the Graduate Faculty in 1967. She, like others at the Graduate Faculty, was interested in the relationship between politics and philosophy, between practice and theory. Although her answers differed from Jonas's, there was an inherent kinship in their thought. Born in 1906 and educated in Königsberg, Immanuel Kant's home, Arendt started reading Kant at the age of sixteen. She began her university training at eighteen and studied philosophy under Heidegger, Husserl, and Karl Jaspers. Although close to Heidegger, she eventually adopted Jaspers's synthesis of phenomenology and Kantian rationalism.[28] Like Jonas, Arendt failed to secure a conventional academic position until her appointment at the University of Chicago in 1963 and later at the New School in 1967.

Her biographer has suggested that Arendt possessed a special gift for friendship. From the very start of her formal intellectual life, she established circles of friends who influenced her thought. In the mid-1920s Arendt participated in the salon of Marianne Weber, the widow of Max Weber, whose members included Alfred Weber and Emil Lederer. Several years later Arendt wrote for *Gesellschaft,* a Social Democratic journal edited by Lederer and Albert Salomon. Following her exile to Paris in 1933 she gravitated toward philosopher Alexandre Koyré, critic Raymond Aaron, Russian Hegelian scholar Alexandre Kojevé, and writer-essayist Walter Benjamin. After coming to the United States in 1940 Arendt associated with the Marxist-oriented *Partisan Review,* and was particularly close to writer Mary McCarthy. Finally, at the New School, she gathered around her a group of devoted graduate students, including her future biographer Elizabeth Young-Bruehl, New School dean Jerome Kohn, and philosopher Elizabeth Minnich, who each found in Arendt a mentor of extraordinary intellectual and personal presence.[29]

Throughout her life, Arendt took seriously the tenuousness of being a Jew in an implicitly Christian culture. Yet her work went beyond what might be called the "Jewish question." In all her writing, Arendt struggled with themes which she believed other intellectuals avoided or found discomfiting, specifically what had become in her terms the "banality of evil." Prior to 1933, by her own admission, she had largely ignored political discussions, but the Nazi succession to power awakened her concern. In Paris, from 1933 to 1940, she worked for the Zionist rescue committee, Youth Aliyah, and married her second husband, Heinrich Blücher, a working-class Marxist who introduced

Arendt to a wide range of leftist political theory. In 1940 she and her husband successfully managed to run the refugee gauntlet from southern France through Spain and Portugal to New York. Ensconced in a small flat on East Ninety-fifth Street, Arendt took a job as a writer for the German-language newspaper *Aufbau,* subsequently became the research director for the Conference on Jewish Relations which Morris Cohen had founded in 1933, and worked as an editor for Schocken Books, where she supervised the posthumous publication of the works of Franz Kafka and her old friend Walter Benjamin. In 1950 she published her first major work, *The Origins of Totalitarianism.*[30]

In *Totalitarianism,* Arendt summarized the political consensus of her fellow European emigrés, many of whom had been associated with the New School. Her notion of totalitarianism—which equated Nazi and Stalinist regimes because of their commitment to terror and propaganda and their common stance as antinational, antiliberal, and antibourgeois—was by now a familiar feature of postwar anticommunist arguments. Arendt, however, went beyond a description of totalitarianism by raising fundamental questions about the nature of liberal democracy as manifested in the West and its relation to totalitarian systems. Leaning heavily on Jaspers's ideas and still struggling to free herself from Heidegger's influence, Arendt offered what she considered a "phenomenology" of totalitarianism.[31] She used philosophical concepts to explore political movements, but found herself caught between two quite different modes of explanation. Her historical account rested on the assertion that totalitarianism was both an attack on and a consequence of the failures of democratic liberalism and the nation-state. In fact, though, the "liberal" institutions that characterized the most liberal nations—England, France, and the United States—were conspicuously absent in prerevolutionary Russia and even in pre-Hitler Germany. Arendt never adequately addressed this discrepancy between her theory and historical fact.

Still, a compelling aspect of Arendt's work in *Totalitarianism* was her criticism, similar to those made by Reinhold Niebuhr and Karl Barth, of the tendency among modern thinkers to dismiss the inherent capacity of all humans to act evilly. She could not accept the horror of Nazi genocide as a historical anomaly or as a peculiarly German problem. As a cultivated German, Arendt denied that German culture was a flawed exception to the prevalent civility of western society or that it could be explained without reference to twentieth-century philosophy. By ignoring the question of evil, or by relegating it to categories of metaphysics and theology, Arendt declared, modern philosophers had failed to recognize an essential aspect of modern, liberal culture and human nature.

In the first and most convincing section of *Totalitarianism,* Arendt dealt with the origins of modern anti-Semitism. Speaking from the Zionist position that criticized the "blindness" of assimilation, she asked: Why the Jews?[32] Her answer only confirmed her position. She saw Jewish emancipation as an aspect of the emergence of the liberal, secular nation-state. Jews became citizens and were thereby tolerated to the extent that they had abandoned their Jewishness. Those Jews most reconciled to liberal nationalism were themselves the most assimilated, the least Jewish. Ironically, she pointed out, the critics of the liberal nation-state singled out Jews as the agents of the de-Christianization of European culture and the cosmopolitan enemies of the nation-state system itself. In the late nineteenth and early twentieth centuries European Jews found themselves in an impossible situation. The secularism of the liberal nation-state denied them their religious identity, while the critics of the liberal nation-state wished to destroy Jews themselves. Zionism seemed to Arendt the only answer. Still, as a Zionist she did not support a wholly independent Israel. A Jewish nation-state seemed to her only to recreate in a Jewish form the dilemma of European nationalism. It offered no acceptable alternatives for religious minorities. It solved only a particular Jewish problem, and even for Jews begged the issue of the enormous diversity of belief and practice among Jews themselves. Instead, to demonstrate her belief that homogeneous groups might establish self-governing communities within a federated polity, she favored a binational solution for Arabs and Jews in Palestine.

Arendt returned to the themes of evil and Jewish assimilation a decade later in her controversial "report" on the trial of Adolph Eichmann, held in Jerusalem in 1961. Originally written for the *New Yorker* magazine, *Eichmann in Jerusalem* raised a storm of controversy.[33] She, in effect, indicted European Jews for a passivity that contributed psychologically to Nazi genocide. Her critics charged that by depicting the Jewish councils in complicitous if not collaborationist roles, Arendt also appeared to be continuing her attack on assimilation. Much of her essay, however, was directed at Eichmann himself. By employing the phrase "the banality of evil," she asked how a completely ordinary human being could commit mass murder. By what system of values could such behavior be understood? Arendt was stunned by Eichmann's utter inability to distinguish good from evil, his incapacity to judge. She attributed his disability to the disability of modern philosophers who seemed incapable of dealing with moral issues. Arendt searched for a philosophical source, an ontological foundation, within the western tradition that would enable her to comprehend Eichmann's quite ordinary and commonplace amorality. His evil could not be explained by German history or his biography. The evil he embodied seemed an essential part of humanity itself.

Following the publication of *Eichmann in Jerusalem*, Arendt, particularly in her graduate seminars at the New School, continued to search for a philosophical foundation for a morally informed politics. Her seminars attracted an almost worshipful group of graduate students. To these disciples Arendt presented two personalities. At home she was informal, even grandmotherly, dispensing food and ideas with equal relish. But in the classroom she remained intellectually unremitting and demanding.[34] She shared with her intimate circle of students her own rediscovery of Kant and to a lesser extent her continuing attraction to Jaspers. Kant provided Arendt a philosophical framework that defined freedom as the "public use of one's reason at every point," the "democratic" implication that all humans were capable of discriminating between truth and falsity, between good and evil.[35] She also endorsed Kant's preference for contemplation over action. Only the spectator, Arendt argued, and not the actor, could properly judge "by the standard of progress" the significance of an event for the individual and for the human race.[36] Political participation denied individuals the detachment necessary to make reliable judgments.

Arendt offered Kant as the antithesis of the unreflective evil represented by Eichmann. As a participant, Eichmann symbolized the "privation" of good, of failed humanity, not just its darker nature.[37] She argued that humanity had to have a "public philosophy" before it could reconstruct a civilized world. Only by subjecting public acts to constant philosophical scrutiny could the "banality of evil" be avoided. In Kant, Arendt had found a language of politics and a rational basis for judgment. In rejecting Heidegger, both Arendt and Jonas, in circuitous ways, returned to what they understood as the essence of eighteenth-century rationalism: a belief in the efficacy of reason, the potential of universal human dignity, and the necessity of intellectual freedom.

This "enlightened prospect" was shared by economist Robert Heilbroner, who with Arendt and Jonas dominated the intellectual life of the Graduate Faculty in the 1960s and 1970s. As a student and friend of Adolph Lowe, Heilbroner came to the New School largely by accident.[38] A New Yorker, born in 1919, he attended the Horace Mann School, at that time a laboratory school for Columbia's Teachers College and therefore strongly influenced by the progressive educational theories of John Dewey. Heilbroner attended Harvard University, where he studied literature and economics. There Paul Sweezy, an American Marxist, introduced him—the son of a successful garment manufacturer—to the "social overtones" of economics. Graduated in 1940, Heilbroner served during the war as a Japanese-language interpreter in the Pacific. He returned to New York with several decorations and a determination to take advantage of the GI Bill.

Following the war Heilbroner worked as an economic analyst in international trade and, restless, he wrote freelance articles on economics, the first of which was published in *Harpers*. Then, in 1946, he took a seminar on Ricardo, offered by Adolph Lowe at the New School. To Heilbroner the faculty at the New School seemed to be serious, yet courtly intellectuals, steeped in European culture and history. Heilbroner viewed his teachers—Lowe, Hans Neisser, and Karl Mayer—as "conservative socialists, both anti-fascist and anti-Stalinist, who were all Mills [John Stuart] at age eleven." Still, he found himself attracted to the place and the people. "I felt at home there, at the New School," he declared, "not at Columbia."[39] The New School confirmed for him what he calls his "New Deal liberal socialism." Sustained by Lowe's intellectual vigor and encouraged by the unique environment, Heilbroner reconsidered his business career as he came to think of himself as a scholar.

The Worldly Philosophers, published in 1953, remains Heilbroner's best-known work.[40] Its phenomenal commercial success enabled him to support himself as a writer.[41] A study of the "lives, ideas, and times" of western economic thinkers, the book was in fact a portrait of Heilbroner's own intellectual world. His ideas have changed over the years, particularly his understanding of Marx and Marxian methodology, but *The Worldly Philosophers* still provides important insights into his thought. Heilbroner identified with Marx the intellectual, not the political revolutionary. Thus, when Heilbroner called himself a "liberal idealist," like Arendt he saw himself as an intellectual who "judges" rather than "acts."[42] A historian of economic thought, rather than a theorist, he consciously avoided the technical concerns that preoccupied most academic economists. Rather, he devoted himself to a critical evaluation of the concept of the market economy, which he believed no longer met the articulated needs of society. He also tried to disabuse his readers of popularly held misconceptions about economic theory. Heilbroner translated the jargon and formulas of the "dismal science" into a language accessible to a literate audience without distorting the often highly technical writing of economists. He understood his audience as informed, yet general readers, very much like those who attended his lectures at the New School.

In *The Worldly Philosophers* Heilbroner described how Marx, starting from classical or Smithian assumptions concerning the mechanism of the marketplace, had gone on to elaborate the dynamics of dialectical materialism.[43] He depicted Marx as trying to demonstrate to his contemporaries that capitalism contained within it the seeds of its own destruction. To Heilbroner, however, Marx was less important as a prophet than as an economist who convincingly explained important features of the nineteenth-century market economy. He presented Marx as an empirical, if not a "positive," economist, ignoring almost entirely Hegel's influence on Marx. Yet Heilbroner struggled less with Marx himself than with "Marxism." Much as Marx in the nineteenth century had sought to determine why the market economy had failed to create social justice, so Heilbroner asked why it had failed to do so in the twentieth century. He also questioned why Marxism had seemed such a jumble of unconvincing contradictions for most western thinkers.

Over the next twenty-five years, Heilbroner published a dozen books in which he dealt with the historical and contemporary nature of modern capitalism.[44] Consistently, he argued that capitalism was limited by both its internal contradictions and its theoretical perspectives. He projected a gradual "socialization" of capitalist organization in which politically imposed choices rather than supply and demand predominated.[45] Heilbroner's sense of himself as a mediator between "capitalism" and "socialism" is similar to that of earlier economists who taught at the New School. Much as Thorstein Veblen, Wesley Mitchell, Adolph Lowe, and Eduard Heimann, Heilbroner accepts the idea of a limited market economy regulated in the public interest by populary elected officials.

In the early 1970s Heilbroner returned to Marxism. *Marxism for and Against* was his first systematic reexamination of Marxism since *The Worldly Philosophers*, where Heilbroner argued in behalf of an alternative to conventional, market-oriented economic theory.[46] At the same time he felt uncomfortable with the Marxist notion of a classless society, and he disapproved of the Soviet economy. Although sympathetic to the possibility of a socialist economy and convinced that Marx's economic theory provided a useful method of analysis, he remained unsure that Marxism offered any practical guidelines beyond a critical vision.[47] Writing in the late 1940s and early 1950s, Heilbroner had accepted the conventional portrait of a scientific Marx. In the sixties, Heilbroner reexamined Marx apart from his nineteenth-century positivist context. As he turned to Marxist revisionists such as philosophers Herbert Marcuse and Louis Althusser, who had resurrected the Hegelian, idealist tendency in Marx's early writing, Heilbroner found a "new" Marxism which relied as much on the idea of a "critical dialectics" as on materially determined historical necessity. In accepting the Hegelian interpretation of Marxism, Heilbroner moved toward the ideas of the neo-Marxist Frankfurt School. Marxian dialectics, he argued, consisted of an analysis that stripped away the surface appearance of economic behavior to reveal the "essential, true, reality" of its subject. Conventional economics, which accepted external behavior as the sole source of economic knowledge and values, simply justified existing behavior by postulating laws that described that behavior. Heilbroner, in effect, accepted the argument of his mentor, Adolph Lowe, who had insisted that conventional economic theory in its "positive" or descriptive mode of analysis represented a form of class ideology, a self-fulfilling prophecy. Heilbroner believed that Marx's dialectical method offered a means to raise critical questions concerning the nature of capitalism. Even so, he was disturbed by the seemingly irresistible tendency of Marxism to become an alternative ideology, complete with its own orthodoxy. Heilbroner wanted economists to use Marxist analysis as a critical perspective to enable them better to penetrate their own conventional beliefs, not as a new faith.

Heilbroner's self-conscious embodiment of the New School's tradition of egalitarian, experimental, and antiprofessional education did not characterize most of the changes taking place at the New School during the 1960s. Heilbroner, who had received his doctorate from the New School in 1963, witnessed its transformation into a modern university. Members of the Graduate Faculty had traditionally offered at least one "open" course in the Adult Division. As the older faculty either left or retired, however, their replacements—with the exception of Heilbroner, Mary Henle, Felicia Deyrup, and Saul Padover— restricted their teaching almost entirely to graduate instruction. The Graduate Faculty's move to its own building—appropriately, in a department store—in 1967 and the division of its faculty into departments, a process that had begun in the late fifties, accelerated this trend. These changes coincided with the loss of many of the school's most important administrators and faculty.

In 1963, after having pushed Henry David out of office and established Robert MacIver as interim president, Alvin Johnson returned to Nyack, this time permanently. He died on June 7, 1971, at the age of ninety-six. In 1962 Clara Mayer, embittered by David's high-handed treatment, retired to her house on the East Side. She remained there until the 1970s when she moved to a more convenient apartment on Central Park South, where she now lives. On his retirement in 1960, Hans Simons joined the Ford Foundation in India. He maintained contact with the New School only through occasional letters to his old friend Arnold Brecht. Hans Staudinger remained actively involved with the New School until his death in 1978, at the age ninety-two, soon after having completed his autobiography. Robert MacIver, the rear-guard of the old guard, retired in 1965; he was succeeded by Jack Everett, who served as president until 1981.

Everett, former president of Rollins College, chancellor of the City University of New York, student of Paul Tillich and protégé of Johnson himself, oversaw the expansion of the New School in a period of unprecedented institutional prosperity. During this time the Adult Division, directed by Allen Austill, more than doubled its enrollments. Austill, a University of Chicago trained political scientist, managed this growth with the help of colleagues Wallis Osterholz and Sal Baldi, each of whom remains associated with the New School today. Only a handful of Alvin Johnson's and Clara Mayer's people remained, such as Esther Levine, the first historian of the New School, who provided personal continuity with the earlier New School. Everett and Austill, together with Vice President for Development Albert Landa, carried on the New School's tradition of eclectic, student-oriented adult education. The prosperity of the 1960s allowed them to develop the New School in directions that some felt undercut the academic seriousness of the school. By the early seventies the Adult Division offered courses in almost every subject imaginable, taught by literally hundreds of part-time lecturers. The New School became more truly than ever the "academic utility" that John Cage had described.

As Alvin Johnson had done before him, Everett expanded the overall programs of the New School as opportunities arose. In the 1960s the New School established the Seminar College, a B.A. degree program directed by Elizabeth Coleman, which coordinated structured undergraduate seminars with course work in the Adult Division. An innovative Master's program in liberal studies was also initiated under the direction of Benjamin Nelson and then Jerome Kohn, a former graduate student of Hannah Arendt. In 1970 the school acquired Parsons School of Design, just across the street from the Graduate Faculty on Fifth Avenue, and in 1979, the Otis Art Institute in Los Angeles. In the wake of the acquisition of the Otis Art Institute, one observer joked that the New School would soon become the McDonald's of adult education, with a franchise in every major American city, as well as Columbus, Ohio. Still, the institutional acquisitions and proliferation of courses were consistent with Johnson's and Mayer's policies since the 1920s. Unabashedly market oriented and profiting from the success of its catalog, a New York institution in itself, the Adult Division had always offered courses on demand as long as the content was consistent with the school's democratic cosmopolitanism. And, as had been the case since the 1920s, the Adult Division not only paid its way, it subsidized the school's more serious scholarly activities, most importantly the Graduate Faculty.

In a similar fashion, the Graduate Faculty flourished during Everett's administration. Student enrollments and faculty size doubled during the 1960s, even as enrollments in the New School as a whole approached 25,000. In the early seventies, however, a period when graduate enrollments were declining nationally, the Graduate Faculty once again found itself in jeopardy. With the deaths of Aron Gurwitch and Hannah Arendt and the retirement of Hans Jonas, the once distinguished philosophy department was devastated. In sociology Karl Mayer and Albert Salomon retired, and in the late 1960s its young stars Peter Berger and Thomas Luckmann both resigned. Adolph Lowe retired from the economics department. In political science and sociology, Arnold Brecht died, and Hans Speier and Hans Morgenthau, each of whom had resumed his teaching career at the New School, re-retired, as did long-time librarian and avid New School supporter Esther Levine. Things became so desperate that in 1978 the New York State Board of Regents rescinded accreditation for the doctorate programs in philosophy, political science, and sociology-anthropology. These problems led to the resignation of the dean of the Graduate Faculty, Joseph Greenbaum, and the appointment of University of Chicago political scientist Ira Katznelson as his replacement.

At the end of the 1970s the school confronted the unhappy prospect of either severely cutting back the Graduate Faculty, perhaps even eliminating it, or investing an enormous amount of money to rejuvenate it. As in the past, the school faced its old dilemma: lacking an endowment and a loyal undergraduate alumni, it had to raise money from private donors or drain off resources from the Adult Division. Raising outside money was always difficult, and diverting resources from the Adult Division threatened to weaken severely the very program that made the New School unique and solvent. The dilemma was familiar, but this time Alvin Johnson was not waiting in the wings, ready at the last minute to step in and miraculously save the school. Everett, in 1979, chose to resign in the belief that more youthful leadership could pull the school through. In 1980 the New School inaugurated Jonathan Fanton, formerly assistant to the president of the University of Chicago, as the seventh president of the New School. The problems were everywhere evident, and the solutions elusive.

The New School's difficulties can be traced to a specific set of institutional problems. Still, the challenge that it faces goes beyond the New School itself and includes the "democratic humanism" that it has so long and faithfully articulated. To some extent, the New School's future depends on whether or not it can convince potential benefactors that the educational and political values it represents are worth saving. Throughout its history, its challenge has been to criticize society and yet to participate actively in it. Critical distance from the mainstream of American academic life has frequently resulted in the New School's dismissal as an eccentric and maverick institution, while its political activism has at times led it to lose some of that same critical distance. In addition, its rejection of traditional standards and its openly skeptical attitude toward conventional professional canons have left the New School vulnerable to intellectual and artistic fads.

Nonetheless, the New School has remained steadfast to the liberal and democratic commitments of its founders. It has advocated personal freedom, artistic and intellectual creativity, scientific rationalism, and democratic politics. Defining itself as nondisciplinary, it has at times encouraged what appeared to be little more than confusing eclecticism, but it has also been the setting for some remarkable collaborative efforts. The dance and music compositions of Doris Humphrey, Aaron Copland, and Henry Cowell, Erwin Piscator's epic drama, the structuralism of Claude Lévi-Strauss and Roman Jacobson, John Cage's influence on abstract expressionism, and Alfred Schutz's phenomenology all developed in the atmosphere of free exchange that characterized the school. Artists and intellectuals in twentieth-century America have found few places as flexible and innovative as the New School.

Revelations of the Nazi death camps, the gulags of Soviet Russia, the atomic explosions at Hiroshima and Nagasaki, and the seemingly self-destructive hedonism of the western democracies have made it difficult for intellectuals since World War II to embrace the defiantly affirmative, if critical, democratic humanism of the New School. Its answers have often seemed either naively irrelevant, philosophically unsophisticated, or too obscure to deal with the chaotic and apparently hopeless condition of the postwar world. The quest of the New School to create a democratic society, informed by a rationalist philosophy and a cosmopolitan culture, is as relevant and realizable today as it was at the turn of the century. Only today, such a vision fails to elicit the utopian enthusiasm that the founders of the New School personified and the school as a whole embraced. The liberalism that inspired the school has become a significant political force, and during its heyday the New School was at the front of the movement that struggled for a more democratic and liberal society.

It may well be that the liberal point of view is no longer compelling, and that, therefore, the New School has lost its most important purpose. The dreams of the New School's past cannot define its future. Yet, to the extent that those dreams have found fulfillment in the history of the New School—dreams of academic freedom, of a cosmopolitan and democratic community, of a social science informed by concern for the world we live in—they may inspire another generation to look beyond the world as it is and establish something new.

NOTES

CHAPTER 1   1917: The Conception of a New School

1. *New York Times* (October 10, 1917).
2. Nicholas Murray Butler, "Annual Report for 1917–1918," Columbia University (New York, 1918), p. 43.
3. A detailed account of the Columbia episode is provided in William Summerscales, *Affirmation and Dissent: Columbia's Response to the Crisis of World War I* (New York, 1970), chapters 3 and 4. See also Richard Hofstadter and Walter P. Metzger, *The Development of Academic Freedom in the United States* (New York, 1955), pp. 470–475, and Richard Hofstadter, *The Progressive Historians: Turner, Beard, and Parrington* (New York, 1970), pp. 285–288.
4. James McKeen Cattell to George L. Rives, chairman of Board of Trustees (May 13, 1913), Cattell Papers, Columbia University.
5. Butler Correspondence (1906–1916), Cattell Papers.
6. Cattell, ed., *University Control* (New York, 1913), p. 5.
7. Twenty-eight members of the Faculty to Cattell (March 3, 1917), Edwin R. A. Seligman Papers, Columbia University. Among those who signed the letter of reprimand were John Dewey, James Robinson, Wesley Mitchell, and Edwin Seligman.

8. Summerscales, *Affirmation and Dissent,* pp. 72–103; Minutes of the Committee of Nine (September 24, 1917), Seligman Papers.

9. Minutes of the Committee of Nine (May 8, 1917; May 11, 1917), Seligman Papers.

10. Seven members of the Committee of Nine to Subcommittee of the Trustees (June 18, 1917), Seligman Papers.

11. Seligman to Cattell (June 18, 1917), Seligman Papers.

12. Committee Minutes (September 14, 1917).

13. Butler, "Annual Report for 1917–1918."

14. Summerscales in *Affirmation and Dissent* and Hofstadter and Metzger in *Academic Freedom* similarly deemphasize the faculty's concurrence.

15. In its statement on academic freedom during wartime, the American Association of University Professors affirmed the idea of "freedom with responsibility," although in the offense for which Butler cited Cattell, the use of university letterhead to ask Congress to oppose conscription, the AAUP sided with Cattell. Report of Committee (AAUP), "Academic Freedom and Tenure" (1917), and Special Committee of General Committee on Academic Freedom and Tenure (AAUP), "Academic Freedom in War Time" (December 24, 1917), carbons of both reports in Seligman Papers; *Columbia Spectator* (October 9, 1917); Charles Beard, "A Statement," *New Republic,* XIII (December 29, 1917), pp. 238–250. At the time of his resignation Beard wrote a detailed account of his long-standing grievances against Butler and the trustees, Beard Papers, DePauw University.

16. Hofstadter, "The Department of History," in R. Gordon Hoxie, ed., *A History of the Faculty of Political Science: Columbia University* (New York, 1955); Beard and James Robinson, *The Development of Modern Europe* (New York, 1907).

17. Burleigh Taylor Wilkins, "Charles Beard on the Founding of Ruskin Hall," *Indiana Magazine of History,* LII (1956), pp. 277–284.

18. Frederic Cornell, "A History of the Rand School of Social Science" (Ph.D. thesis, Columbia University Teachers College, 1976).

19. Beard, *Industrial Revolution* (London, 1901), p. 86.

20. *Ibid.,* pp. 104–105.

21. Beard, "Lessons from Science," *Young Oxford,* II (June 1901), quoted in Bernard C. Borning, *The Political and Social Thought of Charles A. Beard* (Seattle, 1962), p. 15.

22. Luther B. Hendricks, *James Harvey Robinson: Teacher of History* (New York, 1946); Robinson, *The New History: Essays Illustrating the Modern Historical Outlook* (New York, 1927). See also his later books *The Mind in the Making: The Relation of Intelligence to Social Reform* (New York, 1921); *The Humanizing of Human Knowledge* (New York, 1923).

23. Robinson, *New History,* p. 25; *Mind in Making,* pp. 4–5, 13, 61.

24. Robinson, *New History,* pp. 25–27, 134–135.

25. *Ibid.,* pp. 11, 123–127.

26. *Ibid.*, pp. 48, 64-65, 72-73; *Humanizing of Knowledge,* pp. 31-64.

27. Robinson, *Mind in Making,* pp. 12-14, 26-27.

28. *Ibid.*, p. 12.

29. *Ibid.*, pp. 13, 14.

30. *Ibid.*, p. 28.

31. *Ibid.*, p. 36.

32. *Ibid.*, pp. 41, 49.

33. *Ibid.*, p. 165.

34. Robinson, "A Journal of Opinion," *New Republic,* III (May 8, 1915), pp. 9-11; Herbert Croly, "A School of Social Research," *New Republic,* XV (June 8, 1918), pp. 167-171.

35. Harry Elmer Barnes, "James Harvey Robinson," in Howard W. Odum, ed., *American Masters of Social Science* (New York, 1927), pp. 321-408; Lawrence A. Cremin, *The Transformation of the School: Progressive Education in American Education, 1876-1957* (New York, 1961); Laurence R. Veysey, *The Emergence of the American University* (Chicago, 1965); Malcolm S. Knowles, *A History of the Adult Education Movement in the United States* (New York, 1962): David F. Noble, *America by Design: Science, Technology and the Rise of Corporate Capitalism* (New York, 1977); Alexandra Oelson and John Voss, eds., *The Organization of Knowledge in America, 1860-1920* (Baltimore, 1979); Morton White, *Social Thought in America: The Revolt Against Formalism* (New York, 1949); Joseph Dorfman, *Thorstein Veblen and His America* (New York, 1934), pp. 449-496; John Dewey to family (December 28, 1918), Dewey Papers, Southern Illinois University, Carbondale.

36. W. A. Swanberg, *Whitney Father: Whitney Heiress* (New York, 1980), pp. 385, 405-408, 427, 450, 459.

37. Annette K. Baxter, "Emily James Smith Putnam," in Edward T. James, ed., *Notable American Women, 1607-1950* (Cambridge, Mass., 1971), pp. 106-108; *New York Times* (December 23, 1920; January 29, 1921; September 15 and 20, 1931; September 10 and 12, 1919); *Who's Who in America, 1914-1915,* VIII; Straight Family Papers, Cornell University. See also Herbert Croly, *Willard Straight* (New York, 1924), and Swanberg, *Whitney; New York Times* (October 28 and December 31, 1919; February 2, 1920; March 12, 1927; July 23, 1953); *New York Times* (June 8, 1959; June 16, 1938; July 23, 1953; October 20, 1920; March 12, 1941). See also Robert H. Wiebe, *Businessmen and Reform: A Study of the Progressive Movement* (Cambridge, Mass., 1962).

38. "A Proposal for an Independent School of Social Science for Men and Women," printed pamphlet (New York, 1918), New School Archives (hereafter cited as NSA). The first record of plans for a new school are in a letter from Emily James Putnam to Robinson dated January 26, 1916 (Johnson Papers, Felicia Deyrup Collection, Nyack, N.Y.). See also Robinson, "The Need for a New Kind of Education" (typescript, 1918), NSA.

39. Beard and Robinson, *Development of Modern Europe.* See also Borning, *Political Thought of Charles Beard;* Cushing Strout, *The Pragmatic Revolt in American History: Carl Becker and Charles Beard* (New Haven, Conn., 1958), chapters 1, 3, 5, and 7. In many regards the organizers of the New School conformed to an earlier model of social scientists as moral philosophers and reformers described by Thomas L. Haskell in *The Emergence of Professional Social Science: The American Social Science Association and the Nineteenth Century Crisis of Authority* (Urbana, Ill., 1977). See also Carol S. Gruber, "Mars and Minerva: World War I and the American Academic" (Columbia, Ph.D. thesis, 1968). Beard (Oxford Ph.D., 1904); Robinson (Freiburg Ph.D., 1890); Thorstein Veblen (Yale Ph.D., 1884); Horace Kallen (Harvard Ph.D., 1908); Johnson (Columbia Ph.D., 1902); Putnam (Bryn Mawr A.B., 1899); Wesley C. Mitchell (Chicago Ph.D., 1903); Dewey (Johns Hopkins Ph.D., 1884).

40. Dewey, Papers, Family Correspondence (1919–1924), Southern Illinois University, Carbondale.

41. Neil Coughlan, *Young John Dewey: An Essay in American Intellectual History* (Chicago, 1975).

42. Dewey, *Democracy and Education* (New York, 1916), pp. v, 372, 400; *School and Society* (Chicago, 1899).

43. Dewey, *Democracy and Education,* p. 417.

44. *Ibid.,* pp. 358.

45. Dorfman, *Veblen;* Veblen, *The Higher Learning in America* (New York, 1935), pp. 7–11. John Diggins provides a comparative analysis of Veblen's thought of *Bard of Savagery: Thorstein Veblen and Modern Social Theory* (New York, 1978). Veblen, *Higher Learning,* pp. 12–19.

46. *Ibid.,* pp. 199–209.

47. *Ibid.,* pp. 46–63.

48. Dorfman, *Veblen,* pp. 394–396.

49. Veblen, *Higher Learning,* pp. 38–40.

50. *Ibid.,* p. 39.

51. In the 1930s Beard made his implicit absolutism explicit. See particularly his speech at the New School, "Hitlerism and Our Liberties" (April 10, 1934), NSA. Also in the same vein: "In Defense of Civil Liberties," *Current History,* XLIV (April 1936), pp. 228–235; (September 1937), pp. 391–398. See Borning, *Political Thought of Charles Beard,* pp. 140–256; 1955). R. Gordon Hoxie, ed., *A History of the Faculty of Political Science, Columbia University* (New York, 1955).

52. Mary O. Furner, *Advocacy and Objectivity: A Crisis in Professionalization of American Social Science, 1865–1905* (Lexington, Ky., 1975); Burton J. Bledstein, *The Culture of Professionalism: The Middle Class and the Development of Higher Education in America* (New York, 1976).

    See also Richard J. Bernstein in *The Restructuring of Social and Political Theory* (Philadelphia, 1976).

53. Butler, *The Rise of a University*, II (New York, 1937), p. 29. See also Marcia Graham Synnott, *The Half-Opened Door: Discriminations and Admissions at Harvard, Yale, and Princeton, 1800-1900* (Westport, Conn., 1979); Veysey, *Emergence of the American University*, Part III.

54. Cushing Strout, "The Twentieth-Century Enlightenment", *American Political Science Review*, XLIX (1955), pp. 321-339.

CHAPTER 2   The Doors Open in Chelsea

1. *New Republic*, XVII (December 28, 1918), p. iii.

2. "A Proposal for an Independent School of Social Science" (pamphlet printed for public distribution, 1918); "The New School for Social Research" (prospectus printed for public distribution in late 1918 or early 1919), Roscoe Pound Papers, Harvard University Law School Library.

3. E[mily] J[ames] P[utnam] to James Harvey Robinson (January 26, 1916), in Alvin Johnson Papers, Felicia Deyrup Collection, Nyack, N.Y.; Clara W. Mayer, "The New School Tradition" (transcript, circa 1960), NSA (New School Archives). See *New Republic* (July 7, 1915; August 28, 1915; January 6, 1917; February 17, 1917; September 8, 1917; April 6, 1918; April 13, 1918; April 27, 1918; November 30, 1918).

4. Wesley C. Mitchell, diary excerpts (July 16, 1918; July 24, 1918; November 11, 1918; October 2, 1919; February 2, 1920; March 3, 1920; August 20, 1920), contained in Lucy Sprague Mitchell, *Two Lives: The Story of Wesley Clair Mitchell and Myself* (New York, 1953), pp. 333-343. Horace M. Kallen, "Memoir" (typescript, December 17, 1964), NSA. Kallen, interview conducted and taped by Milton Konvitz and Dorothy Kuhn (August 31, 1964; September 3, 1964), tape 623, American Jewish Archives, Cincinnati, Ohio. Joseph Dorfman, *Thorstein Veblen and His America* (New York, 1936), pp. 449-496; Harry Elmer Barnes, "James Harvey Robinson," in Howard Odum, ed., *American Masters of Social Science* (New York, 1927), pp. 317-408; Lewis Mumford, *Sketches from Life: The Early Years* (New York, 1982), chapters 16, 23, and 30.

5. Alvin Johnson, *Pioneer's Progress: An Autobiography* (New York, 1952), pp. 272-279.

6. "Independent School of Social Science: Estimated Annual Cash Requirements to April 30, 1928" (typescript, June 4, 1918), NSA.

7. Johnson, interview conducted by Edward Stettner, Wellesley, Mass. (May 19, 1965).

8. Charles Beard, "The New School for Social Research" (typescript, 1919), NSA.

9. "Early Documents," NSA.

10. New School Course Catalogs (1919-1924), NSA.

11. *Ibid.*

12. "Early Documents"; Johnson, *Pioneer's Progress,* pp. 271-288; Lucy Sprague Mitchell, *Two Lives,* pp. 333-334; Dorfman, *Veblen;* Leo Wolman, interview (March 13, 1957), Columbia Oral History Project.

13. Meriam Beard Vagts, interview (New Milford, Conn., July 1978).

14. Herbert Croly, "A School for Social Research," *New Republic* (June 6, 1918), p. 168; Robinson, "The Need for a New Kind of Education" (typescript, 1919), NSA.

15. New School Catalogs (1918-1925), NSA.

16. Agnes deLima, "New School Associates: 1920-1925" (typescript, May 1959), NSA; Clara Mayer, untitled memoir intended for inclusion in unpublished book (1954), personal papers in possession of Clara Mayer, New York City (a copy is now available at the NSA); Johnson, *Pioneer's Progress,* pp. 276-278.

17. Stella Fogelman, interview (May 22, 1979).

18. Kallen, "Memoir," p. 4.

19. Wolman, interview (March 13, 1957).

20. Kallen to Wolman (July 27, 1923), Kallen Papers, YIVO Institute, New York City.

21. Kallen, "Memoir" (December 17, 1964), pp. 1-4; Barnes, "James Harvey Robinson"; Dorfman, *Veblen;* Lucy Sprague Mitchell, *Two Lives;* Wolman, interview (March 13, 1957).

22. New School, "Report of the Aims, Work, and Financial Condition of the School, December, 1919" (pamphlet printed for public distribution), NSA.

23. "Independent School of Social Science Estimated Cash Requirements" (typescript, June 4, 1918); "Income: 1920-1933" (undated memo), statistical file, NSA.

24. New School, "Work of the First Term; Researches Under Way; Suggestions Concerning Future Development" (typescript, 1919), NSA, p. 1; New School, "Report of December, 1919"; New School, "The New School" (Annual Report, 1922), NSA. The extent of the school's preoccupation with research can be seen in the school's newspaper *The Leaflet* of which three editions are extant (December 1920; January 1921; May 1921). Harry Elmer Barnes wrote *Evolution of Penology in Pennsylvania* (State College, Pa., 1944) (1927), completed *The New History and the Social Sciences* (New York, 1925), and edited *The History and Prospects of the Social Sciences* (New York, 1925). James Harvey Robinson published *The Mind in the Making* (New York, 1921) and while at the New School finished most of *Humanizing of Knowledge* (New York, 1923). Thorstein Veblen published *The Engineers and the Price System* (New York, 1921) and *Absentee Ownership and Business Enterprise* (New York, 1923), Horace Kallen completed *Zionism and World Politics* (New York, 1921), and Charles Beard organized the essays for *Whither Mankind?* (New York, 1928).

25. New School, *Announcement: 1923-1924,* NSA. The 1923-24 course catalog listed twenty-seven courses, including: Veblen, "Economic Factors in Civilization"; Barnes and Robinson, "The Historic Background of the Great

War"; Elsie Clew Parsons, "Sex in Ethnology"; Robinson, "History of the Human Mind"; Wolman, "Statistical Method"; Beard, "Problems of American Government"; Mitchell, "Business Cycles"; Wallas, "Social Inheritance"; Putnam, "Habit in History"; Dewey, "Method in the Social Sciences"; and Roscoe Pound, "Problems of Law Reform in America." The New School also offered courses in social work, education, labor unions, women and work, and psychology.

26. New School, "Preliminary Lectures: February–May, 1919"; *Announcement: 1920-21; Preliminary Announcement: 1921-1922; Supplementary Announcement: Spring Term, 1922; Announcement: 1923-1924,* NSA.

27. Occupations (1919-1929); Academic Training (1919-1929), statistical file (1919-1945), NSA.

28. Total Registrations (1919-1929); Annual Registration Summaries (1930-1935), in statistical file, NSA. Department of Commerce, *Statistical Abstract of the United States, 1920* (Washington, D.C., 1921).

29. Class Lists (1919-1923), in statistical file, NSA.

30. New School, "Report of December, 1919."

31. New School Correspondence (1916-1922), Johnson Papers, Felicia Deyrup Collection, Nyack, N.Y.; Kallen Correspondence (1918-1925), Kallen Papers, YIVO: Kallen Correspondence (1915-1925), Kallen Papers, American Jewish Archives.

32. E. R. A. Seligman, Correspondence, 1900-1930, Seligman Papers, Columbia University; Lucy Sprague Mitchell, *Two Lives;* Joseph Dorfman, "The Department of Economics," and Richard Hofstadter, "The Department of History," in R. Gordon Hoxie, ed., *A History of the Faculty of Political Science, Columbia University* (New York, 1955); Barnes, "James Harvey Robinson"; Luther B. Hendricks, *James Harvey Robinson* (New York, 1946).

33. New School, untitled summary of school's achievements, 1919-1921, written at the conclusion of the reorganization struggle (typescript, 1922), NSA.

34. Lucy Sprague Mitchell, *Two Lives;* Johnson, *Pioneer's Progress;* Kallen Correspondence, 1920-1923, YIVO; Kallen Correspondence, 1920-1925, American Jewish Archives.

35. See Johnson's account, *Pioneer's Progress,* pp. 277-282.

36. Carolyn Bacon, "Report of the Ways and Means Committee" (typescript, 1922), NSA.

37. Johnson, *Pioneer's Progress,* pp. 279-282.

38. Johnson, "Reorganization of the New School" (typescript, 1922), NSA.

39. *Ibid.*

40. Johnson to Dorothy Straight (April 27, 1922), Straight Family Papers, Cornell University.

41. Robinson, "Proposals for the Extension of the Work of the New School in the Direction of Adult Education" (typescript, 1922), NSA; Jack Everett, interview, 1979.

42. No copy of Johnson's "second proposal" has been located, although the substance of the proposal is contained in Mrs. Walton Martin's (Charlotte Hunnewell Sorchan's) resolution to accept Johnson's recommendation (typescript, 1922), NSA.

43. Johnson to Straight, Straight Family Papers.

44. Johnson, *Deliver Us from Dogma* (New York, 1934); *The Clock of History* (New York, 1946); *Ideas Are High Explosives* (private printing, December 8, 1962).

45. Johnson, *Pioneer's Progress,* chapters 1–15.

46. Committee of Fifteen, *The Social Evil* (New York, 1902).

47. Johnson Correspondence, 1900–1920, Johnson Papers, Yale University; Johnson Correspondence (1900–1920), Deyrup Collection; Johnson, *Pioneer's Progress,* chapters 17–26.

48. Johnson, *Pioneer's Progress,* pp. 281–284.

49. New School, "The New School for Social Research" (pamphlet printed for public distribution, 1925), NSA, p. 9.

50. Clara W. Mayer, "New School Tradition"; Esther Raushenbush, "Three Women: Creators of Change, Clara Mayer, Jacqueline Grennan, and Lucy Sprague Mitchell," in Helen S. Astin and Werner Z. Hirsch, eds., *The Higher Education of Women* (New York, 1978), pp. 29–37; Johnson, *Pioneer's Progress,* p. 282.

51. New School Catalogs (1924–1930); Johnson, *Pioneer's Progress,* pp. 270–284; Wolman, interview, Columbia Oral History Project.

52. New School, *Announcement: 1923–1924,* NSA.

53. *Ibid.,* pp. 5–9.

54. "A Proposal for an Independent School of Social Science" (pamphlet printed for public distribution, 1918), NSA.

55. New School, "The New School for Social Research."

56. Quoted in Johnson, *Pioneer's Progress,* p. 283.

57. Wolman, interview (March 13, 1957), p. 86.

58. Johnson, *Pioneer's Progress,* pp. 282–283; Dorfman, *Veblen,* pp. 449–496. John R. Everett, who studied under Johnson and later himself became president of the New School, explained Johnson's decision to fire Veblen with the same ambivalence that characterizes Johnson's own, apparently accurate, account in *Pioneer's Progress* (interview by authors, December 1978).

59. New School, *Announcement: 1926–1927,* NSA.

60. New School, *Announcement: 1927–1928,* NSA, p. 5.

61. See note 25 above. New School, *Announcement: 1924–1925; Announcement: 1927–1928; Announcement: 1928–1929; Announcement: 1919–1930,* NSA.

62. Mumford, *Sketches from Life,* chapters 16, 23, 30, pp. 335, 424ff.; Aaron Copland, *The New Music: 1900–1960* (New York, 1968), pp. 151–170; Doris

Humphrey, *An Artist First: An Autobiography* (Middletown, 1977), pp. 92, 192, 275, 282–284.

63. Occupations: 1919–1929, statistical file: 1919–1945, NSA.

64. Academic Training: 1919–1929, statistical file: 1919–1945, NSA.

65. Class Lists: 1919–1930, statistical file: 1919–1945, NSA. Although the lists are not complete for every year, a random sample of about 300 names for each period revealed little variance.

66. Wolman, interview (March 13, 1957), pp. 24, 83, 90.

67. Mayer, "New School Tradition."

68. New School, "The New School for Social Research."

69. Johnson (untitled draft of report to board partly typed and partly in longhand, 1925), Johnson Papers, Deyrup Collection.

70. Income: 1920–1933, statistical file (1919–1945), NSA.

71. New School, "Report of the Director: 1927–1928" (printed for distribution to board of directors, 1928), NSA.

72. Johnson, *Pioneer's Progress,* p. 320.

CHAPTER 3   Growing Up on West Twelfth Street

1. New School *Annual Report, 1927,* NSA (New School Archives); Alvin Johnson, *Pioneer's Progress: An Autobiography* (New York, 1952), p. 316.

2. Walter Laidlaw, ed., *Population of the City of New York: 1890–1930* (New York, 1932); Jerome Myers, *Artists in Manhattan* (New York, 1940).

3. Johnson to Horace Kallen (September 28, 1926), Kallen Papers, American Jewish Archives, Cincinnati.

4. New School, *Announcement: 1927–1928,* NSA; Seymour Lipton, interview (June 9, 1981). Clara Mayer's family and Vera List were particularly interested in the arts at the New School.

5. New School for Social Research Folder, 1924–1929, Laura Spelman Rockefeller Foundation Collection, Rockefeller Archives, Pontico Hills, N.Y.

6. Daniel Cranford Smith to Rubin Schekter (March 5, 1929), NSA; Johnson to Ruth Wellman (February 7, 1929), NSA; Johnson to Kallen (August 1, 1929), Kallen Papers, American Jewish Archives.

7. Johnson to Agnes deLima (December 26, 1929), Johnson Papers, Yale University; "Building Program: New School for Social Research" (pamphlet, 1930), NSA.

8. Clara W. Mayer, "Building and Murals" (typescript, 1950), private collection, Clara Mayer, New York City; Johnson to Kallen (August 1, 1929); Johnson, *Pioneer's Progress,* pp. 316–320.

9. Joseph Milner to Johnson (December 13, 1929; April 1, 1930; November 7, 1930); Johnson to Mrs. Wesley C. (Lucy Sprague) Mitchell (March 28, 1930,

carbon), Johnson Papers, Felicia Deyrup Collection, Nyack, N.Y. Also in Deyrup Collection are copies of the bond agreements.

10. Johnson, *Pioneer's Progress*, p. 326.

11. "Building Program," p. 3.

12. Caroline Ware, *Greenwich Village: 1920–1930* (Boston, 1935); Francis P. Naughton, "Making the Greenwich Village Counter-Culture: An Analysis of the Construction of an Urban Intellectual Community" (Ph.D. thesis, New School for Social Research, 1978); Albert Perry, *Garrets and Pretenders* (New York, 1960).

13. Ware, *Greenwich Village.*

14. Joseph Bensman and Arthur Vidich, *Metropolitan Communities* (New York, 1975); Erwin A. Gutkind, *The Twilight of the Cities* (New York, 1962); Peter Hall, *World Cities*, 2nd ed. (New York, 1927); Robert E. Park, *Human Communities* (New York, 1952).

15. *Bulletin: New School* (1924–1944).

16. Robert Flint, "Modernity Rules New School of Social Research," *Art News*, XXIX (January 17, 1931), pp. 3–4.

17. Johnson, *Pioneer's Progress*, pp. 320–321; Johnson to Mitchell (March 28, 1930), Deyrup Collection; Mayer, "Building and Murals," Mayer Papers; Henry Russell Hitchcock and Phillip Johnson, *The International Style Since 1922* (New York, 1932).

18. Obituary, Joseph Urban, *New York Times* (July 19, 1933). Peter Vergo, *Art in Vienna: 1898–1918* (London, 1975), pp. 87–178.

19. Johnson, *Pioneer's Progress*, pp. 320–323.

20. deLima, "Trail Blazing in Housing" (typescript, 1942), NSA.

21. Joseph Urban, *Theatres* (New York, 1929); Urban, *The New School for Social Research* (architectural presentation, 1930), NSA.

22. "A Building for Adult Education" (typescript, 1931), NSA; Shepard Vogelsang, "The New School for Social Research," *Architectural Record*, LXVII (April 1930), pp. 305–309, and LXIX (February 1931), pp. 139–150.

23. Johnson to deLima (January 1, 1931), Johnson Papers, Yale University.

24. Alma Reed to Johnson (April 28, 1931) and Johnson to Reed (May 11, 1931), Johnson Papers, Deyrup Collection; Reed, *Orozco* (New York, 1956), pp. 163–164; Lewis Mumford to author (January 5, 1981). The murals can be seen today at the Alvin Johnson Building, New School for Social Research, on Twelfth Street. Photos taken at the time of their execution are available in the Art Collection, New York Public Library and the Smithsonian Institution. Since the Orozco murals have deteriorated somewhat, the New York Public Library photos are useful to determine their original quality. Prints are also available at the Smithsonian Institution.

25. Johnson, *Pioneer's Progress*, p. 164.

26. José Clemente Orozco to deLima (February 9, 1952); Orozco, "Address to Art Committee of the New School for Social Research Associates" (October 17, 1945), NSA.

27. Thomas Hart Benton, *An American in Art: A Professional and Technical Autobiography* (Lawrence, Kans., 1969), pp. 61–64.

28. The best discussion of the intellectual controversy provoked by the term "modern" in American painting is George Roeder, *Forum of Uncertainty: Contradictions with Modern Painting in Twentieth-Century American Thought* (Ann Arbor, Mich., 1981). For a more wide-ranging discussion see the essays in Irving Howe, ed., *The Idea of the Modern in Literature and the Arts* (New York, 1967), and Richard Pells, *Radical Visions and American Dreams* (New York, 1973). See Orozco, *An Autobiography* (Austin, 1962), and Benton, *An American in Art.* For statements by other New School artists see: Aaron Copland, *Our New Music* (New York, 1941) and *Music and Imagination;* (Cambridge, Mass, 1952); John Martin, *Introduction to Dance* (New York, 1939) and *Modern Dance* (New York, 1933); Joseph Urban, *Theatre;* (New York, 1930) Clemente Orozco, *An Autobiography*; Horace Kallen, *Art and Freedom* (New York, 1942); Henry Cowell, *New Musical Resources* (New York: 1930) and *American Composers* (Stanford, Calif, 1933); Ralph Pearson, *A New Art Education* (New York, 1941) and *A Modern Renaissance in American Art* (New York, 1953); John Dewey, *Art and Experience* (New York, 1937); Alvin Johnson, *Delivery Us from Dogma* (New York, 1934); Meyer Schapiro, "Nature of Abstract Art," *Marxist Quarterly,* I (1937), pp. 77–98; Charles Seeger, *Studies in Musicology* (Berkeley, Calif., 1977); Ernst Toch, *Shaping Forces of Music* (New York, 1958) Rosenfeld, *By Way of Art* (New York, 1928); Doris Humphrey, *An Artist First* (Middletown, 1972); Waldo Frank, *Memoirs of Waldo Frank* (Amherst, 1973); William Zorach, "Nationalism in Art: Is It an Advantage," *Art Digest*, VI (March 3, 1932), p. 15; Zorach, "Continuity Between Tradition and Today," *Art Digest*, V (February 1, 1931), p. 12. Mariquita S. Villard, "William Zorach and His Work," *Parnassus*, VI (October 1934), pp. 3–6; Lipton, "Some Notes on My Work," *Magazine of Art*, XL (November 1947), pp. 264–265; Lipton, "Experience and Sculptural Form," *College Art Journal*, IX (1949), pp. 264–265; Eudora Welty, "José de Creeft," *Magazine of Art*, XXXVII (February 1944), pp. 42–47; Elizabeth McCausland, *Changing New York*, photographs by Berenice Abbot (New York, 1939); Lipton, interview.

29. Reed, *Orozco*, p. 165.

30. Johnson to deLima (January 1, 1931).

31. Orozco, *An Autobiography,* pp. 143–150.

32. Laurence Schmeckbier, "The Frescoes of Orozco in the New School for Social Research," *Trend*, I (June 1932); Suzanne LaFollette, "America in Murals," *The New Freeman*, II (February 18, 1931), pp. 540–543.

33. Reed, *Orozco;* Jean Charlot, "José Clemente Orozco," *Magazine of Art*, XL (1947), pp. 258–263.

34. Johnson, "Notes on the New School Murals" (typescript, 1943), NSA.

35. Reed, *Orozco,* p. 48.

36. Edwin Alden Jewell, "Gesso and True Fresco," *New York Times* (Novem-

ber 23, 1930); *Art Digest,* V (February 15, 1931), p. 9; Reed, *Orozco,* pp. 215–228.

37. Laurence Hulburt, "Notes on Orozco's North American Murals," *Orozco Catalog* (New York, 1980).

38. Orozco, *Autobiography,* pp. 143–150.

39. Benton, *An Artist in America* (New York, 1937), pp. 247–252.

40. Matthew Baigell, *Thomas Hart Benton,* New American Edition, (New York, 1975), pp. 73–82; Benton to John R. Everett (June 7, 1968), Public Relations Office, New School.

41. Benton, *An Artist in America.*

42. Johnson, "Notes on the New School Murals."

43. Robert Flint, *Art News,* XXIX (January 17, 1931); *New York Times* (January 2, 1931; January 4, 1931); *New York Times Magazine* (December 28, 1930). See also Edmund Wilson, "Aladdin's Lecture Palace," *The American Earthquake* (New York, 1958), pp. 196–200.

44. Josuha C. Taylor, *The Fine Arts in America* (Chicago, 1979), pp. 151–204; E. P. Richardson, *Painting in America* (New York, 1956).

45. Irving Sandler, *Triumph of American Painting* (New York, 1970), pp. 5–43.

46. Johnson, *Deliver Us from Dogma* (New York, 1934); *Report of the Director: New School for Social Research, 1927–1928,* NSA.

47. New School, *Announcement: 1923–1924,* NSA.

48. New School, *Announcement: 1925–1926,* NSA.

49. Paul Rosenfeld, *Port of New York* (New York, 1924); *By Way of Art* (New York, 1928); *An Hour with American Music* (Philadelphia, 1929); *Discoveries of a Music Critic* (New York, 1936); and Rosenfeld et al., eds., *America and Alfred Stieglitz: A Collective Portrait* (New York, 1934).

50. Edmund Wilson, "Paul Rosenfeld: Three Phases," *Commentary,* V (1948), pp. 111–118; Sherman Paul, biographical sketch in introduction to Rosenfeld, *Port of New York* (Urbana, Ill., 1961); Aaron Copland, *The New Music, 1900–1906* (New York, 1968), p. 106.

51. Copland, *New Music,* p. 158.

52. Julia Smith, *Aaron Copland* (New York, 1955); Copland, *Our New Music*; Copland, *What to Listen for in Music* (New York, 1939).

53. Hugo Weigall, "The Music of Henry Cowell," *Musical Quarterly,* XLV (1959), pp. 488–507; Rosenfeld, *Discoveries of a Music Critic,* pp. 273–280; Nicholas Slonimsky, "Henry Cowell," in Henry Cowell, ed., *American Composers on American Music* (Stanford, Calif., 1933), pp. 57–63.

54. Henry Cowell and Sidney Cowell, *Charles Ives and His Music* (New York, 1955); Henry Cowell, *American Composers.* See also biographical sketch of Henry Cowell in *Baker's Biographical Dictionary of Music,* 6th ed. (New York, 1978).

55. Henry Cowell, "Charles Seeger," *American Composers*; Ann M. Pescatello, "Charles Seeger," *New Grove Encyclopedia,* XVII, pp. 101–102; Charles Seeger, *Studies in Musicology: 1935–1975* (Berkeley, Calif., 1977).

56. Paul Boepple, *Die Elemente der Musikalitat* (Paris, 1910); Emile Jacques-Dalcroze, *The Eurythmics of Jacques-Dalcroz* (Boston, 1913); Lawrence W. Howard, "Emile Jacques-Dalcroze," *New Grove Dictionary,* IX, pp. 554-555; "Paul Boepple," *Baker's Biographical Dictionary,* p. 190.

57. Charlotte Erwin, "Ernst Toch," *New Grove Encyclopedia,* XIX pp. 20-21; David Blake, "Hans Eisler," *New Grove Encyclopedia,* VI pp. 89-92.

58. *Bulletin: New School* (1930-1940).

59. Copland, *New Music,* p. 18

60. Ernst Toch, *The Shaping Forces in Music* pp. 154, 194.

61. Copland, *New Music.*

62. See comments by Henry Cowell, Copland, and Seeger in *American Composers;* Toch, *Shaping Forces;* Eisler, *Musik und Politik,* edited by G. Mayer (Berlin, 1973); Cowell, *New Musical Resources* (New York, 1930); Copland, *Music and Imagination.*

63. Peter Hansen, *An Introduction to Twentieth Century Music* (Boston, 1961), *passim.*

64. Smith, *Aaron Copland,* chapters 6, 7, and 8.

65. Seeger, *Studies in Musicology, passim.*

66. Blake, "Eisler," *New Grove Encyclopedia.*

67. Walter Terry, *The Dance in America,* rev. ed. (New York, 1971), pp. 39-40; Joseph H. Mazo, *Prime Movers: The Makers of Modern Dance in America* (New York, 1977).

68. Doris Humphrey, *An Artist First: An Autobiography,* completed by Selma Jeanne Cohen (Middletown, 1972), pp. 96, 192, 275, 282-284, and Chronology B.

69. *Bulletin, New School: 1933;* Ernestine Stodelle, *The Dance Technique of Doris Humphrey and Its Creative Potential* (Princeton, N.J., 1978), pp. 5-6.

70. "Paul Boepple," *Baker's Biographical Dictionary,* p. 190.

71. Humphrey, *An Artist First,* pp. 96-117.

72. Stodelle, *Dance Technique of Doris Humphrey,* pp. 13-30.

73. "John Martin," *The Dance Encyclopedia* (New York, 1967), pp. 606-607. John Martin, *Introduction to the Dance;* Martin, *The Modern Dance;* Martin, *The Dance* (New York, 1947).

74. Martin, *The Modern Dance,* pp. 53, 93.

75. *Ibid.,* p. 126.

76. *Ibid.,* p. 239.

77. *Ibid.,* p. 306.

78. New School, *Announcement* (1930-1940); *Art Bulletin* (1930-1940); "Art Folders," NSA.

79. *Bulletin: New School* (1930-1940).

80. *First American Artists' Congress* (New York, 1936), copy available at Teachers College Library, Columbia University; Symposium, "Thirty

Years After: Memories of the First American Writer's Congress," *American Scholar* (1966), pp. 495–516; Malcolm Cowley, *The Dream of the Golden Mountains: Remembering in the 1930s* (New York, 1980), pp. 269-279; Richard D. McKinzie, *The New Deal for Artists* (Princeton, N.J., 1973), pp. 78–80.

81. Taylor's *Fine Arts in America;* Richardson, *Painting in America;* Sandler, *Truimph of American Painting;* Ralph Pearson, *The Modern Renaissance in American Art* (New York, 1953). For the artists who taught at the New School in the thirties see New School, *Announcement,* (1930-1940).

82. Pearson, *The New Art Education* (New York, 1941).

83. *Ibid.,* p. 17.

84. *Ibid.,* p. 235.

85. "Peggy Bacon," *Current Biography 1940;* "Berenice Abbott," *Current Biography 1942;* Anne Tucker, "Berenice Abbott," in *The Woman's Eye* (New York, 1973); Benton, *An Artist in America;* "Paul Boepple," *Baker's Biographical Dictionary;* Smith, *Aaron Copland;* "Henry Cowell," *Baker's Biographical Dictionary;* "José de Creeft," *Current Biography 1942;* "Camilo Egas," *Who Was Who in America,* IV; "Hans Eisler," *New Grove Encyclopedia;* Waldo Frank, *Memoirs of Waldo Frank,* ed. by Alan Trachenberg (Amherst, 1973); Humphrey, *An Artist First;* "Yasuo Kuniyoshi," *Current Biography 1941;* Albert Elsten, *Seymour Lipset* (New York, 1970); "John Martin," *Dance Encyclopedia;* Reed, *Orozco;* "Ralph Pearson," *Who Was Who in America,* III: Wilson, "Paul Rosenfeld," *Commentary (1948);* "Charles Seeger," *New Grove Encyclopedia;* "Ernst Toch," *New Grove Encyclopedia;* "Joseph Urban," *New York Times* (July 19, 1933); William Zorach, *Art in My Life* (Cleveland, 1967).

86. Taylor, *Fine Arts in America,* pp. 151–204.

87. Copland, *New Music,* pp. 158–159; Richard D. McKinzie, *The New Deal for Artists* (Princeton, N.J., 1973).

88. See note 28.

89. Horace Kallen, *Art and Freedom* (New York, 1942), 2 vols.

90. *Ibid.,* pp. 963–964.

CHAPTER 4   Alvin Johnson and the *Encyclopedia of the Social Sciences*

1. New School Catalogs (1927–1933), NSA (New School Archives).

2. Of the assistant editors, Clara Mayer and Elizabeth Todd (Staudinger) were associated with the New School throughout their lives. Lerner remained close to Alvin Johnson until Johnson's death and lectured at the New School regularly during the forties and fifties. Of the editorial advisors Carl Becker, Charles Beard, Roscoe Pound, John Dewey, Franz Boas, and Wesley Mitchell served at various times on the board of directors of the New School and Harry Elmer Barnes lectured regularly in the 1920s and 1930s.

3. Joseph Ratner's compendium of Dewey's thought, *Intelligence in the Mod-*

ern World: John Dewey's Philosophy (New York, 1939), exemplifies the "instrumental" revival in the 1930s. Ratner also lectured regularly at the New School in the 1940s and 1950s.

4. Alvin Johnson to David L. Sills (June 22, 1964), Johnson Papers, Yale University.

5. Committee of Fifteen, *The Social Evil* (New York, 1902).

6. Edwin Seligman, Preface, *Encyclopedia of the Social Sciences*, I (New York, 1930). Hereafter cited as *EOSS*.

7. Johnson, *Pioneer's Progress: An Autobiography* (New York, 1952), pp. 305–315.

8. Johnson to Agnes deLima (1927–1935) and Johnson to Sills, Johnson Papers, Yale University; Johnson, *Pioneer's Progress*, pp. 313–315; Edwin Seligman to Johnson (July 21, 1930), Seligman Papers; Edwin Seligman, Preface, I, *EOSS*.

9. Edwin Seligman, "Report of Progress, April 1928," *EOSS*, Seligman Papers.

10. Edwin Seligman, Preface, *EOSS*, I, p. xxii.

11. American Anthropological Association (Robert H. Lowie and Clark Wissler); American Association of Social Workers (Philip Klein and Stuart A. Queen); American Economic Association (Clive Day and Frank Fetter); American Historical Association (Carl Becker and C. H. Haring); American Political Science Association (William B. Munro and John H. Logan); American Psychological Association (Georgia S. Gates and Mark A. May); American Sociological Society (Harry E. Barnes and H. B. Woolston); American Statistical Association (Mary van Kleeck and R. H. Coats); Association of American Law Schools (Edwin A. Patterson and E. D. Dickinson); National Education Asociation (Edward L. Thorndike and J. A. C. Chandler).

12. England (Ernest Barker, John Maynard Keynes, Sir Josiah Stamp, and R. H. Tawney); France (Charles Rist and F. Simiand); Germany (Carl Brinkmann and H. Schumacher); Italy (Luigi Einaudi and Augusto Graziani); Switzerland (W. E. Rappard).

13. Academic members of board of directors: Franz Boas, Walter Wheeler Cook, John Dewey, John A. Fairlie, Carlton J. H. Hayes, Jacob B. Hollander, Alvin Johnson, Wesley C. Mitchell, John K. Norton, William F. Ogburn, Mary van Kleeck, Edwin R. A. Seligman, Margaret Floy Washburn. Lay members of board of directors: James Couzens, Dwight W. Morrow, John J. Raskob, Mortimer E. Schiff, Robert E. Simon, Sinclair H. Strawn, Paul M. Warburg, Owen D. Young, and Mary E. Gleason.

14. Johnson to Edwin Seligman (1928–1935), Seligman Papers.

15. American Anthropological Association, American Association of Social Workers, American Economic Association, American Historical Association, American Political Science Association, American Psychological Association, American Sociological Association, Association of American Law Schools, National Education Association.

16. Harry Elmer Barnes, *Twilight of Christianity* (New York, 1929), is the

most defiant expression of the agnostic views characteristic of the New School. Laurence Veysey, *The Emergence of the American University* (Chicago, 1965); Marcia G. Synnott, *Half-Opened Door: Discrimination and Admissions at Harvard, Yale, and Princeton, 1900-1970* (Westport, Conn., 1979).

17. Johnson, *Deliver Us from Dogma* (New York, 1934); *The Clock of History* (New York, 1946); *Pioneer's Progress.*

18. Max Lerner, interview (New York, January 6, 1981); Elizabeth Todd (Staudinger), interview (Dayton, Ohio, December 20, 1980).

19. Johnson to Sills, Johnson Papers, Yale University; Max Lerner, Introduction to Johnson, *Pioneer's Progress* (Lincoln: University of Nebraska Press, 1960); Lerner, interview.

20. Lerner, interview; Hans Staudinger, interview; Clara W. Mayer, interview (New York, January 1979).

21. "The Handling of Manuscripts" (typescript, n.d.), *EOSS,* Seligman Papers. Johnson, *Pioneer's Progress,* pp. 305-315; Edwin Seligman, Preface, I, *EOSS;* Edwin Seligman, "Report of Progress" (December 7, 1928), *EOSS,* Seligman Papers; Lerner, interview; Todd, interview.

22. "Note to Contributors," *EOSS,* Seligman Papers.

23. Lerner, interview; Seligman, Preface, I, *EOSS.*

24. Johnson to Sills, Johnson Papers, Yale University.

25. Lerner, interview.

26. The reviews included John R. Commons, *American Economic Review,* XX (1930), p. 256; Ralph H. Gabriel, *American Historical Review,* XXXV (1930), p. 285; Ellsworth Faris, *American Journal of Sociology,* XXXV (1930), p. 1112; William MacDonald, *New York Times* (February 2, 1930); W. B. Shaw, *Review of Reviews,* LXXXI (March 1930), p. 9; Felix Frankfurter, *Harvard Law Review,* XLIII (1930), p. 1168; George Soule, *New Republic,* LXIV (August 20, 1930), p. 23.

27. Johnson to Edwin Seligman (May 5, 1929), Seligman Papers.

28. B. B. Seligman, *Commentary,* XL (October 1968), p. 76; Alasdair MacIntyre, *New York Review of Books,* XII (February 28, 1969), pp. 14-16; Thomas C. Cochran, *American Historical Review,* LXXIV (1969), pp. 1573-1576; George Roger Taylor, *Journal of Economic Literature,* VIII (March 1970), pp. 35-40. Examples of radical points of views are Werner Sombart on "Capitalism," III, pp. 195-208; Bernard Stern on "Women's Position in Society," XV, pp. 444-451; Oscar Jaszi on "Anarchism," II, pp. 46-53.

29. See *EOSS, passim.*

30. Morris Cohen, "Scientific Method," *EOSS,* X, pp. 389-395; David A. Hollinger, *Morris R. Cohen and the Scientific Ideal* (Cambridge, Mass., 1975), pp. 139-158.

31. Cohen, "Scientific Method," p. 395.

32. Sidney Hook, "Determinism," *EOSS,* V, p. 111.

33. Horace Kallen, "Pragmatism," *EOSS,* XII, pp. 307, 311.

34. *EOSS*, I, pp. 1–349; Cohen, *Reason and Nature* (New York, 1931), and, with Ernest Nagel, *An Introduction to Logic and Scientific Method* (New York, 1934); Hook, *Reason, Social Myth and Democracy* (New York, 1940) and *John Dewey: An Intellectual Portrait* (New York, 1939); Kallen, "Value and Existence in Philosophy, Art, Religion," in John Dewey, ed., *Creative Intelligence* (New York, 1917), pp. 414–467; Neil Coughlan, *Young John Dewey* (Chicago, 1973); David Hollinger, "The Problem of Pragmatism in American History," *Journal of American History*, LXVII (1980), pp. 80–117.

35. Dewey, "Human Nature," *EOSS*, VII, pp. 531–536; Alexander Goldenweiser, "Social Evolution," *EOSS*, V, pp. 656–662; Franz Boas, "Race," *EOSS*, XIII, pp. 25–35; Bronislaw Malinowski, "Culture," *EOSS*, IV, pp. 621–645; Ernest A. Hooton, "Man," *EOSS*, X, pp. 71–76; Kallen, "Behavioralism," *EOSS*, II, pp. 495–498, and "Psychoanalysis," *EOSS*, XII, pp. 580–588; Joseph Jastrow, "Psychology," *EOSS*, XII, pp. 588–596. See also Dewey, *Human Nature and Conduct* (New York, 1922).

36. Hans Kohn, "Race Conflict," *EOSS*, XIII, pp. 36–41; Louis Wirth, "Segregation," *EOSS*, XIII, pp. 643–646; Benjamin Ginsberg, "Antisemitism," *EOSS*, II, pp. 119–125; Boas, "Race," *EOSS*, XIII, pp. 25–35; Margaret Mead, Bernard Stern, Mary van Kleeck, and Elsie Gluck, "Woman's Position in Society," *EOSS*, XV, pp. 439–459.

37. Hook, "Determinism," *EOSS*, V, pp. 110–114; Kallen, "Behavioralism," and "Psychoanalysis"; Jastrow, "Psychology."

38. Harold Laski, "Democracy," *EOSS*, V, pp. 76–84, and "Liberty," *EOSS*, IX, pp. 442–446. See also Laski, *Authority in the Modern State* (New Haven, Conn., 1928); *Foundations of Sovereignty* (New York, 1921); and *The State in Theory and Practice* (New York, 1938).

39. Laski, "Democracy," *EOSS*, V, pp. 76, 84.

40. See Cohen, with Ernest Nagel, *Introduction to Logic*, p. 402, and *Faith of a Liberal* (New York, 1946), pp. 437–469; Kallen, *The Liberal Spirit: Essays on Problems of Freedom in the Modern World* (Ithaca, N.Y., 1948), pp. 104–105, 133, 208–213; Hook, *Reason, Social Myth and Democracy*, (New York, 1940), pp. 8–9, 283–285, 294–295; Dewey, *Liberalism and Social Action*, (New York, 1935), and *Democracy and Education* (New York, 1916).

41. Hook, *Reason, Social Myth and Democracy*, and *John Dewey: An Intellectual Portrait* (New York, 1939); Edward A. Purcell, Jr., *The Crisis of Democratic Theory* (Lexington, Ky., 1973); Wirth, "Segregation"; Laski, "Liberty"; Kohn, "Race Conflict"; Ginsberg, "Antisemitism"; B. Groethuysen, "Secularism," *EOSS*, XIII, pp. 631–634; Francis W. Coker, "Pluralism," *EOSS*, XII, pp. 170–173; William Munro, "City," *EOSS*, III, pp. 474–482; Kallen, "Modernism," *EOSS*, X, pp. 564–568; Max Boehm, "Cosmopolitanism," *EOSS*, IV, pp. 452–461; Laski, "Democracy."

42. Cohen, *Reason and Nature*, and, with Ernest Nagel, *Introduction to Logic*; Kallen, *The Liberal Spirit*; Johnson, *Clock of History*, and *Deliver Us from Dogma*.

43. Scrapbooks, NSA; John Dewey Papers, Southern Illinois University, Carbondale. The lectures which Dewey gave at the New School are archived at Southern Illinois.

44. Hollinger, *Morris Cohen*, pp. 69-90.

45. Bruce Kuklick, *The Rise of American Philosophy: Cambridge, Massachusetts, 1860-1930* (New Haven, Conn., 1977); Hollinger, "The Problem of Pragmatism in American History," *Journal of American History*; Paul K. Conkin, *Puritans and Pragmatists* (New York, 1968).

46. Hollinger, *Morris Cohen*, p. 54; Kallen, taped interviews (August 31, 1964; September 3, 1964), American Jewish Archives, Cincinnati.

47. New School *Announcement: 1923-1945*, NSA.

48. Kallen Papers, YIVO Institute, New York, and Kallen Papers, American Jewish Archives.

49. Cohen, *A Dreamer's Journey* (Boston, 1949), pp. 241-242; Hollinger, *Morris Cohen*, pp. 208-210.

50. See suggestive article along these lines by Hollinger, "Ethnic Diversity, Cosmopolitanism and the Emergence of the American Liberal Intelligentsia," *American Quarterly*, XXVII (1975), pp. 133-151, as well as Hollinger's more recent article, "The Problem of Pragmatism."

51. For disagreements see Hook, ed., *The Meaning of Marxism* (New York, 1934), which included Hook's "Why I Am a Communist" as well as Cohen's and Dewey's "Why I Am Not a Communist." See also the Kallen/Cohen exchange in the *New Republic* over Zionism: Kallen, "Zionism: Democracy or Prussianism?", and Cohen, "Zionism: Tribalism or Liberalism?", XVIII (1919), pp. 182-183, 311-313.

52. Leonora Cohen Rosenfield, ed., *Portrait of a Philosopher: Morris Cohen in Life and Letters* (New York, 1962), pp. 143-144; Sidney Hook, "Morris R. Cohen: Fifty Years Later," in Joseph Epstein, ed., *Masters: Portraits of Great Teachers* (New York, 1981); Andrew J. Reck, *The New American Philosopher* (Baton Rouge, La., 1968), pp. 164-196; Morton Hoffman, "The Development of American Jewish Thought in the Twentieth Century as Reflected in the Writings of Horace M. Kallen, Ludwig Lewisohn and Morris Cohen" (M.A. thesis, Hebrew Union College, 1953); Louis Kaplan, "Judaism and Jewish Education in Horace M. Kallen's Philosophy of Cultural Pluralism" (Ph.D. thesis, Dropsey University, 1971); Sarah L. Schmidt, "Horace M. Kallen and the Americanization of Zion" (Ph.D. thesis, University of Maryland, 1973).

53. Kallen, *Culture and Democracy* (New York, 1924), p. 43. See also Francis W. Coker, "Pluralism," *EOSS*, XII, pp. 170-173.

54. Kallen, *Culture and Democracy*, pp. 61, 230.

55. Kallen dwelled on his experience at Harvard at length. See extended footnote in *Culture and Democracy*, pp. 186-190.

56. Kallen, *Secularism Is the Will of God* (New York, 1954), p. 95; Kallen, *Individualism: An American Way of Life* (New York, 1933), pp. 235-256; Kallen, ed., *Freedom in the Modern World* (New York, 1928), is a collection

of lectures delivered at the New School which Kallen organized and moderated. See also Kallen, *Indecency and the Seven Arts and Other Adventures of a Prag natist in Aesthetics* (New York, 1930); *Cultural Pluralism and the American Idea* (Philadelphia, 1950); and *The Liberal Spirit.*

57. Kallen, "City Planning and the Idea of the City—Considerations Especially About New York," *Social Research,* XXIII (1956), pp. 186-198.

58. William Munro, "City," *EOSS,* III, pp. 474-482.

59. Max Boehm, "Cosmopolitanism," *EOSS,* IV, pp. 457-461.

60. Hollinger, "Ethnic Diversity and Cosmopolitanism," and "The Problem of Pragmatism."

61. Kallen, interviews, American Jewish Archives.

62. Johnson, *Pioneer's Progress.*

63. Charles Abrams, *Revolution in Land* (New York, 1939); *The Future of Housing* (New York, 1946); and *Forbidden Neighbors* (New York, 1955). Bernard Taper, "Charles Abrams: A Lover of Cities," *New Yorker,* XLII (February 4, 1967), pp. 39-91, (February 11, 1967), pp. 45-115; Charles Abrams, interview (1964), Oral History Project, Columbia University; Roma Connable, interview (New York, June 1981).

64. Berenice Abbott, *Changing New York* (New York, 1939), and *Greenwich Village: Today and Yesterday* (New York, 1949). See Mumford's autobiography, *Sketches from Life* (New York, 1982). Mumford published his New School lectures as *Sticks and Stones* (New York, 1924); for an evocative early statement on New York as an emerging cultural center see Paul Rosenfeld, *Port of New York* (New York, 1924).

CHAPTER 5   Founding a University for Exiles

1. Two works in German have addressed this problem. Both, however, focus on the overall American response and do little justice to the place of the New School in the context of international rescue. See Helge Pross, *Die Deutsche Akademische Emigration nach den Vereinigten Staaten 1934–1941* (Berlin, 1955), and Joachim Radkau, *Die Deutsche Emigration in den USA* (Düsseldorf, 1971). More promising is Karen Greenberg, Yale University, "The American University and the Immigrant Intellectual," which is still in progress.

2. See, for example, Barton Bledstein, *The Culture of Professionalism* (New York, 1979), and Fritz Ringer, *The Decline of the German Mandarins* (Cambridge, Mass., 1969).

3. See Fritz Stern, *The Failure of Illiberalism* (New York, 1976), for a discussion of the problem. See also George Mosse, *The Crisis of German Ideology* (New York, 1946), and Wolfgang Mommsen, *Max Weber und die Deutsche Politik* (Tübingen, 1959), and Bledstein, *Professionalism.* See also Henry F. May, *The End of American Innocence* (London, 1960).

4. Ringer, *German Mandarins.* See also E. Y. Hartshorne, *The National Socialists and the German University* (London, 1937).

5. Hartshorne, *National Socialists,* pp. 47–49.

6. Ringer, *German Mandarins,* pp. 202–213.

7. See Alvin Johnson to Robert MacIver (April 10, 1957), Alvin Johnson Papers, Yale University (hereafter cited as AJPY).

8. See Edmund Purcell, *The Crisis of Democratic Theory* (Lexington, Ky., 1976), and Bledstein, *Professionalism.*

9. See Chapter 4, "Alvin Johnson and the *Encyclopedia of the Social Sciences.*"

10. Stephen Duggan, *The Rescue of Science and Learning: The Story of the Emergency Committee* (New York, 1948), p. 24.

11. Papers of the Rockefeller program in the social sciences, 1928–1932, RFA (Rockefeller Foundation Archives). All references to Rockefeller materials are to series 200, either General Correspondence or specific cartons such as "New School for Social Research." See also Ringer, *German Mandarins,* for an outline of the German university in the 1920s.

12. "Report of the Condition of German Social Sciences in 1932," by Tracy Kittridge, associate director of social services, RFA.

13. Johnson to Agnes deLima (May 6, 1933), AJPY.

14. "Report," RFA.

15. Kittridge to John Van Sicle (March 19, 1933), RFA.

16. Felicia Deyrup, interview (New York, October 15, 1978).

17. *Ibid.*

18. Johnson, Diary (1924), Felicia Deyrup Collection, Nyack, N.Y.

19. See William Leuchtenberg, *The Transformation of American Society* (New York, 1959), pp. 79–103.

20. See the letters of Johnson to deLima (November 22, 1932, and March 4, 1934). "America is intended to be a democracy," AJPY.

21. Johnson to deLima (June 26, 1932), AJPY.

22. *Ibid.*

23. Johnson to Mrs. (Koppel) Pinson (January 1, 1933), AJPY.

24. See the letter of Daniel O'Brien, director of medical sciences at the Paris office of the Rockefeller Foundation, to Raymond Fosdick at the New York office (April 11, 1933), RFA.

25. Hans Speier, interview (Hartsdale, N.Y., October 11, 1978).

26. Kittridge to Van Sicle (March 29, 1933), RFA.

27. A copy of the text, in English and German, may be found at the Rockefeller Archives.

28. O'Brien, "Report," RFA.

29. Johnson to deLima (April 13, 1933), AJPY.

30. Johnson, *Pioneer's Progress: An Autobiography* (New York, 1952), pp. 340–341.

31. Johnson to Seligman (April 21, 1933), Horace Kallen Papers, YIVO Institute, New York.

32. *New York Times* (May 13, 1933).

33. Deyrup, interview (New York, October 1978).

34. Johnson to deLima (May 16, 1933), AJPY.

35. Henry Feingold, *The Politics of Rescue* (New Brunswick, N.J., 1970), pp. 11-14. See also David Brody, "American Jewry; the Refugees and Immigration Restriction, 1932-42," *Publication of the American Jewish Historical Society,* XLV (June 1956), pp. 219-247.

36. Feingold, *Rescue,* p. 14.

37. Johnson to deLima (June 6, 1934), AJPY.

38. Johnson to deLima (May 27, 1933), AJPY.

39. Johnson to deLima (June 6, 1933), AJPY.

40. Johnson to deLima (June 15, 1933), AJPY.

41. Speier, interview (Hartsdale, N.Y., November 1981).

42. Duggan, *Rescue,* pp. 12-36. See also the reports of the meeting in the Rockefeller Foundation Files, RFA.

43. This was essentially the policy of the Rockefeller Foundation. Day to Fosdick (May 23, 1933), RFA.

44. Policy statement, "Special Research Aid Fund" (May 12, 1933), RFA.

45. This is the figure given by Duggan for the Emergency Committee. The total "rescued" in America was probably close to 1,000; 178 were specifically aided by the New School. Duggan, *Rescue,* p. 16, and "List of Displaced Scholars at the New School," NSA (New School Archives).

46. Policy statement, "Emergency Fund," RFA.

47. Policy statement, "Special Research Aid Fund" (February 15, 1935), RFA.

48. Statement of June 18, 1937. "The present aid to displaced scholars represents an attempt . . . to salvage this investment . . . and preserve a leadership." The foundation estimated its "investment" prior to 1933 at $4 million, RFA.

49. Alan Greg, Medical Services Division, to Thomas Applegate, vice president of the Rockefeller Foundation (June 13, 1933), RFA.

50. Raymond Fosdick to John D. Rockefeller II (June 22, 1938), RFA.

51. Johnson to Clara Mayer (May 17, 1945), NSA.

52. Alexander Makinsky, *Diary* (June 1942), RFA. Makinsky, a Rockefeller agent in Paris and Lisbon, interviewed American university personnel after his return to the United States in late 1941.

53. Hans Neisser, "Are Space and Time Real?" *Philosophy and Phenomenological Research* (March 1971), pp. 421-425.

54. See the account of Noman Bentwitch, *The Rescue of Science and Learning* (London, 1947).

55. Johnson to George Bacon (July 1944), AJPY.

56. Johnson to Robert MacIver (April 10, 1957), AJPY.

57. Speier, interview (Hartsdale, N.Y., November 1981).

58. Van Sicle to Rufus Day, memo (April 18, 1933), RFA.

59. There is an entire carton devoted to this subject at the foundation, Series 200, RFA.

60. Van Sicle to Day, memo, RFA.

61. Van Sicle to Day, memo (May 18, 1933), RFA.

62. *Ibid.*

63. Lederer to Van Sicle (April 5, 1933).

64. Adolph Lowe, interview (New York, October 1981, and January 1979).

65. *Ibid.*

66. Hans Staudinger, interview (New York, October 1978).

67. Speier, interview (October 1981).

68. Speier, interview (October 1981).

69. See Arnold Brecht, *The Political Education of Arnold Brecht* (Princeton, N.J., 1969), pp. 310–375.

70. Johnson is "polite" on this in *Pioneer's Progress*, but elsewhere the facts are quite clear. Mannheim's defection was costly to him, and he felt he had to find others to take Mannheim's place. See Johnson to MacIver (April 10, 1957), AJPY.

71. Johnson to deLima (July 28, 1933).

72. Speier, interview (October 1981).

73. *Ibid.*

74. Hans Staudinger, interview (New York, November 18, 1979).

75. Speier, interview (October 1981).

76. Hannah Salomon Janovsky, interview (New York, October 2, 1981). Her father, Albert, was recovering from an attack of polio and did not immediately come to New York.

77. Speier, interview (October 1981).

78. The papers of Frieda Wunderlich are located at the Leo Baeck Institute in New York. Her *vita* is also on file at the New School, NSA.

79. Speier, interview. See also Brecht, *Political Education,* pp. 525–528.

80. Max Wertheimer, "Uber Gestalttheorie," in *Gehalten in Der Kant-Gesellschaft* (Berlin, 1924).

81. These three, in addition to Ascoli and Simons, were the only recipients of Rockefeller assistance prior to 1940, RFA.

82. Erich Hula, interview (New York, March 1979, and October 1981).

83. Johnson to deLima (August 31, 1933), AJPY.

84. Johnson to deLima (May 30, 1934), AJPY.

85. Johnson to deLima (September 18, 1933), AJPY.

86. Minutes of April meeting of the faculty (1935), NSA.

87. Johnson to deLima (August 5, 1934), AJPY. Also Henry Pachter, dean of the School of Politics, interview, 1947–1952 (New York, May 1979).

88. Johnson to deLima (August 31, 1933), and Johnson to Dr. E. Muller (March 23, 1953), AJPY.

89. Each issue of *Social Research*, 1933–1950, contained a list of courses at the Graduate Faculty as well as the topics of the General Seminar.

90. Johnson to MacIver (April 10, 1957), AJPY.

91. Johnson to Clara Mayer (October 25, 1950), NSA.

92. Elizabeth Todd Staudinger, interview (New York, December 1979).

93. Johnson to Horace Kallen (April 10, 1938), Horace Kallen Papers, YIVO.

94. Johnson to Mayer (October 25, 1950), NSA.

CHAPTER 6   The Politics of Disillusionment, 1933–1945

1. Hans Speier and Alfred Kahler, eds., *War in Our Time* (New York, 1939).

2. For a good discussion of their "Enlightenment" commitments, see Ernst Cassirer's *The Philosophy of the Enlightenment* (Princeton, N.J., 1951), which was first published in German in 1932. Cassirer himself became an emigŕe to the United States shortly after the book's publication.

3. The text of Mierendorff's "testimony" and that of sixty-five others may be found in the German Exile Archive, State University of New York, Albany.

4. Max Weber, "Politics as a Vocation," and "Science as a Vocation," in H. Gerth and C. Mills, eds., *From Max Weber* (New York, 1956).

5. See in particular Weber's essay, "Objectivity in the Social Sciences," originally published in *Archiv für Sozialwissenschaft und Sozial-politik* (1904) and reprinted in Edward Shills, ed., *Methodology in the Social Sciences* (New York, 1959).

6. Weber, *The Spirit of Capitalism and the Protestant Ethic* (New York, 1957).

7. Speier, "Emil Lederer: Leben und Werk," in *Kapitalismus, Klassenstruktur und Probleme der Democratic in Deutschland 1910–1940* (Göttingen, 1979), pp. 253–272.

8. Emil Lederer, "Social Control Versus Economic Law," *Social Research*, I (March 1934), pp. 3–21.

9. Lederer, "Social Control," p. 8.

10. *Ibid.*, p. 12.

11. Lederer, "Freedom and Science," *Social Research*, I (March 1934), pp. 219–230.

12. Lederer and Jacob Marschak, "The New Middle Class," trans. by S. Ellison (WPA Publication, mimeo, 1937), pp. 6–45.

13. Kenneth J. Arrow, "Jacob Marschak," *Challenge* (1978), pp. 69–71.

14. Lederer and Marschak, "The New Middle Class," pp. 6–38.

15. *Ibid.*

16. *Ibid.*, p. 45.

17. Speier, *The Salaried Employee in German Society* (New York, 1939).

18. Speier, interview (New York, October 18, 1978).

19. Speier, "The Social Determination of Ideas," *Social Research*, V (1938), pp. 182–206.

20. Speier, "Honor and Social Structure," *Social Research*, II (February 1935), pp. 74–98.

21. Speier, *The Salaried Employee*. See also "Social Stratification," in Eduard Heimann and Max Ascoli, eds., *Political and Economic Democracy* (New York, 1937), p. 30.

22. Speier, interview (New York, October 1978).

23. Speier, *The Salaried Employee*, p. 53.

24. *Ibid.*, pp. 110–120.

25. *Ibid.*, p. 45.

26. Speier, "The Salaried Employee in Modern Society," *Social Research*, VI (February 1934), p. 80.

27. Speier, interview (New York, October 1978).

28. Lederer, *The State of the Masses: The Threat of the Classless Society* (New York, 1939).

29. Sigmund Freud, *Group Psychology and the Analysis of the Ego* (New York, 1959).

30. Lederer, *State of the Masses*, p. 22.

31. *Ibid.*, p. 33.

32. *Ibid.*, p. 73.

33. *Ibid.*, p. 127.

34. *Ibid.*, p. 140.

35. *Ibid.*, p. 152

36. *Ibid.*, p. 173

37. Hans Staudinger, interview (New York, November 1978).

38. *Ibid.*

39. Hans Staudinger, *Individium und Gemeinschaft in der Kulturorganisation des Vereins* (Jena, 1913).

40. See Ferdinand Tönnies's work, *Gemeinschaft und Gesellschaft* (English translation, New York, 1965).

41. Gordon Craig, *Germany 1866–1945* (New York, 1978), pp. 420–431. See also W. F. Bruck, *Social and Economic History of Germany 1888–1938* (Oxford, Eng., 1938), pp. 143–198. Bruck credited Moellendorf with the invention of the term *planwirtschaft* which Staudinger saw as a means to a *gemeinwirtschaft*, a planned or organized community.

42. Arnold Brecht, *The Political Education of Arnold Brecht* (Princeton, N.J., 1971), p. 322.

43. Gustav Stolper, *The German Economy 1870 to the Present* (New York, 1978), p. 118, and *SOFINA*, Belgium utility report, "Memorandum on New Business Development in the Electric Light and Power Industry in Germany 1932–1936" (Brussels, 1936), p. 2.

44. Staudinger told the story of an assistant, a communist infiltrator in his

socialist group, tipping him off at the last moment, "Don't take the ferry tonight." Interview (November 1978).

45. Hans Staudinger, interview (New York, December 1978).

46. Erich Hula, interview (October 15, 1978); Johnson to Else Staudinger (May 8, 1968); Jehuda Riemer, interview (July 25, 1978).

47. Hans Staudinger, interview (New York, November 1978).

48. Hans Staudinger, "The Future of Totalitarian Barter Trade Economy," *Social Research*, VII (1940), pp. 410–429.

49. Hans Staudinger, in Peter M. Rutkoff and William B. Scott, eds., *The Inner Nazi: A Critical Analysis of Mein Kampf* (Baton Rouge, La, 1981). Franz Neumann, *Behemoth: The Structure and Practice of National Socialism* (New York, 1944).

50. Riemer, transcript interview with Hans Staudinger (July 25, 1978), Staudinger Papers, Albany Archives, State University of New York.

51. Hans Staudinger, interview VII (January 1979).

52. Marian Ascoli, interview (New York, November 1979).

53. Max Ascoli and Arthur Feiler, *Fascism for Whom* (New York, 1938), p. 42.

54. See, for example, Wilson H. Coates and Hayden V. White, *The Ordeal of Liberal Humanism*, II (New York, 1970), and H. Stuart Hughes, *Consciousness and Society* (New York, 1963), as well as Benedetto Croce, *History of Europe in the Nineteenth Century* (New York, 1933), for a more elaborate discussion.

55. Allen Cassels, *Two Faces of Fascism* (New York, 1972).

56. Max Ascoli, "No. 38 Becomes a Citizen," *Atlantic Monthly*, CLXV (1940), pp. 168–173.

57. Max Ascoli and Feiler, *Fascism for Whom*, p. 57.

58. *Ibid.*, p. 90.

59. Max Ascoli, "The Fascist March on Scholarship," *American Scholar* (1938), pp. 50–89.

60. Max Ascoli, "On Political Parties," *Social Research*, II (1935), pp. 195–210.

61. Max Ascoli, *Intelligence in Politics* (New York, 1936), p. 182.

62. Max Ascoli and Feiler, *Fascism for Whom*, p. 42.

63. See her obituary in *Social Research* (1966), pp. 1–3.

64. See her article, "The German Unemployment Insurance Act of 1927," *Quarterly Journal of Economics* (1928), pp. 278–305.

65. Frieda Wunderlich, "Kapitalische Philosophie," *Archiv für systematische Philosophie*, III (1916), pp. 219–238.

66. Wunderlich, "New Aspects of Unemployment in Germany," *Social Research*, I (1934), pp. 97–111.

67. Wunderlich, "Some Aspects of Social Work in the German Democratic Republic," *Social Research*, III (1936), pp. 19–36.

68. *Ibid.*, p. 33.

69. Wunderlich, "New Aspects," pp. 109–110.

70. *Ibid.,* p. 99.

71. Wunderlich, "Fascism and the German Middle Classes," *Antioch Review,* V (Spring 1945), pp. 56–66.

72. Wunderlich, "Women's Work in Germany," *Social Research,* III (August 1935), pp. 310–337.

73. Wunderlich, "Germany's Defense Economy and the Decay of Capitalism," *Quarterly Journal of Economics,* III (May 1938), pp. 409–432.

74. *Ibid.,* p. 430.

75. *Ibid.*

76. Henry Pachter, interview (March 1979).

77. Michael Wertheimer, "Max Wertheimer, Gestalt Prophet," in *Gestalt Theory,* II (1980), pp. 3–17; see also Max Wertheimer, "Experimentelle Studien uber das Sehen von Bewegung," *Zeitschrift fur Psychologie,* LXI (1912), pp. 161–265; Wolfgang Köhler, *The Task of Gestalt Psychology* (Princeton, N.J., 1969), p. 35; Mary Henle et al., *Historical Conceptions of Psychology* (New York, 1973), and Michael Wertheimer, "Gestalt Theory, Holistic Psychologies and Max Wertheimer" (unpublished essay), p. 4.

78. Michael Wertheimer, "Max Wertheimer, Gestalt Prophet," p. 12.

79. Köhler, *Task of Gestalt,* p. 42.

80. Henle, "Gestalt Psychology," pp. 209–213.

81. Max Wertheimer, "Uber Gestalttheorie," in *Sondeabdruk des Symposion der Kant-Geselleschaft* (Berlin, 1924), republished as "Gestalt Theory," *Social Research* (1944).

82. Max Wertheimer, "On Truth," *Social Research,* I (1934), pp. 135–136.

83. Max Wertheimer, "Some Problems in the Theory of Ethics," *Social Research,* pp. 353–367.

84. Max Wertheimer, *Productive Thinking* (New York, 1945).

85. *Ibid.,* p. 181.

86. In its methodological sense, gestalt psychology is most derivative of rationalism in general and, according to Michael Wertheimer, anticipates very closely the work of Husserl and phenomenology. Michael Wertheimer, interview (1981).

87. Max Wertheimer, "On the Concept of Democracy," in Max Ascoli and Eduard Heimann, *Political and Economic Democracy.*

88. Michael Wertheimer, interview (Boulder, Colo., October 1981). Wertheimer had worked in 1918 with Einstein and Jacob Marschak to influence the German Reichstag to recognize the claims of the Czech Social Democratic Party.

CHAPTER 7   The Second Refugee Wave

1. Alvin Johnson, *Pioneer's Progress: An Autobiography* (New York, 1952), p. 337. and Joseph Willets, extract from his diary, RFA (Rockefeller Foundation Archives).

2. "Joseph Willets," personnel folder, RFA.

3. Tracy Kittridge to Willets (July 1940), RFA.

4. D. S. Freeman, editor of the *Richmond News Leader*, to Rockefeller (July 18, 1940), RFA.

5. Willets to Thomas Applegate (June 24, 1940), RFA.

6. Johnson, *Pioneer's Progress*, pp. 335–340.

7. Raymond Fosdick, report to John D. Rockefeller, II (July 24, 1940), RFA.

8. Varian Fry to Max Ascoli (February 1941), Max Ascoli Papers, Boston University (hereafter cited as APBU).

9. Willets to Applegate (August 1940), RFA.

10. Willets to Applegate (July 24, 1940), as well as Johnson's report to the foundation (March 19, 1941), RFA.

11. Alexander Makinsky, *Diary*. The diary of Alexander Makinsky of the Rockefeller Foundation has daily entries from early June 1940 to July 1942. Makinsky operated in Paris and Lisbon (from July 1940 to December 1941) and in New York for the foundation, RFA.

12. Report of Thomas Applegate, "Summary of the Refugee Assistance Program" (1946), RFA.

13. See Stephen Duggan, *The Emergency Committee for Assistance of Displaced Scholars* (New York, 1947), p. 53.

14. Fry to Ascoli, APBU.

15. Makinsky, *Diary* (entries of November 29, 1940), RFA.

16. Fry to Ascoli, APBU.

17. *Ibid.*

18. Makinsky, *Diary* (December 7, 1940); Makinsky to Johnson (December 10, 1940), Staudinger Papers, Hans Staudinger Archives, State University of New York, Albany (hereafter cited as H. St. A.).

19. *Ibid.*, (February 7, 1940).

20. *Ibid.*, (March 16. 40).

21. Letter of Marc Bloch to Waldo (July 25, 1940). Copies of this letter are at the Rockefeller Archives and in the papers of Saul Padover, now partially assembled at the Immigrant Archive Collection, Department of German, Albany Archives, State University of New York.

22. The appointment letter is not existent. Bloch's reply by telegram (November 27, 1940), NSA (New School Archives).

23. Warren to Johnson (February 19, 1941), RFA.

24. Makinsky, *Diary* (March 25, 1941), RFA.

25. Bloch had envisaged this as early as December 1940. Bloch to Johnson (December 14, 1940), NSA.

26. Makinsky, *Diary* (March 27, 1940). See also Henry Feingold, *The Politics of Rescue*, p. 148.

27. Bloch to Johnson (July 31, 1941), NSA.

28. Fry to Ascoli (February 1941). APBU.

29. Feingold's study, *The Politics of Rescue* (1970), especially pp. 120–150, provides the framework for the following discussion. Feingold's account coincides with what was happening, as seen at the time by Makinsky, Fry, and Bloch.

30. *Ibid.,* see especially pp. 135–141.

31. *Ibid.,* pp. 42–43. See also Johnson to Adolf Berle (January 14, 1941), and Berle to Johnson (January 16, 1941) concerning Long's role, H. St. A.

32. Makinsky, *Diary* (February 5, 1942), RFA. See also Johnson to Long (December 16, 1941; January 19, 1942; February 2, 1942), H. St. A.

33. Makinsky, *Diary* (January 26, 1942), RFA. See also Johnson to Felix Frankfurter (February 9, 1942), H. St. A.

34. See Chapter 8 on the history of the Ecole Libre des Hautes Etudes.

35. The entire "collection" can be found in a report of Fosdick to John D. Rockefeller, II (July and August 1940), RFA.

36. See minutes of Board of Trustees (1940–1943), NSA.

37. Minutes of Graduate Faculty (July 24, 1940), NSA.

38. Johnson to deLima (April 16, 1935), AJPY (Alvin Johnson Papers, Yale University).

39. Adolph Lowe to Alfred Weber (March 1947), NSA.

40. This was especially true of Arnold Brecht and Hans Speier. See Speier's *From the Ashes of Disgrace* (Amherst, Mass., 1981) for a very specific account. See also Johnson to Horace Kallen (December 21, 1945), NSA.

41. Study Group on Germany, transcribed minutes (November 18, 1941; March 10, 1943), Karl Mayer Archives, Konstanz.

42. In so doing, they anticipated the major historical debates among Anglo–American historians in the twenty years following the war: A. J. P. Taylor, *The Course of German History* (New York, 1962), and Fritz Stern, *The Failure of Illiberalism* (New York, 1977).

43. Study Group (March 10, 1943), NSA.

44. *Ibid.* See also Jack Thompson, *In the Eye of the Storm* (Iowa City, 1980).

45. Study Group (April 21, 1943), NSA.

46. Felix Kaufmann, Study Group Minutes (May 10, 1943). See also his articles on "Methodology in the Social Sciences," *Social Research,* IV, V, VI (1938–1939).

47. *Ibid.* See also Max Weber, "The Meaning of Ethical Neutrality in Sociology and Economics," in *The Methodology of the Social Sciences* (New York, 1949).

48. Confidential memo, "The Italian Situation in Boston," encouraging the use of antifascist materials in American newspapers (June 2, 1941), APBU.

49. Max Ascoli to Johnson (July 29, 1941), APBU.

50. See Ascoli to Lowe (January 9, 1941) and Max Horkheimer to Johnson (March 7, 1941), APBU.

51. Speier and Ernst Kris, *German Radio Propaganda* (New York, 1943). The book was a Book of the Month Club selection.

52. See Chapter 6.

53. Speier, "Nazi Propaganda and Its Decline," *Social Research*, X (1943). p. 63.

54. Kris, Paper 1 (n.d.), General Seminar, NSA.

55. Speier and Kris, "Report of the Research Project on Totalitarian Communism in War Time" (January 31, 1942), NSA.

56. Hans Staudinger to Ascoli (May and June 1941), APBU.

57. See Johnson's inaugural address (November 17, 1943), draft, NSA. Also, Staudinger and Speier to Ascoli (October 1940), APBU.

58. Johnson, address (November 17, 1943), NSA.

59. Lowe, Address to the Institute of World Affairs (November 17, 1943), NSA.

60. See, for example, the following works: Hilde Oppenheimer-Bluhm, "The Standard of Living of German Labor Under Nazi Rule"; Judith Grunfeld, "The Mobilization of Women in Germany." Both are supplements to *Social Research* (1942 and 1943).

61. Arnold Brecht, *The Political Education of Arnold Brecht* (Princeton, N.J., 1970), p. 265.

62. *Ibid.,* p. 301.

63. Brecht, "Regional Differences in Political Opinions in Republican Germany," Institute of World Affairs (March 27, 1944), NSA.

64. Brecht, *Federalism and Regionalism in Germany* (New York, 1945).

65. Erich Hula, interview (New York, November 1978). Hula refused to continue in Cologne when Kelsen's successor Karl Schmitt referred to "that Jew Kelsen."

66. Hula, "The Cooperative Experiment in Austria," *Social Research*, V (1938), pp. 40–58.

67. *Ibid.,* p. 42.

68. Leo Strauss, *Die Religionskritik Spinosas als Grundlage seiner biblewissenschaft Untersachungen zu Spinosas Theologish-Politischem Traktat* (Berlin, 1930). Translated as *Spinoza's Critique of Religion* (New York, 1965), with a new introduction by the author.

69. Hans Jonas, interview (New Rochelle, N.Y., November 1981).

70. *Ibid.*

71. Elizabeth Young-Bruhl, *Hannah Arendt: For the Love of the Mind* (New York, 1982).

72. Strauss, "Anmerkungen zu Carl Schmitt, Der Begriff des Politischem," *Archiv,* LXXVII (August 1932), p. 748.

73. Strauss's papers at the University of Chicago contain many letters to Koyré, Maritain, and Gershom Scholem. Leo Strauss Papers, University of Chicago (hereafter referred to as SPCA).

74. Gershom Scholem, *Walter Benjamin, a Remembrance* (New York, 1982), p. 97. In 1934 Schocken published a long essay by Strauss on Maimonides. Scholem thought so highly of it that he urged Walter Benjamin to review it.

75. Strauss, *The Political Philosphy of Hobbes: Its Basis and Genesis* (Oxford, 1936).

76. Strauss to Jonas (March 1935), SPCA.

77. Strauss, "Persecution and the Art of Writing," *Social Research*, VIII (1941), pp. 488-504.

78. *Ibid.*, p. 489.

79. See his reinterpretation of Spinoza in "How to Study Spinoza" in *Proceedings of the American Academy for Jewish Research*, XVII (1948), pp. 69-131. By refuting the Bible, Spinoza revealed its deeper teaching, argued Strauss.

80. Strauss, *Natural Right and History* (1953), pp. 85-90.

81. Strauss to Helmut Kuhn, letter (undated), about *Natural Right and History*, SPCA.

82. Strauss, *Natural Right and History*, p. 142.

83. *Ibid.*, p. 170.

84. *Ibid.*, p. 196.

85. *Ibid.*, pp. 17-26.

86. *Ibid.*, p. 16.

87. *Ibid.*, p. 44.

88. *Ibid.*, p. 139.

89. *Ibid.*, p. 19. Interviews with Mrs. Leo Strauss, (Annapolis, Md., October 1980) and Joseph Cropsey (Gambier, Ohio, May 1981). In some ways Strauss was a radical hermeneutician, one who studies only the text in search of rules whose veracity can be substituted for the failures of the laws of natural science. To that extent he was both of and apart from the "school" at the Graduate Faculty. Strauss died struggling to recite the words of traditional Jewish prayer.

90. Strauss, *On Tyranny: An Interpretation of Xenophon's Itiero,* Foreword by Johnson (New York, 1948).

91. Strauss, Introduction to *Spinoza's Critique of Religion*, pp. 19-22.

92. Strauss, *Natural Right and History*. Although the book appeared in its final form in 1953, the first four chapters had previously appeared as articles in 1950 and 1951. See particularly "Natural Right and the Historical Approach," *Review of Politics*, XVI (1950), and "The Social Science of Max Weber," *Measure*, II (1951).

93. See H. Stuart Hughes, *Consciousness and Society,* and Peter Gay, *Weimar Culture* (New York, 1970), for a consideration of this tradition.

94. Staudinger, memo (June 23, 1949), NSA.

95. Staudinger to Lowe, memo (January 16, 1948), NSA.

96. Note (May 4, 1948), NSA.

97. Staudinger, interview (November 1978).

98. Ernst Hamburger and Alfred Kahler, *Education for an Industrial Age* (Ithaca, N.Y., 1948).

99. Hamburger, interview (November 1978).

100. Hamburger and Kahler, *Education*, p. 243.

101. Lowe to Hans Merten (April 6, 1949).

102. The Publications of the Institute included papers by Hans Neisser, "The Significance of Foreign Trade for Domestic Employment," and Franco Modigliani, "Fluctuations in the Savings Ratio," along with the analysis in monograph by Brecht, *Federalism and Regionalism in Germany.* See also the extensive report by Lewis Lorwin. "The Place of Research and Related Activities in the New School for Social Research" (December 18, 1953), 80 pp., NSA. Finally, the proposals of the institute can be found in the Rockefeller Foundation Archives, RG 11, B 383, and F 4526.

CHAPTER 8   The Free French in New York

1. Alvin Johnson to Max Ascoli (July 20, 1940) and Aline Caro-Delvaille, aunt of Lévi-Strauss, to Ascoli (September 23, 1940), ABPU (Max Ascoli Papers, Boston University). See also correspondence (February and March 1941) from Johnson to the Rockefeller Foundation, RFA (Rockefeller Foundation Archives). See also "Letters to America: The Correspondence of Marc Bloch, 1940–41," edited and introduced by Peter M. Rutkoff and William B. Scott, *French Historical Studies,* (Vol. 12, No. 2, Fall 1981), pp. 277–303.

2. Madame Pierre Brodin, interview (New York, March 1978). Madame Brodin was with Maritain the day that news arrived of France's defeat in 1940. The Ecole Pratique had been established as a "modern" alternative, in social sciences, to the traditional French university.

3. Johnson to Ascoli (September 16, 1941), APBU. See also Johnson to M. Erskine (n.r., 1944), AJPY (Alvin Johnson Papers, Yale University).

4. Johnson to Ascoli (September 16, 1944).

5. Pierre Brodin, interview (March 1978), APBU.

6. Gustave Cohen to Ascoli, memo (September 1941), APBU.

7. Madame Pierre Brodin, interview (New York, March 1978). See the first Ecole Libre announcement (February 1942), NSA.

8. Johnson to Ascoli (September 16, 1944), APBU.

9. *Renaissance,* "Advertissement," I, No. 1 (1943), pp. 7–16.

10. *Ibid.*

11. Madame A. Koyré, interview, (Paris, June 1978).

12. Raoul Aglion, Papers (August 11, 1941), Archives de Deuxième Guerre Modiale, Paris (hereafter referred to as ADGM).

13. Jacques Maritain, *Le Crépuscule du Civilization* (Paris, 1939).

14. Madame R. Aglion, transcript of interview (December 1948; January 1949), ADGM.

15. G. Tabouis, interview (Paris, June 1978).

16. Documents, France Libre, "Rapport de M. R. Aglion sur la Colonie Française de N.Y." (December 6, 1942), ADGM.

17. *Ibid.* (March 1943).

18. *Ibid.* (December 6, 1942).

19. Minutes of the Editorial Board Meeting of *Renaissance* (January 28, 1944), Claude Lévi-Strauss, Paris.

20. *Ibid.* Letters of Koyré and Lévi-Strauss to Gregoire (February 3, 1944). See also the letter of Johnson to Maritain and Gregoire (April 25, 1944), urging them to stay more closely in touch with him to prevent accusations coming from the State Department that the Ecole was merely the instrument of a foreign government, AJPY.

21. For the subject of intellectual commitment, see Julian Benda, *The Treason of the Intellectuals* (New York, 1957); David Schalk, *Intellectual Commitment in France* (New York, 1979); Marc Poster, *Existential Marxism in Post-War France* (New York, 1978); H. Stuart Hughes, *The Obstructed Path* (New York, 1970); and James D. Wilkinson, *The Intellectual Resistance in Europe* (Cambridge, Mass., 1981).

22. Alexandre Koyré, *L'idée de Dieu et les preuves de son existence chez Descartes* (Paris, 1922).

23. Koyré, *Introduction à la lecture de Platon,* translated as *Discovering Plato* (New York, 1945). Koyré's other work includes *N. Copernic: Des Revolutions des orbes celestes* (Paris, 1934), and *Etudes galilenes,* 3 vols. (Paris, 1939).

24. Cohen, Henri Focillon, and Henri Pirenne, *La civilization occidentale au Moyen Age du XI au milieu de XV siècle* (Paris, 1934).

25. Cohen, *L'histoire du théatre française,* 2 vols. (Paris, 1928 and 1932).

26. Cohen, *La Grand Clarté de Moyen Age* (New York, 1943).

27. Cohen, Focillon, and Pirenne, *Civilization accidentale.*

28. Boris Mirkine-Guetzévitch, *L'influence de la révolution française sur le development du droit international* (Paris, 1928). See also Mirkine-Guetzévitch and Henri Michel, *Les idées politiques et sociales de la résistance* (Paris, 1954).

29. See, for example, Maritain, *La Philosophie Bergoneinne* (Paris, 1914); *La Philosophie de la nature* (Paris, 1935); and a *Preface to Metaphysics: Seven Lectures on Being* (New York, 1939).

30. Maritain's work in social philosophy includes *Humanisme integral* (Paris, 1936) and *Man and the State* (Chicago, 1951). See also the polemical, *Le Crépuscule du civilization* (Paris, 1940).

31. Maritain, transcript of New School speech (April 16, 1940), NSA.

32. Maritain, *Christianity and Democracy*, trans. by Doris Anson (New York, 1944).

33. *Ibid.*, p. 29.

34. *Ibid.*, pp. 30–32.

35. Maritain, New School speech.

36. See, for example, Roman Jacobson, *Main Trends in the Science of Language* (New York, 1973), and *Selected Writings*, 5 vols. (The Hague, 1962–1978). Jacobson's bibliography contains over 200 entries. See also Noam Chomsky and Halle Morris, *The Sound Pattern of English* (New York, 1968).

37. Henri Grégoire, Roman Jacobson, and M. Szefstel, *La geste du Prince Igor*, in *Annuire de l'Institut de Philologie et d'Histoire Orientales et Slaves de l'Université Libre de Bruxelles*, VIII (New York, 1948).

38. See, for example, Claude Lévi-Strauss, *Graccus Babeuf et le Communisme* (Paris, 1928).

39. Lévi-Strauss, *Tristes Tropiques* (1955), pp. 50–56.

40. Lévi-Strauss, interview with Elizabeth Malaquais (Paris, June 1977).

41. Lévi-Strauss, interview (Paris, May 1980).

42. Lévi-Strauss, *Tristes Tropiques*, p. 61. See also James A. Boon, *From Symbolism to Structuralism* (New York, 1972); Howard Gardner, *The Quest for the Mind: Lévi-Strauss, Piaget and the Structuralist Movement* (New York, 1973); and C. Backes-Clement, *Claude Lévi-Strauss*, (Paris, 1970).

43. Lévi-Strauss, *Tristes Tropiques*, p. 63.

44. Lévi-Strauss, interview (Paris, June 1980).

45. Lévi-Strauss, "Le dedoublement de la répresentation dans les arts de l'Asie et de l'Amerique," *Renaissance*, II (1944–1945), pp. 168–186.

46. *Ibid.*, pp. 169–170.

47. *Ibid.*, p. 186.

48. "Structural Analysis in Linguistics and Anthropology," first published as "L'Analyse structurale en linguistique et en anthropologie," *Word, Journal of the Linguistic Circle of New York*, I (August 1945). Republished in *Structural Anthropology* (New York, 1963).

49. *Ibid.*, pp. 35–39.

50. Lévi-Strauss, interview (May 1980).

51. Lévi-Strauss, "Structural Analysis," p. 32.

52. Lévi-Strauss, "Postscript to Chapters III and IV," in *Structural Anthropology*, p. 89.

53. Lévi-Strauss, interview (June 1980).

54. *Ibid.*

55. Lévi-Strauss, "Language and the Analysis of Social Laws" *American Anthropologist*, LIII (1951), pp. 155–163.

56. Lévi-Strauss, *Tristes Tropiques*, p. 391.

57. Lévi-Strauss, interview (May 1980).

58. See, for example, H. Coates and H. White, *The Ordeal of Liberal Humanism*, II, pp. 322–334. See also the suggestion of Georges Gurvitch, "Le Concept de structure sociale," *Cahiers internationaux de Sociologie*, XIX (1955).

59. Pierre Brodin, interview (New York, April 1978) and Lévi-Strauss, interview (May 1978). See also letter of Lévi-Strauss, to Dr. John Marshall (August 9, 1944), RFA.

60. Lévi-Strauss to Bonnet (November 18, 1946), NSA.

61. Pierre Brodin, interview (April 1978) and E. Hamburger to Brodin (June 17, 1947). See also letter of Henri Peyre to Johnson (January 10, 1946) and Henri Grégoire to Louis Weiss (April 28, 1946), AJPY.

CHAPTER 9   Politics on Stage

1. Erwin Piscator Papers, Southern Illinois University, Carbondale, Box 5 (hereafter cited as PSI). See also account in Maria Ley-Piscator, *The Piscator Experiment: The Political Theatre* (Carbondale, Ill., 1967), pp. 45–51.

2. Piscator to Alvin Johnson (May 22, 1939) and Johnson to Piscator (June 6, 1939), Box 5.

3. Ley-Piscator, *Piscator Experiment*, pp. 49–51.

4. Piscator, *The Political Theatre: A History, 1914–1929*, trans. by Hugh Rorrison (New York, 1978). Felix Gassbarra, quoted in John Willett, *The Theatre of Erwin Piscator* (New York, 1979), p. 152.

5. Ley-Piscator, *Piscator Experiment*, p. 51.

6. Piscator, *Political Theatre*, pp. 1–20, 324. See also Willett, *Piscator*, pp. 13–14, 42–45.

7. Piscator, *Political Theatre*, p. 12.

8. Brecht, quoted by Piscator, *Political Theatre*, viii.

9. Willett, *Art and Politics in the Weimar Period: The New Sobriety, 1917–1933* (New York, 1978); Walter Laqueur, *Weimar: A Cultural History* (New York, 1974), Chapter 4; Peter Gay, *Weimar Culture: The Outsider as Insider* (New York, 1968).

10. Willett, *Piscator*, pp. 67–106.

11. C. D. Innes, *Erwin Piscator's Political Theatre: The Development of Modern German Drama*, (Cambridge).

12. *Ibid.*, pp. 23–40. See also Piscator's remarks in *Political Theatre*, pp. 32–327.

13. Willett, *Piscator*, pp. 46–66.

14. Piscator, *Political Theatre*, p. 134.

15. Willett, *Piscator*, pp. 46–66, 88–106.

16. See chronological table of Piscator's productions in Innes, *Piscator's Theatre*, pp. 219–226.

17. Quoted in *ibid.*, p. 74.

18. Piscator, *Political Theatre*, p. 49. See Peter Bauland, *The Hooded Eagle: Modern Drama on the New York Stage* (Syracuse, N.Y., 1968).

19. Much of this analysis is drawn from Innes, *Piscator's Theatre*.

20. Piscator, *Political Theatre*, pp. 188–189.

21. *Ibid.*, pp. 180–184, 193; Innes, *Piscator's*, pp. 131–151.

22. Innes, *Piscator's Theatre*, p. 116. Also Piscator, *Political Theatre*, pp. 50, 121–122, 214.

23. Quoted in Innes, *Piscator's Theatre*, p. 206.

24. Willett, *Piscator*, pp. 127–151.

25. For material on early years of the Dramatic Workshop see Boxes 5 and 6, PSI; Dramatic Workshop, Scrapbooks, NSA; Ley-Piscator, *Piscator Experiment*, chapters 4, 8, and 9.

26. Jurgen Stein, "Production Chronology," PSI.

27. See "The Dramatic Workshop, a memorandum prepared for Mrs. [Thomas] Lamont [long standing member of the board], approved by Dr. Johnson" (Spring 1941), Box 5, PSI.

28. Johnson to Piscator (August 7, 1945), Box 15, PSI.

29. Piscator, "Theatre of the Future," *Tomorrow* (February 1942), p. 6, Box 45, PSI.

30. Tennessee Williams to Piscator (August 13, 1942) and Piscator to Stella Adler (November 26, 1942), Box 12, PSI; John Gassner, *The Theatre in Our Times* (New York, 1954), pp. 337–341, 510; Willett, *Piscator*, p. 166.

31. Boxes 7–12, 169, PSI; Dramatic Workshop, Scrapbooks, NSA; and Ley-Piscator, *Piscator Experiment*, chapters 9, 11, and 12.

32. See the comments of Marlon Brando, Walter Matthau, Ben Gazzara, and Harry Belafonte in Walter Rigdon, ed., *The Biographical Encyclopedia and Who's Who of the American Theatre* (New York, 1966).

33. For a comparison of acting styles see Piscator, Strasberg, and Adler in Toby Cole and Helen Drich Chinoy, eds., *Actors on Acting* (New York, 1970), pp. 301–306, 601–605, 621–628. Also, Piscator to Adler (November 26, 1942), PSI; Lee Strasberg, Introduction, in Toby Cole, ed., *Acting: A Handbook of the Stanislavski Method* (New York, 1947); and Ley-Piscator, *Piscator Experiment*, p. 119.

34. Gassner, *Theatre in Our Times*, pp. 11–30, 65–95.

35. Ley-Piscator, *Piscator Experiment*, pp. 94–97.

36. Gassner, *Theatre in Our Times*, r. vii.

37. Dramatic Workshop, Scrapbooks, NSA; Box 169, PSI; Ley-Piscator, *Piscator Experiment*, chapters 11 and 12. The first of these was *King Lear* with the distinguished actor Sam Jaffee as Lear. Piscator turned Lear into a symbol of dictatorships and related him to contemporary fascist govern-

ments. He followed up this largely unsuccessful production with Klabund's adaptation of the Chinese classic *Circle of Chalk*. These were followed by Philip Yordan's *Any Day Now*, Frank Gabrielson's *Days of our Youth*, Ferdinand Bruckner's *The Criminals*, Bruckner's adaptation of Lessing's *Nathan the Wise*, Piscator's and Alfred Neuman's adaptation of *War and Peace*, and Daniel James's *Winter Soldiers*. *Circle of Chalk* and *Winter Soldiers* were Piscator's most successful Studio Theatre productions. *Winter Soldiers*, an account of Napoleon's siege of Moscow, actually made money, no doubt in part because of the current interest in Hitler's invasion of Russia. *Nathan the Wise*, which explored the insidious character of anti-Semitism and the necessity of religious toleration, moved to Broadway for a short engagement. Piscator's most ambitious effort, *War and Peace*, presented in the epic style, complete with a narrator, gauze screens, and five separate stages, proved a commercial and critical disaster.

38. Bauland, *Hooded Eagle*, chapters 4 and 5; Gassner, *Theatre in Our Times* (New York, 1954), pp. 337–341; Willett, *Piscator*, pp. 165–167; Jane DeHart Matthews, *The Federal Theatre, 1935–1938; Plays, Relief, and Politics* (Princeton, N.J., 1967); Eric Bentley, *The Theatre of Commitment* (New York, 1967); Brooks Atkinson, *Broadway* (New York, 1970).

39. Clara Mayer to Walter Greaza (May 15, 1940), Box 7, and correspondence in Boxes 10, 12, and 13, PSI.

40. Piscator to Johnson (November 1943; February 4, 1944) in Box 14; Piscator to Bryn Hovde (November 15, 1948), Box 29, PSI.

41. "Report on Survey of the Dramatic Workshop" (January 1945), Box 15, PSI.

42. Dramatic Workshop, Budgets, 1940–1945, Box 160, PSI; Dramatic Workshop, Financial Summary (1944–1947), NSA.

43. Boxes 14 and 170, PSI.

44. Keith W. Olson, "The G.I. Bill and Higher Education: Success and Surprise," *American Quarterly*, XXV (1973), pp. 596–610.

45. Boxes 166, 167, and 171, PSI.

46. Dramatic Workshop, Scrapbooks, NSA. Piscator–Hovde Correspondence (1945–1946), Boxes 15 and 16, PSI; John Chapman, ed., *The Burns Mantle Best Plays of 1947-48* (New York, 1948); Piscator to Hovde (December 10, 1945), Box 15, PSI; Ley-Piscator, *Piscator Experiment*, chapters 14 and 15.

47. Box 171, PSI.

48. The scripts of nearly all of Piscator's Dramatic Workshop productions with his stage notes and changes are in PSI. See also Ley-Piscator, *Piscator Experiment*, Chapter 15; Dramatic Workshop, Scrapbooks, NSA.

49. *New York Times* (December 8, 1946).

50. Hovde, interoffice memo (January 17, 1947), and Piscator to Paul Ransom, interoffice memo (January 17, 1947), Box 17, PSI.

51. See Issai Hosiosky to Mayer (January 21, 1947), Box 17, PSI; Johnson to

Mary Urban (December 9, 1948); Johnson to Mr. Berger (April 1950); Johnson to Edith Brie (1950?), AJPY (Johnson Papers, Yale University).

52. *New York Times* (February 5, 7, 9, 19, 1947; May 10, 13, 1947; September 25, 26, 1947). See also Hans Eisler file, RFA (Rockefeller Foundation Archives).

53. *New York Times* (September 26, 1947); Johnson to Urban (December 8, 1948), AJPY; Johnson, *Clock of History* (New York, 1946), pp. 101–107.

54. *New York Times* (March 20, 26, 27, 1949).

55. See Piscator–Johnson Correspondence (1948–1950), AJPY; Piscator-Hovde Correspondence (1947–1949), Boxes 16, 17, 19, 24, PSI.

56. Hovde to Piscator (October 17, 1946), Box 16, PSI.

57. Henry Wendriner to Piscator (December 31, 1947), Box 22, PSI.

58. Piscator to Board of Trustees of New School (March 1, 1948), Box 24, PSI.

59. Piscator to Hovde (March 9, 1948) and Hovde to Piscator (March 12, 1948), Box 24, PSI.

60. Piscator to Hovde (June 16, 1948), Box 26, PSI.

61. See Hovde to Piscator (June–December 1948), Boxes 26–29, and Johnson to Piscator (December 3, 1948), Box 29, PSI; Johnson–Piscator Correspondence (June 1948–June 1950), AJPY; Hovde to Piscator (June 28, 1949), Dramatic Workshop, NSA.

62. Press release (February 15, 1949), Dramatic Workshop, NSA.

63. Johnson to Piscator (January 16, 1949), Dramatic Workshop, NSA; Piscator–Johnson Correspondence, Johnson Papers, NSA.

64. Willett, *Piscator,* pp. 162–182; Innes, *Piscator's Theatre,* pp. 181–207.

CHAPTER 10   A Return to Social Theory

1. Robert Heilbroner, interview (October 1981).

2. Hans Staudinger, interview (New York, December 1978).

3. Erich Hula, interview (New York, May 1979).

4. Hannah Salomon Janovsky, interview (New York, October 1981).

5. See, for example, Solomon Asch, *Social Psychology,* (Englewood, N.J., 1952), and Rudolf Arnheim, *Art and Visual Perception* (Berkeley, Calif. 1954).

6. See especially Howard White, *Peace Among the Willows: The Study of the Political Philosophy of Francis Bacon* (The Hague, 1968), and *Shakespeare and the Classical Polity* (The Hague, 1970).

7. Arnold Brecht, *Political Theory: The Foundations of Twentieth Century Thought* (Princeton, N.J., 1959).

8. See the biography of Riezler by Wayne C. Thompson, *In the Eye of the Storm, Kurt Riezler and the Crisis of Modern Germany* (Iowa City, 1980).

9. Kurt Riezler, *Man, Mutable and Immutable* (Chicago, 1950).

10. Thompson, *Eye of the Storm*, p. 220.

11. Staudinger, interview (December 1978).

12. Alfred Schutz, *The Phenomenology of the Social World* (Evanston, Ill., 1959). Schutz's work was intended as a critique of logical positivism of Rudolph Carnap's *Der Logische Aufban der Welt* (Vienna, 1920).

13. See Edmund Husserl, "Philosophy and the Crisis of Modern Man," in *Phenomenology and the Crisis of Philosophy* (New York, 1965). Also, Richard Bernstein, *The Restructuring of Social and Political Theory* (Philadelphia, 1978), and Morris Cohen, *Reason and Nature* (New York, 1931). More specific studies abound, for example: Carl Schorske, *Fin de Siècle Vienna* (New York, 1980); H. Stuart Hughes, *Consciousness and Society* (New York, 1963); Paul Fussell, *The Great War and Modern Memory* (New York, 1978); Roger Shattuck, *The Banquet Years* (New York, 1958); and Robert Wohl, *The Generation of 1914* (Cambridge, Mass., 1979).

14. Thomas Luckmann, interview (Constance, Switzerland, May 1980).

15. Schutz, *Phenomenology*, p. 244. Biographical material on Schutz is available in most of the introductions to his collected papers. Cf. the works listed below edited by Maurice Natanson. More importantly, Mrs. Alfred Schutz provided many personal details in an oral interview (New York, June 1979). Many of Schutz's personal papers are in the care of Helmut Wagner, Geneva, N.Y.

16. Unpublished ms. by Dr. Ilja Srubar, "Schutz Reception of Bergson," lent by the author, University of Konstanz. See also Helmut Wagner, "The Bergsonian Period of Alfred Schutz," *Philosophy and Phenomenological Research*, XXXVII (1977), pp. 187–200.

17. See the article by Kaufmann on "Methodology in the Social Sciences," *Social Research* (Fall 1939 and Spring 1941). In addition, Richard Bernstein, *The Restructuring of Social and Political Theory* (Philadelphia, 1978), contains excellent material on Schutz.

18. Richard Grathoff, ed., *The Theory of Social Action: The Correspondence of Alfred Schutz and Talcott Parsons* (Bloomington, Ind., 1978). The comment is in Maurice Natanson's introduction to the volume, p. 2. See also Natanson, ed., *Phenomenology and Social Reality* (The Hague, 1970).

19. A good example is in Carnap, "Psychology in Physical Language," in A. J. Ayer, ed., *Logical Positivism* (New York, 1959).

20. Schutz, Introduction to *Phenomenology*, p. xv.

21. *Ibid.*, p. 46.

22. *Ibid.*, p. 221.

23. *Ibid.*, p. 222.

24. *Ibid.*

25. *Ibid.*, p. 244.

26. See Grathoff, *The Theory of Social Action*. Parsons's work, *The Theory of Social Action*, was published in 1937.

27. Natanson, interview (New Haven, Conn., March 1979). The supporting story holds that Johnson himself "told" Schutz to "Americanize" his ideas.

28. Schutz in Grathoff, *The Theory of Social Action*, p. 62.

29. Schutz, "William James' Concept of the Stream of Thought Phenomenologically Interpreted," *Philosophy and Phenomenological Research*, I (1941), pp. 3–15.

30. *Ibid.*, p. 6.

31. *Ibid.*, p. 13.

32. See Schutz, "Common Sense and Scientific Interpretation," *Philosophy and Phenomenological Research*, XII (1953).

33. *Ibid.*

34. See Schutz, "Concept and Theory Formation in the Social Sciences," *Journal of Philosophy* (1954).

35. Adolph Lowe, "The Hope of Small Catastrophe," interview for German radio (1982); transcript provided to authors by Lowe. Original title was "Die Hoffnung auf kliene Katastrophen."

36. Kenneth Boulding, review "on Economic Knowledge," *The Nation* (September 1960).

37. Lowe, interview (Bronx, N.Y., February 1979).

38. *Ibid.*

39. Lowe, "Some Notes on the Institute" (1941), NSA (New School Archives).

40. Claus-Dieter Krohn, "An Overlooked Chapter of Economic History: The New School's Effort to Salvage Weimar Economic Policy," *Social Research* (Fall 1982). See also Krohn, *Wirtschaftstheorien als politische Interessen* (Frankfurt, 1981). See also Lowe, "Wie ist Kojunkturtheorie uberhaupt moglich," *Weltwirtschaftliches Archiv*, II (1926).

41. Theodore H. Vogelstein, "Joseph H. Schumpeter and the Socialsierung-Kommission," unpublished paper, Papers of Adolph Lowe.

42. See, for example, E. Heimann, *Soziale Theorie des Kapitalismus* (Tübingen, 1929), and *Liberalism, Socialism and Marxism* (New York, 1946).

43. Paul Tillich, "Grundlinien des Religiosen Sozialismus," *Blatter für Religiosen Sozialismus,* translated as *Basic Principles of Religious Socialism* (New York, 1971).

44. *Ibid.*, p. 743.

45. *Ibid.*, p. 82.

46. Lowe, *The Price of Liberty* (London, 1935), and *Economics and Sociology* (London, 1937).

47. Lowe, "The Hope for a Minor Catastrophe."

48. Lowe, interview (Bronx, N.Y., February 1979).

49. Letter, Lowe to Robert Heilbroner (July 10, 1972). Heilbroner has made his correspondence with Lowe available to the authors. It is hereafter referred to as PRH (Papers of Robert Heilbroner). Lowe, "A Reconsideration of the

Laws of Supply and Demand," *Social Research,* IX (November 1942); "On the Mechanistic Approach in Economics," *Social Research,* XVIII (December 1951); "The Classical Theory of Economic Growth," *Social Research,* XXII (1954), p. 130.

50. Lowe to Heilbroner (July 10, 1954), PRH. Lowe, interview (Bronx, N.Y., February 1979). Lowe used free association in this "draft" of an experiment he said derived from an earlier encounter with psychoanalysis.

51. Lowe to Heilbroner (May 30, 1957), PRH.

52. Lowe, *On Economic Knowledge,* 2nd ed. (New York, 1976; hereafter referred to as *OEN*), pp. 6–20.

53. *Ibid.,* pp. 59–95.

54. The issue of "control" is more completely developed in the postscript to the second (1976) edition.

55. *OEN,* p. 130.

56. *Ibid.,* p. 85.

57. Lowe to Heilbroner (September 4, 1962). Also, interview (Bronx, N.Y., February 1979).

58. See, for example, Richard Bernstein, *Praxis and Action* (Philadelphia, 1973).

59. Lowe to Heilbroner (September 4, 1959), PRH.

60. *OEN,* pp. 193–199.

61. Lowe, interview (Bronx, N.Y., February 1979).

62. *Ibid.*

63. Albert Salomon, "German Sociology," in Georges Gurvitch, ed., *Twentieth Century Sociology* (New York, 1945). See also his *In Praise of Enlightenment* (New York, 1957).

64. Albert Salomon, "Max Weber's Sociology," *Social Research,* II (1935), pp. 60–74. See also his "Max Weber's Methodology," *Social Research,* I (1934), pp. 147–169.

65. *Ibid.,* p. 61.

66. *Ibid.,* p. 65.

67. Salomon, *"German Sociology,"* p. 600

68. Hannah Salomon Janovsky, interview (New York, November 1981).

69. Papers of Albert Salomon, Leo Baeck Institute, New York. Hannah Salomon Janovsky, interview (New York, November 1981.

70. Karl Mayer, "Sekte und Kirche" (Ph.D. dissertation, Heidelberg University, republished University of Konstanz, 1967), Konstanz, Germany,

71. Mayer, ms. notes, *Karl Mayer Archives,* Konstanz.

72. Maurice Natanson, *The Social Dynamics of G. H. Mead* (The Hague, 1973), p. 2.

73. *Ibid.,* p. 4.

74. *Ibid.,* pp. 81–82.

75. *Ibid.*, p. 85.

76. Thomas Luckmann and Peter Berger, *The Social Constitution of Reality* (New York, 1963) p. 15.

77. *Ibid.*, pp. 186–188.

CHAPTER 11   New Students for a New Era

1. Alvin Johnson, *Pioneer's Progress: An Autobiography* (New York, 1952), pp. 395–505.

2. *New York Times* (September 27, 1949).

3. Johnson, Correspondence (1945–1950), Johnson Papers, Yale University (AJPY). Johnson to Horace Kallen (September 22, 1949), Kallen Papers, YIVO Insitutute.

4. Bryn Hovde, "The Education of This Generation" (December 27, 1945); Hovde, "A Report and a Blueprint" (1947); "Appeals for Support for 1944–1947" (1944), NSA (New School Archives). Max Ascoli to Hans Simons (March 24, 1949); Simons to Ascoli (April 2, 1949, Ascoli Papers, Boston University (APBU).

5. News release (May 6, 1950), NSA.

6. Simons, biographical sketch (June 14, 1950), NSA.

7. Johnson Correspondence (1950–1955), Johnson Papers, NSA. Arthur L. Swift, Jr., "The New School Study" (November 26, 1952); "The New School's Development Program" (April 6, 1954); Simons, "Annual Report of the President" (December 1953), NSA.

8. News release (May 5, 1955), Building File, NSA; *New School Bulletin* (December 15, 1958; May 4, 1959).

9. Statistical Reports (1955–1965), NSA.

10. "Enrollment Statistics: A Summary, 1919–1924," in loose-leaf notebook, NSA. After 1944 see Annual Statistical Reports, NSA. United States Department of Commerce, *Historical Statistics of the United States* (Washington, D.C.: Government Printing Office, 1975), pp. 360–388.

11. *New School Bulletin* (1919–1965), NSA.

12. *New School Bulletin* (Fall 1943); "Bachelor of Arts Program" (1944); "The Senior College: The Program Leading to the Bachelor of Arts Degree" (April 28, 1959), NSA.

13. Saul Padover File, Dean's Office, Graduate Faculty, New School.

14. Gerda Lerner, *The Majority Finds Its Past* (New York, 1979), pp. xiii–xxxii.

15. Statistical Reports, 1945–1965, NSA.

16. *Ibid.*

17. *Ibid.*

18. *Bulletin: New School* (1945–1965).

19. M. F. Ashley Montagu, "It Is a Privilege to Teach at the New School," *Bulletin: New School* (October 29, 1951), NSA.

20. Johnson to "Mr. Berger" (April 29, 1950); Johnson to Mary Urban (December 9, 1948), AJPY; Johnson, *Ideas Are High Explosives* (private printing, December 18, 1962; Johnson, *Pioneer's Progress.*

21. Max Lerner, interview (New York, January 1979); Johnson, taped interview, Southern Illinois University, Carbondale; Clara Mayer, interview (New York, 1979).

22. Johnson to Urban (December 9, 1948), JPYU; memorandum (January 27, 1942), Hans Eisler File, Rockefeller Foundation Archives; Sidney Hook, telephone interview with Professor Roy Wortman, Kenyon College (June 20, 1981), typescript of interview in author's files; Lerner, interview. Johnson Correspondence (1947–1952), AJPY.

23. Johnson–Piscator Correspondence (1947–1952), Piscator Papers, Southern Illinois University, Carbondale; *Bulletin: New School* (1957–1967); Maria Ley-Piscator, interview (June 1981); Johnson, *Ideas Are High Explosives;* Kallen, "Are There Limits to Toleration in a Free Society?" (address given at New School, January 21, 1950), NSA; Kallen, *Secularism Is the Will of God* (New York, 1954), pp. 149–164; Mayer, *Manmade Wilderness;* Simons, "The New School: Fortress of Freedom," *New School Bulletin* (October 10, 1950).

24. *New York Times* (May 22, 1953); Agnes deLima to Mr. Arkins (interoffice memo, April 2, 1951); Alma Reed, report to Artists Equity (April 3, 1951), Mural File, NSA; Student Petition (1953) and Student Mural Committee (1953), Mural File, NSA.

25. Reed to deLima (April 17, 1953); Simons to deLima (April 20, 1953); deLima to Reed (April 21, 1953), all in Mural File, NSA.

26. Johnson, "Notes on the New School Murals" (New School publication, n.d.), Mural File, NSA; Johnson, *Pioneer's Progress,* pp. 327–331.

27. Executive Meeting of Board of Trustees (May 1953); Simons to deLima (April 1, 1953); William H. Davis, "Orozco Murals," *New School Bulletin* (November 9, 1953), NSA.

28. Johnson to Edith Brie (draft, 1953), AJPY.

29. Peter Scarpa, chairman of Student Mural Committee, to William H. Davis, chairman of Board of Trustees (November 17, 1953), Mural File, NSA.

30. Robert Gwathmey, interview (New York, 1979).

31. Minutes, Special Meeting of Executive Committee of Board of Trustees (May 1, 1957), Minutes File, NSA.

32. Simons, correspondence (1951–1956), Simons Papers; Hans Staudinger, Correspondence (1951–1956), Staudinger Papers, Albany Archives, State University of New York.

33. Clarence Mitchell to Simons (January 21, 1954) and Simons to Mitchell (February 5, 1954), Simons Papers.

34. *New School Art Bulletin* (1934), NSA.

35. See Chapter 4. Patterson Sims, "Decade of Transition, 1940–1950" (Whitney Museum of American Art, April 30–July 12, 1981); Frank Getlin, *Chaim Gross* (New York, 1974); Albert Elsen, *Seymour Lipton* (New York, 1972); John L. Cunningham, *José de Creeft* (Athens, Ga., 1950); E. C. Gossen, *Stuart Davis* (New York, 1959); "Leonard Baskin," *Current Biography: 1964*, pp. 27–29; Davis, "What About Modern Art and Democracy?", *Careers Magazine* (December 1943); and Berenice Abbott, quoted in *Current Biography* (1942).

36. Gorham Munson, *The Written Word* (New York, 1949); Munson, *Style and Form in American Prose* (Garden City, N.Y., 1929); Munson, "The New School—Pioneer Writing Center," *New School Bulletin* (November 11, 1950). See also "Gorham Munson," in Stanley Kunitz, ed., *Twentieth Century American Authors* (New York, 1942), p. 1000.

37. *New School Bulletin* (October 18, 1948; January 23, 1950; February 4, 1952), as well as the introductions to *American Vanguard* and *New Voices*, all of which are available at the Fogelman Library at the Graduate Faculty.

38. Maxwell Geismar, *Nation* (June 6, 1953), p. 487.

39. *New School Bulletin* (1930–1965).

40. Richard Kostelanetz, ed., *John Cage* (New York, 1970), pp. 3–44; "John Cage" *Current Biography* (1961), pp. 90–92; Irving Sandler, *The New York School: The Painters and Sculptors of the Fifties* (New York, 1978), pp. 163–173; Michel Nyman, *Experimental Music: Cage and Beyond* (New York, 1974); John Cage, *For the Birds* (Boston, 1981).

41. Cage, interview (New York, June 1981); Lipton, interview (Locust Valley, N.Y., June 9, 1981).

42. Martin Duberman, *Black Mountain: An Exploration in Community* (New York, 1972), pp. 99–100, 277–279, 350–358.

43. Sandler, *New York School*, pp. 163–173.

44. Cage, "The New School," in Kostelanetz, ed., *John Cage*, pp. 118–119.

45. Cage, *For the Birds*, pp. 35–72.

46. Henry Cowell, "Current Chronicle," *Musical Quarterly* (January 1952), reprinted in Kostelanetz, ed., *John Cage*, p. 95.

47. Sandler, *New York School*, provides an excellent brief account of Cage's thought which is neither hostile nor apologetic.

48. Cage quoted in interview by Sandler, *New York School*, pp. 164–165.

49. *Ibid.*, p. 166.

50. Cage, interview (New York, June 1981).

51. Cage, *For the Birds*, pp. 42–57.

52. Cage, interview.

53. Elsen, *Seymour Lipton*, pp. 11–63.

54. Lipton, interview.

55. *Ibid.*

56. *Ibid.*, and *New School Bulletin* (1955–1965).

57. Lipton, interview. Also, Lipton, "Some Notes on My Work," *Magazine of Art* (November 1947), pp. 264–265; Elsen, *Seymour Lipton.*

58. Lipton, interview.

59. *Ibid.*

CHAPTER 12   The Changing of the Guard

1. Adolph Lowe, "The Future of the Graduate Faculty," 1958, NSA (New School Archives).

2. See the enrollment figures which show the concurrent growth of the two departments, Office of the University Registrar, compiled 1982.

3. The most important of these studies was the McGrath report of 1958, which suggested that the Graduate Faculty be curtailed significantly. Curiously, the judgment of that report bore strange fruit in the late 1970s when several graduate departments were discredited, prohibited from granting Ph.D.s, on the ground that they were not in the "mainstream" of American graduate education.

4. See the statements of Hans Neisser, Alfred Schutz, and others on "The Future of the Graduate Faculty," 1958, NSA.

5. Hans Simons to Arnold Brecht, others (1957–1958), Brecht Papers, State University of New York.

6. "The Future of the Graduate Faculty."

7. Lowe, *Ibid.*, 1958.

8. "Recommendations of the Faculty Presidential Advisory Committee, 1959–60," NSA.

9. Henry David, memo (September 1961), NSA.

10. Faculty wrote letters and petitions and held meetings in 1961 and 1962, NSA.

11. Hans Staudinger Papers, given to the authors in 1978 with "Destroy" written on them. Staudinger was animatedly dramatic in this respect. He presented the papers to us with the injunction to "use them wisely." (Hereafter cited as HSP).

12. Staudinger to Alvin Johnson, memo (February 1963), HSP.

13. Letters of Staudinger and Johnson to Joseph Halle Schaffner (February and March 1963), HSP.

14. The telegram, dated February 18, 1963, is in the Staudinger Papers, HSP.

15. Elizabeth Young-Bruehl, *Hannah Arendt, For the Love of the World* (New Haven, Conn., 1982), p. 109.

16. *Ibid.*, p. 46.

17. Hans Jonas, *The Gnostic Religion,* 2nd ed. (Boston, 1963), p. 320.

18. *Ibid.*, p. 331.

19. Jonas, interview (New Rochelle, N.Y., 1982).

20. Jonas, *The Gnostic Religion,* p. 340.

21. Jonas, interview (New Rochelle, N.Y., 1983).

22. Much of this material is contained in Jonas's personal file at the Graduate Faculty of the New School for Social Research.

23. Jonas, interview (New Rochelle, N.Y., 1982).

24. *Ibid.*

25. Hans Jonas, "The Practical Uses of Theory," *Social Research,* XXVI, No. 2 (1959), pp. 127–151, reprinted in *The Phenomenon of Life* (Chicago, 1982). Jonas recalled that Strauss's student, Howard White, was "deeply offended" by his position. Interview (New Rochelle, N.Y., 1982).

26. Jonas, "Nature and Ethics," *The Phenomenon of Life,* pp. 282–285.

27. *Ibid.,* p. 283.

28. Much of the biographical information in this section comes from Elizabeth Young-Bruehl's excellent biography, *Hannah Arendt, For the Love of the World.*

29. See not only the reporting of Young-Bruehl, but as well the recollections of Henry Pachter (interview, New York, 1979) and the unpublished article by Louis Coser, "Hannah Arendt."

30. Hannah Arendt, *The Origins of Totalitarianism,* 2nd ed. (New York, 1958).

31. This point is well made by Young-Bruehl; see especially Chapter 7, "Being at Home in the World," pp. 263–327.

32. Arendt, *The Origins of Totalitarianism,* pp. 27–85.

33. Arendt, *Eichmann in Jerusalem: A Report on the Banality of Evil* (New York, 1963).

34. Elizabeth Young-Bruehl, interview (Gambier, Ohio, 1983).

35. Arendt, "Kant's Critique of Judgment." Written lecture notes for her New School, Graduate Faculty Seminar (1969 or 1970) provided by Jerome Kohn. Published in 1983 as *Lectures on Kant's Political Philosophy* (Chicago, 1983).

36. Arendt, *Kant's Political Philosophy,* p. 39.

37. *Ibid.,* pp. 59–60.

38. Robert Heilbroner, interview (New York, 1979).

39. *Ibid.*

40. Heilbroner, *The Worldly Philosophers,* 3rd ed. (New York, 1953), 1967.

41. Heilbroner to Lowe, letter, May 1964. Papers of Robert Heilbroner (see Chapter 10, note 49).

42. See, for example, Heilbroner, *The Worldly Philosophers,* p. 62.

43. *Ibid.,* pp. 123–154.

44. For example, *Between Capitalism and Socialism* (1970), *Beyond Boom and Crash* (1978), and *The Limits of American Capitalism* (1966). See also the

interview with Heilbroner (October 16, 1978); "Robert Heilbroner on the Doom of Capitalism," *The Chronicle of Higher Education.*

45. Heilbroner, interview (New York, 1979).

46. Heilbroner, *Marxism for and Against* (New York, 1980).

47. See particularly the chapter entitled "The Dialectical Approach to Philosophy," pp. 29–59 in *Marxism for and Against.*

INDEX

INDEX